'The scholarship of this book is meticulous . . . Hutchinson brilliantly conveys the atmosphere of terror . . . a gripping narrative . . . Hutchinson provides an across-the-spectrum grand slam portrait of the second Tudor monarch. No one writing about Henry VIII in the future will be able to ignore this magnificent book'   Frank McLynn, *Daily Express*

'Hutchinson's narrative, level-headed and carefully researched, is the more enjoyable for being so consistently unedifying'
Jonathan Keates, *Spectator*

'This book may be called biographical history at its best and the corruption it portrays still has the power to shock'
Contemporary Review

'The genuinely original chapters aim to relate Henry's character to his medical condition. These and an intriguing sequel on his failed mausoleum project are fresh and interesting'   John Guy, *Sunday Times*

'This is a scholarly but racy account focusing on the final four years, 1543 to 1547, of Henry's long reign'   David Edelsten, *The Field*

Robert Hutchinson is a Fellow of the Society of Antiquaries of London and an expert on the impact of the Reformation in England. He is a tutor in church archaeology for the University of Sussex Centre for Continuing Education and the consultant on church monuments to the Diocese of Chichester Advisory Committee. He was a contributing author to *The Archaeology of the Reformation* and has written numerous papers on ecclesiology and church monuments.

THE LAST
DAYS OF
HENRY
VIII

Conspiracy, Treason and Heresy at the Court
of the Dying Tyrant

ROBERT
HUTCHINSON

PHOENIX

A PHOENIX PAPERBACK

First published in Great Britain in 2005
by Weidenfeld & Nicolson
This paperback edition published in 2006
by Phoenix,
an imprint of Orion Books Ltd,
Orion House, 5 Upper St Martin's Lane,
London WC2H 9EA

5 7 9 10 8 6 4

The Orion Publishing Group's policy is to use papers that are natural,
renewable and recyclable products and made from wood grown in sustainable
forests. The logging and manufacturing processes are expected to conform
to the environmental regulations of the country of origin.

A CIP catalogue record for this book
is available from the British Library.

ISBN 0-75381-936-8
EAN 978-0-75381-936-4

Printed and bound in the UK by
CPI Mackays, Chatham ME5 8TD

www.orionbooks.co.uk

For my beloved wife, Sally

Contents

Author's Note 9

Acknowledgements 11

Prologue 13

ONE A Dangerous Honour 19

TWO God's Imp 63

THREE The Hunt for Heretics 82

FOUR The Final Quest for Military Glory 104

FIVE 'Anger Short and Sweat Abundant' 126

SIX The New Levers of Power 151

SEVEN The Plot to Burn the Queen 161

EIGHT Protestants Ascendant 175

NINE The Mystery of the Royal Will 205

TEN 'Dogs Should Lick His Blood' 221

Epilogue 233

Sequel: 'Tombs of Brass are Spent' 259

Notes 274

Bibliography 314

Chronology 328

Dramatis Personae 333

Index 340

Author's Note

Henry VIII is the most famous king in England's history, and you may think that the story of this psychotic and ruthless ruler is well known. However, it was during the last few years of his long reign that his uncertain health finally broke down, he mounted his final foreign military adventures and the conspiracies over politics and religion within his own court reached fever pitch. These years, 1543–7, were the defining moments of his time as king and sowed the poisoned seeds that were to bear bloody fruit when his offspring successively occupied the throne.

Such dramatic events require a new, detailed examination. Instead of forming the last pages of the many excellent published descriptions of the entire thirty-seven years of Henry's reign written by a host of distinguished and learned historians, this study examines, in depth, the events of that short, tumultuous period. I have also endeavoured to convey a graphic sense of exactly how precarious an existence Henry's courtiers and officials led during his final years in the whispering corridors of his sumptuous palaces, in the face of an aggressive, vengeful, cunning and pain-racked king.

This book also examines his all-important medical condition. Unknown to his cohorts of doctors – the best available at the time – the king was probably suffering from a disease that turned his waking hours into a paranoid nightmare, emotionally detached him from those he was fond of and threw him into troughs of melancholy from which only his faithful fool, or jester, could rouse him. Henry was no theatrical caricature: he was a huge, devious man-mountain capable of remorse-less cruelty – a true bully who was never afraid to exercise his total power of life or death over those he ruled, friend and foe alike. He must have been truly terrifying. In his moments of paranoia, he was certainly mad; he was undoubtedly bad and clearly dangerous to know.

This is a sad, violent story of a once splendid prince who could not cope with old age or the limitations that disease and pain put upon him. The sixteenth-century techniques of government – for example, the cynical use of propaganda and the isolation of the ruler from reality by a handful of largely self-seeking men – will seem familiar to us today, mirrored as they are in many contemporary regimes. So also will the harsh methods of his totalitarian state. In many ways, Henry's charac-ter closely resembles those who held and wielded absolute power in the world in the twentieth century and who continue to do so in the twenty-first. Certainly that power corrupted government in the middle of the sixteenth century in England. None the less, Henry, for all his faults, did much to create the nation we live in today.

Acknowledgements

This book could not have been written without the help and active support of many friends and colleagues, not least my dear wife who has had to live with Henry VIII for many months.

In particular, I would like to thank Bernard Nurse, Librarian, and Adrian James, Assistant Librarian, of the Society of Antiquaries of London; the ever-willing and helpful staff at the former Public Record Office (now the National Archives) at Kew; the enthusiastic team at the library of the Wellcome Institute for the History of Medicine; the manuscripts and rare-book departments at the British Library; Robin Harcourt Williams, Librarian and Archivist to the Marquis of Salisbury at Hatfield House; Julia Hudson, Assistant Archivist at St George's Chapel, Windsor; Patricia Robinson of the Bodleian Library, Oxford; the Gloucestershire Record Office; Claude Blair for details of Henry's armour and his new research regarding that worn by the king on the Boulogne campaign; Dr Seonaid Simpson for her kindness in helping with many details concerning the king's medical condition; the Revd Father Jerome Bertram for much help with Latin translations; David Chipp for his helpful comments on the manuscript; Ian Drury of Weidenfeld & Nicolson for all his encouragement; Caroline Cambridge, Managing Editor, for much kindness and always willing help; Lisa Rogers for her painstaking care and considerable editing skills; Celia Levett for her proofreading; Alison Waggitt for the index; and finally to Marcel Hoad for his invaluable support in so many ways.

To all these kind people, I would like to pass on my grateful thanks.

I must point out, however, that any errors or omissions are entirely my own responsibility.

Robert Hutchinson

WEST SUSSEX, 2005

Prologue

'The Pope has news from France confirming the death of the king of England and attaches great importance to it, saying this opportunity must not be allowed to slip without endeavouring to bring the country to submission again.'

JUAN DE VEGA, SPANISH AMBASSADOR IN ROME, IN A CONFIDENTIAL DISPATCH TO HIS EMPEROR, CHARLES V, 19 FEBRUARY 1547.[1]

Henry VIII – 'by the grace of God, King of England, France and Lord of Ireland, Defender of the Faith and of the Church of England ... on earth the Supreme Head'[2] – finally departed his long, troubled life, friendless and lonely, at around two o'clock in the morning of Friday 28 January 1547.[3] The golden glory of his spry, gallant youth had years ago faded away and the radiant European prince of the Field of the Cloth of Gold in 1520 had decayed into a bloated, hideously obese, black-humoured old man, rarely seen in public during his last months. The bloody-handed tyrant now lay lifeless in the magnificently carved walnut great bed in his opulent secret apartments in the sprawling Palace of Westminster. His unpredictable, dangerous moods and Tudor low cunning had at long last been neutralised by the omnipotent hand of Death. After thirty-seven years, nine months and five days of absolute power, ruthless and rapacious government and the judicial murder of up to 150,000[4] of his hapless subjects – some his wives, best friends and distant relatives – Henry expired dumb and helpless, his cruel belligerence ultimately silenced. The royal hand firmly squeezed that of the faithful and obsequious Archbishop of Canterbury Thomas Cranmer, the only sign that he died 'in grace', secure in the faith of Christ. The 'old fox', as one French ambassador called him, was aged fifty-five years and seven months, a good age for those times[5] – particularly considering the king's known fondness for gin,[6] his latterly sedentary existence and persistent overindulgence in entirely the wrong kinds of food.

Later that morning, as the huge, stinking corpse stiffened and grew cold, the members of Henry's turbulent Privy Council, led by Cranmer; Thomas Wriothesley, his scheming Lord Chancellor; Sir William Paget, the king's Chief Secretary and Sir William Paulet, Lord St John, Lord Steward of the Household, filed thoughtfully through the silent, darkened bedchamber, primarily to confirm formally that the royal life really had expired. They were also there to pay their respects to the monarch they had feared, maybe loathed, but to whom they certainly owed much for their considerable lands, income and status. These strutting dignitaries had all survived a precarious existence at Henry's court, always living under the cosh of his erratic temper and overdeveloped ego. Dread of sudden disfavour had pervaded every corner of his many magnificent royal palaces and houses like an ever-present but invisible contagion. One moment, perhaps, they could be riding high in the king's esteem; the next, arrested by the captain of the guard, accompanied by a file of halberdiers, on a trumped-up charge of treason or heresy. Life or death, poverty or wealth, could all hang merely on the irascible whim of a king both stricken with pain and frustrated by the immobility and limitations imposed by old age and his several ailments – or on the outcomes of the devious plots hatched by the politico-religious factions at his court in furtherance of their own quests for power and influence. As the always realistic courtier Sir Anthony Denny later told his friend Roger Ascham, tutor to Princess Elizabeth:

The court ... is a place so slippery that duty never so well done is not a staff stiff enough to stand by always very surely; where you shall many times reap most unkindness where you have sown greatest pleasures and those also ready to do you much hurt, to whom you never intended to think any harm.[7]

Watching the hushed figures as they moved slowly around the bed were Denny and Sir William Herbert, the two powerful Chief Gentlemen of the Privy Chamber who had efficiently guarded Henry's isolation from the bustling world of his court and realm over the last years and months of his life and ministered even to the most intimate needs of his malodorous and diseased body.

Whether in sixteenth-century England or 500 years on in today's sleazy authoritarian states, a change in regime is an uncertain, perilous time for those accustomed to the ample pleasures and comforts of authority. The small government of largely self-seeking men that Henry had left behind him now moved swiftly to sustain their precarious grip on power and to secure the person of his successor, the precocious and intelligent nine-year-old Prince Edward, the long-awaited legitimate son and heir provided by Queen Jane Seymour.

His uncle, Edward Seymour, the ambitious and conniving Earl of Hertford, and Sir Anthony Browne, Master of the King's Horse, with a force of 300 mounted troops, rode post-haste to Hertford Castle where Edward was staying, later moving the prince, under close guard, to Enfield, Middlesex, where his half-sister Princess Elizabeth was living. Both were then told of their father's death and due homage was paid to Edward as the new king.[8] From here, at around three or four o' clock in the morning of 29 January, Hertford sent Paget the key to the small casket containing Henry's recently revised last will and political testament. In a covering letter, he agreed that the king's will

should [not] be opened until further consultation and that it might be well considered how much ought to be published. For diverse [reasons] I think it not convenient to satisfy the world [yet].

Hertford's letter was endorsed: 'Post-haste, with all diligence, for your life.'[9] As an additional security measure, England was sealed off from Europe by closure of the ports and the roads around London were also blocked by troops by government order.

For three days, news of Henry's death was kept secret – even within the corridors of his own court – thereby maintaining the pretence of everyday normality. Francis van der Delft, the well-informed Spanish ambassador to London, wrote to his imperial master, the Emperor Charles V, on 31 January:

> I learnt from a very confidential source that the King, whom may God receive in His Grace, had departed this life, although not the slightest signs of such a thing were to be seen at court, and even the usual ceremony of bearing in the royal dishes to the sound of trumpets was continued without interruption.[10]

The same day, a Monday, still under Hertford's close protection, Edward rode south through the City of London to the Tower, where he was publicly proclaimed king amid the roar of cannon firing salutes from the battlements and from ships moored in the River Thames. The arch-conspirator Wriothesley, his voice choking with emotion and insincere tears trickling down his cheeks, had that morning announced Henry's death to a genuinely grieving Parliament. Paget then read out the salient terms of the king's last will and Parliament was immediately dissolved.

Close by, as the power-broking and deals were done in countless behind-the-hand conversations in the galleries and darkened closets of the Palace of Westminster, the efficient bureaucracy was setting in train the elaborate arrangements for Henry's obsequies. In 1547, as in 2002 with the funeral of Queen Elizabeth, the Queen Mother, the establishment knew how to put on a good show full of pomp and circumstance, splendour and pageantry. Every last detail of form and protocol had already been laid down in the Westminster *Ordo*[11] by the heralds of the College of Arms and according to rules established by the dead king's domineering grandmother, Margaret Beaufort, before she died nearly four decades earlier.

The first priority was to stabilise Henry's body, already corrupted by the blood and pus of his ulcerated legs,[12] by 'spurging, cleansing, bowelling, searing, embalming, furnishing and dressing with spices'.[13] Paulet ordered the royal household's gentleman apothecary, Thomas Alsop, to supply unguents – including cloves, oil of balm, tow, myrrh and sweet-smelling nigella and musk – either powdered and divided into seven lots for the surgeons to use in embalming, or contained in ten bags to put into the coffin,[14] at a total cost to the exchequer of £26 12s 2d – more than £6,600 at today's prices. Alsop and the yeomen apothe- caries of the royal household assisted the surgeons and wax-chandlers in the embalming process now under way. It must have been a thor- oughly unpleasant and exhausting experience: at his death, Henry probably weighed more than twenty-eight stone[15] and the 6 ft. 3 in.-tall obese corpse cannot have been easy to manhandle. None the less, the cleansing and purging were successfully completed and the royal bowels removed before the embalmed cadaver was wrapped in layers of waxed cerecloth, in turn covered with lengths of the finest velvet and finally trussed up with silken cords. A label, probably cast in lead, was secured to the breast with 'writing in great and small letters ... containing his name and style, the day and year of his death'. The king's serjeant plumber and carpenters were then called in to seal the body inside an anthropoid lead shell and to construct the 6 ft. 10 in.-long coffin's huge outer casing of solid elm.[16]

The king's entrails and bowels were buried in a lead box in the chapel of the Palace of Westminster amid solemn Masses and the weighty coffin set upon trestles within the presence chamber, resting beneath a rich pall of cloth of gold with a cross on top, surrounded by candles. Thirty of Henry's chaplains and the Gentlemen of the Privy Chamber took turns to mount their loyal twenty-four-hour watch over the body for five days.[17]

Above the coffin, as a reminder of the glories of the reign now ended, was the huge *Whitehall Mural*, painted ten years before, showing the magnificent, imposing figure of Henry at the height of his powers. He stands proudly before the figures of his parents, Henry VII and his queen Elizabeth of York, the demure Jane Seymour – mother of the king's lawful successor – to his right.[18] It was, and is, a powerful propaganda image. Many watching in that hushed room must have wondered what the future held for England and the uncertain Tudor dynasty.

Some conspirators already knew.

CHAPTER ONE

A Dangerous Honour

'The King's Majesty was married on Thursday last to my Lady Latimer, a woman in my judgement, for virtue, wisdom and gentleness, most meet for his Highness, and sure I am his Majesty had never a wife more agreeable to his heart than she is. Our Lord send them long life and much joy together.'

THOMAS WRIOTHESLEY, SECRETARY TO THE PRIVY COUNCIL,
IN A LETTER TO THE DUKE OF SUFFOLK, 16 JULY 1543.[1]

Henry had always been unlucky in his women. Throughout his life, a number of wives failed him in his desperately important political mission to provide healthy, legitimate male heirs to carry on the precarious Tudor line. During those tempestuous years, some of his wives had plotted and intrigued, and others, in his eyes, had cuckolded or betrayed him. In the 1530s, full in the teeth of the Holy Catholic Church, he had annulled his union with his first wife, Catherine of Aragon, on the grounds of the uncertain consummation of her marriage with his elder brother Arthur before his death aged fifteen, from tuberculosis, on 2 April 1502, less than five months after their wedding. Henry's reckless infatuation with Anne Boleyn ended brutally on Tower Green on 19

May 1536 with an executioner specially brought from St Omer in France to behead her with a mighty two-handed sword. After the political pain and agony of nearly three decades and his cataclysmic break with Rome, Henry finally got his long-sought-after lawful son at two o'clock on the morning of 12 October 1537 by his third wife, the modest, charming and fragile Jane Seymour. She died twelve days later, just before midnight, from a puerperal fever and septicaemia caused by an infection contracted during the arduous two days and three nights of labour in her newly decorated chamber at Hampton Court.

Despite Henry's honest and genuine grief at his queen's death, it was not long before his counsellors were pressing him to take a fourth wife, primarily for diplomatic reasons, but also to provide the all-important 'spare' male heir, a Duke of York, in case the infant Prince Edward fell victim to the constant epidemics of plague and other diseases that afflicted London. Unofficial ambassadorial enquiries, possibly without Henry's knowledge, were immediately put in hand regarding a number of potential candidates even before Jane's solemn burial in a vault beneath the choir of St George's Chapel, Windsor, on 12 November.[2]

Initially, a French match looked politically advantageous, which might block a threatening alliance emerging between France and Spain. Reports of a voluptuous tall widow, Marie of Guise, had captivated Henry and, as he told his cronies, he was 'big in person and have need of a big wife'.[3] But she had already become betrothed to James V of Scotland[4] and Henry had bluntly told the French envoy in London that he 'would not take the Scots' leavings'.[5] Other nubile French ladies were suggested, including Marie's attractive sisters, Louise and Renée. Amongst her many other charms and allurements, the blushing Louise was known to be a virgin. The French ambassador Louis de Perreau, Sieur de Castillon, lasciviously told the king: 'Take her! She is a maid, so you will have the advantage of being able to shape the passage to your measure.'[6] Laughing uproariously, Henry slapped the bawdy diplomat on his shoulder and piously went in to attend Mass. Marie of Vendôme was also available, but unfortunately already professed as a nun. However, the boisterous Constable of France was 'sure the king of England, who considers himself

Pope in his own kingdom, would choose her in preference to all others'.[7]

Henry was always wary of making a physically unattractive match. Consequently, he demanded to inspect personally seven or eight French princesses within a marquee pitched on the border between France and English-held Calais before making his final choice of bride. Even though they would be properly chaperoned by the French queen, the king, Francis I, was outraged at the suggestion, and Castillon was instructed to tell Henry in August 1538:

> It is not the custom of France to send damsels of noble and princely families to be passed in review as if they were hackneys [horses] for sale.[8]

More accepted methods of royal selection, involving sedate diplomatic reports about suitability and appearance, were firmly rejected in London, with Henry insisting:

> By God! I trust no one but myself. The thing touches me too near. I wish to see them and know them some time before deciding.

The audacious French ambassador archly replied, to Henry's palpable embarrassment:

> Then maybe your grace would like to mount them one after the other and keep the one you find to be the best broken in. Is that the way the knights of the Round Table treated women in your country in times past?[9]

His laddish jibe hit home at the priggish monarch's well-known fondness for chivalry and courtly love and occasional prudery over matters moral. Castillon reported afterwards:

> I think this shamed him, for he laughed and blushed at the same time and recognised that the way he had taken was a little dis-courteous. After rubbing his nose a little, he said, 'Yes, but since the king [Francis I], my brother, has already so great an amity with the [Spanish] emperor, what amity should I have with him? I ask

because I am resolved not to marry again unless the emperor or
king prefer my friendship to that which they have together.'[10]

The ambassador adroitly ducked the question, replying tactfully that it
would take a wiser man than he to answer that. Henry's choice of partner
manifestly rested not just on sexual attraction – diplomacy was an all-
important consideration, too.

Privately, some may have thought that the matter of a new wife was
daily becoming increasingly unseemly – more like an ageing stallion
being brought to stud with a young, prancing filly than part of a grand,
sweeping diplomatic strategy and a vital means to further safeguard
the crown of England for the Tudor dynasty. If anyone did think this,
no one dared, at the risk of the king's notorious and awesome rage, to
mutter more than uncouth whispers amongst the swaggering courtiers
in the corridors of Henry's palaces.

But the king was not dissuaded from pursuing the arcane process
of princely courtship by his French failures in love. Perhaps, his fawning
advisers murmured discreetly, a Hapsburg candidate, then? They had in
their sights another prospective bride: Christina, daughter of the deposed
Christian II of Denmark, niece of the Spanish Emperor Charles V and
great-niece to Henry's first wife, Catherine of Aragon.

She was slim, also very tall and said to be 'soft of speech and very
gentle in countenance'[11] with dimples appearing on her chin and cheeks
when she smiled 'which becomes her right exceeding well'.[12] The sixteen-
year-old widow of Francesco Sforza, Duke of Milan, was universally
admired for her beauty and the portrait that the court artist Hans Holbein
the Younger had frantically painted in just three hours and brought
back from Brussels enchanted Henry and awakened joy and fresh
romance in his cynical old heart.

She was, however, less than enamoured with the prospect of marital
bliss with the English king, even though Thomas Wriothesley, then one
of Henry's two principal secretaries, persuasively told her that his master
was the 'most gentle gentleman that lives, his nature so benign and
pleasant that I think till this day, no man hath heard many angry words

pass his mouth'.[13] No doubt he paused expectantly for her reaction to this outrageous canard. Confronted by her silence, Wriothesley hastened on: Henry, he said, was 'one of the most puissant and mighty princes of Christendom. If you saw him, you would [talk of] his virtue, gentleness, wisdom, experience, goodliness of person, all ... gifts and qualities meet to be in a Prince'.

Truth was never at a premium amongst the sycophantic courtiers, and Christina knew it. She listened carefully to his saccharine words but giggled, Wriothesley reported afterwards, 'like one, methought, that was tickled'.[14]

The duchess's doubts mounted as her advisers talked openly of the widespread rumours of the sinister demise of the king's previous wives: 'Her great-aunt was poisoned, that the second wife was put to death and the third lost for lack of keeping her childbed.'[15] There was also the necessity (but, realistically, remote chance) of obtaining a papal dispensation to allow marriage to her great-aunt's widower.

Henry's reputation abroad was the real problem, however: on 2 January 1539, the Marquis de Aguilar wrote to the imperial emperor that the English king 'is every day growing more inhumane and cruel',[16] a stark and telling accusation in the sixteenth century when life was cheap and judicial execution both uncivilised and universally practised. Henry Pole, Lord Montague, who had been caught up in Henry's brutal and violent purge of his blood royal cousins the Courtenays and Poles (the last of the royal Plantagenet line) and executed the previous month, had prophetically told his servant: 'Jerome, the King never made man, but he destroyed him again with displeasure or with the sword' – a prediction that would become repeatedly true, as many were to discover at the cost of their lives or their lands. In the end, with a wit and wisdom far beyond her teenage years, Christina reportedly declared that if she had two heads, one would be at Henry's disposal.[17] She would not become his new bride.

Despite by now being well practised in the marriage stakes and in choosing a handful of mistresses in the past, Henry was finding it difficult to make a decision on a bride. Diplomatic events abroad overtook him as he continued to cast wearily about for a new wife, surrounded by portraits of eligible Continental princesses and piles of glowing testimonials to their beauty and demeanour provided by his energetic envoys. On 18 June 1538, France and Spain agreed on a diplomatic *rapprochement*, signing a ten-year truce in Nice. Urged on by Pope Paul III, they planned co-ordinated action against religious heresy, beginning with a trade embargo. An invasion of England by the Catholic powers now suddenly seemed likely, sparking the frantic construction of a rash of new fortifications along her vulnerable south coast. The German Protestant princely houses began to look a more attractive option, both as a source for a bride and as Continental allies to prevent Henry's total isolation in European politics.

And so the king embarked on the farce, if not disaster, of his fourth marriage.

His fumbling choice settled on twenty-four-year-old Anne of Cleves, who came from very much a ducal backwater on the Lower Rhine. She was one of two unmarried sisters of the ambitious Duke William who had succeeded to the Clevois title in February 1539. All the warning signs, however, were apparent for those with the skill to spot them. Anne did not hunt, nor could she sing or play a musical instrument – three of Henry's favourite pastimes – but she *was* an accomplished needlewoman. She was unsophisticated, unworldly and unused (if not totally innocent) in the ways of both men and love. She could command only a few words of English; indeed, she could not read or write in any language aside from her own unattractive nasal and guttural Low German dialect. When Henry's envoy, Nicholas Wotton, complained that he could not see her face beneath her voluminous headdress, her scandalised chancellor retorted, 'What, do you want to see her naked?' And the full-face portrait brought back to Henry generously flattered her appearance, showing her with a solemn, almost serene countenance, an oval face, a prominent, slightly bulbous long nose and heavy-lidded eyes, demurely cast down.

Henry, persuaded by the artful skills of Master Holbein and the enthusiastic reports of his ambassadors, finally assented to the marriage.

So it was that, accompanied by an entourage of fifteen ladies and a 245-strong household including thirteen trumpeters and two kettle drummers,[18] Anne of Cleves arrived in English-held Calais from Düsseldorf on 11 December 1539, to face the perilous and uncertain voyage across the Channel. But gales and bad weather delayed the new queen's departure for England and the loving embraces of her egotistical bridegroom. The Earl of Southampton, then Lord High Admiral, occupied the time whilst awaiting calmer seas teaching Anne, at her request, the game of piquet, no doubt in the happy knowledge that playing cards was an enjoyable entertainment for the king. Southampton wrote enthusiastically of her to Henry, who was celebrating Christmas at Westminster, in words and phrases he was later to regret bitterly. Afterwards, he admitted, rather ruefully, that:

> Upon the first sight of her, [he] considered it was no time to dispraise her there, whom so many had by reports and paintings so much extolled, [so he] did by his letters much praise her.[19]

But who could blame Southampton for his eagerness to please his royal master, 'the English Nero'?[20] The bearer of bad tidings to the all-powerful has traditionally always paid an unenviable price and he saw no sensible reason to test Henry's uncertain temper.

Eventually, the winds in the Channel abated and, accompanied by a fleet of fifty English ships, Anne and her English escorts landed at Deal in Kent at five o'clock on the cold afternoon of 27 December. The party pushed on by easy stages, via Dover and Canterbury, arriving three days later at the bishop's palace at Rochester. There they would remain until their planned final ride to Greenwich, where Henry was due to welcome her officially on 3 January 1540.

The king, impatient and headstrong as ever and excited at the prospect of meeting his new bride, decided on a surprise visit to present Anne with a New Year's gift 'to nourish love', as he told his chief minister, the Lord Privy Seal Thomas Cromwell. The delicate flower of romance had not yet died in his heart. Throwing aside rigid court protocol and the careful plans of state pageantry, Henry and five of his Gentlemen of the Privy Chamber, wearing gay multicoloured cloaks and hoods, rode pell-mell to Rochester, arriving on the afternoon of New Year's Day. He was more like an ardent young lover again than a forty-eight-year-old monarch long past his prime, suffering from painful, badly ulcerated legs.

A stunning disappointment awaited the merry party.

Sir Anthony Browne, Master of the King's Horse, politely called on Anne in her lodgings at Rochester to warn her of the king's imminent arrival. When he clapped eyes on the new queen, Sir Anthony was 'never more dismayed in all his life, lamenting in his heart ... to see the lady so far and unlike that was reported'.[21] He had no time to warn Henry, as the impetuous bridegroom and two of his jolly, laughing companions were hard on his heels. There must have been an awkward and embarrassed silence, with blushes and nervous smiles on the faces of Anne and her German ladies-in-waiting, after the boisterous king burst impatiently into the room, anxious to embrace and kiss his bride.

Henry's first glimpse of his new queen left him 'marvellously astonished and abashed'[22] as she stood at a window of the palace, shyly watching the holiday entertainment of bear-baiting noisily going on down in the courtyard outside. She looked older than her years; she certainly lacked her reported beauty – and smallpox scars disfigured her sallow face.[23] Sir Anthony immediately saw 'discontentment' in the king's expression, and 'a disliking of her person'.[24] Henry, who could never hide or control his emotions, stayed scarcely long enough to utter twenty polite, stilted words. He snatched up his gift to her – a richly garnished partlet of sable skins to be worn around the neck – and hastily departed amid the low bows of his friends and courtiers, leaving behind a perplexed bride. The king sent his present around the next morning with as 'cold and single a message as might be' before hurriedly and sulkily departing Rochester for Greenwich. On the way back, Henry angrily asked his friend, Sir John Russell:

How like you this woman? Do you think her so fair and of such beauty as has been reported to me? I pray you tell me the truth.

Russell, no doubt hesitantly, told Henry that he did not think her fair, 'but to be of a brown complexion'. The king, 'sore troubled', cried out:

> Alas! Whom should men trust? I promise you I see no such thing
> in her as hath been showed me of her and am ashamed that men
> have so praised her as they have done. I like her not.[25]

There was no escape from the potential dishonour of the situation. Henry had to put a brave face on events, if only for the all-important diplomatic objectives of the match. He greeted a sumptuously dressed Anne as planned at Shooter's Hill, Blackheath, on 3 January 1540, gallantly pulling off his jewelled bonnet 'and with most lovely countenance and princely behaviour saluted, welcomed and embraced her, to the great rejoicing of the beholders' – an escort of 5,000 horsemen and invited luminaries from the City of London. But beneath the smiling face of regal propriety and all that pomp and circumstance lurked a burning, resentful anger and an overwhelming desire to halt the wedding.

Safely within his Privy Chamber at Greenwich Palace, he snapped, 'What remedy now?'[26] to his hapless chief minister, Thomas Cromwell, adding, 'If I had known as much before as I now know, she should not have come within this realm.' Cromwell could only reply, rather unconvincingly, 'I thought she had a queenly manner.'[27]

The Lord Privy Seal, thinking hard and fast, seized on the unresolved issue of an old pre-contract of marriage between Anne and Francis, the son of the Duke of Lorraine, mooted in 1527 when she was aged twelve and he just ten. To the future queen's continued mystification and disappointment, the marriage was suddenly postponed for two days while Cromwell's lawyers and the king's Privy Council wrestled with the issue in a desperate, frenetic attempt to revoke or in some way nullify the unwanted nuptial agreement. But it was all to no avail: Duke William's taciturn ambassadors were naturally less than helpful and 'made a light matter of it'. Unfortunately, they said, they had brought no documents with them to clear up the matter, but they emphasized, reassuringly, that there was really no problem as the pre-contract was made in Anne's minority and had never taken effect. They promised to send over the requisite papers 'as should put all out of doubt'.[28]

So, to Henry's great chagrin, the wedding went ahead. Ironically, despite the lengthy diplomatic negotiations and niceties, this match ended up just like Henry's earlier marriages, overshadowed with doubts regarding its legal validity. Archbishop Thomas Cranmer solemnized the marriage in the queen's closet at Greenwich on 6 January 1540, Twelfth Night – traditionally a time of merriment and laughter in Henry's court, a coincidence that could only fuel his anger and increase his despair. For the wedding, Anne was dressed in a gown in the Dutch fashion made of rich cloth of gold, embroidered with flowers and decorated with 'great and Oriental pearls'. She wore her yellow hair long, 'hanging down' beneath a golden coronet 'replenished with a great stone and set about full of branches of rosemary'.[29] She must have looked rather like a Christmas tree. Her wedding ring was engraved with the motto 'God send me well to keep'. Unbeknown to her, divine intervention would indeed be necessary to safeguard her future, as the king had lost all interest in his bride. She respectfully curtsied low, three times, as Henry came into the chapel.

The thwarted king was resentful and 'nothing pleasantly disposed'.[30] His friends and courtiers were careful in their choice of words to him. The evening before, he had asked Cromwell, 'Is there none other remedy that I must needs, against my will, put my neck in the yoke?'[31] Before he limped towards the chapel, he growled that he had been 'ill served [by] them' he had trusted. The king paused before entering to tell Cromwell, 'My lord, if it were not to satisfy the world, and my realm, I would not do that [which] I must do this day for no earthly thing.'[32] Never was there a more unhappy, reluctant and bad-tempered bridegroom and Henry's words were to bode very ill for his chief minister.

Inevitably, the wedding night was an embarrassing physical disaster. The next morning, a prurient Cromwell unwisely asked the king, 'How liked you the queen?' One can imagine his nudge and the leer on his coarse, heavy-jowled, almost bovine features. Glowering, Henry told him brusquely, 'I liked her before not well, but now I liked her much worse.'[33] He added:

I have felt her belly and her breasts and thereby, as I can judge, she should be no maid, which struck me so to the heart when I felt them, that I had neither will nor courage to proceed further in other matters. I left her as good a maid as I found her.[34]

The king then stumped grumpily off. Worse was to come: after four nights of dutiful manly effort, the king still had not consummated the marriage, and clearly now did not ever intend to.

He confided to the Gentlemen of his Privy Chamber the very intimate problems of his marital bed. Sir Thomas Heneage, Groom of the Stool, later testified:

In so often that his Grace went to bed to her, he ever grudged and said plainly he mistrusted her to be no maid, by reason of the looseness of her breasts and other tokens. Furthermore, he could have no appetite with her to do as a man should do with his wife, for such displeasant airs as he felt with her.[35]

Henry told his Privy Chamber confidant Anthony Denny, 'Her body was of such indisposition ... that he could never in her company be provoked and stirred to know her carnally.'[36] Henry, ever interested in matters medical, also diligently consulted his physicians. One of the royal doctors, John Chambre, comfortingly counselled the king not to 'enforce himself' for fear of causing an 'inconvenient debility' of his sexual organ.[37] Word of the king and queen's unhappy state of affairs was, no doubt, the secret, sniggering talk of the court. Henry's all-consuming and dangerously inflated ego was threatened by these whispers, and he told another of his physicians, William Butts, that he had experienced *duas pollutiones nocturnas in somno* (two nocturnal ejaculations or 'wet dreams') and believed 'himself able to do the act with others but not with her'.[38] Ribald suggestions that he was impotent were firmly quashed by Butts' repeating these statements around Henry's household, as intended.

It may be, as some have speculated, that the king was always keenly aroused by the odour of a woman's body. The queen's 'displeasant airs' could hardly have spurred his husbandly duty or stimulated his physical ability to consummate the marriage.

Poor Anne of Cleves – truly an innocent abroad. Just before midsummer, the forthright Lady Jane Rochford told her directly, 'I think your grace is still a maid.' The queen replied, 'How can I be a maid ... and sleep every night with the king?' The unworldly Anne added, ingenuously:

> When he comes to bed, he kisses me and takes me by the hand and bids me 'Good night sweetheart' and in the morning kisses me and bids me 'Farewell darling'. Is not this enough?

Lady Eleanor Rutland said diplomatically,

> Madam, there must be more than this, or it will be long [before] we have a Duke of York, which this realm most desires.

Still puzzled, the queen replied,

> No, I am contented with this, for I know no more.[39]

Henry was now counting the days before he could end the farce of his fourth marriage. Wriothesley, 'right sorry that his majesty should be so troubled', urged his friend Cromwell – 'for God's sake' – to quickly devise some stratagem to rid the king of his unwanted wife, 'for if he remained in this grief and trouble they should all one day smart for it.' Cromwell could only answer hopelessly: 'Yes! How?'[40]

But time had run out for England's chief minister. After dinner on the afternoon of Saturday 10 June 1540, Cromwell attended a routine meeting of the Privy Council at Westminster. On entering the chamber, he found the other members already seated around the table. As he walked to his chair, the Duke of Norfolk barked out, 'Cromwell, do not sit there. That is no place for a traitor! Traitors do not sit amongst gentlemen!' Shocked, Cromwell could only lamely retort, 'I am not a traitor.' Behind him, the captain of the guard had come into the Council room and he now seized Cromwell's arm, saying, 'I arrest you.' Cromwell asked, 'What for?' The captain replied ominously, 'That you will learn elsewhere.' Norfolk then stepped forward: 'Stop, Captain! Traitors must not wear the Garter.'[41] He ripped the jewelled Order of St George from around Cromwell's neck, followed by Southampton tearing the glittering Garter insignia from his robes. Norfolk repeated: 'You are a traitor. You shall be judged by the bloody laws you yourself have made.'[42]

They were like hyenas around the still-living carcass of their luckless prey. As the Councillors pounded the table with their fists and chanted, 'Traitor, traitor, traitor,' Cromwell, red-faced, his eyes starting out of their sockets with fury, threw his cap down on the floor in tearful frustration and was dragged away, still struggling, by the captain and his six halberdiers to a boat waiting to convey him to the Tower. Cromwell, arch-intriguer and architect of the financially fruitful Dissolution of the Monasteries, had tarried too long to save himself. Now he would pay with his life for one of his few failures in his dutiful performance of the king's business.

On 24 June, Anne was dispatched to Richmond Palace, Surrey, for 'her health, open air and pleasure' under the guise of a convenient threat of plague in London. In reality, Henry had delicate matters to settle and in order to achieve his objective, the queen had to be absent from court. The marriage was to be nullified by his two archbishops, sixteen bishops and 139 learned academics on the legally subtle grounds that Henry did not consummate it (since he knew it to be unlawful) because of Anne's elusive pre-contract with Francis of Lorraine. Henry had, to all intents and purposes, never agreed to the marriage: 'I never for love to the woman consented to marry; nor yet if she brought maidenhead with her, took any from her by true carnal copulation,' he wrote in his 'brief, true and perfect declaration'[43] to the commission. The king liked such matters to be tidy and to appear legal, but there were still a few loose ends to tie up. His disgraced and discarded chief minister could provide one last faithful service before execution. Cromwell, incarcerated in the Tower, was instructed to provide testimony fully confirming Henry's case if he wanted to avoid the traitor's hideous death of half-hanging, evisceration whilst still living and then beheading.[44] Cromwell signed the required full statement of events, concluding:

I am a most woeful prisoner, ready to take the death when it shall please God and your majesty. Yet the frail flesh incites me continually to call to your grace for mercy and grace for my offences. And thus Christ says preserve and keep you.

Written at the Tower, this Wednesday the last of June, with the heavy heart and trembling hand of your Highness's most heavy and most miserable prisoner and poor slave.[45]

Desperation and despair then overwhelmed him and he added, as a shaky postscript, 'Most gracious prince, I cry for mercy, mercy, mercy.' His piteous, anguished plea inevitably fell on deaf ears, although Archbishop Cranmer had bravely pleaded with Henry for Cromwell's life on 11 June, writing that he

much magnified his diligence in the king's service and preservation and had discovered all plots as soon as they were made. [Cromwell] had always loved the king above all things and [had] served him with great fidelity and success.

Cranmer added that if the minister really was a traitor, he was glad he had been arrested, but he prayed God earnestly

to send the king such a counsellor in his stead who he could trust and who, for all his qualities, could serve him as he had done. I am very sorrowful: for whom shall your Grace trust hereafter, if you may not trust him?[46]

But Cromwell was finished and as good as dead already, as far as the king was concerned: Henry was already seizing his considerable wealth. Only hours after the arrest, around £14,000 of moveable assets – gold and silver-gilt plate, such as crosiers and chalices, and ready cash (worth nearly £6 million at 2004 prices) – were rapidly inventoried and removed during the night from Cromwell's home at Austin Friars, near the north wall of the City of London. The bullion and coinage were taken, escorted by fifty archers under the command of Sir Thomas Cheyney, to Henry's secret jewel house at Westminster.[47] Cromwell's other household goods were systematically looted soon after.[48] There were also his considerable holdings of lands and revenues elsewhere to sequester, all of it a welcome windfall for the ruthless and avaricious king.

Cromwell – 'a person of as poor and low degree as few be within [the] realm' – was condemned without trial by Act of Attainder on 29 June[49] for being 'the most false and corrupt traitor, deceiver and circumventor against your royal person and the imperial crown of this realm that had ever been known in your whole reign'. He was also labelled a heretic and accused of circulating many erroneous books amongst Henry's subjects, particularly some that contradicted the belief in the holy sacrament of communion, as well as licensing heretics as preachers. He had taken bribes in exchange for permission to export money, corn, horses and other commodities, contrary to Henry's own proclamations. He had issued many commissions without the king's knowledge and, being of base birth, had confidently said that 'he was sure of the king'.[50] Cromwell's conveniently discovered crimes knew no bounds.

After the enjoyable and profitable diversion of sequestering his chief minister's wealth, Henry still faced two major problems in seeking his new annulment. Firstly, there was the reaction of Anne herself – her contradictory evidence could damage or invalidate his claim of non-consummation – and secondly, the continuing and pressing diplomatic need to keep the Duke of Cleves, Henry's all-important Protestant ally in Germany, happy, even after the rejection of his sister as a wife and the queen of England. The typically Henrician solution was copious quantities of hard cash and maintenance of status. It was dire news for the always hard-pressed royal exchequer, but that was a factor that never entered the king's head when he wanted something badly enough.

In return for remaining in England as 'the king's good sister', where she would be firmly under Henry's surveillance and control, Anne was to receive a generous annual pension of £500 for life (£216,265 in today's values), together with a number of manors and lands, most of them, with heavy irony, forfeited by Cromwell himself, who was to pay the scapegoat's horrific price on the scaffold for his hand in arranging the disastrous marriage. What the king taketh away, the king giveth. Anne would remain the premier lady in all England after any new queen and Princesses Mary and Elizabeth. She could keep all her clothes, jewels and plate. She was given a fifteen-strong household of German servants appropriate to her rank and station, including Schoulenburg, her own cook. No doubt she could also keep her pet parrot.

Wriothesley, Southampton and Suffolk journeyed to Richmond by river to tell her the awful news. There were wild rumours afterwards that she fainted when told of the annulment, possibly with relief at the prospect of freedom from further nights of fumbling attention by the grunting, obese and probably flatulent Henry, but these naturally do not figure in the courtiers' report of this difficult meeting. More likely, their unexpected appearance sparked instant fears that *she* was to be taken to the Tower, where a violent death perhaps awaited her. The frightened queen was swiftly reassured. Anne listened to their silky, flowing phrases through an interpreter, apparently 'without alteration of countenance' and, with little thought, meekly agreed to the terms of the settlement. Behind that stolid, pockmarked face, she was no fool. All in all, it was not a bad deal and to turn it down, Anne must have fancied, could well lead to an appointment with the executioner, given Henry's usual method of dispensing with inconvenient wives such as Anne Boleyn. Self-preservation was a more powerful emotion now than the remote possibility of her romantic attachment to a vindictive monarch with a known violent streak in his character. She seized the chance of freedom with a zest that speaks volumes for the absolute sterility of the royal marriage and with an alacrity strongly suggestive of her own frustrations and fears.[51]

There only remained some tiresome formalities. After the Clerical Convocation had ended her marriage on 9 July, confirmed by Parliament just four days later, she docilely wrote to Henry on 16 July promising to be 'your Majesty's must humble sister and servant', signing herself merely as 'Anna, daughter of Cleves'.[52] Her surrender of the status and trappings of royalty was complete. In a letter to her brother, Duke William, almost certainly dictated by Henry's officials, she said, 'I account God pleased with [what] is done and know myself to have suffered no wrong or injury' and averred that her body was still 'preserved in the integrity which I brought into this realm'. The English king was 'a most kind, loving and friendly father and brother' and he was treating her 'as honourably and with as much humanity and liberality as you, I myself, or any of our kin or allies could wish or desire'. She earnestly begged him not to be difficult about the agreement.[53] For his part, Duke William was 'glad his sister had fared no worse'. And for Henry, it was the tidiest and most convenient end to any of his marriages, wrapped up not in the six uncomfortable years it took to rid himself of Catherine of Aragon, but in just six days.[54]

France's new ambassador in London, Charles de Marillac, reported disapprovingly, 'As for her who is now called Madame de Cleves, far from pretending to be married, she is as joyous as ever and wears new dresses every day.'[55] After six months and three days of an arranged marriage choked by dark humiliation and intimate despair, a golden life now beckoned after Henry. Anne of Cleves began to enjoy drinking wine, casting aside her previous abstinence. She had metamorphosed into a rich, merry widow in all but name or title. In the very ending of the marriage, and probably for the first time, Anne had not disappointed the king.

The reasons behind Henry's desire for a speedy annulment of his marriage were not only those of physical revulsion, or even royal protocol and diplomatic convenience. He had another matter on his mind, one that was very much closer to his heart and dipping libido: the frivolous and vivacious eighteen-year-old Katherine Howard, a first cousin to Anne Boleyn and niece to the reactionary Thomas, Third Duke of Norfolk. The king probably saw Katherine in March 1540 at a grand banquet given by the conniving Bishop of Winchester Stephen Gardiner in the great hall of Winchester House in Southwark, his palatial home on the South Bank of the River Thames, built in the shadow of St Saviour's Church. No more flattering portraits, no envoys' carefully euphemistic reports now for Henry. He immediately fell in love with the diminutive, sensual, auburn-haired girl as she danced and frolicked in the rainbow light thrown down by the huge rose window above Gardiner's feast. She was fashionably plump and considered attractive rather than beautiful.

The love match looked incongruous, if not grotesque. She was more than thirty years younger than the king; indeed, she was six years younger than Princess Mary and probably stood well over a foot shorter than the man-mountain the monarch had become as a result of frequent overindulgence at the festive board since Jane Seymour's death. But in Katherine's presence, Henry felt and acted like a romantic young man again – in stark contrast with the bored, empty feelings he had experienced for his unwanted queen, Anne of Cleves. Norfolk, his eyes ever firmly set on increased political power, actively and enthusiastically encouraged the relationship, praising Katherine's 'pure and honest condition' to the king, whose amorous appetites were thoroughly roused.

Henry was already shamelessly showering gifts on the Howard girl by the Easter of 1540. Ralph Morice, Cranmer's secretary, wrote that the 'king's affection was so marvellously set upon that gentlewoman as it was never known that he had the like to any woman'.[56] To Henry, she was a 'blushing rose without a thorn'.[57] He *had* to make her his fifth wife, and his regal desires would never brook denial, once expressed. As the Spanish ambassador, Eustace Chapuys, perceptively wrote later:

> For if this king's nature and inclination be taken into account; if we consider that whenever he takes a fancy to a person or decides for an undertaking, he goes the whole length, there being no limit or restriction whatever to his wishes.[58]

Although a Howard, Katherine came from a far from wealthy background. Her education had been neglected because of the poverty of her father Lord Edmund Howard, the feckless son of the Second Duke of Norfolk. Her bluff and ambitious uncle Thomas Howard, who succeeded his father to the title in 1524,[59] was a soldier, Earl Marshal and Lord High Treasurer of England, the third most important office in the realm. He was also one of the leaders of the religiously conservative party. That year, 1540, he had told a clerk in the exchequer who had married a former nun:

> I never read the Scripture, nor ever will read it. It was merry in England before the new learning came up: yes, I would all things were as has been in times past.[60]

He and Gardiner, the Bishop of Winchester (an even more fervent opponent of liturgical reform), could not believe the luck that Henry's roaming eye had brought them. If Katherine became queen, they would capture greater influence at court, providing the opportunity to return the troubled realm to the traditional religion and to exploit the possibility, albeit dim, of reconciliation with Rome. They were already triumphant at the fall of Cromwell – that scorned and hated religious reformer. Their hopes that their lascivious bait would be snapped up were soon realised. With perfect timing, they led the other members of the Privy Council to humbly beg the king 'to frame his most noble heart to love' – indeed, to marry again and to create, they coyly added, 'some more store of fruit and succession to the comfort of his realm'.[61]

Henry needed no second bidding. A bare nineteen days after the clerical annulment of his marriage to Anne of Cleves, he wed Katherine at Otelands Palace, near Weybridge in Surrey, on 28 July 1540, the same day that the unpopular Cromwell met his bloody fate, 'barbarously' at the hands of a clumsy and unskilled axeman at Tower Hill.[62] Deliberately and ignominiously, his fellow victim on the scaffold was selected to be Walter, Lord Hungerford, who was beheaded for committing buggery and for raping his own daughter.[63] Norfolk's arrogant son Henry Howard, Earl of Surrey, said scornfully of Cromwell's end: 'Now that foul churl is dead, so ambitious of others' [noble] blood; now is he stricken with his own staff.' These 'new erected men [want to] leave no noble man in life'.[64]

The royal couple were now sternly cautioned to use the marital bed 'more for the desire of children, than bodily lust', as their marriage was 'a high and blessed order, ordained of God in paradise'.[65] Henry was almost delirious with happiness about his new bride and on 8 August,

Katherine was publicly displayed as queen at a spectacular banquet at Hampton Court. The wedding seemed to have given the king a fresh zest for life, coupled with a new willingness to listen to his hard-pressed doctors' advice to curb his overeating and control his burgeoning weight.

Marillac reported that the king, then at his house at Woking, Surrey,

> has taken a new rule of living. To rise between five and six, hear mass at seven and then ride [hunt] till dinner-time which is ten a.m. He says he feels much better thus in the country than when he resided all winter in his houses at the gates of London.[66]

He took Katherine on an energetic and triumphant progress that scorching summer – the hottest in living memory – through the counties of Surrey, Berkshire, Buckinghamshire and Oxfordshire, hunting and feasting, dancing and singing all the way. It was truly pastime with good company and marked one of the few periods of real settled happiness for the king. But in September, on the way south to London, at Ampthill in Bedfordshire, he fell sick with malaria and the ulcers on his legs flared up again, forcing him to take to his bed. After recovering and returning to Windsor, he discovered that his niece, Lady Margaret Douglas, senior lady of Katherine's Privy Chamber, was involved in an affair with the queen's brother, Lord Charles Howard. The king could sometimes be prudish over matters sexual. She was banished to Syon Abbey in Middlesex for a year for her 'over-much lightness'. There were also fears about an outbreak of plague outside the walls of Windsor Castle: Henry ordered the sick to be taken from their beds and carried out to the fields alongside the Thames to die, to prevent the threat of infection spreading to the court.[67]

In February 1541, Henry, already walking with the aid of a staff, alarmingly suffered more problems with his ulcerated legs that probably led to a dangerous infection, as he was reported feverish, with a blackened face. But following fearsome losses of temper, he recovered both his good humour and his health. Two months later, there were reports that Katherine was pregnant but these came to nothing and Henry, for the first time, seemed displeased with her.

A curious little drama was played out in London in late June 1541 that vividly demonstrates Henry's vindictiveness and spite. It also reveals just how capricious he could be in the dispensation of his royal prerogative of mercy. Twenty-three-year-old Thomas Fiennes – Lord Dacre of the South, of Herstmonceux Castle, Sussex – was amongst 'eight rakish youths' who had killed 'a poor old man', John Busebridge, in an 'unpremeditated affray' in the neighbouring parish of Hellingly after they were caught poaching deer. With the others, Dacre was tried and sentenced to death. Sir William Paget reported that on 27 June, members of his jury of peers met the Privy Council in the Star Chamber in the Palace of Westminster to discuss their concerns about the case. Some 'spoke so loud' that the royal clerk could plainly hear their voices through the two closed doors between him and the meeting. Amongst those who could not agree to the charge of wilful murder was Lord Cobham, whose remarks, reported Paget, were 'vehement and stiff'. After dinner, the Council passed on these concerns to Henry, together with Dacre's humble submission to the king, 'hoping thereby to move his majesty to pardon him'. The appeals had no effect.[68] Chapuys reported to the Queen of Hungary that despite being both of noble blood and wealthy – Dacre owned property worth more than £1,200 a year (around £450,000 in today's money) – the youth was

> hung from the most ignominious gibbet and for greater shame, dragged through the streets to the place of execution [Tyburn][69] to the great pity of many people, and even of his very judges who wept when they sentenced him and in a body asked his pardon of the king.[70]

Significantly, another youth who was present at the old man's death had been 'freely pardoned' on 29 June, the day of Dacre's execution. He was the son of Sir Thomas Cheyney, former Lord Warden of the Cinque Ports, who had been appointed Treasurer of the Royal Household in 1539[71] and had organised that lightning nocturnal grab of Cromwell's bullion. Patronage, in Henry's England, was everything. At other times, he was also more free in the act of mercy towards those close to him:

on 28 January 1538, Henry had reprieved a servant of his young favourite Thomas Culpeper (of whom we shall hear more shortly) at the very last moment 'to the great comfort of all the people' crowding around the scaffold in the tiltyard in front of the Palace of Westminster. The boy servant had stolen his master's purse, containing a jewel of the king's, and £12 in cash. 'He was brought to the place of execution ... and the hangman was taking down the ladder from the gallows, [when] the king sent his pardon and so saved his life.'[72]

Fresh from these excitements, on 30 June 1541 the king and queen, with an escort of 1,000 soldiers, began the long-promised, glittering and stately progress to the restive North of England, reaching York on 16 September, where their subjects had hopes, subsequently unfounded, that Katherine was to be formally crowned queen. In the quiet of the early hours, after the splendid feasts and banquets had ended, it was the queen's secret nocturnal activities on this progress that were to become her fatal undoing.

Henry returned to Hampton Court from this progress at the end of October and ordered that on 2 November – All Souls' Day – there should be special prayers offered for 'the good life he led and trusted to lead' with 'this jewel of womanhood'. Crushingly and cruelly, on that very day he was to have the veil torn from his old eyes about his young, flirtatious queen. Cranmer had received confidential information from John Lassels, a religious reformer (who would be burnt at the stake five years later for his Protestant beliefs), about Katherine's unchaste life before her marriage to the king. Her previous behaviour now proved to have been far from 'pure and honest'. Henry arrived in the Chapel Royal at Hampton Court to hear a Mass for the Dead and found a sealed letter from Cranmer waiting for him in his pew. The inscription on the cover urged him to read it in private. Within, the note accused the queen of having 'lived most corruptly and sensually'.

An incredulous king was informed that his wife had behaved improperly with Henry Monox, a lute-player who had taught her the virginals (an ironic pun) at her step-grandmother's home when she was just fifteen. Discovering them alone together, Agnes, Dowager Duchess of Norfolk, had administered 'two or three blows' to Katherine and told them to behave.[73] Katherine had also had an affair with Francis Dereham in the autumn of 1538, when she was seventeen. Only three months earlier, in August 1541, Katherine had unwisely appointed him her private secretary and usher of her chamber. Henry's self-belief suffered a stunning blow at this news and he initially refused to believe Cranmer's allegations. Then he asked his old friend Southampton, now Lord Privy Seal, secretly to investigate the charges levelled against his queen.

Dereham was taken to the Tower of London and interrogated by the Privy Council. He claimed he had been betrothed to Katherine in 1538 and consequently the relationship had not been sinful in the eyes of the Church. Stunningly, he also named Thomas Culpeper, one of Henry's especial favourites in his Privy Chamber, as having 'succeeded him in the queen's affections'. This ambitious courtier was a less than attractive character: two years before, he had raped a park-keeper's wife in a wooded thicket while three or four of his companions had held her down. He later killed a villager who tried to arrest him.[74] Henry, who did not want to lose Culpeper's jolly company or his frequent tender ministrations to his painful legs, had then astonishingly pardoned him. This time, Culpeper was arrested and questioned by Wriothesley under the threat of torture on the rack – a notorious machine in the bowels of the Tower nicknamed 'the Duke of Exeter's daughter' by apprehensive Londoners.[75]

Back in the Palace of Westminster, Culpeper's rooms were being searched for evidence and his goods and chattels listed and valued. He had started his life at court as a page, later being appointed a groom and finally, two years before his arrest, he had been created a Gentleman of the king's Privy Chamber, which allowed him privileged access to the sovereign's person. His possessions included two caps of velvet given to him by the king, plus numerous gowns, coats and other clothing, together with swords and daggers. Other items included horses and bedroom furniture. In total, his possessions were valued at £214 18s 1d (£80,500 at 2004 prices) and were delivered up to Sir Thomas Heneage of the Privy Chamber. Culpeper's debts, to the king and six others, amounted to £195 2s 8d (£73,050),[76] some of it probably gambling debts. A disapproving bank manager today might well say that, on paper, Culpeper was living only just above the line of penury; the figures certainly speak volumes about his fast and loose life. But the courtier also had considerable potential earnings from the positions showered upon such a favourite by a doting Henry. The inventory of his goods includes them all: Keeper of the Gallery at Greenwich Palace; Clerk of the Armoury; Keeper of the parks and houses at Penshurst and North Lye; Lieutenant of Tonbridge Castle; and Steward of Ashdown Forest. There were also substantial incomes from property holdings. His lustful dalliance with the queen had flaunted and risked all this, as well as his life.

The king's Council sorrowfully reported the scandal to Henry's ambassador to France, Sir John Paget, on 12 November, saying, 'A most miserable case lately revealed ... Now may[be] you can see what was done before marriage. God knows what hath been done since.'[77] Armed with his own intelligence, King Francis I of France – probably delighted at Henry's discomfiture – wrote to his 'good brother' of England the same day, declaring that he felt the 'grief of the king as his own'. Henry, he wrote, 'should consider that lightness of women cannot bind the honour of men – and that the shame is confined to those who commit the crime.' It was not intended to cheer Henry's dark hours, nor did it.[78]

While the interrogations were discreetly under way at the Tower, the French ambassador Marillac reported that Henry avoided Katherine's company at Hampton Court as much as possible and that the queen

> who did nothing but dance and amuse herself, now keeps her apartments without showing herself ... When musicians with instruments call at her door, they are dismissed, saying it was no longer time for dancing.

The Spanish ambassador Chapuys, puzzled at what was going on at court, confirmed that Henry 'feigned indisposition' and was ten or twelve days without seeing his queen or allowing her to come into his room,

> during which time there was much talk of divorce but owing to some surmise that she was with child, or else the means for a divorce were not arranged, the affair slept until 5 November when the king went into the Council room and remained there till noon.[79]

Meanwhile, all the queen's coffers and chests were sealed by her investigators and palace guards were stationed at the doors of her apartments to prevent any incriminating evidence from being removed.

Katherine's brother Lord Charles Howard, another Gentleman of the king's Privy Chamber, was also exiled from court – without being told the reason. Marillac added:

> The Duke of Norfolk must be exceedingly sorry and troubled, for the queen happens to be his own niece and the daughter of his brother, just as Anne [Boleyn] was also his niece on his sister's side and his having been the chief cause of the king marrying her.

Piece by piece, the evidence was being covertly gathered concerning the queen's promiscuity. The Privy Council was told that while the royal party were staying at Lincoln, Culpeper had entered her chamber 'by the backstairs' at eleven o'clock at night and had remained there until four the next morning. Another tryst had taken place in the cramped and hardly romantic surroundings of the queen's stool chamber. On another occasion, she had given him a gold chain and a rich cap. The allegations of adultery and betrayal continued, on and on, poured out by Katherine's maids and ladies of her bedchamber, who were no doubt attempting to save their own necks.

Given all that had passed in Henry's turbulent marriages, the queen must have been mad to embark on this dangerous liaison with the king's favourite. Was her extraordinary, almost suicidal recklessness motivated by an immature young girl's physical and emotional disgust with an old, diseased man whom she had married for duty rather than love? Did she crave affection from a virile gallant nearer her own age in compensation for a conjugal life more concerned with siring a new heir than with sexual pleasure?[80] Did she merely gain a forbidden *frisson* from the secrecy and incredible risks of the affair? Or was she, as some must have supposed, even planning to conceive a child with Culpeper and pass it off as a Duke of York, so safeguarding her own future as queen and fulfilling the ambitions of her uncle and Bishop Gardiner? She certainly lived up to every syllable of her reputed personal motto: 'No other will but mine own.'

During a torrid all-night Council meeting at Gardiner's home in Southwark on 6 November, the sordid details of the queen's activities were revealed to a still-disbelieving Henry. Finally, after he was convinced by the tide of evidence placed diffidently before him, the expected royal reaction was terrible to behold. The king had suffered twin, numbing assaults on his vanity, his bloated egotism, his self-esteem. His queen had betrayed him – and with his trusted favourite, Culpeper. Confronted by the awful truth of the double duplicity, this, probably his last sexual love, swiftly transformed into raw, naked hatred. He called for a sword so that he could slay Katherine 'that he loved so much'. Vengeance, as always when Henry was crossed, was uppermost in his tortured mind. That 'wicked woman' had 'never such delight in her incontinency as she should have torture in her death' he screamed at the amazed courtiers. He struck out at his Council, abusing them for 'soliciting' him to marry her. It was all their fault! His anguished cries of animal rage broke down into wrathful tears, and he sobbed about his 'ill-luck in meeting with such ill-conditioned wives'.[81] His awestruck and frightened Councillors believed his anger had driven him insane and they shrank back, with fearful glances at each other, from his grief and rage. Henry stormed off and, like a child whose favourite toy has been broken, sought comfort and distraction in an unplanned treat: killing other defenceless quarry in the hunting field.[82]

English ambassadors abroad were given an official sanitised description of the king's grief for consumption at their accredited courts – that his 'heart was so pierced with pensiveness that long was it before his majesty could speak and utter the sorrow of his heart to us and finally, with plenty of tears, which was strange in his courage, opened the same'.

Many of those close to Katherine – her family and household – 'light young men ... privy to the naughtiness of the queen and Dereham, besides advancing Dereham to her service' were dragged off to the Tower. The lieutenant there informed the Privy Council that there were not enough rooms 'to lodge them all severally' unless the king and queen's own lodgings were used. The king agreed to this, but his double keys to the royal apartments could not be found and accommodation for some prisoners had to be arranged elsewhere.[83]

Meanwhile, Marillac set spies to watch the comings and goings at Hampton Court. They reported that the queen's jewels and rings had been inventoried and that Cranmer arrived at the palace alone on 8 November.

He was there again to question Katherine, and the archbishop reported later that her state 'would have pitied any man's heart to see'. He immediately promised her mercy, if she would only confess, 'for fear that she would enter into a frenzy'.[84] The promise calmed her and she told him, 'Alas, my lord, that I am still alive, the fear of death grieved me not so much before, as doth now the remembrance of the king's goodness' and her thoughts of what 'a gracious and loving Prince I had'.[85] At six o'clock that evening, reported the archbishop, the queen fell into another 'pang' which was caused, she said, by her 'remembrance ... for about that time [every day], Master Heneage was wont to bring her knowledge of the king'.[86] Was this feminine guile, or the genuine emotional outbursts of an innocent teenager? Cranmer did not mention her marriage, being interested only in the talk of a pre-contract with Dereham as a possible solution to the scandal. Stupidly, Katherine told him there was no such contract, but she admitted that Dereham had carnal knowledge of her. The queen's statement, written after the archbishop's interrogation, graphically describes her teenage romps. It said that many times,

[Dereham] hath lain with me, sometime in his doublet and hose and two or three times naked; but not so naked that he had nothing upon him, for he had always at the least his doublet and as I do think, his hose also. But I mean naked when his hose were put down.

And diverse times, he would bring wine, strawberries, apples and other things to make good cheer after my lady [Agnes, Dowager Duchess of Norfolk] was gone to bed.[87]

After the archbishop left, Katherine's vice-chamberlain, Sir Edward Baynton,[88] told the king that she began to excuse her actions and water down the things she had admitted to Cranmer. She claimed, he wrote, that what Dereham had done to her had been achieved by force.[89]

On 13 November, Wriothesley went to Hampton Court and, summoning all the members and servants of the queen's household into the great chamber, 'there openly afore them declared certain offences that she had done in misusing her body with certain persons afore the king's time, wherefore he there discharged all her household'.[90]

Katherine naïvely believed that she would be left alone after making her free confession. When she discovered that her inquisitors were far from finished with her, she refused 'to drink or eat and weeps and cries like a madwoman, so that they must take away things by which she might hasten her death', according to her uncle, Norfolk.

The duke cuts an unappealing figure during this *cause célèbre* that struck so close to home and to his political ambitions. Now perhaps fearing the loss of his head, he was at some pains to distance himself from his niece, telling Marillac 'with tears in his eyes, of the king's grief', who had loved Katherine 'much, and the misfortunes to his [Norfolk's] house in her and Queen Anne [Boleyn], his two nieces'.[91] All this, of course, was faithfully reported to Francis I. Later, Norfolk confided to Chapuys, 'I wish the queen was burned.'[92]

What was to be done with her while her fate was decided? Her new domestic arrangements demonstrate the cold efficiency of Henry's administration. On 14 November, she was sent to the former Bridgettine nunnery at Syon House, Middlesex, under the charge of Sir Edward and Lady Isabella Baynton and three gentlewomen.[93] The accommodation was to be furnished 'moderately as her life and condition deserved'. Rich, ornate hangings were firmly denied; instead, they were to be 'mean stuff, without any cloth of estate'. Katherine was allowed six of her favourite dresses, edged with gold and in the fashionable French style. Her jewels were all removed, carefully inventoried and returned safely to the king's jewel house. At Syon, on the banks of the Thames, in the two rooms allotted to her, she waited anxiously for news of her fate amid constant rumours that Henry would show clemency. Her moods swung between utter despair and adolescent hope. During her wilder optimistic moments, perhaps she fancied that some kind of settlement like that enjoyed by Anne of Cleves could save her head. Her composure certainly returned, for she made 'good cheer, [and was] fatter and handsomer than ever' and 'more imperious and commanding and more difficult to please than ever she was when living with the king'.[94] Katherine, in her heart, knew her time to enjoy the trappings of royalty was limited and perhaps she wanted to savour them while she could. She put out of her mind any thoughts of the king's retribution.

In truth, Katherine was as guilty as sin itself. She was also particularly dim-witted. As her passionate affair raged, she had sent a number of love letters to Culpeper via one of her servants. One billet-doux, no doubt found during searches of Culpeper's rooms at Westminster, survives today amongst the state papers in the National Archives. It leaves little doubt as to where her affections really lay:

> I heartily recommend me unto you, praying you to send word how that you do. I heard you were sick and never longed [so] much for anything as to see you. It makes my heart die to think I cannot always be in your company.

She signed herself, 'Yours, as long as life endures, Katheryn.' She may as well have been signing her own death warrant.[95]

Meanwhile, Anne of Cleves travelled to Richmond to be near Henry

– she nurtured hopes of reconciliation in the disgrace of her successor [96] – but these, inevitably, came to naught. Pathetically, her only contact with the court was a messenger who claimed back a ring given to Anne by the fallen queen.

Lady Jane Rochford, one-time lady-in-waiting to Anne Boleyn and widow of George Boleyn (who was executed in May 1536 for an alleged incestuous relationship with his sister Anne Boleyn), had acted as a procuress for Culpeper. She was too deeply embroiled in the scandal to escape and, inevitably, was one of those arrested and cross-examined at Hampton Court before being taken to the Tower. Lady Rochford was seized with a fit of madness on the third day of her imprisonment 'by which [her] brain was affected'. Chapuys noted that 'now and then she recovers her reason and that the king takes care that his own physicians visit her daily, for he desires her recovery chiefly that he may afterwards have her executed as an example and warning to others'.

Katherine's anxious wait for the king's verdict lasted less than ten days. On 22 November she lost the title of queen and two days later she was indicted for having led 'an abominable, base, carnal, voluptuous and vicious life' before the royal marriage and behaving 'like a common harlot with diverse persons, as with Francis Dereham of Lambeth and Henry Monox of Streatham, at other times maintaining ... the outward appearance of chastity and honesty'. She had misled the king 'by word and gesture to love her' and 'arrogantly coupled herself with him in marriage'. The marriage pre-contract with Dereham had been concealed from Henry 'to the peril of the King and of his children to be begotten by her' and after the royal wedding, she had shown Dereham 'notable favour' and had incited Culpeper to sexual intercourse, telling him she loved him above the king.[97]

On 1 December 1541, Culpeper and Dereham were arraigned before the Lord Mayor, Sir Michael Dormer, at the Guildhall, London, for high treason, with Norfolk sitting uncomfortably at his left hand. Culpeper cravenly maintained that he had secretly met the queen only because of her royal commands. Katherine had made all the running in the affair. She was, he alleged, 'languishing and dying of love for him'.[98]

Hardly the words or actions of a chivalrous gallant. After a hearing lasting around six hours, Dereham and Culpeper were unsurprisingly found guilty. Both were executed at Tyburn on 10 December, with the king unexpectedly commuting the sentence to simple decapitation for Culpeper alone, rather than the hanging, drawing and quartering[99] that Dereham cruelly suffered. It was the last and least act of mercy that Henry had shown Culpeper.

Norfolk, his ambitions now in ashes and facing the prospect of a second niece being executed while queen, wrote to Henry from the safe isolation of his estates at Kenninghall, near Norwich, eloquently deploring the roles played by his family in the scandal and firmly denying any involvement in their 'false and traitorous proceedings against your royal majesty'. After writing of 'the abominable deeds by two of my nieces', with breathtaking temerity he sought reassurance that he still remained in good standing with the king, writing obsequiously:

> Prostate at your royal feet, most humbly I beseech your Majesty that by such, as if it shall please you to command, I may be advertised [told] plainly how your Highness doth weigh your favour towards me.
>
> Assuring your Highness that unless I may know your Majesty to continue my good and gracious Lord, as ye were before their offences [were] committed, I shall never desire to live in this world any longer ...[100]

Henry's reaction to the letter is not known, but the noble house of Howard suffered grievously. Norfolk was soon to discover that his influence at court had waned for ever. For hiding Katherine's promiscuity, his step-brother Lord William Howard and his wife Margaret, Lady Katherine Bridgewater (the queen's aunt), Anne Howard (wife of her brother Henry), and her step-grandmother Agnes (the 'old and testy' dowager Duchess of Norfolk) were found guilty at Westminster Hall on 22 December of misprision[101] of treason and forfeited their estates and possessions. They were also sentenced to perpetual imprisonment – although within a year, all were pardoned and released.

Chapuys wrote on 3 December that Henry 'wonderfully felt the case of the Queen ... and that he has certainly shown greater sorrow and regret at her loss than at the faults, loss or divorce of his preceding wives'. The ambassador added shrewdly:

I should say that this king's case resembles very much that of the woman who cried more bitterly at the loss of her tenth husband than she had cried on the death of the other nine put together.[102]

On Saturday 11 February 1542, Royal Assent was given by a commission, appointed by letters patent, to an Act of Attainder[103] condemning Katherine to death for treason, to spare Henry the pain of having to hear 'the sorrowful story and wicked facts' all over again.[104] Henry wasted no time. The previous day she had been transferred to the Tower of London. The cold light of reality had hit her like a douche of icy water and she had panicked, resisted and had to be forced, screaming, into a small covered boat at Syon. Four of her ladies, with four sailors to man the vessel, accompanied her. She was brought down the river in a sombre little procession, escorted by the Duke of Suffolk and a troop of armed soldiers in a large barge and the Earl of Southampton, Lord Privy Seal, in another, all propelled by oars. Nearing the end of her journey, Katherine's boat would have shot the narrows beneath London Bridge where the severed heads of her former lovers had been impaled. One hopes that, in the fading light of that grim afternoon, she was spared the gruesome spectacle. A few minutes later, dressed appropriately in black velvet, she landed at the steps of Traitor's Gate 'with the same honours and ceremonies as if she was still reigning',[105] before being taken to the comfort of the queen's lodgings within the Tower.

On Sunday 12 February, Katherine was finally told that she was going to die the following day and should therefore 'dispose her soul'. That night she asked, with a curious morbid fascination, to see the headsman's block, 'pretending that she wanted to know how she was to place her head on it. This was granted and the block being brought in, she herself tried and placed her head on it by way of experiment,' reported Chapuys.[106] The next morning at a little after seven, she was swiftly beheaded on Tower Green. 'After her body had been covered with a black cloak, the ladies of her suite took it up and put it on one side.'[107] Lady Rochford immediately followed her on to the bloodstained straw of the scaffold, her madness apparently calmed. Always anxious to cover his actions with the cloak of legality, the king had hurried an Act through Parliament permitting the execution of insane persons who had committed treason.[108]

Both women were acquiescent in their fate. Neither spoke much on the scaffold, merely confessing their guilt and dutifully praying for the king's welfare and prosperity. This reticence was not just mere misplaced loyalty or tradition (although it satisfied the onlookers from the Privy Council).[109] The queen was absolutely terrified. Katherine, reportedly 'so weak [from fear] that she could hardly speak', died, mercifully, with one sweep of the axe severing her once frivolous, dizzy head cleanly from her young body. Henry's fifth marriage was over and his wife's corpse was buried in the Church of St Peter ad Vincula within the Tower of London – alongside that of Anne Boleyn, Henry's second wife, who had been executed almost six years earlier.

The king was now aged fifty-one, in poor health and grown very stout. For the first time after ridding himself of a wife in thirty tempestuous years of wedlock, there were no plans to find him another, even though Parliament had now passed an Act making it a treasonable offence for a woman to marry the king without disclosing her unchaste past. This measure was, in the bland words of today's Whitehall civil servants, intended purely as an enabling measure 'to avoid doubts for the future', as well as providing Queen Katherine's demise with a more substantial veneer of legitimacy, albeit retrospective. Chapuys, in a thinly veiled comment on the notoriously loose morals of Henry's household, wrote: 'Few, if any, ladies of the court nowadays [are] likely to aspire to such an honour of becoming one of the king's wives or to desire that the choice should fall on them.'[110]

It was not that Henry did not feel the need for female company in his declining years. There were some who believed that Henry's amorous habits would die hard and that he would swiftly seek another wife; some hopefuls even suggested, vainly, that Anne of Cleves, now apparently grown 'half as beautiful again since she left court', could attempt a return match with the English king. Elizabeth Basset and Jane Rattsey, two of her ladies-in-waiting, were hauled up before Henry's Council on 4 December 1541 and jailed for adding fuel to the fire of rumour by indiscreetly asking, 'What! Is God working his own work to make the Lady Anne of Cleves queen again?' and 'What a man is the King! How many wives *will* he have?'[111] No doubt, many of his 2.7 million subjects may have pondered the same question.

In truth, he now required a consort to look after his three children by different mothers: Mary, aged twenty-six and still without a husband, Elizabeth, eight-and-half, and Edward, approaching five. He also needed a woman's tender touch in dressing his painful and debilitating ulcerated legs, to comfort him in the loneliness of his old age and to distract him from the daily problems of kingship. The idea of further procreation to produce a Duke of York may have finally disappeared from Henry's mind with his poor health, increasing corpulence and the searing pain of Katherine Howard's betrayal. For the king had again taken to food as a solace in his grief: Marillac, in his diplomatic dispatches, talks openly of the monarch's 'marvellous excess' in eating and reports him 'daily growing heavier'. Henry's weight had increased so substantially that his great bed of walnut in the Palace of Westminster had to be widened and strengthened to support his growing bulk.

Chapuys, the mischievous Spanish ambassador, suggested to William Paget, then clerk of the king's Council (who for 'a long time [has] been on intimate terms with me'), that if Henry cast Katherine aside

on account of her having had connexion with a man before her marriage to him, he would have been justified in doing the same with Madam dé Cleves, for if the rumour current in the Low Countries was true, there were plenty of causes for a separation considering the queen's [Anne of Cleves'] age [and] her being fond of wine, as they [the English] might have had occasion to observe, it was natural enough to suppose she had failed in the same manner. The Clerk did not deny the strength of my argument, but said he did not believe the King would again retake her or marry another woman until Parliament positively forced him to it.[112]

Ambassadors always deal in rumours, and here the gossipy Chapuys was being unkind to Anne of Cleves, as the talk of her lack of chastity seems totally unfounded. There were, however, some official attempts by the Duchy of Cleves to reinstate Anne to the unlikely royal affections. Its ambassador sought to speak to Henry about Anne, 'but as the king's grief did not permit it' he had to make do with addressing the Privy Council in the middle of December 1541. After passing on the Duke of Cleves' thanks for Henry's 'liberality to his sister, he prayed them [to find] means to reconcile the marriage' and restore Anne as queen. The Council, on the king's behalf, answered 'that the separation had been made for such just cause that he [Henry] prayed the duke would never make such a request'. The ambassador, perhaps experiencing difficulty with his English, asked for this very definite statement to be repeated. Bishop Gardiner 'with every appearance of anger, said that the king would never take back the said lady and that what was done was founded on great reason, whatever the world might allege'. The man from Cleves dared not reply, Marillac reported to Francis I, 'for fear that they might take occasion to treat [Anne] worse'.[113]

Aside from mischief-making in the corridors of Westminster, Chapuys meanwhile had more important diplomatic imperatives: the envoy was at some pains to dissuade Henry from the possibility of seeking a sixth wife in France. Chapuys reported to his imperial master how the English king had told him that

the French were continually presenting him ladies to marry [but] I answered that no doubt they would do as they had done when he himself pursued the princess who is now the queen of Scotland[114] and that in point of marriage, the French had always employed their usual tactics, and gone against the treaties between England and France ... Since the French had not been ashamed to do such things openly and to his very face, they must all the time have played him in secret more devilish tricks still; adding, the more to darken the picture, many anecdotes I knew of King Francis and his ministers.[115]

Henry's spirits were dramatically lifted by a new English victory against the Scots at Solway Moss on 24 November 1542,[116] quickly followed by the death of their king, James V, on 14 December from a fever and despair that his wife had delivered a daughter. On 15 January 1543, Chapuys wrote that

> ever since his late queen's misconduct [Henry] has been sad and dejected, showing no inclination for carousels and pageants or paying his court to ladies. No sooner did the news from Scotland arrive than he began to invite and entertain them at court.[117]

Princess Mary was recalled from her quarters at Hunsdon, Hertfordshire, to act as hostess at her father's palaces. She was greeted warmly and was given rings, silver plate and other jewels including two rubies of 'inestimable value' by Henry as New Year gifts. Chapuys added:

> Many here think that in the midst of all this feasting and carousing, the King may well take a fancy to some lady of the court and marry her, but I must say I see no appearance of that.[118]

Henry returned to staging the grand court occasions he had loved so much. At the end of January, he threw a great supper for sixty-one ladies at the Palace of Westminster, having personally stumped around their lodgings beforehand, fussily checking that everything was in pristine readiness for his guests. The king's rheumy old eyes dwelt upon a number of the laughing company around him, including Anne Basset, a girl reportedly of very limited intellect. Marillac afterwards described her as a 'pretty creature with wit enough to do as badly as the other [Katherine], if she were to try'. While watching Anne Basset's silly, giggling frivolity at his dinner table, Henry was perhaps painfully reminded of his last executed queen.[119] Youth, beauty and gaiety were not now requirements for a king's consort; morality, companionship and kindness would be more proper attributes in anyone else Henry sought to keep him warm at night. Although he received the ladies 'with much gaiety', he showed no 'particular attention for any of them', according to Chapuys.

At this time, a central character in the last days of Henry VIII emerged: Katherine Parr, who was to become his sixth and final wife.

The king would have known her for much of her life; indeed, her brother William was a long-time favourite of his. Probably born in 1512, she was the eldest child of a powerful northern magnate, Sir Thomas Parr of Kendal in Cumberland, who was knighted at Henry's coronation in 1509 and fought at the Battle of the Spurs against the French in 1513. Her mother had been a lady-in-waiting to the king's first wife, Catherine of Aragon. Katherine Parr had been married at fifteen to the ailing Edward, Lord Borough of Gainsborough, Lincolnshire, who suffered from a 'distracted memory', and she was widowed, childless, in 1529. In the late spring of 1532, she had married the rich widower John Neville, Baron Latimer of Snape Castle, Yorkshire. He was forty-two, more than twenty years older than his bride, had been married twice before and had two children, a son and a daughter. The Latimers were to be caught up dangerously in the northern Pilgrimage of Grace rebellion in 1536. Katherine's husband was taken hostage by the ringleaders and became their spokesman to the king's Council in London, before switching sides to rescue Katherine and her stepchildren unharmed from the hands of the rebels at Snape. During Thomas Cromwell's subsequent virulent witch-hunt for those in any way involved in the rebellion, the Duke of Norfolk came to the Latimers' aid, pointing out that he was unable to find any evidence that Katherine's husband had done anything wrong, except when under the duress of violence. He added, 'No man was in more danger of his life,' and so they were spared from the heavy hand of Henry's chief minister's retribution.

Katherine was frequently at court: her sister, Anne, married William

Herbert, one of Henry's confidants amongst the Gentlemen of his Privy Chamber, then an esquire of the king's body, whose father was an illegitimate son of the 1st Earl of Pembroke.[120] Latimer, sick and infirm, died in London, probably in December 1542, and Katherine arranged for him to be buried in St Paul's Cathedral beneath an impressive tomb, recorded as having been 'broken all in pieces' seventy years later.[121] His will was proved in March 1543.

The previous month, Henry cautiously began to pay her court.

Despite the widow insisting on a seemly period of mourning, the king had decided to pursue her as his sixth wife. She was the ideal candidate. Her personal motto – 'To be useful in all I do' – has the ring of a sensible, practical and dutiful Girl Guide captain. After nursing two older men, she was experienced in the ways of the sick room, as well as being gentle and kind. As the childless widow of two dead husbands, there could be no question of unpleasant surprises lurking in her past; indeed, her virtue was one of her proudest and most praised assets.[122] Portraits of her show a dignified and graceful matron of some strength of character, with a fashionably pale complexion, tightly brushed-back auburn hair and light-brown eyes. She was slim, around 5 ft. 2 in. tall,[123] lively in conversation and, for the time, very well educated. She enjoyed intellectual discussion – and could be very forthright in her views. Some have portrayed her as a kind of sixteenth-century bluestocking; true, Katherine could speak fluent French and Italian and later learnt to both read and write in Latin, but she also loved music and dancing, lavish jewels and expensive, fashionable clothes. She was known to be pious, but not overtly associated with either the religiously conservative or reformist groups still slugging it out brutally for dominance at court. Katherine Latimer, *née* Parr, Henry concluded, would make the ideal wife and stepmother in his declining years. With the king's self-belief now restored, he convinced himself it might even be possible that she could bear him a Duke of York, despite the fact that the first flush of youth had long departed her. Finally, there was a political dimension, a factor never lost on the canny Henry: marriage to the daughter of such a powerful and respectable northern family would bring him benefits in that traditionally most troublesome region of his realm. What the king desired, the king would get.

As a lame and sick man with five unfortunate marriages behind him, Henry resorted to his most powerful asset in pursuing her affections. He used hard cash to woo her, placing an order on 16 February 1543 with his tailor, John Skutt, for a generous package of pleats and sleeves, followed by gowns in the latest Italian, Dutch and Venetian fashions and 'French hoods', all valued at a total of £8 9s 5d (just over £3,000 in today's money). Although grotesquely obese and afflicted with painful and stinking leg wounds, Henry still vainly believed that he knew how to turn a woman's head.

He also had patronage to employ as a telling weapon: it can be no coincidence that a string of honours and appointments were pointedly awarded to Katherine's brother William, Baron Parr of Kendal, at the same time as Henry was courting her, although William had long been a favourite of the king, called 'his Integrity' by Henry. In March, he was made a member of the Privy Council[124]. This was followed by his election in April as a Knight of the Garter and his appointment as Warden of the Scottish Marches, the border territories where he had shone in the latest military campaigns against England's intractable neighbour.

The king faced another strong contender for the hand of the rich widow: his brother-in-law by marriage to Jane Seymour, the debonair and roguish Sir Thomas Seymour, who had returned to court that month after eight months based in Vienna, serving as a military observer studying the tactics and weaponry employed in the wars against the Turks. Katherine had fallen heavily for his piratical good looks, his renown as a courageous soldier and his courtly manners and dress. Her head had been turned by his glamour, dash and derring-do; her prim heart excited, after a dull life with two sick husbands, by his wild reputation. She was not even deterred by his notorious bad temper. Henry, however, was apparently aware of their developing relationship. In order not to be outdone and to ensure that the way remained clear for an acceptance of his proposal of marriage, he appointed Sir Thomas, within two weeks of his return, special ambassador to the queen regent in Brussels.

Katherine was clearly deeply in love with Seymour. Four years later, in a letter, she admitted to him:

> For as truly as God is God, my mind was fully bent the other time I was at liberty, to marry you before any man I know. Howbeit, God withstood my will ... most vehemently for a time and through His grace and goodness made that possible which seems to me most impossible; that was, made me to renounce utterly my own will and to follow His will most willingly.[125]

Perhaps Katherine weighed up how long the king had to live and realistically calculated that if Seymour would be patient, their love might not have to wait many years before being sanctified by marriage. Henry, for his part, cunningly made it his business to see that Sir Thomas was almost continuously out of the country during the remaining years of his reign. Seymour later served under Sir John Wallop in the English military operations in the Low Countries, and at sea with the fleet under John Dudley, Viscount Lisle who was appointed Lord High Admiral in 1542.

Lisle wrote to William, Lord Parr, on 20 June 1543 that after Henry had inspected two new havens at Harwich, he returned to London, where 'none but my lady Latimer, your sister, and Mrs Herbert be both here in the Court' with Princesses Mary and Elizabeth.[126]

Henry was certainly in a hurry to marry his widow woman. Cranmer issued a special licence in Latin on 10 July at Lambeth Palace, authorising the marriage to take place between Henry and 'Lady Katherine Latimer, late wife of Lord Latimer, deceased'[127] without the need for banns being said in any church, oratory or chapel. No time was wasted in arranging the king's sixth wedding. And this was not to be a hole-in-the-corner, secret ceremony, like those to Anne Boleyn, Jane Seymour and Katherine Howard.

The wedding, held two days later, was – unusually for Henry – a family affair. Crammed into an upper oratory – 'the Queen's privy closet'

– within Hampton Court were Prince Edward, Princesses Mary and Elizabeth and the king's niece Lady Margaret Douglas (who carried Katherine's train), as well as a bevy of twenty senior and close courtiers and their wives. Of those attending, only John, Lord Russell, now Lord Privy Seal, and Sir Anthony Browne, Captain of the King's Pensioners,[128] were members of the religiously conservative faction at court. The others were firmly in the reformers' camp.

Gardiner conducted the marriage in English, putting the statutory questions to the couple. Henry impatiently answered each with a loud 'Yea' and, taking Katherine's right hand in his, repeated after the bishop:

I, Henry, take thee, Katherine, to my wedded wife, to have and to hold, from this day forward, for better for worse, for richer for poorer, in sickness and in health, till death us depart, and thereto, I plight thee my troth.

Katherine then said her vows, adding after 'sickness and in health':

to be bonair[129] and buxom in bed and at board, till death us depart, and thereto I plight thee my troth.[130]

With that, the wedding ring was slipped on to her finger and gifts of gold and silver proffered. After Gardiner blessed the marriage, Henry commanded his notary, Richard Watkins, to make the promises public.

Strangely, history had repeated itself. It was like the king's first marriage all over again. In both cases, the bride had declared for a close relative – Henry's elder brother Arthur in the case of Catherine of Aragon, and the king's brother-in-law – Thomas Seymour – in the case of Katherine Parr. The Christian name of the king's bride was the same in both cases. Psychologists have read much into this, claiming that Henry had an unconscious desire for an incestuous union.[131] Whatever his motives, the marriage turned out a happy one despite a very bumpy patch in 1546, as we shall see later.

Edmond Harvel, the English ambassador to Venice, rejoiced in a letter to Russell at the king's marriage to 'so prudent, beautiful and virtuous a lady, as is by universal fame reported'. The Venetian government had declared 'no mean congratulations on this marriage', he added.[132]

Chapuys reported the royal wedding to the crown prince of Spain and described Katherine as possibly being 'about thirty-two years of age. May God be pleased that this marriage turn out well and that the king's favour and affection for the princess [Mary] continue to increase'.[133]

The plague was meanwhile raging in London, and a proclamation was issued on 15 July from Hampton Court forbidding Londoners from entering any house occupied by the king and queen, and banning any servant of the household from visiting the capital.[134] The court then beat a hasty retreat a few miles further west to the manor of Otelands. From there, on 20 July, the new queen, writing to her brother, talked of the marriage being 'the greatest joy and comfort that could happen' to her. She prayed that he would write and visit her 'as frequently as if she had not been called to this honour'. The letter was enclosed in another to Lord Parr by Wriothesley, who told him rather prissily that he should frame himself to be 'more and more an ornament to her majesty'.[135]

The royal party then embarked on the traditional summer progress through the Home Counties – Buckinghamshire, Bedfordshire and Hertfordshire. It was just another honeymoon for Henry, but the first taste of royal rank and privilege for Katherine.

Anne of Cleves' prominent nose was put out of joint by the marriage. On 27 July, Chapuys wrote to the queen of Hungary that he had heard 'from an authentic quarter' that Anne

> would greatly prefer giving up everything that she has ... to remaining any longer in England, treated as she is and humiliated and hurt as she has lately been at the King marrying this last lady, who is by no means so handsome as she herself is.
>
> Besides which there is no hope of her [Katherine] having children, considering that she has been twice a widow and has borne none from either of her deceased husbands.[136]

Anne's reported comments are full of childish pique. 'A fine burden Madam Katherine has taken upon herself!' she is supposed to have remarked acidly, for she was marrying a king 'so stout, that such a man has never been seen'. Moreover, 'three of the biggest men that could be found could get inside his doublet'.[137] Perhaps her situation should excuse her outbursts. Her beloved mother had died and she was trapped, bereft of any man's affection, in a foreign country. She was locked out of the glittering society of the royal court, now presided over by yet another of Henry's wives. She could only watch from the sidelines, albeit very comfortable sidelines. Who could begrudge her the outpourings of a little jealousy? All her plans to return to the limelight of society had failed. The Duke of Cleves' ambassador, whom Henry's Council suspected was merely Anne's agent, had been living meanly in a room above a tavern with one manservant and had been called to court twice or three times in the early part of 1543, probably on business connected with the discarded queen. All came to naught, however, and although Chapuys tried hard to obtain an exit passport for him, he remained stranded in London: 'The poor devil ... must very much wish to get out of this country for he does nothing here and gets no assistance in money.'[138]

Katherine now began to enjoy life as a queen. She had a pet dog, a small spaniel named 'Rig' that wore a collar of crimson velvet embroidered with gold.[139] Henry showered jewels upon her. The inventory of her jewels taken after the king's death includes several very personal bespoke items:

> A brooch containing the image of king Henry the eight with the queen's image, a crown of diamonds over them and a rose of diamonds under them ... [140]

> A tablet the one side with 'H' and 'K' a rose and G[arter] all of diamonds with ostrich feathers and five small rubies and on the other side, a fair diamond holden by an image with four other diamonds.[141]

A tablet of gold having on the one side the king's picture painted and on the same side is a rose ... containing therein five diamonds and six rubies. On the border thereof is five very small diamonds and one ruby in the top and another underneath and in the border ... four very small diamonds. On the other side is two men lifting of a stone, being a diamond, containing on that side twenty-two diamonds, two rubies and a fair emerald.[142]

More than 120 items are listed, contained in a coffer 'having written upon it "the Queen's Jewels"',[143] held in the king's jewel house in the Tower.

For all the splendour and new riches around her, Katherine did not forget her duties as stepmother to the royal children: already she was being reported as behaving 'very affectionately' towards Princess Mary. Nor did she forget her other responsibilities: some of the first articles ordered after her marriage were eleven yards 'of black damask for a nightgown' and 'for making a nightgown of black satin with two burgundian gardes [sleeves] embroidered and edged with velvet'.[144] On 13 July she ordered perfume for her bedchamber at Hampton Court from the court apothecary, although this may prosaically have had more to do with the smell from the kitchens positioned beneath her room than with the wiles of an *affaire de coeur*. Katherine knew well how to handle elderly husbands and was not going to make the same mistakes as poor Anne of Cleves.

CHAPTER TWO

God's Imp

'I shall, during my life, while I am here, pray to Almighty God that ... [the] most noble imp,[1] the prince's grace, your most dear son, may succeed you to reign long, prosperously and felicitously to God's pleasure ...'

LETTER FROM THOMAS CROMWELL, IMPRISONED IN THE
TOWER OF LONDON, TO HENRY VIII, 30 JUNE 1540.[2]

In 1542, one of Prince Edward's doctors told the inquisitive French ambassador Marillac that he could not predict a long life for the four-year-old 'fat' and 'unhealthy' heir to the English crown.[3] Such remarks have helped to create a persistent tradition that the child was weak, sickly and prone to constant infection. If any sickness was in the offing, it was believed that Edward would catch it.[4] In reality, this seems far from the truth: only seven months before, the same diplomat had reported Edward to be 'handsome, well-nourished and remarkably tall for his age'[5] and from the end of October 1541, the prince was recovering from a quartan fever[6] – suffering high temperatures every fourth day – far more quickly than his elder half-sister Mary.[7] Edward became an active youth, enthusiastically hunting, jousting, playing tennis and regularly trying his hand at archery.

However, his fever of 1541 – by any reckoning dangerous to a child of tender years – came at a terrible time for the ageing king, struggling as he was to contain his shock and grief over the allegations of promiscuity and, afterwards, reckless adultery committed by his queen, Katherine Howard. Was the heir to both the crown and the future of the Tudor dynasty now also threatened? Henry, in those terrible weeks, must have thought his once ordered, secure world was tumbling all around him. All the uncertainties of both past and future had returned to haunt the king's waking hours. For ten days or so, the prince's life may have been in danger, and Henry desperately consulted a number of doctors regarding suitable cures.[8] But to the relief of the king and his physicians, Edward recovered and grew strongly into a slim, confident, attractive child, adorned with blond hair and the waiflike facial features of his mother, Jane Seymour.

His birth on 12 October 1537 was marked by salutes fired from cannon along the battlements of the Tower of London: more than 2,000 rounds boomed out in 'a great peal of guns' to mark the jubilation of the capital and 'the rejoicing of all Englishmen' in the arrival of the long-sought male heir. All the parish churches within the city walls celebrated a *Te Deum* and their bells rang out in celebration until late into the evening. The citizens rejoiced in more secular style with celebratory bonfires in the streets and the consumption of large quantities of fruit and wine.[9]

The child's christening, at midnight on Sunday 15 October 1537, was a spectacular affair staged in the Chapel Royal at Hampton Court. Gertrude Courtenay, Marchioness of Exeter,[10] carefully carried the infant on a cushion from his own lodgings in the palace, beneath a canopy of cloth of gold, in a winding procession through the echoing council chamber, the great hall and thence into the recently (and expensively) refurbished chapel. Henry's complex preparations for the ceremony were made with one eye on practicality, the other on the all-important pomp and circumstance of the occasion.[11] Within the chapel, a silver-gilt font was elevated on a stepped dais within a screened area, with a temporary side-room to the south heated by a brazier filled with perfumed [char]coals 'for making ready the Prince [for] the christening'. Silver basins held warm water to 'wash the Prince if need be'.[12] Favoured courtiers Sir John Russell, Sir Francis Bryan, Sir Nicholas Carew and Sir Anthony Browne, prosaically wearing aprons and carrying towels, took charge of the font. Edward's nurse and the midwife who had delivered him after Queen Jane's drawn-out confinement were also close by, ready to provide instant assistance if necessary.

Archbishop Cranmer christened the prince, who was wrapped in a richly embroidered white 'chrisom' or robe.[13] Henry's choice of Christian name was highly symbolic: the child was named Edward after his maternal great-grandfather, King Edward IV, and also because his birth came on the eve of the feast of St Edward the Confessor, England's own royal saint of special pious and sacred memory. At the moment of naming, the torches of virgin wax carried by all the esquires, gentlemen and knights amongst the 400-strong congregation[14] standing packed in the chapel were simultaneously lit. Garter King at Arms, the chief herald, then proclaimed in a loud voice:

> God, of his infinite grace and goodness, give and grant good life and long to the right high, excellent and noble prince, Prince Edward, duke of Cornwall and earl of Chester, most dear and most entirely beloved son to our most dread and gracious lord, King Henry VIII.[15]

Then twenty-four of the king's trumpeters sounded a strident fanfare that echoed around the fan-vaulted ceiling of oak timbers, completed the previous year and now resplendent with bright blue paint and gleaming gold leaf.

As usual on such occasions, the proud parents did not attend. Cranmer and the Duke of Norfolk were godfathers, and Princess Mary the godmother. It must have been a galling experience for Mary, as the tiny child had now quashed her hopes of being heir to the throne of England. If it did, she showed no sign of such jealous thoughts: the cup of gold[16] she had given as a baptism present was carried out of the chapel by the Earl of Essex as the first of the gifts lavished on the young prince by the fawning royal household. Her half-sister, the four-year-old Princess

Elizabeth, was also present, carried by the Viscount Beauchamp, assisted by Lord Morley 'on account of her tender age'.[17]

The prince was immediately confirmed as a full member of the Church of England, with Henry's old friend and sparring partner at the jousting lists, Charles Brandon,[18] First Duke of Suffolk, as his godfather.

Edward was afterwards taken triumphantly to his mother's apartments in the palace where his parents were waiting to give him their fond and grateful blessing. A proud Queen Jane, smiling wanly after her long ordeal, was propped up in bed, wearing a splendid mantle of crimson velvet and ermine.[19] Henry took the child up in his arms and blessed him loudly and fervently, invoking the names of Mary, the Blessed Mother of Christ, and St George, the patron saint of England. His mind must have recalled the tragic loss of Prince Henry, after just fifty-two days of life, way back in 1511, and Anne Boleyn's repeated failures to bear him a son, for emotion suddenly overwhelmed him. The king wept unashamedly with joy as he tenderly held the little prince: at long last, here was a legitimate and incontestable heir to inherit a firmly Tudor England. The queen's own proud announcement of the birth, in circular letters to the great and good, had earlier emphasized the legality of the joyous event: '[Jane the Queen] be delivered and brought in childbed of a prince conceived in most lawful matrimony between my lord the king's majesty and us.'[20]

All that marital pain, all those hard travails and bitter disappointments of Henry's past were now swept away as the tyrant cooed and burbled incongruously over the baby in his arms.[21] No doubt the ingratiating guests, all their thoughts unconsciously mirroring those of the king, spontaneously burst into applause. All too quickly, the prince's nurses reclaimed the child to return him to his own quarters in the north range of the palace's Chapel Court[22] and his canopied cradle in the 'rocking chamber'. But the merry christening celebrations in the queen's apartments went on until nearly dawn, with hippocras[23] and sweet French wine drunk by the nobility and gentry, whilst they nibbled politely on wafers and bread. To mark the occasion, the king knighted six courtiers, including Thomas Seymour, who was raised to membership of Henry's Privy Chamber, Thomas Wyatt and William Parr, son of a former Comptroller of the Royal Household.[24] The ragged poor, crowding in front of the barred gates of Hampton Court, were not forgotten: Henry ordered generous alms in cash – 'great largesse', the heralds called it – to be distributed to those waiting outside in the cold October night.

Twelve days later the queen was dead. Her end came swiftly. Sir John Russell wrote to Cromwell on 24 October: 'She was in great danger last night and today but if she sleeps tonight, the physicians hope that she is past danger.'[25] Alas, their optimism was ill-founded. Norfolk, at eight o'clock that night, sent a letter post-haste by mounted courier, again to Cromwell at Westminster, urging him to be at Hampton Court early the next morning 'to comfort our good master, for as for our mistress, there is no likelihood of her life, the more pity, and I fear she shall not be alive at the time you shall read this'.[26] Cromwell claimed later that Jane had died because of 'the neglect of them that were about her, who suffered her to take great cold and to eat such things that her fantasy in sickness called for',[27] but the reported symptoms and the lack of medical hygiene in the sixteenth century leave little doubt as to the real cause or major factor in her death.

The king of France had quickly written to congratulate his brother England on the birth of a son. A stunned Henry, now a sudden and unexpected widower, sadly replied:

Divine Providence has mingled my joy with the bitterness of death of her who has brought me this happiness.[28]

Norfolk, talking to the grief-stricken king on 3 November ('not wisely, yet plainly'), exhorted him 'to accept God's pleasure in taking the queen and to comfort himself with the treasure sent to him and his realm, namely the prince'. Recounting the conversation the next day in a letter to Cromwell, the duke said he had urged Henry 'to provide for another wife' – advice that carried, unspoken, the need to sire a Duke of York. Graspingly, charmlessly and with a tactless sense of timing, he also tried to manipulate the king into agreeing to share out the lucrative spoils of the dissolved priory of St Pancras at Lewes, Sussex, between himself and Cromwell: 'I was content [Cromwell] should have two parts,' Norfolk told the king. Henry distractedly replied, 'As you showed unto to me' – a sign, Norfolk believed, that the king thought the property 'well bestowed'.[29]

Henry's main concern now was that the future security of the Tudor royal dynasty had to be protected from both his enemies and that equally deadly adversary, disease. As 'God has the devil repugnant to Him and Christ hath Antichrist',[30] so there might be more threats, real or intangible, to the heir to the throne. Were there not reports circulating of evil-doers, practitioners in witchcraft, using a 'wax child' or dummy of the baby prince as a means of harming him? Under interrogation, one Richard Guercey confessed that he had spoken, in the kitchen of Corpus Christi College, Oxford, of information given to him by a man called Osmond – 'one of Peckwater's Inn' – that there was

> a wax image found in London way with a knife sticking through his head or his heart, representing the prince, and as that did consume, so likewise the prince.[31]

Edward spent some of the early weeks of his life at Hampton Court before being moved on to another of Henry's houses, Havering-atte-Bower in Essex. Henry had begun construction work at Hampton Court in May 1537, preparing confidently for a male heir. These extensions included the provision of a new 'jakes' or lavatory, a kitchen and a washing house.[32] With an eye to the necessities and trappings of the child's regal future, a small chamber of presence was created, approached by a processional staircase.[33] A household for the infant prince was set up in March 1538, led by Sir William Sidney as chamberlain, who was instructed to witness the child's daily bath and supervise the preparation of his meals in a dedicated kitchen. All food was carefully tasted before royal consumption in case of contamination by an assassin's poison.

The king issued strict instructions concerning the domestic arrangements for the prince – the 'whole realm's most precious jewel' – to Sidney and Sir John Cornwallis, steward.[34] They should ensure 'that all dangers and adversaries of malicious persons and casual harm shall be vigilantly foreseen and avoided'. Irrespective of rank, no one was allowed to approach the infant's cradle or to touch the prince (and this limited to only kissing his hands when it was permitted) without a written permit from the king. No pages were employed near the prince, as youths were regarded as frivolous, clumsy and forgetful of their duties.[35] Members of the household were also forbidden from entering London during the dangerous hot summer months when the plague was rife in the capital. If one fell sick, they had immediately to quit the precincts of the prince's establishment. Three times a day, the passages and rooms in the apartments had to be scrubbed with soap to ward off infection. In the same vein, the serjeant porters regularly drove the poor from the gates of wherever the prince was lodged, for fear that they harboured disease. 'If any beggar shall presume to draw near the gates, then they shall be ... grievously punished, to the example of others', the king's ordinance laid down. Every want and need of the child was considered and catered for: Joan Mewtes, one of his nurses, was paid out of the king's household accounts for 'a dozen handkerchiefs garnished [embroidered] with gold' at ten shillings each in 1540 and again the following year.[36]

On 8 September 1538, some members of the Privy Council were granted Henry's special licence to see the infant prince at Havering for the first time. Sir Thomas Audley, writing to Cromwell, the sycophancy almost oozing off the vellum, enthusiastically reported that he had never seen

> so goodly a child of his age. So merry, so pleasant, so good and loving [of] countenance and [with] so earnest an eye as it were a sage judgement towards any person that repaireth [approaches] to his grace.

The eleven-month-old child, said the Lord Chancellor,

has shot out in length and waxes firm and stiff and can steadfastly stand and would advance himself to move and go if they would suffer [let] him ... But ... they do best, considering his grace is yet tender, that he should not strain himself, as his own courage would serve him, till he come above a year of age.

I am right glad to hear the king's majesty will remove him from Havering against winter time: it is a cold house in winter, though in summer, it [has] a good air.[37]

At the end of November, Lady Honor Lisle, the formidable wife of Arthur Plantagenet – the illegitimate son of Edward IV who was now the Captain of Calais – was allowed to see the child. She, too, was enthusiastic in a letter to her husband:

I have seen my lord prince who is the goodliest babe that ever I set mine eyes upon. I pray God make him an old man, for I should never be weary of looking on him.[38]

The household became peripatetic, moving from one royal residence to another in search of fresh country air and to avoid any epidemics: from Havering to Hunsdon in Hertfordshire, thence to Ashridge in the same county. Costs of the prince's household for the first twelve months amounted to £6,500, or £2,920,000 in 2004 monetary values,[39] according to bills submitted by Richard Cotton, comptroller; a huge sum, despite the king's penny-pinching as he urged the household to avoid 'superfluous charges or waste' and operate at 'the least charges'. (Despite this, the prince had his own troupe of players, or actors, who were paid £4 for performing before the king at Christmas 1538.)

'Mistress Jak' was appointed Edward's wet nurse and the infant was reported to be sucking well, 'like a child of his puissance',[40] before her departure from this most intimate of services in October 1538. There were also four rockers of the cradle, two of them named as Jane Russell and Bridget Forster.[41] Margaret, Lady Bryan, who was a member of Princess Elizabeth's household, was created 'lady mistress' of the prince's establishment, and she reported to Cromwell in 1538 that Edward was 'in good health and merry. His grace has four teeth and three full out and the fourth approaching.'[42] Henry was a frequent visitor, checking on his son's health and progress. In May of 1538, the king set aside a day to spend with his longed-for heir at a hunting lodge at Roydon, Hertfordshire, 'and there solaced all the day with much mirth and joy, dallying with him in his arms a long space and so holding him in a window to the sight and great comfort of all the people'.[43] No doubt they were kept at a safe distance.

New Year's gifts to the prince throw some light on the tastes of the dysfunctional Tudor family and their immediate courtiers. On 1 January 1538, Henry's splendid presents included a gilt basin (forty ounces in weight) with a design of a Tudor rose in the bottom, a gilt ewer and a standing cup and cover of antique design with the figure of a man on the top. Princess Mary gave a coat of crimson satin, embroidered with gold, and Elizabeth, with a nice touch of girlish domesticity, 'a shirt of cambric of her own making'. Amongst the household's presents of gold and silver-gilt cups, salts, bowls and pots, Henry Bourchier, Second Earl of Essex, more realistically offered a 'bell of gold with a whistle', noted by Edward's careful accountants as weighing $1\frac{1}{4}$ ounces.[44] He also very practically gave two oxen and twenty mutton sheep as provisions for the prince's kitchen. The Earl of Southampton, for his part, gave a bonnet in black velvet, adorned with a white feather and a gold brooch.

The young prince spent his early years almost constantly in the company of deferential governesses and nurses, firstly Lady Bryan and Sybil Penn,[45] sister-in-law of Sir William Sidney, who was appointed in October 1539 as Mistress Jak retired. The child was brought up, his own chronicle recorded later, 'until he came to six years old among the women'.[46] Their constant fussing attention may well have instilled into his character a priggishness and a perhaps understandable insistence on always having his own way. Despite the fawning reports of his appearance and character, he sometimes behaved badly, like any other child. Bishop Gardiner related an incident sometime before 1540 when the infant became tearful during a visit by ambassadors from Protestant

Saxony and Hesse. Despite all efforts by Lady Bryan and his nurse in 'cheering ... and flattering', Edward 'ever cried and turned away his face' and comical face-pulling by the Earl of Essex was required to stem the flow of royal tears. The earl put his 'great beard' near Edward's face, tickled him and made him laugh.[47] The conservative Gardiner stuffily believed that the tantrum was a sure sign of the child's godliness because he was shunning the Protestant envoys.

A letter from Dr William Butts,[48] one of Edward's physicians (who was also in the king's service as his favourite and most trusted doctor), to his colleague Dr Chambre in 1542 provides a vivid snapshot of the medical attention paid to the five-year-old prince, as well as his developing wilfulness:

> Thanks to God, the prince's grace ... [is] taking of meats and took yesterday broths; conveniently keeping and well digesting the same and exercise [sic] himself on foot in his accustomed pastimes, so that now I think shall be no less business to dissuade him from taking of meats than hither ...
>
> This night he has slept quietly from nine of the clock to this present hour and now having drunk, turneth him again to sleep.
>
> He had yesterday, after his meat, one sege[49] of corrupt matter and no disposition to vomit but good appetite to his meat. This, fare you well, at three of the clock ...[50]

Butts adds as a postscript: 'He has prayed me to go away and has called me a fool. If I tarry till he call me "knave" then shall I say: "Lord, let now thy servant depart in peace."'

It was not long before one of the prime roles of an heir to the crown became apparent: to be a partner in a diplomatically advantageous marriage. In the immediate aftermath of the stunning English victory of Solway Moss over the Scots in November 1542, Henry hatched a plan to win control of Scotland that included marriage of the week-old infant Mary, Queen of Scots, to Edward. Nothing came of it due to the proclamation of the Earl of Arran, appointed in the New Year as governor during her minority. But the royal children of both nations were betrothed as part of a peace treaty agreed by Scottish ambassadors at Greenwich in July 1543, which stipulated that the infant daughter of the now dead James V would come to England when she was aged ten. This agreement also disappeared without trace into the quicksand of Scottish politics, with Mary being removed to France in 1548.[51]

Edward's education began when he was six with the appointment of two of the most advanced thinkers of the day: John Cheke,[52] the Regius professor of Greek at Cambridge, and Richard Cox,[53] first dean of Christ Church, Oxford, and later chancellor of that university. Both men, later professed Protestants and imprisoned during Mary's reign and then exiled to Europe, focused on teaching the boy the accepted classics, such as Aesop's *Fables*. Elizabeth's tutor, the author Roger Ascham,[54] was also sometimes seconded to Edward's household to help teach him to write and improve his penmanship.

The prince was a bright little boy, quickly learning Latin and, from October 1546, French,[55] and, later, Spanish and Italian. Dr Cox told Cranmer in August 1546 that his pupil was 'of such towardness in learning, godliness, gentleness and all honest qualities' and that he should be regarded as 'a singular gift sent of God, an imp worthy of such a father'.[56] Some of Edward's handwritten arguments in Latin and Greek are contained in a 222-page quarto volume entitled *Orationes* or Declamations, now in the British Library, possibly including a small contribution by one of his schoolfellows, Henry Brandon, later Duke of Suffolk, who died of the sweating sickness at Cambridge in 1551.[57] There seems little doubt that a select few were taught with the prince: Edward, in a letter to Dr Cox dated 2 April 1546, from Hertford, mentions 'other boys' – his schoolfellows – who were more negligent than himself in writing.[58]

Edward also received tuition in music, geography, astronomy and geometry – a true and rounded Renaissance education, as befitted the son of a king who believed himself to be firmly of that mould, in the full European sense. Amongst John Cheke's possessions, probably used by the prince, was an astronomical calendar in Latin dating from 1463, with tables for finding the dates of Easter[59] and annotated by Edward's tutor. Cheke also designed and had engraved an astronomical brass quadrant, used for measuring the positions of stars, for the prince.[60] Playing music was at that time regarded as a physical recreation in the education of royal children, as shown by the guidelines drawn up in 1525 for Princess Mary:

> To use moderate exercise for taking open air in gardens, sweet and wholesome places which may confer [upon] her health, solace and comfort, as by the said lady governess, shall be thought most convenient.
>
> And likewise to pass her time most seasons at her virginals or other instruments musical so that the same be not too much and without fatigue or weariness to intend to her learning of the Latin tongue and French.[61]

The composer Dr Christopher Tye directed Edward's music education and he was also taught to play the lute by the Dutchman Philip van Wilder,[62] Keeper of Instruments at the Palace of Westminster and a Groom of Henry's Privy Chamber.[63] The prince also enjoyed the singing of metrical psalms.

He saw little of his father as he grew up, and Henry remained a distant, rather awesome figure, the very personification of majesty with his massive bulk, intimidating presence and splendour of dress. When he wrote, his son addressed him as 'Most noble Father and most illustrious King', and was always fully aware that in all his deeds he had to 'satisfy the good expectation of the King's Majesty'. A later letter written to Henry from the little boy fiercely promised that he would be 'worthy to be tortured with stripes of ignomiy if, through negligence, I should omit even the smallest particle of my duty'. Reassurance of the king's continued regard seemed uppermost in the young prince's mind.

Edward's rather unattractive prissiness grew as the years went by. In a letter to Henry's queen, Katherine Parr, written on 2 May 1546 from Hunsdon when he was just eight, he scolded his half-sister Mary, thirty years his elder, as well as indulging in subtle little sideswipes at the queen herself:

Pardon my rude style in writing to you, most illustrious Queen
and beloved Mother, and receive my hearty thanks for your loving
kindness to me and my sister.

Yet, dearest Mother, the only true consolation is from Heaven
and the only real love is the love of God.

Preserve, therefore, I pray you, my dearest sister Mary from
all the wiles and enchantments of the evil one, and beseech her to
attend no longer to foreign dances and merriments, which do not
become a most Christian princess.[64]

Another letter to Katherine, written in the same year, concludes: 'I
pray to God to keep you and to grant you learning and virtue, the most
sure of riches.'[65]

His religious education was almost certainly organised by Archbishop Cranmer, one of the leaders of the reformist faction at Henry's
court, with some influence exerted by Katherine herself; some of his
later tutors became exiles during the Marian Counter-Reformation
after 1553. Edward had a great interest and erudition in religious issues
and his library contained many books on the subject. These volumes
included *Lectures in Latin on the First Three Chapters of Genesis*, given
to him as a New Year's gift by Glaterus Doloenus, later attached to the
royal household. At the end, the donor pointedly seeks a stipend for
ministers of the Dutch Protestant Church in England.[66] Nothing in life
is ever free. Another, later acquisition was the *Ecclesiastes* and the *Song
of Solomon*, translated into Latin elegiac verse by the Parisian Martin
Brione on forty-nine pages of vellum with illuminated initials to each
chapter and dedicated to Edward as king.[67] This all seems heavyweight
reading for a young prince, but he lapped it up.

John Bale, the fiercely Protestant Bishop of Ossory, wrote in 1552
of the excellence of the prince's education:

His worthy education in liberal letters and godly virtues and his
natural aptness in retaining the same, plenteously declares him
to be no poor child but a manifest Solomon in princely wisdom.

His sober admonitions and open examples of godliness at

this day shows him mindfully to prefer the wealth of his commons [people] as well as ghostly [spiritual] as bodily, above all foreign matters.[68]

There is little doubt that the ideas developing regarding religious change within the mind of the heir to the throne would find echoes in the beliefs held by his new stepmother, who was probably increasingly responsible for the ordering of the prince's education, bringing in Anthony Cooke and William Grindal, as well as John Cheke.[69]

Both princesses and Edward lived in separate households, but with the arrival of Katherine Parr as Queen Consort, Mary was finally allowed to stay at the royal court as a member of her entourage while Henry lived. It was part of Katherine's campaign to create a family for her elderly husband in his remaining years, although she probably would not have dared to express her plans in such stark terms to the king. Whilst separate establishments were maintained for Elizabeth and Edward up to December 1542, Henry's children by three different mothers were brought together for special occasions. The first opportunity came in August 1543 when Henry was persuaded by Katherine to take a detour to Ashridge, Hertfordshire, to visit the royal children, while they were journeying on their royal progress to Ampthill.

Katherine had a substantial household of her own. The humanist scholar Sir Anthony Cope was her Vice-Chamberlain before her uncle, Lord Parr of Horton, was appointed in his place. Her sister Anne, wife of William Herbert, became her chief lady of the bedchamber and her stepdaughter from her last marriage, Margaret Neville, one of her maids of honour. Her almoner was George Day, Bishop of Chichester, and her chaplains included John Parkhurst. Her household payments provide a detailed insight into her new life and interests. In 1544, Richard Bell was paid a shilling for going to Oldford to fetch Lady Audley's fool, or jester, to court to entertain the queen. She had her own ensemble of Italian viol-players, who were each paid 10d a day. In 1546, there were a number of payments to William Coke, Groom of the Leash, for milk and straw for Katherine's greyhounds; Thomas Beck received 4d for hempseed for the queen's parrot (which lived in the Privy Chamber) and 12s 4d was paid to Maurice Ludlow, Groom of the Chamber, for transporting her hawks. Giles Bateson, crossbow-maker, received 44s 8d for various contrivances, 'a crossbow case and one dozen crossbow strings for the queen's grace',[70] and John Chapman, freemason, 20s for carving a wooden beast – a panther – for the queen's barge on the River Thames. In September, Edward Fox received 3s for riding from Byfleet, Surrey, to London with one of her clocks to be mended. There are several payments for fetching the queen's furred gowns, stored at Baynard's Castle in London, and for travelling from the palace at Eltham in Kent to London for 'pins, starch and other necessaries'.[71] Some of these gowns had been made for Katherine Howard, but now were economically altered by the royal seamstresses to fit the new queen. Not that Katherine Parr was parsimonious in her expenditure on fashion: the accounts mention the purchase of forty-seven pairs of shoes in one year.[72] But aside from the hunting, music and other pastimes, Katherine's sense and prudence shine through the dull listing of her expenditure. Again and again, cash outlays were paid to those tasked in advance with searching out cases of sickness in the areas around the court's next destination: the queen was anxious to avoid any risk of infection by the plague both for her husband's sake and for that of her stepchildren.

There is no doubt that Katherine's kindness and compassion engendered great affection for her amongst Henry's disparate brood. Edward's forms of address to the queen in his letters, *Mater Charissima* – 'my dearest mother' – or 'most honourable and entirely beloved mother', are strongly indicative of the warm relationship that had developed between them.[73] They must have had very regular correspondence, as Katherine wrote to him several times, gently chiding him for his lack of letters to her.

One of Edward's letters, written on 12 August 1546 from The More, the house Henry had earlier acquired from Cardinal Wolsey, near Rickmansworth in Hertfordshire, thanks the queen for her kindness to him during his visit to Westminster and apologises for not writing sooner:

It seems to me an age since last I saw you. But I wish to entreat your highness to pardon me for that I have not addressed letters to you for so long. Indeed I intended to, but everyday expected I should see you.[74]

At other times, he clearly showered her with letters. Earlier that year, on 24 May, he wrote to the queen in Latin:

Oh most noble queen, perchance you are amazed that I write to you so often in so short a time but 'twere as like you would marvel that I do my duty unto you.

This I now do most willingly, for I have a fitting messenger, my servant, so that I cannot fail to send letters ... to bear witness to my devotion to you.

Your most obedient son, Edward the Prince.[75]

His correspondence to Katherine was mainly written in Latin but sometimes in English and French. One letter from Hunsdon, dated 10 June 1546, was concerned with the queen's penmanship and her efforts to learn Latin herself. It is a remarkable insight into the precocity of the eight-year-old, who was writing to a stepmother more than four times his age. With ponderous humour, the prince expresses 'much surprise' that a letter, in Latin, had been written by her and not by her secretary: 'I hear besides that your highness makes progress in the Latin language and in good literature, on which account I feel no little joy, for literature is lasting while other things perish.'[76]

Six months earlier, he had written to thank Katherine for sending him a new portrait of Henry and herself, saying that the pleasure of looking at the features of those 'he desired so much to see in person was so great that he was more thankful for such a new year's gift than if he had received costly robes or chased gold or anything of the highest estimation'.[77]

Now a mystery emerges from the dark recesses of the royal court: the lasting enigma of 'a child named Ralfe Lyons, that was given to Henry' in 1546.[78] The wording is quite clear: 'given to our late sovereign lord

Henry the eight' is pointedly repeated on each of four pages of accounts for the last year of the king's reign and for 1547–8, the first year of Edward's. In twenty-first-century understanding, 'given' clearly implies offered up for adoption or fostering, but this interpretation seems unlikely in mid-Tudor England, although something very unusual had obviously happened to justify the constant use of this tantalising phrase and to warrant maintaining separate accounts for him. Certainly, special care was lavished on the child for the two years that the Privy Purse was responsible for his upkeep. Ralfe Lyons was sent to be taught by Robert Phillips at the Chapel Royal, based since 1533 at St James's Palace, across the fields from the Palace of Westminster. Payments were made for new clothes – 5s 4d for a doublet, 8d for a purse in 1546 – and for board and wages within the allowances. History is silent on how young Ralfe came to be cared for so well, why he was singled out for this generous attention and what eventually happened to him. Was he the son of a favoured junior member of the royal household whose parents had both died, leaving him an orphan? Can one detect in this the kind, caring hand of Katherine Parr? Given the king's medical condition and reduced sexual capacity, the child was unlikely to be another royal bastard. Alternatively, was he merely a boy chorister with a fabulous singing voice who was sequestered from another institution, as it is known that efforts were made to employ the best singers for the Chapel Royal?[79] The answer maddeningly remains a mystery.

Within the royal family, one particular issue had to be overcome before Katherine's long-desired normalisation of relations could be achieved. This was Henry's suspicion regarding Princess Elizabeth and her own distrust of her father after the numerous unsuccessful attempts to marry her off for diplomatic or political ends. By 1545, she was an articulate twelve-year-old well-educated girl who had copious quantities of the low cunning that was an integral part of the Tudor genes. Part of her rehabilitation into family life came with the restoration of both princesses into the line of succession to the crown after Edward and his heirs, enshrined in an Act passed by Parliament in 1544.[80] It is not difficult to see Katherine's quietly manipulative hand in this decision by Henry to legitimise his daughters in the eyes of the law, an action that irrevocably bound both princesses to her patronage and affection.

In July 1544, Henry went to war in France for the last time, appointing Katherine as regent of England. He also changed the structure of Edward's household, appointing Cox to be almoner and Cheke as a deputy 'both for the better instruction of the prince and the diligent teaching of such children as be appointed to attend upon them'.[81] Edward moved to Hampton Court for greater security, apparently with the two princesses, as on 25 July Katherine wrote from that palace to Henry: 'My lord prince and the rest of your Majesty's children are all (thanks be to God) in very good health.'

Elizabeth, who apparently departed soon after, ruefully sent a letter to Katherine on 31 July from St James's Palace, complaining at her separation from her stepmother:

> Envious fortune for a whole year deprived me of your presence and not content therewith has again despoiled me of that benefit.

The princess, however, knew she had Katherine's love, whom, she heard, had not forgotten her in her letters to the king, campaigning in France.[82]

Katherine, firmly rooted in modern humanist thinking, was not quite so close to the staunchly Catholic Princess Mary, although she showered gifts upon her and encouraged her to translate into English Erasmus' *Paraphrase of the Gospel of St John*.[83] The queen also persuaded Elizabeth to translate from the French Queen Marguerite of Navarre's devotional poem *The Mirror or Glass of the Sinful Soul*, happily delivered by Elizabeth to Katherine as a New Year's gift on 31 December 1544,[84] and Erasmus' *Dialogues Fidei*.

Katherine herself also produced religious books – *Prayers Stirring the Mind unto Heavenly Meditations*, which became something of a best seller after it was first published in 1545,[85] and *Lamentations of a Sinner*, copies of which were circulating in Henry's court by November 1545[86] but which, significantly, only appeared in print after his death in 1547, portraying the king as a Moses who had led England out of the thraldom of Rome. When she was aged twelve, Elizabeth also translated Katherine's expanded *Prayers and Meditations* into Latin, French and Italian. This 117-page book, with a crimson silk binding deftly embroidered by Elizabeth herself in gold and silver thread with the initial 'H' and a large monogram of the name 'Katherina', includes a dedicatory letter to Henry written in Latin and dated 'Hertford, December 20 1545'.[87]

Katherine's interest in religion and her views on its development were reflected in the make-up of her household and those who benefited from her patronage: for example, Thomas Cromwell's friend Miles Coverdale, who translated the Bible into English; the psalmist Thomas Sternhold; and Nicholas Udall, the 'thrashing'[88] headmaster of Eton, who took part in the translation of Erasmus' *Paraphrases of the Gospels*[89] with Princess Mary.

Although she loved dancing and fine clothes and jewels, Katherine's chambers were also a citadel of learning and liberal thought. As a reflection of the religious discussions that constantly went on within her apartments, a Mr Goldsmith who had unsuccessfully sought a position in her household congratulated the queen for her 'rare goodness [that] has made every day a Sunday, a thing hitherto unheard of, especially in a royal palace'.[90] Udall described life in Katherine's apartments as embracing 'virtuous exercises, reading and writing and with most earnest study'; she and her ladies 'early and late, apply themselves to extending [their] knowledge'. The queen's beliefs and opinions were to lead her into very dangerous waters indeed: the maelstrom caused by the continuing conflict within Henry's Privy Council over religious reform. It was almost to cost the queen her life.

CHAPTER THREE

The Hunt for Heretics

*'Consider, gentle reader, how full of
iniquity this time is, in which the high mystery
of our religion is so openly assaulted ...
Be desirous of the very truth and seek it as thou
art ordered, by direction of Christ's church,
and not as deceitful teachers would lead
you, by their secret ways.'*

BISHOP STEPHEN GARDINER,

A DETECTION OF THE DEVIL'S SOPHISTRY (LONDON, 1546).

On 16 November 1538, King Henry publicly grasped the nettle of heresy. John Lambert, alias John Nicholson, had been arrested for persistently denying the holy presence of Christ in the consecrated wafer and wine of the Mass, the so-called 'Real Presence'. The prisoner had been educated at Cambridge – he had been a fellow of Queens' College in 1521 – and later had become a radical evangelical, serving as a chaplain to the English community in Antwerp. He was jailed in England in 1532 for his beliefs but later released and went on to run a school in London. Arrested again, Lambert now had to confront Henry personally in an elaborately staged propaganda trial for his life.

The king's religious policies sometimes seem contradictory during the second half of his reign, as he flip-flopped between conservative and reformist measures pressed upon him by the vociferous opposing factions within his court. Whilst remaining very much an orthodox and devout Catholic in many aspects of doctrine and liturgy, he veered to and fro between executing members of both the evangelical and conservative factions,[1] sometimes as heretics, more often as traitors, as well as staging very public bonfires of profane books.[2] Much earlier in his reign, he had been an ardent supporter of the Holy Catholic Church, yearning for what he saw as due papal recognition of his piety. It came on 11 October 1521, when the spendthrift Pope Leo X declared Henry – his 'most dear son in Christ' – *Fidei Defensor*, 'Defender of the Faith', for his authorship of a 30,000-word book in Latin, the *Assertio Septem Sacramentorum* or 'Assertion of the Seven Sacraments'. This had been written, with some academic assistance, specifically to mock and attack the new Protestant beliefs then being promulgated by the apostate monk Martin Luther in Germany. The book went through twenty editions, eagerly devoured by Henry's pious and loyal subjects.[3] Then came the thorny and self-serving issue of the king's divorce from his first wife, Catherine of Aragon. Henry's assumption of the supremacy of the Church in England and the break with Rome followed in December 1533, when the Privy Council ordered that Pope Clement VII no longer had authority over the realm and should henceforth be referred to merely as 'the Bishop of Rome'. The Act of Supremacy, passed in November 1534,[4] confirmed Henry's rule over the Church in English law and was to cause much bloodshed amongst those, great and low, priest and secular, who could not bring themselves in good conscience to take the oath of allegiance to the king as head of the Church. The subsequent Act for Extinguishing the Authority of the Bishop of Rome of 1536 impolitely railed against

> The pretended power and usurped authority of the Bishop of Rome, by some called the Pope ... which did obfuscate and wrest God's holy word and testament a long season from the spiritual and true meaning thereof, to his worldly and carnal affections, as pomp, glory, avarice, ambition and tyranny, covering and shadowing the

same with his human and politic devices, traditions and inventions, set forth to promote and establish his only dominion, both upon the souls and also the bodies and goods of all Christian people, excluding Christ out of his kingdom and the rule of man his soul as much as he may and all temporal kings and princes out of their dominions which they ought to have by God's law upon the bodies and goods of their subjects.[5]

Most importantly, not only did the pope 'rob' the king as supreme head of the realm of England 'immediately under God of his honour, right and pre-eminence due to him by the law of God, but spoiled this realm yearly of innumerable treasure'. It was typical Henrician propaganda: smug, self-justifying and arrogant. A staunch Lutheran in Germany could happily have written it. The Act marked an important continuum of the king's campaign against Rome, should any of his subjects be reckless enough to retain any doubts as to the wisdom of his religious policy.

Cromwell staged a public and very graphic demonstration of the royal supremacy in London on 17 June 1539. Today we would regard it as crude, obvious propaganda, but the chief minister knew his audience well and unsubtly combined his political and religious message with a spectacular designed to entertain and amuse, as well as subliminally create support for the king's policies. Two vessels – the king's barge and a 'papal' barge – rowed up and down the River Thames between Westminster and the King's Bridge. On board the pontifical barge were a number of men dressed as the pope and cardinals who 'made their defiance against England'. The two boats exchanged gunfire (presumably firing blanks) and 'at last, the pope and cardinals were overcome and all his men cast overboard into the Thames' to the great merriment of the watchers on the banks,[6] including Henry himself. Other, less ambitious pageants against the pope were also staged in towns and cities throughout the realm.

Religious Injunctions of 1536 and 1538, issued by Cromwell, also required the clergy 'to the uttermost of their wit, knowledge and learning, purely, sincerely and without any colour of dissimulation' to preach against the 'Bishop of Rome's usurped power and jurisdiction' as a direct means of re-educating the minds of Henry's subjects. Moreover, the Injunctions prohibited the setting up of images (religious statues) or extolling 'relics or miracles for any superstition or lucre, nor allure the people by any enticements to the pilgrimage of any saint'. The later set of injunctions went further, imposing on the clergy of England the duty, once every three months, of warning their congregations

> not to repose their trust ... in any other works devised by men's fantasies besides Scripture; as in wandering to pilgrimages, offering of money, candles or tapers to images or relics ... saying over a number of beads not understood or minded on, or in such-like superstition.[7]

Most importantly, the Injunctions of 1538 required priests to provide

> on this side of the Feast of Easter next coming [1539], one book of the whole Bible of the largest volume in English and the same set up in some convenient place within the ... church that you have cure of, whereas your parishioners may most commodiously resort to the same and read it.[8]

This refers to the so-called *Great Bible*, printed in London in 1539–40 by Richard Grafton after the French Inquisition stopped production of it in Paris, which showed Henry in a woodcut on the main title page, as well as Cranmer and Cromwell,[9] and the people loyally crying '*Vivat Rex*' and 'God Save the King'. It boldly declared: 'This is the Bible appointed to the use of the churches.'[10] But Henry's subjects' enjoyment of the Bible in their own language was short-lived. The Act of 1543 for the Advancement of True Religion[11] withdrew his government's permission for everyone to read the English Bible, limiting it to noblemen, gentlemen and merchants (who could peruse it in private), but women, workers, apprentices and others were strictly prohibited from reading it in public or privately. Generously, the Act allowed those of noble or gentle rank of both sexes to read it to themselves silently – certainly not to others.

Back in November 1538, Chief Minister Cromwell and Archbishop Cranmer had launched an active campaign against members of the growing Anabaptist[12] sects throughout the realm – in particular, those who argued against the 'Real Presence' in the sacrament of communion. The chief minister, now also the king's vice-regent in matters spiritual, had decided that a public example was needed to underline Henry's fervent opposition to heresy. Lambert was selected as that example, probably by Bishop Stephen Gardiner. Lambert had earlier appeared before Cranmer on a charge of heresy and had been found guilty. Henry's propagandists then turned his appeal into a show trial in all but name. Within the banqueting hall of the Palace of Westminster, temporary wooden scaffolding had been erected along the walls to seat spectators, to enable them to witness their king determinedly defending the sacred beliefs of the Church of England – 'the reverence of the holy sacrament of the altar', as Cromwell remarked. The nobility and clergy were specially invited to attend. They would have seen what transpired, but as virtually all the proceedings were to be conducted in Latin, not everyone would have understood what was said. Promptly at noon, Henry entered the hall attired head to foot in the splendour of white silk, escorted by his yeoman guards, also dressed in white uniforms. He climbed the short flight of steps to his throne beneath the canopy of estate and sat, flanked on his right by Cranmer and the bishops, and on his left by the temporal peers, led by Cromwell, and the Gentlemen of the Privy Chamber. The great hall was hushed as Lambert was brought in to stand on a special wooden stage, facing his accusers, 'fearful and timorous'.[13]

The beginning was cheery enough. 'Ho! Good fellow, what is thy name?'[14] Henry asked Lambert, after the buzz of the audience had died away. It sounded very much like a jocular 'hail fellow, well met' sort of greeting, but what followed was not anything like so genial. When the prisoner explained that he had changed his name to escape persecution, the king, his 'look, his cruel countenance and his brows bent unto severity', told him bluntly, 'I would not trust you, having two names, although you were my brother.' Lambert naïvely then tried flattery, humbly thanking Henry for hearing his case and commending his 'great judgement and learning'. But the king, now standing before the throne, an imposing, tall figure in the hall, quickly interrupted him: 'I did not come here to hear my own praises.'

George Day, provost of King's College, Cambridge, and a famed public orator,[15] explained the true reason why everyone was gathered there. The 'assembly was not at all convened to dispute about any point of faith, but the king, being supreme head, intends openly to condemn and confute that man's heresy' – and he pointed accusingly at Lambert – 'in all their presence'.

So Henry pressed on with the grave business of the day. Removing his cap piously as he mentioned the Name of Christ, he demanded to know whether the defendant believed that the consecrated wafer and wine in truth represented the body of God the Son.

Lambert answered that he was 'with St Augustine, that it is the body of Christ – after a certain manner'.

Back swiftly came the king's bullying, hectoring retort: 'Answer me neither out of St Augustine, nor by the authority of any other, but tell me plainly whether you say it is the body of Christ, or no.'

The prisoner, abashed, answered, 'It was not his body. I deny it.'

'Mark well,' said the king, 'for now you shall be condemned even by Christ's own words: "This is my body."'

Lambert had been forced to produce a written statement in advance of his trial, laying down ten cogent reasons for his denial of the 'Real Presence'. Cromwell, always the careful stage manager, had wanted to allow him enough wooden faggots to burn himself with. One after the other, Henry's bishops took each of the prisoner's reasons and, well prepared, argued strongly against them during the five gruelling hours of the trial. The reactionary and impatient Bishop Gardiner believed the good-natured Cranmer was 'arguing but faintly' and rudely interrupted his discourse with his own forceful opinions.[16]

As the hearing drew to an end, 'the general applause of the hall gave victory to the king'. As the polite clapping died down, Henry asked the prisoner: 'Wilt thou live or die? You have yet a free choice.'[17]

But Lambert obstinately refused to change his beliefs. He

committed his soul to God and submitted his body to the king's clemency. Henry shrugged his shoulders and told him loudly: 'That being the case, you must die, for I will not be a patron unto heretics.'[18] He pointedly looked up at the serried ranks of spectators as his words rang around the hall, now lit by torches in the late-winter afternoon. The culmination of the trial had served his purpose well.

Cromwell stepped forward and loudly pronounced Lambert an incorrigible heretic and condemned him to be burnt. Six days later, on 22 November, he was to suffer a markedly cruel death at Smithfield. When his legs and thighs had been burnt to the stumps, the fire sank lower, so two officers raised up his still living body on their halberds and let him fall back into the flames. He cried out 'None but Christ, none but Christ' before he was burnt to ashes.[19]

The chief minister wrote after the 'open and solemn' trial of this 'miserable heretic sacramentary' that it was

> a wonder to see how fiercely, with how excellent gravity and ines-
> timable majesty his highness exercised there the very office of a
> supreme head of his Church of England; how benignly his grace
> assayed to convert the miserable man, how strong and manifest
> reasons his highness alleged against him.

He added sycophantically that if the potentates of Christendom had seen the king in action, they would have marvelled at his wisdom and thought him 'the mirror and light of all other kings and princes'.[20] The London agent of the orthodox Catholic Viscount Lisle wrote to his master in Calais:

> His grace alone had been sufficient to confound [Lambert] ...
> It was not a little rejoicing unto all his grace's commons and also to
> all others that saw and heard how his grace handled and used this
> matter, for it shall be a precedent while the world stands. I think
> there will be none so bold hereafter to attempt any such like cause.[21]

On the same day as the trial, to emphasize Henry's strong beliefs on religious doctrine, the government issued a proclamation banning the printing of any Bible without an official licence and ordering his subjects to denounce Anabaptists promptly to the religious authorities. Married priests were to lose their livings and any who married thereafter were to be imprisoned. Rituals such as creeping to the cross during the Good Friday services and the use of candles at Candlemas would continue. One senses the firm hand of Gardiner in the announcement. Two Anabaptists, a Dutch man and woman, were burnt as heretics at Smithfield on 28 November, and a 'goodly young man about twenty-two years of age' was executed for being a Sacramentarian at Colchester, Essex.[22]

Ironically, less than a month after the trial in December 1538, Pope Paul III prepared to promulgate the long-awaited Bull excommunicating Henry, first drawn up in 1533 by Clement VII and later revised. The decision was triggered by the sacking of the shrine of St Thomas Becket, that much-revered martyred archbishop, in Canterbury Cathedral. The Bull declared Henry irrefutably a heretic and thus legally deposed him from the throne of England. His subjects were solemnly discharged from their oath of allegiance to him, and all Catholic monarchs in Europe were urged to unite to return England to her proper, traditional allegiance to papal authority in Rome. Cromwell, 'that limb of Satan',[23] was cast into Hell's all-consuming fire. The Bull obviously could not be published in England, so it was rather lamely read out at various safe locations closest to Henry's realm: in the north at St Andrew's and Coldstream in Scotland, and in the south at Boulogne and Dieppe in France.

Bishop Gardiner was also probably the inspiration behind the creation of the 'Six Articles' of religion in 1539, the legal instrument that stopped Protestant reforms dead in their tracks – they called it the 'whip with six strings' – and pulled the Church back to orthodox doctrine. Henry, far more conservative in his religious beliefs than many realised, was a fervent supporter of the Six Articles, as he was painfully aware that the vast majority of his subjects were probably 'more inclined to the old religion than the new opinions'. The Act, introduced into Parliament by Norfolk in May 1539, laid down that the body of Christ was truly and legally present in the consecrated bread and wine during Mass. The penalty for denying this was death by burning at the stake

– even after a recantation. The other Articles covered the validity of vows of celibacy within the religious orders, a repeated prohibition of the marriage of priests, the continuation of private Masses, the importance of the sacrament of confession and the administration of communion. Penalties for denying these were death by hanging and forfeiture of the miscreants' lands and goods. In addition, anyone who tried to flee England to escape such prosecutions was also guilty of treason and would be hanged, drawn and quartered if captured. Those priests already married had to leave their wives and those who married after the law came into force were also to face the death penalty.

Moreover, the Six Articles comprehensively defined heresy as a secular offence: any person 'by word, writing, imprinting, ciphering[24] or in any other wise, to publish, teach, say, affirm, declare, dispute, argue or hold any contrary opinion' together with their aiders and abetters 'shall be adjudged heretics and shall therefore have [to] suffer judgement, execution, pain and pains of death by way of burning'. It was a piece of uncompromising, harsh legislation intended to brook no argument in the enshrinement of the doctrines of the Church of England in law. Many were to die in the flames of martyrdom as a result.

Cranmer, himself married, had vigorously disputed the terms of the Six Articles during a hotly contested three-day debate in the House of Lords in May 1539, attended each day by Henry himself. The archbishop lost the argument, probably because of Henry's personal intervention, and An Act Abolishing Diversity in Opinions[25] was granted the Royal Assent on 28 June. Cranmer promptly sent his wife back to Germany.[26] What his enemies' eyes could not see, they could not use against him.

Protestants in Germany were horrified by news of the new legislation. The Lutheran reformer Philip Melanchthon wrote to Henry on 1 November 1539, his words tumbling angrily on to the page, protesting that the Articles 'play into the hands of the Pope'. Presumably

> it was your bishops who were responsible ... not you. Really wise
> Princes are capable of reconsidering their decisions ... Do not take

up the cause of the Antichrist against us. Your bishops may pretend to take your part but they are in league with the Pope.

The Articles are full of sophistry and deceit. They are inconsistent with church history, for example, in saying private Masses as necessary and [that] the marriage of priests is against Divine Law.

I blame the bishops, especially Winchester. They are concerned about their own incomes.

No one can deny that the Church has come through a period of horrible darkness, like paganism, as is still the case in Rome.

Now at the end of time, God has intervened against the Antichrist [but] I thought England was leading the way. But your bishops are still plotting to retain idolatry, hence the Articles.[27]

Melanchthon pleaded, 'I suggest you think again. Otherwise your bishops will tyrannise the church. Christ will judge.' Strong stuff indeed. But his appeal fell on deaf ears; indeed, as Henry played so active a part in the creation of the legislation, the letter may well have incensed him.[28]

There is a bizarre anecdote about the aftermath of the Six Articles. Cranmer later wrote detailed notes on the reasons behind his opposition to them, backed up by citations from the Bible and from accepted learned scholars' writings, which he planned to present to Henry. His secretary, the faithful Ralph Morice, made a fair copy of them in a small book and on his way to Westminster with it met with a startling accident on the Thames. Bishop Burnet, in the next century, related the story:

Some others that were with him in the wherry[29] needed to go to the Southwark side to look at a bear-baiting that was near the river, where the king was in person.

The bear broke loose into the river [with] the dogs after her. Those that were in the boat leaped out and left the poor secretary alone there. But the bear got into the boat, with the dogs about her, and sank it. The secretary, apprehending his life was in danger, did not mind his book, which he lost in the water.

But being quickly rescued and brought to land, he began to look for his book and saw it floating in the water.

So he desired the bearward [bear-keeper] to bring it to him; who took it up, but before he could restore it, put it into the hands of a priest that stood there, to see what it might contain.[30]

Turning the sodden pages, the priest immediately realised that the contents disputed the Six Articles and told the bearward that whoever claimed it would be hanged. Burnet, always partisan, adds: 'This made the bearward more intractable, for he was a spiteful papist and hated the archbishop, so no offers or entreaties could prevail on him to give it back.' Morice, panicking, urgently sought assistance from Cromwell, and the next day they discovered the bearward at court, seeking to hand the book over to one of Cranmer's enemies, no doubt in return for a handsome reward. Cromwell 'took the book out of his hands, threatening him severely for his presumption in meddling with a privy councillor's book'.[31] Cranmer was thereby saved. Others were not so fortunate.

Amongst the earliest to be arrested, held in the Tower and put on trial were a number of priests and soldiers from the Calais garrison who, like Lambert, were also accused of denying the 'Real Presence'. Legally, their heresy dated from before the Six Articles became law, so they were spared after making full recantations. They were merely paraded through the London streets as a humiliation, carrying a faggot or bundle of wood – the fuel normally used to burn heretics alive – on their shoulders before beginning various terms of imprisonment.

On 12 April 1540, Cromwell, in the king's name, told a new session of Parliament of the importance of a 'firm union' amongst all of Henry's subjects. He knew that

there were many incendiaries and much cockle grown up with the wheat. The rashness and licentiousness of some, and the inveterate superstition and stiffness of others in the ancient cor-ruptions, had raised great dissensions, to the sad regret of all good Christians.

Some were called papists, other[s] heretics; which bitterness of spirit seemed the more strange, since now the holy Scriptures, by the king's great care of his people, were now in all their hands, in a language they understood.

But these were grossly perverted by both sides who studied rather to justify their passions out of them than to direct their belief by them.

Significantly, he added:

The king leans neither to the right nor to the left hand, neither to the one nor the other party, but set[s] the pure and sincere doctrine of the Christian faith only before his eyes.[32]

Henry was anxious to see 'decent' religious ceremonies continued, Cromwell went on, 'and the true use of them taught, by which all abuses might be cut off and disputes about the exposition of the Scriptures cease'. The king was also 'resolved to punish severely all transgressors of what sort or side, [who]soever they were' and was determined, Cromwell added portentously, 'that Christ, the gospel of Christ and the truth should have the victory'.

In just over fourteen weeks, Cromwell himself was dead, beheaded as a traitor and heretic. Despite his considerable political and administrative skills and his eloquence in laying out the king's religious policies, Henry's chief minister fell because many of his noble and episcopal rivals had become intolerant of his influence with the king and jealous of his continued advancement, both in status and wealth. They chose his failure over the disastrous marriage to Anne of Cleves as the moment to strike, as Henry nursed his burning resentment at being 'ill used' by Cromwell. His alleged heresy was his declaration on 30 March 1539, in the parish of St Peter the Poor in London, that teaching in the reformed religion was 'good' and 'if the king would turn from it, yet I would not turn'. If Henry did reject it 'and all his people, I would fight in this field in mine own person with my sword in my hand against him and all other'. Then he pulled out his dagger, held it up and vowed:

'Or else this dagger thrust me to the heart, if I would not die in that quarrel against them all.'[33]

He was not the only one to perish for heresy. Three notorious evangelical priests – William Jerome,[34] Robert Barnes and Thomas Garret[35] – had been arrested in 1540. Barnes had returned to London from exile in Antwerp in 1535 at Cromwell's invitation. He made the great mistake of preaching against Gardiner during Lent 1540 at Paul's Cross (a covered churchyard pulpit outside the north-east wall of the great London cathedral). Barnes punningly and mockingly referred to the bishop as a 'gardener setting ill plants in a garden'.[36] A vibrant sense of humour was not one of the prickly Bishop of Winchester's most abundant assets. The preacher was forced to seek Gardiner's pardon and the bishop 'being twice desired by him to give some sign that he forgave him, did lift up his finger'. All three were brought before the king soon after and Garret, for his part, signed a document acknowledging that 'his highness, being assisted by some of his clergy, had so disputed with him that he was convinced of his rashness and oversight and promised to abstain from such indiscretions'. The Tudor propaganda machine was at work again. Barnes also submitted to the king, but was quickly snubbed. Henry walked to the altar within his chamber, devoutly genuflected and told him: 'Submit not to me. I am a mortal man, but yonder is the Maker of us all – the author of truth.'[37] The three accused were required to preach at St Mary's Church, Spitalfields, in London that Easter, to demonstrate their new support of orthodox doctrine. But this was not enough for Gardiner. Despite his denials, it seems plain that he was behind their immediate imprisonment in the Tower after their interview with Henry on charges of heresy. Once behind bars and only too conscious of their impending fate, they withdrew their recantations.

On 30 July 1540 they were burnt at Smithfield. In a macabre public demonstration of Henry's even-handiness in his determination to stamp out heresy and treason, they were dragged face down on sheep hurdles through the streets alongside three papists – Richard Featherstone, Thomas Abel[38] and Edward Powell – who themselves faced execution by hanging, drawing and beheading for treason because of their denial of the royal supremacy. Thus, one heretic and one papist were strapped to each hurdle and as they were bumped along the cobbles through the mud, horse droppings and foul sewage, they reportedly argued furiously about which one of them was truly facing a martyr's death.[39] Barnes generously reassured his fellow victim: 'Cheer up, brother, today we shall be in glory.'[40]

At the place of execution, standing at the stake above a huge pile of wood faggots, Barnes raised his voice to ask Sir William Laxton and Martin Bowes, the two sheriffs of London, the reason why he was about to die. The wretched sheriffs, shaking their heads, did not know.[41] Barnes then repeated the question to the watching crowd and asked them whether 'they had been led into any errors by his preaching'. Defiantly, he went on: 'Let them now speak and I will make them answer.' No one spoke out. Then, said Barnes, he had 'heard I was condemned to die by act of Parliament, seemingly for heresy, since we are to be burned'. He prayed to God to forgive those responsible and, in particular, the Bishop of Winchester:

> If he had sought or procured my death either by word or deed, I pray to God to forgive him, as heartily, as freely, as charitably and as sincerely as Christ forgave them that put Him to death.

In a strange display of loyalty in his last moments of life, Barnes urged the people to pray for the king 'and after him that godly prince Edward'. He added:

> I have been reported a preacher of sedition and disobedience to the king's majesty. But here, I say to you that you are all bound by the law of God to obey your prince with all humility, not only for fear, but for conscience.[42]

All three evangelicals prayed for the pardon of their sins and the constancy and patience to endure their sufferings. They embraced, kissed each other and then were tied to their stakes. A horror-struck silence fell on the crowd as their pyres were lit.

Their deaths were not popular in Protestant London. One contemporary commentator wrote:

> Most men said it was for preaching against the doctrine of Stephen Gardiner ... who chiefly procured this their death. God and he knoweth, but a great pity it was that such learned men should be so cast away without examination, neither knowing which was laid to their charge, nor never called to answer.[43]

The burnings and executions continued, including three in Salisbury and two in Lincoln on the same day. In January 1541, Henry issued instructions to Edmund Bonner, Bishop of London, and Sir Richard Gresham, the Lord Mayor, to root out once and for all those in the capital who rejected the 'Real Presence' during communion. One case stands out from many: that of the orphan Richard Mekins, 'a boy not above fifteen years of age and both illiterate and very ignorant' who denied the corporeal presence of Christ in the sacrament and, additionally, praised Robert Barnes for his beliefs. When he appeared on trial for his life at the Guildhall, two witnesses reported his words, but the jury foreman said the case had not been proved.

> Upon which Bonner cursed and was in a great rage and caused them to go aside again.
>
> So they being overawed, returned and found the indictment [true].
>
> But when he was brought to the stake, he was taught to speak much good of Bonner and to condemn all heretics and Barnes in particular.[44]

The chronicler Edward Hall said contemptuously that

> the poor boy would for the safeguard of his life have gladly said that the Twelve Apostles taught it him, for he had not cared of whom he had named it, such was his childish innocence and fear.[45]

Mekins was executed anyway at Smithfield on 30 July.

Another youth called John Collins, who lived in Southwark, within

Gardiner's diocese of Winchester, had objected to what he saw as idol-
atrous worship of a wooden statue of Christ within a chapel used by
Spanish sailors arriving in the port of London to offer up prayers of
thanks for their safe passage. He shot an arrow at the statue, which
lodged in one of its feet, and loudly called on the crucifix to defend itself
and punish him for his sacrilege.[46] Collins had been kept in prison for
two or three years and had been confined with Lambert. He was quite
possibly insane, but Henry's Act, passed for use against Lady Jane
Rochford, which permitted the execution of those found guilty of heresy
or treason even if they were deemed insane, was conveniently used
against Collins. He, too, was burnt to death.[47] Again, he was popularly
thought to have been a victim of Gardiner.

Despite his continued pleas for religious unity in his realm, by
1540 Henry's Privy Council and court were riven by what had become
two opposing factions over the proper future direction of the Church of
England. Those supporting the more traditional doctrines were led by
Gardiner and Norfolk and included the king's long-time friends
Southampton and Sir Anthony Browne, Master of the King's Horse,
as well as Sir William Paulet, Lord St John; Sir John Baker, Attorney-
General; Sir Richard Rich (who had perjured himself so shamefully
at the trial of Sir Thomas More in 1535 and was a prime informant
against Cromwell)[48] and Wriothesley. Opposing them were the evangelicals: Cranmer and Sir Edward Seymour, Earl of Hertford and Suffolk,
Henry's old jousting partner. In view of the constant plots and counter-
plots, it is not surprising that Henry's religious policies during this
period of his reign appear sometimes incongruous as he tried to
maintain a precarious balance by cunningly playing off one faction
against the other.

Two weeks after Henry's marriage to Katherine Parr, there was
another case against Sacramentarians, this time rather closer to home
– at the court in Windsor. John Marbeck, organist of the Chapel Royal,
St George's, and local men Anthony Pearson – a priest from Winkfield,
Berkshire, Henry Filmer – a tailor, Robert Testwood – 'a singing man',
and another called Bennet had been charged with heresy and held in

the Marshalsea Prison, Southwark. They were brought to trial on Thursday 26 July 1543 at Windsor before the former Benedictine monk John Capon, now Bishop of Salisbury, William Franklin, Dean of Windsor, and a jury drawn from the Chapel Royal's own tenants. Testwood was so ill that he arrived in court only with the aid of crutches; Bennet was sick with the plague and was left in the Marshalsea,[49] the sickness incongruously saving his life. Therefore only four appeared in the dock and all were found guilty after a controversial trial in which the case against Testwood included the vacuous charge that he avoided looking at the Host when it was raised during Mass, instead of acknowledging it devoutly. Marbeck was, however, reprieved by royal pardon because Gardiner apparently enjoyed his music[50] and pleaded with Henry for his life.

No one was entirely safe from the devious intrigues at court. Almost certainly encouraged by Gardiner and Sir John Baker, some of the seven conservative canons of Canterbury Cathedral accused Cranmer himself of encouraging heretical sermons within the diocese of Canterbury in 1543. Their complaints and accusations were dispatched to the king. As Henry was rowed upriver on his royal barge one evening, he saw Cranmer standing outside the gates of his palace at Lambeth. The vessel pulled into the bank and the archbishop, coming aboard, was stunned by the king's light-hearted greeting: 'Ah, my chaplain! I have news for you. I know now who is the greatest heretic in Kent.' Henry then pulled the paper listing the accusations against Cranmer from his sleeve and showed it to him.[51] The king liked Cranmer, perhaps was even fond of him, for his easy-going honesty, otherworldliness, compassion and total lack of personal ambition. With a neat sleight of hand, Henry appointed him to head the commission of inquiry into the accusations against himself. After lengthy deliberations, a general pardon was issued to all concerned.

The Bishop of Winchester also moved against a number of Cromwell's former protégés who remained in court and shared his reformist views on religion. At Easter 1543, Gardiner seized his opportunity to 'bend his bow against the head deer', as he described it, and arrested the diplomat Sir Philip Hoby, shortly to join Katherine Parr's household as receiver of foreign receipts, for sheltering a Sacramentarian. Hoby's companions Sir Thomas Carwarden, Edmund Harman, Thomas Sternhold (a Groom of the Robes) and Thomas Weldon were also caught up in Gardiner's sweep for heretics but all were later pardoned, presumably because of their closeness to the royal family.[52]

Gardiner himself had a narrow escape in January 1544 when his cousin and secretary Germain was executed for upholding the papal supremacy. Suffolk believed that the miscreant had been protected from justice by his powerful patron and urged Henry to bring Gardiner to trial as a traitor. But the bishop's allies on the Privy Council warned him and he hastened to the king's side to head off any attempt to arrest him. Gardiner humbled himself, was forgiven and kept both his head and his position at court.

Cranmer was the target of the conservative conspirators once more, probably in November 1545 after the archbishop had been permitted to publish an English primer earlier in the summer. Henry was again told of his archbishop's heresy and was urged to send him to the Tower. The king agreed to Cranmer's arrest, which was planned for the next day during a Privy Council meeting at Westminster. But that night, at eleven o'clock, Henry sent the ubiquitous Sir Anthony Denny to Lambeth to summon Cranmer to his presence. The archbishop was roused from his bed, immediately crossed the River Thames and met the king in a darkened gallery of the Palace of Westminster. He was quickly warned of the plot against him. Henry told him:

I have granted their requests but whether I have done well or not, what say you my lord?

Cranmer thanked his royal master for the information but said he was happy to be committed to prison and to be tried for his beliefs, because he knew Henry would not allow him to have an unfair hearing. Always realistic, the king tried to make him understand what he was now confronting:

Oh Lord God! What fond simplicity you have!

If you permit yourself to be imprisoned, your every enemy may take advantage of you. Do you not think that once they have you in prison, three or four false knaves will be procured to witness against you and to condemn you? Whilst at liberty, [no one] dares to open their lips or appear before your face.

No, not so, my lord, I have better regard towards you than to permit your enemies to so overthrow you.

At least Henry fully understood how his leading administrators could be entrapped. He gave the archbishop his ring, which 'they well know I use for no other purpose but to call matters from the Council into my own hands to be ordered and determined'. Show them the ring, said the king, when they make their accusations and order your arrest, and all will be well.

The next morning at eight o'clock, the Privy Council sent for Cranmer but kept him waiting outside the door of their chamber. He stood 'among serving men and lackeys above three-quarters of an hour, many councillors and other men now and then going in and out'. Presently, the king's favourite doctor, William Butts, another well-known evangelical, arrived and chatted to Cranmer. Then the physician went inside and told Henry:

Yes, I have seen a strange sight ... my lord of Canterbury has become a lackey or a serving man, for he has been standing among them for almost an hour ... so that I was ashamed to keep him company there any longer.

Cranmer was immediately called inside and told that a 'great complaint' had been made both to the Council and the king. Cranmer and others, 'by his permission, had infected the whole realm with heresy and therefore it was the king's pleasure that they should commit him to the Tower ... [to] be examined for his trial'. Cranmer, pale-faced but calm, replied:

I am sorry, my lords, that you drive me to this exigency – to appeal from you to the king's majesty, who, by this token has taken this matter into his own hands and discharges you thereof.

And with that, he held up Henry's ring. There was an astonished silence. John, Lord Russell, was the first to speak. 'Did I not tell you, my lords, that the king would never permit my lord of Canterbury to have such a blemish as to be imprisoned, unless it were for treason?' Henry taunted them:

> Ah! My lords, I had thought that I had a discreet and wise council but now I perceive that I am deceived. How have you handled my lord of Canterbury here?
>
> What makes you [treat him like] a slave, shutting him out of the council chamber amongst serving men? Would you be so handled yourselves?

Then he became deadly serious:

> I would you should well understand that I believe Canterbury as faithful a man towards me as ever was prelate in this realm and one to whom I owe many ways beholden, by the faith I owe to God (and he laid his hand upon his breast) and therefore, who so loves me will regard him [so] thereafter.

Norfolk, who had undoubtedly played a leading role in the conspiracy against Cranmer, hurriedly told the king, rather disingenuously,

> We meant no manner of hurt to my lord of Canterbury in that we requested to have him in durance [prison]. We only did [so] because he might, after his trial, be set at liberty to his own glory.

Just who was he fooling? Certainly not Henry:

> Well, I pray you not to use my friends so. There remains malice among you, one to another. Let it be avoided out of hand, I would advise you.[33]

So the councillors – some of them who had, mere minutes before, been planning to burn Cranmer alive – hastened to shake his hand warmly as a token of their friendship and goodwill, under the stern eye of the king.

Henry's motivation in this tense little human drama remains unclear, if not downright Machiavellian. He had patently agreed to his archbishop's arrest, if not actively encouraging his enemies amongst the conservative faction. But Henry then proceeded to tip Cranmer off about his impending doom in a melodramatic late-night meeting. From that moment, in the empty corridor at Westminster, the archbishop was never in danger. Yet the king happily let the plot run its course before firmly and publicly stamping upon it. Humiliation plays an important part in the story – Henry teases his advisers about it: the humiliation of Cranmer, kept waiting amongst the common lackeys; the humiliation of his Privy Council accusers by the sudden production of the life-saving king's ring mere moments before the planned arrest; the humiliation caused by Henry's rebuke. That flourish by Cranmer, in holding up the royal ring, immediately showed Gardiner, Norfolk and the rest of his enemies that the game was up and that they had been outmanoeuvred. And that must have been Henry's intention all along. His aim, this time, was to mortify the conservative faction as part of his delicate balancing act in the difficult area of developing religious policy. The constant conspiracies and divisions amongst his councillors must also have exasperated him, as did similar controversy amongst his subjects.

Much of what we have as evidence of what actually happened during those turbulent times comes from obviously militant Protestant sources or apologists. After nearly 500 years, it is difficult to separate true fact from skewed propaganda, a weapon as freely and effectively used by both sides during the Reformation as it is in politics today. But there is no disputing the bloodshed, cruelty and horror as so many died on both sides, as martyrs, for their faith and beliefs. Richard Hilles wrote of those years:

> It is now no novelty among us to see men slain, hung, drawn, quartered, beheaded. Some for trifling expressions, which were explained or interpreted as having been spoken against the king; others for the Pope's supremacy; some for one thing, some for another.[54]

It is all too easy in the twenty-first century to shrink back in revulsion at the endless slaughter caused by religious differences in the sixteenth. It was, to our modern eyes, a cruel, hard time and it is difficult for us to distinguish what happened in Henry's reign from the conditions we tragically witnessed in twentieth-century totalitarian states. But we should judge the remedies aimed at curing dissent and punishing crime by the standards of mid-sixteenth-century England and by what was occurring concurrently in Europe. No doubt the population supped deeply from the spoon of horror when they saw those suffering harsh penalties for transgression, but some may have judged the crimes just as terrible. And horror there was. One example may serve to illustrate the point. In 1531, Parliament passed an Act against poisoners[55] that decreed that those found guilty should be sentenced to the hideous death of being boiled alive. It was a swift riposte to a crime that was, according to the Act, 'most rare, and seldom committed or practised' in England, a knee-jerk official reaction to assuage what they perceived to be mounting public concern. The law was passed following the case of Richard Roos who, for unknown motivations aside from his 'wicked and damnable disposition', poisoned porridge that was being heated in the kitchen of John Fisher, Bishop of Rochester. Not only were 'seventeen persons of his family which did eat of that porridge' poisoned, one later dying, 'but also certain poor people which resorted to the said bishop's palace and were there charitably fed with the remains of the porridge' were also afflicted. One pauper woman also died. Roos was duly boiled to death at Smithfield.[56] There was another case in March 1542, when Margaret Davy, 'a maid', was boiled alive after she poisoned people in the three London households she had lived in, murdering three individuals.[57] Life was cheap for the great and mighty of the land as well as for the lowborn and poor. Judicial execution, for transgression against the king's will or against the law of the land, had to be a spectacle to prove a deterrent. Almost always, these were synonymous. These were hard, merciless days in Henry Tudor's England.

CHAPTER FOUR

The Final Quest for Military Glory

'Rejoice Boulogne in the rule of the eighth Henry! Thy towers are adorned with crimson roses, now are the ill-scented lilies uprooted and prostrate, the cock is expelled and the lion reigns in the invincible citadel.'

TRANSLATION OF A LATIN INSCRIPTION ON THE BLADE
OF A SWORD MADE FOR HENRY VIII.[1]

After the Franco-Spanish truce of 1538 with its consequent threat of invasion, Henry's attention turned to his northern border with the troublesome Scots in the early 1540s. The English border forces had launched frequent hit-and-run raids on Scottish villages across the frontier, burning and destroying homes and driving back captured livestock into England. After negotiations to secure the marriage between Prince Edward and the infant Mary, Queen of Scots, broke down and a dispute flared up over the English capture of some Scottish ships on the high seas, the king's impatience boiled over. He ordered Suffolk to attack Edinburgh when the winter rains ended in March 1544, with his army of 8,000 men, based in Darlington. These plans were dropped when a much larger force under Hertford, drawn from Ipswich, King's Lynn, London and Hull, was embarked in 114 ships at Tynemouth at the end of April for a punitive assault on the Scottish capital. The Privy Council coldbloodedly told Hertford that Henry's pleasure 'was that you shall put to fire and the sword' all the communities along the shores of the Forth Estuary and burn Edinburgh 'without taking either the castle or town to mercy, though they would yield, for you know the falsehood of them all'. On 4 May, the English force successfully landed near the port of Leith, entering nearby Edinburgh three days later after blasting open its gates, and burnt the city – although the virtually impregnable castle, high up above on its sheer cliffs of volcanic rock, withstood Hertford's assaults.

With the Scots now thoroughly cowed by this scorched-earth policy, the king could turn his martial attentions to his old enemy, France. In an unlikely diplomatic alliance between the Imperial Emperor Charles V and the heretic Henry, both sides pledged themselves to invade the realm of that 'Most Christian' king, Francis I. Imperial forces had been fighting the French in the Low Countries to further Spanish claims to Burgundy and in an effort to end France's relations with the Turks, 'the inveterate enemy of the Christian name and faith'. The Spanish were aided by 5,600 English troops under Sir John Wallop in the Siege of Landrecies, and by Henry's subsidies for mercenaries. England and Spain were now committed to fielding armies, numbering 42,000 each, by 20 June 1544 in a twin-pronged offensive aimed at the French capital – the so-called 'Enterprise of Paris' – from the springboards of English-held Calais and the emperor's lands to the north. War preparations began.

But Henry's health had deteriorated, delaying his departure to Europe, and his army set out before him under the command of the experienced generals Suffolk and Norfolk. Through his sheer determination (if not bloody-mindedness) and the anxious ministrations of his physicians, Henry recovered and happily and enthusiastically prepared for war – his last great adventure as a military leader. Finally, on the evening of 14 July, he landed at Calais to take the field of battle at the head of his troops, proudly riding 'a great courser' or heavy-armoured horse, with an absurdly large wheel-lock pistol martially, if not nonchalantly, laid across the pommel of his saddle. The banner of St George flew bravely behind him. His great helm and lance were borne by William Somerset, Lord Herbert, son of the Second Earl of Worcester,[2] riding ahead of the king. Henry's final chance for military glory irresistibly beckoned.

It was the first time he had worn armour in the field since his campaign against France long ago in 1513; indeed, he may not have ridden in armour since a bad jousting accident in 1536.[3] In preparation for the wars, an existing armour had to be enlarged to fit what was now his vast bulk, but Henry changed his mind[4] about the alterations after work had begun. He probably ordered two new field armours to be made in his Almain (German) armoury at Greenwich, but settled on an Italian design imported by the Milanese Francis Albert. This beautifully etched, blackened and gilt three-quarter armour[5] was almost certainly the one Henry wore on his journey to Boulogne.[6]

It is difficult not to compare and contrast Henry's gamecock self-certainty with his bloated immobility: the Shakespearian caricature of Sir John Falstaff somehow lurks in the back of one's mind, but the king clearly lacked his constant joviality. The violent thunderstorm and torrential rain that greeted him and his column of English troops when they arrived at Marquise, twenty miles from Calais, on 25 July may have considerably dampened Henry's ardour for campaigning.

Before embarking for France, he had needed to ensure that England was secure and stable, particularly on the borders with Scotland, traditionally an ally of the French kings and potentially the source of a crippling diversionary attack that would disrupt the campaign across the English Channel. Like all responsible soldiers about to go into action, he prudently made a new will and, cannily, appointed Queen Katherine as regent to rule in his stead, with the Earl of Hertford as the military lieutenant or commander of all homeland forces. At the same time, as a mark of his especial favour, he settled the rich manors of Mortlake, in Surrey, and Chelsea and Hanworth, both in Middlesex, upon her.

The commission of regency signed on 7 July 1544 instructed that Prince Edward should be moved to Hampton Court for security and laid down that Katherine should use 'the advice and counsel of the Archbishop of Canterbury, Lord Chancellor Wriothesley, the Earl of Hertford, the Bishop of Westminster and Sir William Petre, secretary of state, in her judgements',[7] a carefully balanced mix of conservative and radical members of the Council. A draft commission in the hand of Sir William Paget, newly appointed principal secretary to the king, dated 11 July, made arrangements for the financial running of the realm:

> Commission to Queen Katherine and [blank] at the least[8] of the councillors named in the commission of regency (which the king taking his voyage at the present time over the seas to invade the realm of France has made her) to address warrants to the king's treasurers, receivers etc for the payment of money.[9]

Hard intelligence about what was going on within England was vital for its good governance, and Henry's efficient civil servants instructed commissioners in every county to report regularly: 'Once a month they shall certify to the Queen and council ... upon the state of the county and their proceedings and all noteworthy occurrences.'[10] One such report came from York, informing the queen that during the month-long assizes of oyer, terminer and gaol delivery[11] at the castle there, seventeen persons had been convicted of murders and felonies, of which sixteen had been executed and one committed to the bishop's prison. There was no mention of any acquittals.

Katherine revelled in her new-found power and demonstrated an extraordinary level of administrative competence as well as knowledge and expertise about military matters, particularly over issues in the dangerous Scottish border region.

Soon after Katherine assumed the regency, Francis Talbot – Earl of Shrewsbury and the king's lieutenant in the North – and others wrote to her about the problem of Scottish prisoners held by the English[12] who were not to be allowed to return home. Those able to pay for their upkeep were to be imprisoned 'this side of the Tyne' and the others consigned to gaols 'as Hertford knows'. However,

> It appears that with the Scottish prisoners being at least 100 and the prisoners already there, the gaols will be so pestered that they must die of hunger unless relieved at the king's charge.

They begged her to decide with the Council whether to send the prisoners back to Scotland or to feed them at a cost to the exchequer,

> for the gaols are so full that many die daily for lack of food and that number being so much increased, the penury and famine must needs be the greater.

Furthermore, the towns of Durham, Newcastle, Alnwick, Morpeth and Darneton were

> infected with a very contagious disease of which two or three people die daily so that the writers may not lie here without danger.

Could they withdraw twenty or thirty miles south to Barnard's Castle, for safety? The earl ended that they 'did not think it convenient to remove without knowing her pleasure'.

Two days later, by command of the queen at Westminster, they were firmly instructed how to resolve the problem. Those prisoners 'of the poorer sort' who are 'stout, busy or otherwise like to do any hurt being at liberty' were to be sent to several prisons, and the others 'if extreme necessity shall so require' should be fed at the king's charge. The remainder should be released upon a bond for good behaviour. The letter was signed 'Kateryn the Queen Regent'.[13]

On 25 July, Katherine wrote from Hampton Court to Henry, who was directing the campaign against Boulogne, informing him that £40,000 was being sent to pay for the fighting and that the Council would be 'diligent to advance to him, against the beginning of next month, as much money as possible'. Four thousand men were also being made ready to reinforce the English army 'at one hour's warning', with arrangements in progress to transport them across the English Channel. She ends on a homely note: 'The prince and the rest of the children are well.'[14]

Today, one can still sense the excitement Katherine felt about being at the heart of events in the surviving state papers and correspondence. On 31 July, she wrote again to the king to relate a report she had received that afternoon that the fishermen of Rye in Sussex had captured a

Scottish ship 'wherein were certain Frenchmen and Scots sent with letters and credentials to the French king and others'. The plain-speaking queen thought the lucky seizure was 'ordained of God to shame the crafty dealing and juggling of that [Scots] nation'.[15] She enclosed the most important of the letters, which clearly indicates that she had read all the papers and had decided their significance.

On 6 August, she informed Henry of rumours that Frenchmen had landed in England, adding – with a flash of humour – that 'fearing that some seditious person had spread the rumour (for a landing of French about Gloucester was unlikely)', she had instructed the justices of the peace in the region to quieten the excitement in the country and to make diligent inquiries. She had received replies that showed 'all was well' and that the rumour was founded merely on the departure from Bristol of English warships.[16]

There were more serious issues to tackle, such as the problem of deserters from the English army. On 9 September, she issued a proclamation from Westminster 'for the examination of persons returned from the king's army in France and punishing of such as have insufficient passports to do so'.[17] There was another proclamation relating to the plague then raging in 'sundry parts of London and Westminster'. This banned from the court those infected or living in infected homes and prohibited members of the household from visiting such places 'to avoid danger to the prince, Queen Katherine and the other children'.[18]

Katherine was also adept at praising those who served the king well. In early September, she wrote to the Lords Evers and Wharton, Wardens of the Scottish Eastern and Western Marches, for whose

> diligent service ... in the defence of the realm and the chastising of the king's enemies, we give you hearty thanks and require you to give the like in our name to the captains and gentlemen that have served you.[19]

The queen also required them to continue their diligence 'especially now in the time of harvest, so as their [the Scots] corn may be wasted as much as may be'.

This new war leader did not forget Henry's requirement for a humble, loving wife at home. From Greenwich, soon after his departure for France, she wrote to tell him that although he had not been long away, she could not be satisfied until she had heard from him:

> The want of your presence, so much beloved and desired by me, makes me that I cannot quietly enjoy anything until I hear from your Majesty.

She knew Henry's absence was necessary, she continued,

> yet love and affection compels me to desire your presence ... Love makes me in all things to set apart my own commodity and pleasure and to embrace most joyfully his will and pleasure whom I love.
>
> God, the knower of secrets, can judge these words not only to be written by ink, but most truly impressed in the heart ... I make account with your Majesty as I do with God for His benefits and gifts heaped upon me daily ...
>
> And even such confidence I have in your Majesty's gentleness, knowing myself never to have done my duty as were requisite and meet to such a noble Prince, at whose hands I have received so much love and goodness that with words I cannot express it.
>
> Lest I should be too tedious unto your Majesty, I finish this, my scribbled letter, committing you into the governance of the Lord, with long life and prosperous felicity here, and after this life to enjoy the kingdom of His elect.

She dutifully signed the letter:

> By your Majesty's humble, obedient loving wife and servant. Kateryn the Queen. K.P.[20]

Meanwhile in France, after a brief armed reconnaissance mission by Suffolk, the English forces, short of soldiers, had partially invested Boulogne, twenty miles from Calais, whilst others, under Norfolk, besieged Montreuil. Bad weather in the Channel and in Flanders delayed deliveries of gunpowder, shot and other supplies – Norfolk complained that his men had to drink water rather than beer – and Henry had to wait impatiently until early August before the full force of the English artillery could be brought to bear on the French defences at Boulogne. The chronicler Raphael Holinshed records the huge array of military earthworks thrown up by the besiegers:

> Beside the trenches which were cast and brought around the town, there was a mount [artificial hill or earthwork] raised upon the east side and divers pieces of artillery planted aloft on the same. The which, together with the mortar pieces, sore annoyed them within [the town] and battered down the steeple of Our Lady's church.[21]

For six weeks the deafening cannon roared, lobbing 100,000 gun stones into the town, and assaults were mounted on Boulogne's outworks. The military operations were observed and directed by Henry, who was safely out of the range of French retaliatory fire on the north-east side of the town, near the sea and with easy access to fresh water. There was no shortage of that; no doubt he was also protected from the constant rains and high winds that afflicted operations that summer. In a postscript to a letter written to Queen Katherine on 8 September, Henry excitedly reported:

> At the closing of these letters, the castle ... with the dike [defensive ditch] is at our commandment and not like to be recovered by the Frenchmen. Castle and town are like to follow the same trade for this day we begin three batteries and have three mines[22] going; besides one which has shaken and torn one of the greatest bulwarks. I am too busy to write more but send blessings to all my children and recommendations to my cousin Margaret[23] and the rest of the ladies and gentlemen and to my Council.[24]

Three days later, the castle exploded spectacularly and those inside Boulogne knew the game was up. They sought the English terms for capitulation and negotiations for an honourable surrender began.

The chronicler Hall describes the king's campaign against the town:

He so assaulted and so besieged with such abundance of great ordnance that never was there a more valiant assault made. Beside the undermining of the castle, tower and walls, the town was so beaten with the ordnance that there was not left one house whole therein ...[25]

The English noted with delight that the beleaguered town was 'in great necessity, for many eat horseflesh and some of the gentlemen Italians are glad to eat of a cat well larded and call it dainty meat'.[26] Boulogne surrendered and Henry, who had been invigorated both in spirits and health during the siege, entered its gates in triumph on 18 September:

having the sword born [sic] before him by the lord marquis of Dorset, like a noble and valiant conqueror, he rode into Boulogne and the trumpeters standing on the walls of the town sounded their trumpets at the time of his entering to the great comfort of all the king's true subjects.[27]

It was the crowning moment of a hitherto lacklustre military campaign.[28]

Ironically, that was the same day that Charles V, Henry's ally, deserted him. The imperial emperor had attacked through Champagne and had advanced to within fifty miles of Paris before a logistical shortage of supplies forced his retreat. After secret negotiations with the French, a separate peace treaty was concluded at Crépy and announced on 18 September, surrendering Savoy and Milan to the Spanish, who in turn dropped their territorial claims on Burgundy. The Duke of Orléans was to marry Charles' daughter. The Dauphin, heir to the French throne, now freed of an imperial threat to Paris, was able to concentrate a 36,000-strong army against the English and later in September he marched on Montreuil to relieve the garrison there, forlornly besieged by Norfolk and his starving troops. Henry, still supervising the extensive refortification of Boulogne, ordered Norfolk to withdraw and fall back to the main English force on the coast. Henry covertly left France on 30 September, and despite the desertion of his ally and the almost total failure of the allied war aims he returned in triumph to England. But in truth, he knew he was likely to face French retribution wreaked on his own realm.

By November, looking about him, Bishop Gardiner was downcast by the progress of the war and by Henry's government's problems at home and abroad. On the 13th, he wrote to Secretary Paget from Bruges:

> I am very much troubled with the state of our affairs ... I cannot forebear to hold my pen still ... as my mind is [so] encumbered with the matters to be busy in writing and devising.
>
> I consider we be in war with France and Scotland. We have an enemy [in] the Bishop of Rome.
>
> We have no friendship assured here.
>
> We have received such displeasure of the Landgrave, chief captain of the Protestants, that he has cause to think we are angry with him.
>
> Our war is noisome to the wealth of our own realm and it is so noisome to all merchants that must traffic by us and pass the narrow seas, as they cry out here wonderfully.
>
> Herewith we see at home a great appearance of lack of such things as the continuance of the war requires.
>
> When we put away this war, we show ourselves content to make a peace, we may have it, but so miserable, to speak the truth, as the French men offer, that thereby the king's majesty's noble courage should be so touched as we ought to fear the danger of his person after so long [a] travail in honour, in rule and government of the world, to sit still with such a peace as to render Boulogne and let the Scots alone only for a little money, not paid but promised.[29]

Gardiner's gloom was fully justified. In early February 1545, Henry launched a pre-emptive strike on Scotland to keep the Scots firmly in their box. Sir William Evers, Warden of the Eastern Marches, led a raid into the border country, successfully burning the town of Melrose. His mission accomplished, he was ambushed on the way back at Ancrum Moor, near Jedburgh, and heavily defeated (Evers was killed in the fighting), providing the Scots with ample revenge for Solway Moss.

Elsewhere, domestic and international problems burdened the king and his advisers. The year 1545 saw a famine in England – a 'great dearth of corn and victuals'[30] – which forced the purchase of cereals from Denmark and 'Bremberland', the country around Bremen in Germany. Four thousand quarters of corn[31] were delivered to London in one month alone, paid for by a tax levied on the companies of the city. In the face of a new, more serious French threat, the military mobilisation necessary to maintain three armies in the field (in Scotland, at Boulogne and for defence of the south coast) as well as manning the navy[32] meant that there were few men to maintain law and order in London. At midsummer, only constables kept watch in the wards of the city. However, bills had been pasted on to houses warning of 'certain priests and strangers' – a French fifth column – that would set fire to London. The king's Council ordered the mayor to impose a curfew on strangers and set a special watch of citizens from nine at night until four the next morning. The blowing up of a ship, the *Hedgehog*, on the Thames at Westminster on 19 July must have raised levels of anxiety about enemy agents or saboteurs within the realm.[33] It was a time of great anxiety, for the French were determined to take the war to England.

Francis I had earlier threatened invasion to force the surrender of English-held Boulogne. On 3 January 1545, Francis had written to Denmark about his powerful fleet now being formed

> to invade England when the season arrives, as the best way to constrain the enemy to make restitution and satisfaction and perhaps with God's grace, deliver the people of England from his tyranny.

With the assistance of the Danes and the Scots, Francis predicted that Henry

> who is hated by his nobility and subjects for well known reasons and exhausted by two years of great expense, will like most of his predecessors, find himself deserted by his own subjects.

If the king of Denmark joined the enterprise,

it would cost him little, seeing that his ships are always ready and many of his subjects would [take part] ... for their own profit, if he gave them permission.[34]

But much of this was empty posturing: France probably did not have the resources to mount a full-scale invasion nor the ability to resupply its forces' bridgehead. Probably the French king envisaged a series of stinging hit-and-run attacks on the English coast to goad Henry into returning Boulogne.

As far as Henry was concerned, however, a landing was expected at any time that summer. In July, his spies reported a French army 40,000-strong to be ready to board their ships. A sophisticated system of beacons was hastily set up on the downs of southern England to provide warning of any French incursion. Three defending armies, totalling more than 90,000 men under arms, were based in Kent and Sussex under the command of the experienced Duke of Suffolk, in East Anglia under Norfolk and in the West Country under John, Lord Russell, the Lord Privy Seal.[35] At Darlington, the Earl of Hertford had mobilised forces in preparation for countering any French attempt to invade the North of England in support of their Scottish allies.[36] More soldiers had also been sent to Boulogne: 1,000 from London and another 4,000 from the Home Counties. The watchful defenders of England's shores would not have long to wait for action.

In May 1545, the ailing Spanish ambassador Eustace Chapuys took his leave of London and the royal court. His last encounter with Queen Katherine further reveals her to have been an adept diplomat, as well as kind and discreet. The ambassador arrived early for his farewell audience at the Palace of Westminster:

> When I entered the back door of the king's apartments, having traversed the garden facing the queen's lodgings and arrived nearly at the other end, close to the principal entrance of the king's apartments, my people informed me that the queen and the princess [Mary] were following me quickly.
>
> I hardly had time to rise from the chair in which I was being

carried, before she [the queen] approached quite near and seemed from the small suite she had with her and the haste with which she came, as if her purpose in coming was specially to speak to me.

Katherine, accompanied by four or five women of her chamber, had been told the previous evening by the king of Chapuys' retirement.

Whilst on the one hand she was very sorry for my departure as she had been told that I had always acted well in my office and the king had confidence in me; on the other hand she doubted not that my health would be better on the other side of the water.

The queen hoped that the friendship between England and Spain would be maintained. Chapuys wrote afterwards to Charles V:

She ... begged me affectionately, after I presented to your majesty her humble service, to express explicitly all I had learned here of the good wishes of the king towards you ... She asked me very minutely, and most graciously, after your majesty's health and expressed great joy to learn of your ... amelioration, adding many courteous and kind expressions.

The envoy asked to be allowed to salute Princess Mary, 'which was at once accorded', Katherine being anxious that Chapuys should not stand too long. Sensitively, the queen withdrew seven or eight paces so that she could not overhear his conversation with Mary.[37]

The ambassador then met with Lord Chancellor Wriothesley and Charles Brandon, Duke of Suffolk, and after dinner they asked if the emperor could supply 'a few men, wagons and victuals' to Henry's army to 'keep the French quiet' outside the English enclaves of Calais and Boulogne. They also asked his opinion on how to bring about a peace or truce and begged him, perhaps significantly, to believe 'that what they had said was entirely on their own account and without the king's knowledge'.[38] Chapuys was then called into Henry's presence, who 'received [him] most graciously and ... said some kind things about my convalescence and my departure from England'. Then the king got quickly down to business, displaying a surprising grasp of detail about the issues raised: the question of an alleged French spy; complaints about the presence of the Scottish ambassador at Charles V's court; and the welcome given to four French warships in Dunkirk harbour. Henry would prefer a settled peace to a truce with the French, he told the ambassador, but the enemy were short of men, money and food, so they could hardly resist him, 'as had been proved by the successful exploits of the English on land and sea against them'. Henry bragged that during the past ten days

> the English privateers, not in his service, had captured twenty-three French vessels and shortly before as many more had been sunk, burnt or captured. He calculated that his people had taken no less than 300 French ships since the beginning of the war.[39]

So the gossipy Chapuys departed, taking with him a 'thorough-bred dog' given to him by Sir William Paget, principal secretary to the king.

In June, Francis I inspected his assembled fleet of 324 warships under Admiral Claud d'Annebaut, near Rouen, before it set sail for England in the middle of the following month. On 18 July, a detachment of twenty-two galleys raided and burnt the fishing village of Brighton in Sussex. Forewarned by fishermen of the French approach, Henry began to concentrate his forces near the Hampshire coast. On the evening of 19 July, he dined aboard the flagship *Great Harry* at the important naval base at Portsmouth with Charles V's new ambassador, Francis van der Delft, and angrily rejected his suggestion to surrender Boulogne. The next morning, a Sunday, the enemy fleet, deployed in a battle array of three squadrons, arrived off Portsmouth and anchored threateningly off St Helen's Point on the Isle of Wight. The outnumbered English ships [40] later sailed out in two lines to fight them, watched anxiously by Henry from the ramparts of nearby Southsea Castle with his land commander, Suffolk, alongside him. As both sides opened fire for the first time, one of the two leading English vessels, the seventy-one-gun *Mary Rose*,[41] 700 tons, her decks crowded with soldiers in armour, was caught by a freak gust of wind. Watched by the horrified onlookers on land, she heeled to starboard and the sea rushed in through her open lower gun ports. Within minutes she had disappeared beneath the waves. Only thirty of her 415-strong crew survived; the rest drowned horribly, ensnared beneath the netting spread across her upper deck to prevent attack by enemy boarders. The piteous cries of the trapped and dying men could be clearly heard on land, barely a mile away. Henry cried out loud: 'Oh, my gentlemen! Oh, my gallant men!' With surprising compassion, he limped over to where Lady Carew, wife of Sir George, the Vice-Admiral of the English fleet, was standing, tears streaming down her face. The king sought inadequately to comfort her: she had just watched her husband go down with the *Mary Rose* beneath the blue waters of the Solent.

The French, triumphantly crowing at this great propaganda *coup*, landed 2,000 troops at Bembridge on the Isle of Wight on the evening of 21 July. Local militia forces skirmished with the invaders in the woods and on the slopes of Bembridge Down before retreating and destroying the bridge over the River Yar. A day or two later, a French party sent to fill their water casks at a spring in Shanklin Chine, on the island's east coast, were attacked and cut to ribbons.[42] The French fleet meanwhile mounted attacks on the English shipping in Portsmouth harbour at

> every tide with their [oared] galleys and shot their ordnance at the king's ships in the haven, but the wind was so calm that the king's ships could not sail, which was a great discomfort to them.[43]

The City of London sent 1,500 hastily recruited men towards Portsmouth as reinforcements, but they turned back for home when they reached Farnham in Hampshire because the French had gone. Having been defeated by the militia on the Isle of Wight with great loss, including the French general, after twenty-four hours Admiral d'Annebaut retreated.[44] Heading for home, he paused further east along England's south coast only to sack the towns of Newhaven, recently granted a charter by Henry VIII, and Seaford before, once again, local forces drove his troops ignominiously back to their ships.[45] The pursuing English vessels were becalmed off Beachy Head, Sussex, and the French escaped safely back to their home ports after only a brief and inconclusive skirmish at sea.

Henry sought the pleasures of hunting to distract him from the highly symbolic loss of one of his major warships and, characteristically, to flee the dangers of the plague now rampant amongst his fleet in Portsmouth harbour. But a second more terrible blow, this time a very personal one, afflicted him on 22 August: the sudden death of his old jousting comrade, the Duke of Suffolk, at Guildford, Surrey, where the court was staying. After the king heard the stunning news, he told his courtiers that Brandon had been the best of friends, generous and loyal as well as truly magnanimous towards his political enemies. Glaring, he pointed out that few of his Council could boast the same about themselves. Henry arranged for a sumptuous state funeral for his friend, who was buried, perhaps significantly, at St George's Chapel, Windsor; the king, although in straitened financial circumstances, picked up the bill for the funeral.[46]

The Earl of Hertford had earlier been appointed commander of the English forces in Boulogne and had defeated a determined French attempt to retake the town in January 1545. Almost seven months later, Francis I had sent another large army against the town, resulting in daily skirmishes, and had built siege works near by, including the construction of a large tower at Basse Boulogne from the top of which French guns fired into the English fortifications. Hertford was then recalled to command the English forces on the Scottish borders and was replaced by the old soldier Norfolk. The French war was digging deep into the English coffers of both money and men, and Henry, always needful of cash anyway, was forced to raise funds from the Antwerp moneylenders, such as the Fuggers banking family, and had to resort to the expensive and troublesome hiring of foreign mercenaries.[47] Spanish, Albanians, Italians, Clevois, Swiss and Germans had all been recruited to reinforce English forces in the Scottish borders and to augment the army in France. The Spanish in Newcastle complained about the local food and resorted to cooking their own meals in the kitchens of their billets, causing friction with their landladies.[48]

One episode assumed what would otherwise have been farcical overtones, if it had not also had serious diplomatic and fiscal implications for the king, who was perhaps unused to employing hard-nosed Continental mercenaries. Henry had hired the German soldier Captain Frederick von Reiffenberg after the mercenary, writing from Cologne, had offered his services, 'moved by [the king's] pre-eminence in kingly virtues'.[49] In June 1545, Philip, Landgrave of Hesse, had provided von Reiffenberg with a letter of commendation and urged Henry to take up his services as he 'may have cause to be grateful'. The German and his 8,000 war-hardened foot soldiers and 1,500 cavalry were hired for three months at the high cost of 52,000 florins or £15,550 a month (more than £5 million in today's monetary value). Unfortunately, Charles V refused the freelances (or mercenaries in the modern expression) permission to enter Brabant *en route* to Boulogne and they caused mayhem. The emperor wrote complainingly that the mercenaries had caused 'inestimitable damage' in the Treves area and had then passed by Aix through his territories beyond the River Meuse and 'forced their way into the Bishop of Liege's town of Wesel'. The German commanders then began to argue about the precise terms and conditions of their contract with Henry, taking hostage their English liaison officers (Thomas Chamberlain, governor of the English court of merchants at Antwerp, and Sir Ralph Fane, lieutenant of Henry's pensioners or bodyguard) until the disputed fees were paid. The English were furious and Henry's principal secretary Sir William Paget wrote to von Reiffenberg on 2 November from Windsor complaining of the 'disloyal and evil service' done to the English king 'and his strange usage of his commissioners'.

> I am grieved both for the dishonour to yourself and the diminution of the credit of him who recommended you to his majesty. The king has commanded me in his name to charge you to observe your covenants with him and set his commissioners free to execute their [missions].[50]

Paget added a dire threat: 'Or else, be assured that wherever you may be in all Christendom, it will cost you your life, even if his majesty pays 50,000 crowns for it.'[51] His words remind us of the threats uttered by an American president nearly five centuries later: 'You may run, but you cannot hide.'

But the English threats were easily shrugged off and the money was not returned, although the luckless English hostages were at least freed.[52] Henry had learnt an expensive lesson regarding the unreliability of European mercenaries – beware Germans bearing arms – although his son later hired substantial numbers of them to help put down the insurrections in England in 1549. Stephen Vaughan, the king's financial agent in Antwerp, wrote harshly of the German nation:

> Happy is he that has no need of Almaines [Germans] for of all the nations under the heavens, they be the worst, most rudest and unreasonable to deal with.[53]

Philip, Landgrave of Hesse, was rather embarrassed by the behaviour of the mercenary he had recommended. On 16 December, he wrote to Henry of his indignation that von Reiffenberg and 'his fellow soldiers did not deal uprightly'[54] with the English king. But, after all, he pleaded, he had nothing to do with their decisions and this he had emphasized to Henry's ambassadors. It was a somewhat lacklustre apology.

On 4 August, the City of London sent another 1,000 soldiers – gunners, bowmen and pikemen dressed in new white coats – off in barges from Tower Wharf to Dover for embarkation on to ships waiting to take them across the Channel.[55] The king's Council, stretched militarily on two fronts, ordered Cranmer 'as victories come only at the appointment of God within the remembrance of man' to organise prayers in English and religious processions throughout the kingdom on 10 August[56] to seek a victory against the French.

It was also a year for bad weather: on June 25, there were tempests in Derbyshire, Lancashire and Cheshire, uprooting trees, damaging houses and the spires and towers of churches and producing hailstones 'as big as a man's fist [that] had prints [impressions] on them like faces and some like gun holes'.[57] France was not spared, either. In Paris, too, in July lightning burnt down four of the great churches and the tower wherein was stored much of the army's artillery.[58] At Havre-de-Grace in Normandy, a major French warship, the oddly named carrack *Rumpy le Conte*, was also burnt and lost with all hands, together with £1 million in gold – payment for the sailors of Francis I's battle fleet. At least destiny was even-handed in dealing out catastrophe to the two combatant nations.

Cornelius Sceppurus, a member of the imperial emperor's Council, told Dr Louis Schore, President of the Council of Flanders, that he saw no fighting ships on the Thames in London during this period, 'but many ships and small craft carrying soldiers to Boulogne. The people desire peace but must dance to their leader's tune.'[59]

Well they might. The war was crippling England's fragile economy and its people were burdened by taxation to pay for it. The campaign in France in 1544 had cost Henry's exchequer a total of more than £700,000, well over £200 million at today's prices, compared with the £250,000[60] budgeted for the war by his government. The armies and fleet consumed another £560,000, or £196 million, the following year up to 8 September. A 'benevolence' – a less than voluntary gift to the exchequer – was planned in early 1545, with the king writing to the commissioners for collection:

> Our people ... Be of so loving and kind disposition towards us that they will gladly contribute by way of benevolence that, for the necessity of the affair, shall be requisite as if the same was granted by Parliament.[61]

Richard Read, a London alderman, unpatriotically refused to pay up and for his pains was forcibly conscripted into the army and sent to fight on the Scottish borders. The Privy Council, writing to Sir William Evers, Lord Warden of the Eastern Marches, in January 1545, said that the vengeful Henry thought

> that he [Read] should do some service with his body and for that purpose sends him to your school, as you shall perceive by such

letters as he shall deliver unto you, there to serve as a soldier, and yet both he and his men at his own charge.

Read was dispatched 'on pain of death' to take part in

any enterprise against the enemy.

He is to ride and do as the other poor soldiers do in all things that he may know what pains other poor soldiers abide and feel the smart of his folly.

Use him after the sharp military discipline of the northern wars.[62]

Read was captured by the Scots in the disaster at Ancrum Moor. In December 1545, his wife entreated the Privy Council to agree to exchange a Scottish prisoner held in the Tower for her imprisoned husband, offering to pay cash in lieu of the Scot's ransom. The Scottish prisoner was Patrick Hume, servant to Cardinal David Beaton, Archbishop of St Andrew's, who had been seized by English forces earlier that year, in September. He was brought to the Council and after 'a general declaration of his cruelty to Englishmen and namely the murder of Sir Bryan Layton, late captain of Norham, the king's clemency was declared unto him for his return to Scotland, upon procuring Read's release'.[63]

The clergy were also asked to pay the next instalment of their subsidy at 3s in the pound to the crown in June instead of at Christmas. But still Henry's exchequer struggled to pay the mounting bills. In November 1545, Lord Chancellor Wriothesley had further gathered a meagre £20,000 to pay for the wars, but told Paget on 11 November:

I assure you master secretary, I am at my wits' end how we shall possibly shift for [the] three months following and especially for the two next. For I see no great likelihood that any good sum will come in until after Christmas.[64]

Early in 1546, the MP Thomas Hussey wrote to the Earl of Surrey that 'the king's majesty is indebted at this time, four hundred thousand marks, to the levying ... by subsidy and other practices at this

Parliament, there is not to be received above £200,000'. In addition to sales of monastic lands, England's coinage was being debased through the addition, by the Mint, of base metal, and Henry turned his attentions to dissolving the rich ecclesiastical chantries and hospitals as a means of raising extra cash. Henry was also borrowing heavily overseas, but later in 1546, Stephen Vaughan, his long-suffering financial agent in Antwerp, told his master in London that the cautious Fuggers' Bank would part with no more money 'unless your majesty would find the means by act of Parliament that all the subjects of your majesty's ream shall be bound for the repayment thereof again'. The Privy Council said that Henry did not want to enter into such an agreement as required 'by the Fuggers ... for repayment' as it would 'seem to the world to be brought so low as he should need for that sum to give them assurance by act of Parliament'. Wriothesley cast around for other methods of raising cash, such as collecting debts owed to the government, but the money came in slowly.

> Our daily travail is with such as appear here for the king's ... debts, and we send out letters in great number for more debtors ... As for money, all the shift shall be made that is possible, but yet the store is very small. The contribution comes very slowly in.[65]

Plaintively, Wriothesley added: 'The Mint is drawn dry.'

Eventually even Henry had to overcome his enormous ego and cave in to the financial pressures posed by his empty exchequer. Consequently, in April 1546, Paget, John Dudley – Viscount Lisle, Hertford and Dr Nicholas Wotton, Dean of Canterbury and York and Henry's ambassador in Flanders, were commissioned to enter into peace talks with the French, with an agenda tucked into their doublets that included English insistence on holding on to Boulogne, demands for war reparations in cash and for the French to stop mischief-making in Scotland. Henry initially asked for eight million crowns in French payments: 'Eight millions quoth they [the French envoys]. You speak merrily! All Christendom has not so much money. We may as well offer you again

THE FINAL QUEST FOR MILITARY GLORY

one hundred crowns.'[66] Backwards and forwards went the negotiations, with Henry inevitably interfering in the detail of the discussions. At times, the wrangling was almost more than the English delegation could bear. On 27 May, Paget, who had vowed that he and his colleagues would 'show ourselves men of stomach and intend to be revenged on this proud nation', wrote to Sir William Petre from Guines:

> Instead of the grace and peace, which I sent you last, help to send unto us now on this side, fire and sword, for other things cannot bring these false dogs to reason.
>
> God give them pestilence, false traitors!
>
> The king's majesty has been trifled [with] too long already and seeing these false, wicked men work after this fraudulent fashion, God shall revenge us upon their iniquity and falsehood.

So much for the polite niceties of diplomatic language! Fatalistically, he added: 'All this is for the best. God's will is fulfilled in all things.'[67] At last, a peace treaty was signed on 7 June in a tent pitched at Campe[68] between Ardres and Guines. The agreement stipulated that the town of Boulogne would be handed back to France in 1553, but only after payment of two million crowns (£13 million in today's money) by the French[69] in reparations for the war. That thirsty drain on England's economy had finally been plugged.

CHAPTER FIVE

'Anger Short and Sweat Abundant'

'"I dreamed now that the king is dead ..." Two days after, he said in his great chamber at Bockmar: "The king is not dead but he will die one day suddenly, his leg will kill him and we shall have jolly stirring."'

INTERROGATION OF HENRY POLE, LORD MONTAGUE,
7 NOVEMBER 1538.[1]

For much of his life, the king had always enjoyed rude health, except for an attack of smallpox (or possibly measles) when he was twenty-two and the first of a number of recurrent bouts of malaria seven years later.[2] As a slim, handsome youth, his athleticism in the joust, the hunting field and other manly sports such as wrestling was famous throughout the realm and in foreign courts and was admired by his subjects much more widely than any latter-day international soccer superstar's skill and prowess.[3] He was the very personification of a new, confident England, no longer an isolated island off the coast of Europe, as he attempted to dominate the stage of Continental politics.

But in 1527, when Henry was a dashing and robust thirty-six, this love of sport and physical activity caused the first of several injuries that were continually to try the king's patience and unsubtly remind him that his imperial crown did not protect him from very human pain and suffering. In April that year, Henry apparently hurt his foot during an energetic game of tennis,[4] probably at the Palace of Westminster, and the next month he was forced to wear a black velvet slipper to ease the pain still troubling him. The weakness, in a tendon, may have persisted, as he wrenched a foot again two years later.

Worse was to come. During one of the royal progresses in 1527–8, the king was confined to bed at Canterbury with a 'sore leg' believed to be a varicose ulcer on the left thigh, probably caused by the constrictive garters he fashionably wore below the knee,[5] or alternatively by a traumatic injury sustained while jousting.[6] Thomas Vicary,[7] a local surgeon, was called in and managed to heal the ulcer quickly and relatively painlessly – much to the king's relief. Vicary was rewarded with a medical appointment to the household at a salary of 20s a year and was promoted to serjeant surgeon in 1536, a post worth £26 13s 4d annually (or more than £10,000 a year at 2004 prices), which he retained during the reigns of Edward, Mary and Elizabeth. A still-grateful Henry later granted him a twenty-one-year lease on the dissolved Abbey of Bexley in Kent.

Out of this sore leg was born the much-quoted tradition that Henry suffered from syphilis, contracted during the wild salad days of his youth in England, or while he was campaigning in France in 1513, or even that he was infected by his first wife, Catherine of Aragon.[8] Many still believe that he died in 1547 from the terminal effects of this venereal disease. However, the king was not, by contemporary European standards, the great royal libertine of folklore. Aside from mere court dalliances and flirtations, surviving accounts document his extramarital relations with just three women: Elizabeth Blount, mother of his bastard son Henry Fitzroy,[9] later Duke of Richmond; Mary Boleyn; and Margaret Shelton. No doubt he had other flings, particularly in the hale and hearty days before he ascended the throne in 1509, at which point his life fell under the scrutiny of the prying eyes of foreign ambassadors. His varicose ulcer of 1527–8, say proponents of this theory,[10] was in reality a broken-down gumma or swelling – an obvious symptom of tertiary syphilis, although the thigh is an unusual location for this.[11] Moreover, gummata are not normally painful and the king certainly suffered intolerable agony with his legs. As syphilis can also damage foetuses, the frequent miscarriages and stillbirths by both Catherine of Aragon and Anne Boleyn are also offered up as further evidence of Henry's venereal infection. Several portraits and sketches of Henry completed during or immediately after 1536 show a very slight 'lesion' or depression on the right side of the king's nose – again, a supposed symptom of syphilis. Other paintings, however, omit this slight deformity, perhaps for reasons of royal vanity. Finally, Wolsey, in his downfall in 1529, was accused by the trumped-up Act of Attainder of attempting to infect the king with syphilis:

> the same lord cardinal, knowing himself to have the foul and contagious disease of the great pox, broken out upon him in diverse places of his body, came daily to your grace, rowning [whispering] in your ear and blowing upon your most noble grace with his most perilous and infective breath to the marvellous danger of your highness if God, of his infinite goodness, had not better provided for your highness.[12]

The allegations about Wolsey's syphilis, however, were treacherously provided to the Boleyn party at court by the cardinal's own doctor, the enigmatic Venetian Augustine de Augustinis, who became a physician to the king in late 1537 and was also employed on various diplomatic missions by both Henry and his Lord Privy Seal, Thomas Cromwell.[13] The wording of the accusation, asserting that Henry was protected against infection by divine providence, is perhaps indicative of the king's perceived special relationship with God.

And there is no evidence of syphilis in his children, Mary, Elizabeth and Edward – none of them bore its visible stigmata – and Tudor doctors, well versed in the symptoms of what was euphemistically called 'the French disease', would have swiftly recognised a gumma as an indication of syphilis and treated the king accordingly. The rudimentary medical treatment of this venereal disease in the sixteenth century consisted of six weeks of sweating the patient and the administration of successive doses of mercury (although poisonous) which made the patient's gums red and sore and created 'copious flows of saliva'.[14] The ever-present ambassadors, constantly seeking scurrilous gossip to report to their royal masters abroad, would surely have spotted either a pro-longed absence of the king from public life or the visible symptoms of the treatment. Neither was reported.

So, as we have seen, it is more probable that Henry suffered from varicose ulcers, which are sometimes linked to deep-vein thrombosis. More seriously, it is likely that injuries to the royal legs, perhaps sustained while hunting or, more likely, jousting, damaged the tibia and also caused chronic osteitis, a very painful bone infection. If the wound healed over with the bone still infected, then fevers would occur and the legs would become further ulcerated,[15] requiring changes of dressings several times a day as the stench of the ulcers filled his Privy Chamber. This condition closely matches his known symptoms and had grave implications for his future life and health.

No wonder that Henry would today be recognised as a hypochon-driac, always obsessed with his health and anxious to hide his infirmi-ties from his subjects, as revealed in a letter to the Duke of Norfolk written on 12 June 1537 (which provides evidence of both legs being afflicted by ulcers):

> To be frank with you, which you must keep to yourself, a humour has fallen into our legs and our physicians advise us not to go so far in the heat of the year ...[16]

A public image of the strength and omnipotence of a ruler means every-thing for a government, then as now. The king was also fascinated with medicine for its own sake – part and parcel of a Renaissance prince's interests and continued education in the fashionable subjects of theology, astronomy and music. A law passed early on in Henry's reign intended to regulate medical practice discloses that quackery was

> daily within this realm exercised by a great multitude of ignorant persons of whom the great part have no manner of insight into [medicine] nor any kind of learning ... so far that common

artificers such as smiths, weavers and women boldly ... take upon them great cures and things of great difficulty in which they partly use sorcery and witchcraft, partly apply such medicine unto the disease as be very noyous [noxious] ... to the high displeasure of God ... and the grievous hurt, damage and destruction of many of the king's liege people, most especially of them who cannot discern the uncunning from the cunning.[17]

Henry was also curious about new pharmaceutical cures and had clearly acquired some practical knowledge of the medicinal properties of a large number of plants and herbs even before he became the unwilling and testy recipient of some of the less pleasant potions and nostrums. His interest is demonstrated by around 100 recipes for ointments, balms and poultices, apparently developed personally by him,[18] contained in a water-damaged but still-legible book of prescriptions for Henry's own use preserved in the British Library. The constituents of the 'king's own plaster' included

roots, buds, different plants, raisins without stones, linseed, vinegar, rosewater, long garden worms, scrapings of ivory, pearls powdered fine, red lead, red coral, honeysuckle water, suet of hens, fat from the thighbone of calves.

The concoction would be poisonous and is certainly not one to be tried at home. Henry sent his own recipe for curing 'the sweat' to the courtier Sir Bryan Tuke, Treasurer of the Privy Chamber and Henry's secretary, during the great epidemic of 1517–18, which involved drinking a little wine 'with the pills of Rasis' – probably Rhases, an Arabian physician. But following his normal cautious, if not neurotic, practice, Henry himself fled diseased London to the safety of the countryside, moving from palace to palace ahead of the spread of the scourge. Henry also had his own patent recipe for curing bubonic plague. His ingredients were exotic in the extreme:

Take one handful of marigolds, a handful of sorrel and a handful of burnet,[19] a handful of feverfew,[20] half a handful of rue[21] and a quantity of dragons[22] of the top or else the root and wash them clean in running water and put them in a pot with a potel[23] of running water and let them seethe easily. From a potel on to a quart of liquor and then set it back till it be almost cold and strain it with a fine clothe and drink it. If it be bitter, put thereto sugar. And if it be taken before the purpulls [buboes, swelling in the glands of the armpit or groin] do appear, it will heal the sick person with God's grace.[24]

Divine intervention therefore remained essential.

The royal staff of doctors, surgeons and apothecaries was extensive and frequently consulted, but their advice not always obeyed due to Henry's obstinacy and relentless, restless energy. The king was, in all senses, a difficult patient,[25] ignoring pleas to rest and the protests of his doctors. But he was also very generous in his gifts and rewards to his medical team, possibly a sign of his growing concern over his declining health.

Henry began his reign with three doctors on the Privy Purse payroll – Thomas Linacre, who had been tutor to his sickly brother, Prince Arthur; John Chambre; and the Spaniard Fernando de Victoria or Vittoria, who had arrived in England with Catherine of Aragon's entourage in 1501. The king granted letters patent in 1518 to all three to set up

a college in perpetuity of learned and wise men who make any practice of medicine in our City of London and suburbs and within seven miles thereof.[26]

However, this college was not established until 1523 because Parliament had to override the Bishop of London's traditional right to grant licences to practise medicine in the city. What became the Royal College of Physicians was granted its own, very appropriate arms in 1546, displaying *'an ermine cuff with a hand feeling the pulse of an arm'*[27] as a heraldic pun.

In addition, in 1540, Henry approved a parliamentary Act[28] that merged two city companies, the Mystery of Barbers and the Company of Pure Surgeons, into one incorporated body, creating a powerful regulatory authority that, like the physicians' college, strove to take the magic out of medicine.

Despite these attempts to put medical science on a more rational footing, religion and ancient dogma continued to play important roles in the careers of the leading doctors of the time. Medicine was still rooted in the ideas of the classical anatomists and physicians of centuries before, such as Galen, the Greek who became doctor to the Roman Emperor Marcus Aurelius in AD 163. New ideas were now emerging, some bizarre, such as the requirement for 'lusty singing' recommended in 1537 by the diplomat and scholar Sir Thomas Elyot as an exercise for those confined to the sick bed,[29] but others more familiar such as the belated recognition that an irregular pulse could be a sign of ill health. The patient's room could have been a noisy place. The colour and appearance of urine also figured strongly in diagnosis, samples being taken in straw-covered bottles from midnight to midday, with physicians sternly urged not to shake the specimens.

Sixteenth-century medical treatment, to modern eyes, was crude, if not downright cruel. Enemas, to which Henry was subjected increasingly in his last years for frequent bouts of stubborn constipation, were firmly applied to a patient's anus by means of a pig's bladder to which a greased metal tube was fixed. The bladder normally contained more than a pint of a weak solution of salt and infused herbs that had to be retained by the patient for between one and two hours. Another favourite mixture was soothing honey and 'pap' – cow's milk[30] – used particularly for the treatment of haemorrhoids, a common affliction particularly prevalent in those who spent long hours in the saddle in all weathers, perhaps wearing armour.

Medical care of 'humours' or ulcers – the chief amongst Henry's painful afflictions – was based on the principle of counter-irritation: draining them by means of a chronic inflammatory reaction, maintained, if necessary, as a running sore. This involved the so-called 'seton', a horsehair or silk filament threaded through a loose fold of skin around the ulcer, tightened and left to suppurate. The wound, of course, stank. With what seems a surprising nod to modern ideas of hygiene, the needle used in this process would be first heated red hot and then handled by the doctor with forceps. At other times, an 'issue' was deployed: a bulky object such as a small gold or silver ball would be inserted below a flap of skin, previously cut open with a lancet,[31] to achieve the same efficacious effect.

Who comprised this diagnosis of doctors responsible for the increasingly difficult, if not dangerous, task of maintaining Henry's health and wellbeing in the face of his numerous temper tantrums and irascibility?

Linacre, born in 1460, translated a number of Greek and Latin treatises on medicine and was the first president of the College of Physicians, with their meetings held at his house in Knightrider Street in the City of London. He was appointed tutor to the seven-year-old Princess Mary in 1523 but died the following year 'from the [gall] stone'[32] and was buried, as a mark of his status, in St Paul's Cathedral, where his fulsome Latin epitaph was recorded more than a century later, just before the Great Fire of London destroyed the medieval cathedral[33] and all the grand tombs within it.

Chambre, or Chamber (1470–1549), fellow and later warden of Merton College, Oxford, became a doctor to the king after studying medicine at the University of Padua and was promoted to chief physician on Linacre's death in 1524. He also collected a number of lucrative ecclesiastical appointments such as Canon of St George's, Windsor, and Dean of St Stephen's, Westminster. He supervised the confinement of Queen Anne Boleyn and safely delivered Princess Elizabeth on 7 September 1533. Chambre also probably attended (with two other royal doctors – William Butts and George Owen) the prolonged labour of Jane Seymour in 1537 and her subsequent infection, from which she died soon afterwards.

Fernando de Victoria, who qualified at a Spanish university, inevitably fell from royal favour when he was dispatched by Catherine of Aragon to inform Charles V of Henry's attempts to divorce his aunt. He died in 1529[34] and was succeeded by Edward Wotton, born around 1492, the son of the beadle of Oxford University and a natural historian of some repute. His studies included the use of insects as a source of medicinal drugs. Wotton died in 1555 and was buried in St Alban's, Wood Street, in London's Cheapside.

We have already met Augustine de Augustinis who, when working for Wolsey, famously asked Cromwell for leeches for bloodletting – 'hungry ones' – to be procured for his master, then lying ill at Esher, Surrey. They were to be applied by another Italian, Balthasar Guersie, surgeon to Catherine of Aragon. After Wolsey's disgrace and death, Augustine was employed on diplomatic service overseas for the Duke of Norfolk and Cromwell, as well as suffering a spell of imprisonment in the Tower,[35] before being appointed a physician to the royal household around 1537 at £50 a year, receiving a good brooch from the jewel collection of the recently deceased Jane Seymour[36] for his pains. In addition to his royal medical duties, he was also engaged in shadowy, if not sinister, diplomatic espionage on behalf of the king. For example, the Spanish ambassador Chapuys wrote to the emperor on 31 October 1540:

> Last week, an Italian physician attached to this King's household and very familiar with the Lord Privy Seal[37] came to dine at this embassy on four different days.
>
> He is the king's spy and has come, as I have reason to think, for no other purpose than to learn what I am about and persuade me to intercede with your majesty for a closer and particular friendship and alliance to be made with him ...
>
> The Italian at first dissembled as much as he could, trying to make me believe the suggestions came from him, not from anyone else; yet I had no difficulty in guessing, by various loose remarks he made, who had sent him onto me. For in the course of conversation he alluded to various facts which could not be known to him except through the channel of the Lord Privy Seal.[38]

Augustine may have also liaised with the French ambassador Charles de Marillac, perhaps in furtherance of the Howard faction's interests.[39] Later, as the king's health deteriorated, Augustine, long personally and irretrievably linked to the Duke of Norfolk, probably decided that public affairs at court were becoming unhealthy for him, too, and he applied for and was granted a passport to leave England in early July 1546, with £50 as a reward from Henry in his purse. He went to Venice and died in the walled city of Lucca in Tuscany on 14 September 1551.[40]

William Butts (?1485–1545) was Henry's favourite and most trusted physician, with a handsome salary to match and, later, a knighthood. He attended two of Henry's queens – Anne Boleyn and Jane Seymour, the king's bastard son Henry Fitzroy and Princess Mary, as well as Prince Edward. A strong intellectual, he was a supporter of religious reform and a friend and ally of both Queen Katherine Parr and Archbishop Cranmer. He died of malaria and was buried beneath a monumental brass depicting him in armour, now sadly lost, in Fulham Church[41] in West London, then a fashionable country parish in Middlesex. His personal loss as friend and confidant to the king is difficult to overestimate.

Thomas Wendy, born about 1500, succeeded Butts as chief physician and was one of the witnesses to Henry's will, together with fellow royal doctors George Owen and Robert Huicke, who each received a legacy of £100 from Henry. Wendy, who took his MD at Ferrara in northeast Italy, was reappointed physician to Edward VI and Mary, the latter granting him the lordship and manor of Chatteras, Cambridge, in 1558, just before she died.[42] He witnessed her will and died at Hasingfield, Cambridgeshire, in 1560.[43]

Other physicians in the royal medical team included George Owen, who died in 1558 from 'an epidemic of intermittent fever' and was buried in St Stephen Walbrook, London;[44] Walter Cromer, 'the Scot', who was dead by 1547; and Robert Huicke, whose relative William fell foul of Bishop Gardiner over his unorthodox religious beliefs, particularly his denial of the transubstantiation of bread and wine during holy communion, but escaped unscathed after a personal appeal to the king. The doctor was not an attractive character, however, and was involved in a very messy divorce from his wife, Elizabeth, in 1546. After hearing his appeal at Greenwich against a legal finding in favour of his wife, the Privy Council wrote that

we never in all our lives heard matter that more pitied us: so much cruelty and circumvention appeared; the man, so little cause ministered by the woman.[45]

Huicke again survived the scandal and was appointed physician extraordinary to Edward VI at £50 a year and witnessed Katherine Parr's will. He became physician to Elizabeth when she ascended the throne in 1558. He is believed to have died in 1581 and was buried in the chancel of Harlington Church, Middlesex.

If these levels of medical knowledge were not sufficient, special medical advice was also called in from time to time from a variety of sources, notably Andrew Boorde – 'merry Andrew' – who had been recommended by Norfolk. This former Carthusian monk examined Henry in 1542 and reported, in the terse manner of most doctors, that the king was 'fleshy' with large arteries, ruddy cheeks and pale skin, with his 'hair plenty and red, pulse great and full digestion perfect, anger short [and] sweat abundant'.[46] But Boorde was alarmed by Henry's overeating and obesity, a concern shared by his household doctors who feared that the royal constitution did not augur well for long life. Following a colourful career, Boorde died in the Fleet Prison in 1549 after being accused, almost inevitably given his lusty, spirited character, of maintaining prostitutes in his home in Winchester.

The king also employed surgeons, notably Sir John Ayliffe, Master of the Barbers' Company, in 1538,[47] who successfully treated Henry for a fistula – a narrow-mouthed ulcer – at Brinkworth, Wiltshire, 'for which the king bestowed on him great estate in gratitude' and later bequeathed him £100 in his will.[48] Others included John Monforde, or Mumford, and Richard Ferris, who is believed to have attended the king during his last illness in 1546–7. A 'nurse-surgeon', William Bullein, author of a book on pleurisy and the sweating sickness, was also a member of the royal household's medical team.

Three barbers also worked for Henry during his time on the throne – these were privileged players in the closed, regimented world of the court. The king's barber was one of just fifteen courtiers allowed access to the monarch's secret apartments for the early-morning ritual of the trimming of the regal beard.[49] Henry's ordinances for the organisation of the Privy Chamber prohibited them from consorting with 'vile persons or misguided women', warned them not to disclose anything they heard while in the king's company and ordered them to keep themselves and their clothing clean.[50]

This was a formidable array of medical talent, probably unrivalled in its corpus of expertise anywhere in the courts of Europe of the day. Their regular duties included frequent and profound examination of the royal stools, sputum and urine, as well as bleeding and cupping, in line with the changing lunar phases, to maintain the balance of Henry's bodily humours, as suggested by the classical philosophers.[51] Such procedures must have been purely routine in the halcyon healthy days of the king's youth. Then came the first of many emergencies.

Henry's real medical problems began on 24 January 1536, when he was forty-four. He had taken a carefully orchestrated starring role in a dazzling display of jousting at Greenwich, on the eve of the conversion of St Paul.

> The king, mounted on a great horse to run at the lists, both fell so heavily that everyone thought it a miracle that he was not killed, but he sustained no injury.[52]

Due to his showy enthusiasm and braggart recklessness, Henry had suffered accidents in the lists before. In 1524, whilst tilting with lances with his old friend the Duke of Suffolk, the king had been injured above the right brow after he unwisely rode out with his helmet visor raised. Although he was lucky not to lose an eye and, daredevil-like, ran six more courses at the lists that day, he suffered frequent migraine headaches afterwards.[53]

This latest jousting incident was far more serious even than it seemed at the time. His armoured horse reportedly fell on top of him as he was unseated by his opponent's blunted lance. Five days later, Anne Boleyn miscarried of a male foetus aged about three and a half months after her uncle, the Duke of Norfolk, told her of the accident. More indicatively, two months later, a report from Rome quoting the French king said that Henry, having fallen from his horse, 'had been for two hours without speech', possibly through severe concussion or, worse, bruising of the cerebral cortex.[54] Although Cromwell wrote to Bishop Gardiner in February that the 'king is merry and in perfect health', one can smell deceit in that devious minister's reassuring weasel words, which were probably only intended for outside consumption. Then, in March, Lord Montague unwisely and famously blurted out his premonition of the king's death and paid with his life for his hasty words, for it was high treason to presage the king's death. But they were patently true: the next month, Henry was said to 'go seldom abroad because his leg is something sore'.[55] The fall almost certainly broke open the varicose ulcer he was treated for in 1527–8 and thus it became chronic, discharging freely. No doubt the royal doctors tightly bandaged up the wound.

This was the beginning of all the king's debilitating medical problems that constantly and painfully afflicted him until his death. On 14 May 1538, one of the fistulas on his leg closed up and

> for ten or twelve days, the humours which had no outlet were like to have stifled him so that he was some time without speaking, black in the face and in great danger.[56]

In today's modern medical terms, the king was suffering from a thrombosed vein in his leg and, dangerously, a clot may have detached from this vein. He was lucky to escape with his life: even with the benefits of twenty-first-century medicine, the condition still remains hazardous. In November that year, Sir Geoffrey Pole reported that Henry had

> a sore leg that no poor man would be glad of and that he should not live long for all his authority next to God.[57]

By Good Friday 1539, the king's legs must have improved, as he was able to take part in that strange pre-Reformation liturgical rite of 'crawling to the cross'. This ritual involved veneration of the crucifixion scene, temporarily positioned in the Easter Sepulchre on the north side of the chancel of a church, by reverently shuffling forward on the knees from the chapel door during Mass.[58]

But in September, he was clearly suffering from acute constipation. This recurrent and very intimate problem would not come as a surprise to today's dietitians, given the menus of the huge, unhealthy meals daily consumed by the court and other wealthy households in the Tudor period. The English were famous for being big meat eaters (remember the 'roast beef of old England') with plenty of game, hoofed and feathered, heaved on to the groaning banqueting tables. The slaughter of birds for food was both prodigious and catholic in choice: larks, stork, gannets (and other gulls), heron, snipe, bustard, quail, partridge, capons, teal, cranes and pheasants all regularly appear on menus that would send horrified shivers down the corporate spine of today's Royal Society for the Protection of Birds. One of the court's favourites was stewed sparrows. The king was said to be fond of galantines,[59] game pies and haggis – a sheep's stomach stuffed with minced offal and oats. Today, it is a traditional Scottish dish.[60] Impressive quantities of salted and smoked cod, plus herrings, fresh salmon and eels were also consumed after the hot meat course. Most meats and fish, if not downright unpalatable, were heavily flavoured with spices to disguise their lack of freshness. Little roughage appeared on the dinner table: fresh fruit was widely shunned as it was believed to cause diarrhoea and fever. Green vegetables, as well as turnips, carrots and parsnips, were also avoided because 'they engender wind and melancholy'[61] but cucumbers, lettuces and the succulent herb purslane[62] were eaten in more healthy salads as a first course. Butter was usually rancid and used mainly in cooking. One writer has ingeniously suggested that most of Henry's ailments were attributable to scorbutic disease, or scurvy, caused by a chronic lack of vitamins supplied in our modern diet by fresh vegetables and fruit.[63] Whatever, his food bingeing aggravated his medical condition and regularly blocked the healthy movement of his bowels.

Henry's physicians prescribed as a cure for his constipation that the

King's majesty went betimes [early] to bed, whose highness slept until two of the clock in the morning.

And then his grace was to go to the stool which by waking of the pills and glister [an enema] that his highness had taken before had a very fair siege as the physicians have made report, not doubting but the worst is past by their perseverance to no great danger or any further grief to remain in him.

The hinder part of the night until ten of the clock this morning his grace had very good rest and his grace finds himself well, saving his highness says he has a little soreness in the body.[64]

So reported Sir Thomas Heneage, Groom of the Stool of Henry's Privy Chamber, in a salaciously detailed letter to Cromwell written from Ampthill. No doubt the king's soreness came from the enthusiastic application of the pig's bladder enema.

Henry normally consumed three meals a day, plus probably frequent snacking in the evenings. His average day began with the page of the Privy Chamber lighting the fires in his secret apartments at seven and he rose half an hour later for breakfast in his bedchamber.[65] He went to Mass and consumed 'dinner' at around ten o'clock. Most of the day could then be spent hunting, before supper at four. Afterwards, his secretaries and intimates dealt with state papers with him in his study – it was a difficult task, sometimes, to curb his impatience – before he spent the rest of his evening gambling at cards or dice, or playing chess with his cronies.

In late February 1541, the king probably suffered another severe infection caused by the fistulas on his legs closing up. Henry had talked of inspecting his fortifications of the south coast as he was considering rebuilding some of the ramparts, particularly at Dover. However, this trip was prevented by 'an illness' he suffered at Hampton Court – a slight fever – followed by a recurrence of the dangerous infection. The French ambassador Marillac reported to Francis I that

One of his legs, formerly open and kept open to maintain his health, suddenly closed to his great alarm, for five or six years ago, in like case, we thought him to have died.

This time, prompt remedy was applied and he is now well and the fever gone. Besides the bodily malady, he had a *mal d'espirit*.[66]

Marillac was being diplomatic. In fact, Henry was incandescent with rage. Nothing could or would please him as he lay in great pain upon his sick bed. He lashed out ferociously at anything and everything. The ambassador recounted his rantings:

He had unhappy people to govern whom he would shortly make so poor that they would not have the boldness nor the power to oppose him ...

Most of his Privy Council, under the pretence of serving him, were only temporising for their own profit but he knew the good servants from the flatterers and if God lent him health, he would take care that their projects would not succeed.[67]

Even in his agony and labouring under the all-pervasive fear that death was beckoning him, Henry could not resist the temptation to verbally assault his courtiers, ensuring that they knew he was fully aware of their continual profiteering from their royal patronage. He even blamed them for Cromwell's death:

Upon light pretexts, by false accusations, they made him put to death the most faithful servant he ever had.[68]

Whilst still more than capable of cunning, the king was really very ill, and his constant gluttony following the death of Jane Seymour was taking its toll. In addition to his anger and violent mood swings, he displayed frequent and capricious changes in his opinions and decisions. On 3 March, Marillac said in a dispatch:

The king's life was really thought to be in danger, not from the fever, but from the leg which often troubles him because he is very stout and marvellously excessive in drinking and eating so that people worth credit say that he is often of a different opinion in the morning than after dinner.[69]

Shrovetide came and went quietly at Hampton Court, while Henry, sequestered in his secret apartments, exploded in tantrum after tantrum. Life there passed 'without recreation, even music which [the king] used to take so much pleasure [in] as any prince in Christendom'. With visitors turned away at the gates, Marillac said there was so little company in the palace 'that the court resembled more a private family than a king's train'.

On 14 March, Henry was still 'indisposed', but then surprisingly made a good recovery, enabling his energetic royal progress to the North to show off his new queen, Katherine Howard. But he was to fall into the hands of his doctors again at the end of December, taking their prescribed medicines as he 'did not feel quite the thing', possibly because of his shock and dreadful despair at her adultery.

Henry was now huge. As a young man in 1514, his harness of armour, specially made for him, shows that he was 6 ft. 3 in. in height and had a trim waist measurement of 35 in. and a chest diameter of 42 in. – a powerful, muscular picture of chivalry. That manly physique had now gone. At the age of forty-nine, Henry's waist had swelled to a gargantuan 54 in. and his chest to 58 in. The deterioration in his appearance was awe-inspiring.

Gone were the magnificent propaganda images painted only five years or so before when he was in his mid-forties,[70] showing the barrel-chested king in familiar three-quarter view. In these portraits, an arrogant monarch stares back defiantly at us out of the canvases, daring us not to be humbled by his bravura. His haughty, regal glance is designed to bring us to our knees. He is clearly fit and healthy, swaggering, overbearing and domineering. This is an imperious Henry, God's true deputy on earth, shown at the peak of his powers.[71] At the time these portraits were created, the Spanish ambassador Eustace Chapuys wrote tellingly of Henry: 'He has no respect or fear of anyone in the world.'[72] The king's contempt for all around him radiates out malevolently from his eyes. No wonder Henry was the first English king to adopt the word 'majesty'.

Half a decade or so later, how things had changed! The metamorphosis is dramatic. Now the artist portrays him as a pathetic, hugely overweight old man. The years of misuse and abuse of his body have patently had a dire impact on his frame. His small eyes peer out pig-like from a jowled, fat, lined face. He holds a heavy embossed staff in his left hand for support.[73] He is the personification of geriatric decay. One can almost smell the putrid stench of the rank pus oozing from his ulcers, staining the bandages on his swollen legs. Chapuys labelled them 'the worst legs in the world'.

Henry could no longer fully pursue his much-loved pastime of hunting: although he was still able to ride, long hours in the saddle were now beyond him. Instead, the quarry was driven before him to be shot by crossbow, or he was forced to watch as an impatient onlooker while his keepers drove the game towards a choreographed kill before him.

Yet the coming years of 1544–5 were a critically important period of high mental and physical activity for Henry, during which he personally led his last campaign in France and superintended plans to protect England from invasion,[74] despite being in continual pain and suffering from the debilitating effects of his massive bulk. His driving determination to lead, to rule effectively, to succeed, must have been terrible to behold.

In March 1544, the ulcers on Henry's legs flared up yet again, confining him to bed with a fever. The royal doctors urged him not to personally lead the 42,000 English troops then being assembled for the Anglo-Spanish invasion of France and his ministers flapped about in the same cause, ever fearful of provoking another of the king's rages. But for Henry, the issue was clear cut: he *was* the king, and the king belonged at the head of his army. To do otherwise on such an important international military undertaking would be a great dishonour both to him and to the prestige of England. The practical and realistic Chapuys urged his imperial master to intervene to persuade Henry against taking to the field of battle, with all the discomforts and inconveniences of campaigning. The emperor sent a special envoy who 'found Henry so determined upon the voyage that he dared not try to dissuade him'. Once again, with a grim fortitude, Henry recovered and in early June wrote to his ally, promising that he was sufficiently well to embark for Calais 'where he would resolve whether to go further'. In the event, he crossed the Channel to the field of battle, but it is very doubtful whether Henry went particularly close to the fighting. A mere whiff of gunpowder in the siege of Boulogne was probably enough for the proud old warhorse to prove his point to himself and the watching world.

Another key player in the last days of Henry VIII enters now upon the stage: the king's fool or jester, Will Somers. He strikes a very human note of sanity amid the recurrent bouts of anger, the low cunning and the bloody ruthlessness of his ageing psychopathic master and the plots and conspiracies being waged in dark corners as the various factions in the court began to vie for power when the king finally died. Of all the royal household, this humpbacked little man with his pet monkey was trusted totally by Henry. His ability to make the sad, pained old man laugh enabled him not only to tell the king things that others would not dare to, but to survive happily this most dangerous reign and its immediate successors.

Robert Armin (*c.*1568–1615), one of the principal actors in Shakespeare's plays late in Elizabeth's reign, wrote of Somers' first meeting with Henry at Greenwich in 1525 in his *Nest of Ninnies*:[75]

A comely fool indeed, passing more stately:
who was this forsooth? Will Sommers! And not
meanly esteemed by the king for his
merriment; his melody was of a higher strain
and he looked as the noon broad waking.
Will Sommers, born in Shropshire, as some say
was brought to Greenwich on a holy day.
Presented to the king, which fool ordained
to shake him by the hand, or else ashamed.
Lean as he was, hollow-eyed, as all report
and stoop he did too; yet in all the court
few men were more beloved than was this fool

whose merry prate kept with the king much rule.
When he was sad, the King and he would rhyme
Thus Will exiled sadness many a time.

Tradition maintains that Richard Fermer, a Northamptonshire merchant of the Staple of Calais, had employed Somers and introduced him at court.[76] Somers succeeded the elderly Sexton as the chief royal fool and constantly delighted Henry with his wicked sense of humour and his acrobatics.[77] No one amongst Henry's court or administration, no matter how high their status, was safe from his jokes or his dartlike witticisms. Soon the king was promising to fulfil any favour Will desired and the fool undertook to apply when he had the grace to ask, meaning that he would decide when to make the request. 'One day I shall,' Somers is said to have commented, 'for every man sees his latter end, but knows not his beginning.' With this quip, the jester left the royal presence and 'laid himself down among the spaniels to sleep'.[78]

One story recounts that soon after his arrival at court, Somers cheekily cheated Henry's then chief minister, Wolsey, out of £10. It is probably apocryphal, like so many of the tales about the fool, but it provides a flavour of Somers' wit and the unrestricted access he enjoyed to his royal master. According to the story, the fool had entered the royal apartments while the king and cardinal were privately discussing state business. Somers apologised for his interruption and said that some of Wolsey's creditors were outside, demanding their money. The cardinal pompously replied that he would forfeit his head if he owed any man a penny, but gave Somers £10 in gold on the promise that it would be paid to whom it was due. Somers then left, but returned later, asking Wolsey: 'To whom do you owe your soul?' 'To God,' came the reply. Somers then asked: 'And your wealth?' 'To the poor,' said the cardinal piously. Then, said the fool quickly, Wolsey's head was forfeit to the king 'for to the poor at the gate I paid the debt which he agrees is due'.

Henry laughed long at the joke and the cardinal no doubt feigned his merriment, but 'it grieved him to give £10 away so' – a large sum of money, equivalent to more than £4,000 in today's purchasing power.

Somers apparently played a number of other practical jokes on the minister, who was always ready to stand on his dignity, and the cardinal 'could never abide him'.[79]

Thomas Wilson (who thirty years later became a secretary of state in Elizabeth's government) in his *Art of Rhetorique*, published in 1551 or 1553, quotes some pointed repartee between Somers and the king, who was then, as ever, in need of hard cash. His fool told him, 'You have so many frauditors, so many conveyers and so many deceivers' – clever puns on 'auditors', 'surveyors' and 'receivers', administrators in the Tudor government – 'that they get all to themselves.'

Somers enjoyed a very close relationship with Henry, following him from palace to palace, playing with his children. One ferryman's bill records the passage of his horse across the Thames from Lambeth on Christmas Eve when Henry and his entourage moved to Hampton Court.[80]

The strange rapport between sovereign and fool that endured for more than two decades (when many others fell so easily in and out of royal favour) and the great affection in which Somers was obviously held are reflected in his appearance in several royal portraits and contemporary illustrations. A painting of a chubby Edward, aged six, now in the Kunstmuseum, Basle, shows the prince holding a monkey, probably Somers' pet.

Most poignant of all is a miniature of Henry, with Somers close by, that appears in the *King's Psalter*, preserved in the British Library.[81] The 176-page book, bound in red velvet now worn through usage over time, was written for Henry on vellum in the Italian style of calligraphy by John Mallard around 1540.[82] Much of it is concerned with the biblical story of David and Goliath, and its content clearly associates the king with David. It contains many marginal notes in the king's own handwriting as well as several miniature paintings of Henry, one, for example, portraying him sitting in his great bedchamber, reading a book.[83] Sometimes the king's handwritten notes are poignant and telling indicators of his thoughts. Alongside verse 25 of Psalm 17 – 'I have been young and now am old' – Henry writes rather pathetically '*Dolus dictum*' – 'a painful saying'. The years were running away for the king and he was all too conscious that his mortal span was nearly ended. In his letters, he writes that time 'is of all losses the most irrecuperable, for it can never be redeemed for no manner, price nor prayer'.[84]

In the *Psalter*, the Somers picture accompanies Psalm 52 and shows an aged Henry as David, seated, hunched up on a coffer, his legs crossed, playing a small harp. The king has a wistful if not melancholic expression on his wrinkled face, perhaps dreaming of glories past. Although he wears a heavy furred robe, his back looks distinctly humped (of which more anon in Chapter 9). Somers, his fingers intertwined, faces right, out of the illustration, obviously rejected as the content of the psalm dictates. He is wearing a green hooded jacket, a purse and green-blue stockings, probably the 'coat ... of green cloth, with a hood to the same, fringed with white crule [wool embroidery]' ordered for him on 28 June 1535[85] by Henry from Lord Windsor, Keeper of the Great Wardrobe, to be made by John Malt, the king's tailor.

Somers also appears in the huge dynastic family portrait of Henry, Jane Seymour and the royal children Edward, Mary and Elizabeth, painted around 1545 by an unknown artist, which once hung in the Palace of Westminster.[86] On either side of the main figures are two archways, providing a glimpse of the ornate and lush Privy Gardens outside. In the right-hand archway stands Will Somers, a clothed monkey wearing a cap squatting on his left shoulder, busily scratching the fool's bowed head. In the left arch stands a female figure who is probably Jane, Princess Mary's own fool.[87] Beneath the subliminal propaganda signals of the painting, intended to suggest the continuity and legality of the Tudor line of succession and the power and prestige of the dynasty, lies a very human message: all the figures depicted, both royal and humble, must then have been very close to Henry's heart.[88]

The king's household accounts for the last twelve months of his reign include a number of references to Somers, relating to his care and upkeep. On the bottom of a bill for 7s 4d for the carriage of two chests from the Palace of Westminster to Windsor is a note in Secretary Wriothesley's hand: 'Remember Will Somer shirts.' And later in 1546 there is a bill from Robert Callyniuod for laundry and clothing for the fool that illustrates how his movements followed the king's:

> For washing William Summer[s' garments], Michaelmas to
>   Candlemas to the laundry 11s.
> For W. Somer, his shaving, 4d.
> For a pair of boot hose, 8d.
> For William Sommer for two pair of black hose 10s and two
>   pairs of stock[ing]s, 3s 4d at Windsor, October 6.
> Two pair of black hose at Windsor against ?Hallowtide, 10s.
> Two pair of black stock[ing]s at Oteland, December 1, 3s 4d.
> Two pair of black stock[ing]s at Westminster, against Christmas,
>   10s. and two pairs of black stock[ing]s at Westminster,
>   January 24, 3s 4d.
> Received for William Summer for Michaelmas to Candlemas,
>   three pairs of lined shoes at 10d; seven pairs unlined at 8d,
>   two pairs of summer buskins at 2s, one pair of winter
>   boots, 3s.[89]

Paradoxically, given Henry's frequent illnesses, it was a firm belief amongst his subjects that the king had the power to cure scrofula, or tuberculosis of the lymph glands in the neck.[90] This healing process was known as 'The King's Evil' and sufferers merely had to touch his sacred person to be healed by the royal powers. The massive inventory of Henry's possessions drawn up after his death includes 'A black velvet bag ... containing three rings, whereof one, a ruby, that the king wore at the healing of poor folk'[91] that was used in this regularly staged ceremony.

In the spring of 1546, Henry's mobility deteriorated considerably as his legs had become very swollen and made walking difficult: the king had become a semi-invalid and had to rely on other means to move around his palaces. In July that year, an entry in the meticulously kept household accounts for the Palace of Westminster records:

Stuff made by the king's commandment and the same delivered in charge unto ... Anthony Denny:

Item: two chairs called 'trams' for the king's majesty to sit in, to be carried to and fro in his galleries and chambers covered with tawny velvet all over quilted with tawny silk with a half place [92] underneath either of the said chairs and two foot stools standing on either side of the half place, embroidered upon the backs of them and the top of the high pommels on either of them with a rose of Venice gold fringed round about with tawny silk.

Item: one other like chair cover with russet velvet likewise quilted and embroidered with silk and gold and fringed with a like half place and like stools. [93]

A belief grew up amongst Victorian historians that some mechanical contrivance such as a lift or elevator was constructed to raise the corpulent king from floor to floor of his palaces. This view is based solely on the testimony of the Duke of Norfolk's mistress, Mrs Elizabeth or 'Bess' Holland, [94] at the trial of Henry, Earl of Surrey, in January 1547. This 'churl's daughter', as the spurned and discarded Duchess of Norfolk bitterly called her, [95] confessed to the court that the duke had told her

that the king was much grown of his body and that he could not go up and down stairs and was let up and down by a device. And that his majesty was sickly and could not long endure

– the last words alone condemning the duke for treason.

It seems very likely that the king's 'trams' described in Denny's accounts refer to some form of what later came to be called a sedan chair – fitted with horizontal poles and carried by four attendants, one at each corner. Indeed, the Spanish ambassador van der Delft in his dispatches reports Henry 'passing in his chair' on 7 October that year, [96] probably in the Palace of Westminster. The chairs may have been fitted with wheels because of the king's great weight, the Old English word 'tram' meaning not a vehicle in the modern sense, but a two-shafted cart, wagon or hand-barrow. They were kept in the king's study, now called 'the chair house' in the inventory of the contents of the Palace of Westminster. There is no mention of a lift or any other contrivance in the household accounts and probably there was little need of one: the king's secret apartments were always on one floor.

Denny's terse accounts of the time paint a vivid, human picture of Henry as an old man in constant pain, needing comfort for his ulcerated legs and frequent respites from the agony caused by standing for long periods or by prolonged periods of movement. Payments for the same month of July 1546 also include delivery of 'two foot stools of wood ... covered with purple velvet and fringed with silk' and later there are frequent orders for 'new made' chairs and cushions of purple velvet and six more matching foot stools.[97] The popular image of an elderly king seeking solace by resting his leg on the lap of a compassionate and caring Queen Katherine may not be so far from the truth.

Some of the last items ordered for the king before his death were new close stools, or commodes. William Green's bill, dated 28 December 1546, totalled £4 10s 6d for making 'a close stool for the king's majesty' covered with black velvet and 31 lb. of down for stuffing the seat, arms and sides, fixed with 2,000 gilt nails. Elizabeth Slanning was also paid 27s 6d for supplying silk fringes and ribbons to Green on 28 November for this commode, delivered to Anthony Denny.[98] Early the following month, William Hustwayt was paid 5s to make 'a great pewter cistern' for one of Henry's close stools at Westminster and another 5s for a similar very intimate utensil for Windsor. He was also paid 2s for mending an old cistern. On 14 January 1547, two weeks before the king's death, his Privy Chamber purchased a yard and a half of black velvet 'to make two pairs of large slippers newly devised'.[99]

By then, Henry's medical condition had rendered such homely comforts too little, too late to benefit him.

CHAPTER SIX

The New Levers of Power

'Councillors shall apply themselves diligently, uprightly and justly in the premises, being every day in the forenoon by ten of the clock and at afternoon by two of the clock in the King's Dining Chamber not only in case the King's pleasure shall be to commune or confer with them upon any cause or matter but also for hearing and direction of poor men's complaints on matters of justice.'

HENRY'S PRIVY COUNCIL ORDINANCES, 1526[1]

Outside the bear pit of religious dispute and political argument that Henry's Council had become lay the king's Privy Chamber, increasingly now the real seat of power in the realm. This small group of ambitious men was closest to the royal person, not only always within hearing and sight of the king, but also privy to Henry's innermost thoughts and changing moods. In addition, they were concerned with his most personal bodily needs. Such familiarity always spawns power. The members of this élite had constant, privileged access to Henry, and consequently the lucrative asset of royal patronage was very much in their hands. They also controlled the burden of his administrative load, doubly significant because of Henry's notoriously low boredom threshold for paperwork.

The head of this small, very select organisation was the Chief Gentleman of the Privy Chamber and Groom of the Stool, Sir Thomas Heneage, who had made his mark as head of Cardinal Wolsey's Privy Chamber back in the late 1520s before his promotion into this, the king's most intimate service, in 1536. But Henry's real 'fixer', his man-about-the-court, trusted messenger and true confidant was Anthony Denny, who had been knighted on the field of battle after the surrender of Boulogne in September 1544. Then Heneage was suddenly and summarily dismissed as Chief Gentleman in October 1546 for reasons that are unclear, but may have been the result of a deliberate palace *coup* by religious reformers.[2]

Denny's relationship with the king was totally different from that enjoyed by the court fool, the shrewd Will Somers, who was there to cheer the king and distract him from his ever more frequent bouts of melancholy. His role was that of a discreet sounding board, with whom the king could safely discuss delicate issues of state, away from the vested interests and entrenched positions of his conspiratorial Privy Council and his government officers. Denny's colleague William Herbert testified after Henry's death that the king 'would always, when Mr Secretary [Paget] was gone, tell us what passed between them'. As such a loyal adviser, upon whom Henry grew increasingly reliant, Denny rapidly became the true authority lurking behind the throne, a role only recently identified by historians.[3] His talents and attributes were recognised by his contemporaries. Sir William Cecil, reporting the news from London in 1549, wrote that 'Sir Anthony Denny is dead, whereof none have greater loss than very honest [and virtuous] men'.[4]

Denny was born in Howe, Norfolk, in January 1501, the second surviving son of Sir Edmund Denny, Chief Baron of the Exchequer, by his second wife Mary, of Cheshunt, Hertfordshire.[5] He was educated at St Paul's School under the famous humanist thinker William Lily and at St John's College, Cambridge,[6] before joining the household of the favoured courtier Sir Francis Bryan in 1531. When Bryan became a Chief Gentleman of the Privy Chamber in 1536, Denny followed him into Henry's service, becoming King's Remembrancer and a groom, a

Yeoman of Robes and then Keeper of the Palace of Westminster in September 1537. The king wrote to the Sheriff of Norfolk and Suffolk, probably in December 1535, recommending Denny's election as a Member of Parliament for the prosperous east coast port of Ipswich.[7] When Bryan was ousted in late 1538 during Cromwell's last purge of royal officials, Denny cheerfully replaced his mentor.[8]

He had good court connections.[9] His youngest sister Martha married Sir Wymond Carew, former receiver-general to Anne of Cleves and later treasurer of the Court of First Fruits and Tenths[10] in 1545–9; the widow of his eldest brother, Thomas, remarried Robert Dacres, Master of Requests[11] and a Privy Councillor in 1542–4.[12] He also had a reputation for the new learning and scholarship and was a close friend of the author Roger Ascham, tutor to Princess Elizabeth and later to Prince Edward. Denny apparently told Ascham: 'If two deities did not command him to serve, the one the prince, the other his wife, he would surely become a student [again] in St John's [College].'[13] He was charming, level-headed and always more than sympathetic to Henry's many trials and tribulations. Of the marriage charade with Anne of Cleves in 1540, Denny commented comfortingly:

> The state of princes in matters of marriage is far worse a sort than the conditions of poor men. For princes take as is brought to them by others and poor men be commonly at their own choice and liberty.[14]

One can see why the king was so fond of him. There is no talk here of diplomatic imperatives or the strict requirements of protocol, such as Henry must have constantly heard from Cromwell and his other advisers. Sir John Cheke said that Denny was 'able to mould Henry's mind, now mixing the useful with the sweet, now weaving the serious things with the light ones, great with small'.[15] But despite his skill in manipulating the king, the fear of Henry's uncertain temper and his ever-changing moods, together with the stealthy machinations of those around him, must have caused Denny many a sleepless night.

He lived in Aldgate, on the eastern edge of the City of London, quite close to Hans Holbein the Younger, who painted a portrait of his neigh-bour in 1541.[16] The painting shows an intense, earnest face, bearded, with a lively expression and quizzical eyes peering out from beneath a sombre cap.[17] Denny married Joan, daughter of Sir Philip Champer-nown, of Modbury, Devon, in February 1538, in a match probably encour-aged by the king[18] and eventually had twelve children. Joan was an attractive and intelligent woman and a strong adherent of the reformed religion. She became a lady-in-waiting, first to Anne of Cleves on her arrival in England in 1540 and later to Queen Katherine Parr.

Denny was an influential supporter of the evangelical party at court, although he took pains to discreetly hide his religious beliefs. He was cer-tainly a friend of Thomas Cranmer.[19] As he blossomed in Henry's esti-mation, he began to amass considerable holdings of land and sinecure offices, thoughtfully provided by a grateful monarch. These included: the lucrative job of collector of tonnage and poundage in the port of London (1541);[20] a grant of the dissolved priory of Hertford (1537); steward of the manor of Bedwell and Little Berkhamsted, Hertfordshire, the manors of Butterwick and Great Amwell and the nunnery of Cheshunt in the same county (1539); lands belonging to the abbey of St Alban's (1541); Mettingham College, Suffolk, with six manors in East Anglia (1542); and a thirty-one-year lease on more than 2,000 acres of Waltham Abbey land in Essex in 1544. He was also granted, for life, houses in close prox-imity to the Palace of Westminster, charmingly called Paradise, Hell and Purgatory, probably to enable him to be near his job as Keeper of the Palace, paid at the modest rate of 6d a day. After he died, his lands probably totalled about 20,000 acres in the counties of Hertfordshire and Essex alone, and his annual income amounted to around £750, or more than £220,000 a year at current prices.[21]

As the king's reliance on Denny grew, the courtier set up a small administrative unit within the Privy Chamber. It was led by his brother-in-law John Gates, something of a thug and the original sixteenth-century 'Essex' man, who was used as the hard man to ensure that things got done around the court. The pen-pushers were William Clerk, who had charge of the 'dry stamp' that created a facsimile of Henry's signature, and Nicholas Bristow, who was the accountant overseeing the expenditure by the Privy Purse – Henry's own private bank account. Denny and Gates had no compunction in exploiting their unique access to the king with the many subjects who wished to press their suits. Two examples vividly illustrate the patronage system:

5 September 1546. John Dodge to Mr Gates, 'steward to the right worshipful Mr Denny. The parson of Leyborne, Kent, with the consent of the archbishop of Canterbury, his patron, and bishop of Rochester ... will lease to me a free chapel in Leyborne for as many years as the law will permit ... The king has ordered his archbishops and bishops to make no such leases without his consent. I beg you to get the king's confirmation of the lease and to move your master [Denny] to get the king's commandment directed to the said bishops.'

22 November 1546. Richard Norlegh to an unknown recipient. 'As you are a friend to my master Mr Gates, I will do what otherwise I would not for £40, for honesty is to be esteemed above all things and thereto I never forsook my first client. I will not hinder you but cannot be a suitor for you that were too apparent. If you were not a friend to Mr Gates £100 would not stop my mouth but I should speak for my first client.'[22]

All were aware of Denny's influence and power. Edmond Harvel, the English ambassador to Venice, kept a close eye on Denny's nephew John, who was studying in that Italian city-state. John seems to have been a gullible youth, distracted by its cosmopolitan environment. In May 1543, Harvel wrote to Denny saying that his nephew was 'forcing himself' to increase his virtuous qualities, but 'being weak and delicate of nature, it [would not be helpful] to load him with a greater burden than he may well sustain'. John himself later wrote to Denny, praying God to inspire him to observe his uncle's loving admonitions.[23] When Sir Thomas Cheyney, Treasurer of the Royal Household, broke his son's engagement with Denny's niece, he was warned that Henry's favourite was a man

near about the king and one unmet to be trifled or mocked with.

Your slipping away may not only lose you friendship but cause displeasure. My advice is that you consider that.[24]

Denny's role as keeper of the Privy Purse entailed handling large sums of money for the king's personal use, from payment of his some-times substantial gambling debts – Henry was a keen card player[25] – to settling bills for his many construction projects. During the last five years of the reign, Denny received a total of £243,387 1s 6d for Henry's use, or more than £61 million in today's monetary values, spent accord-ing to the king's verbal orders.[26] This Tudor monarch, unlike his father, was a profligate spender, pushing the exchequer's balance sheet into the red in both 1544 and 1545, mainly because of expenditure on the fighting in France and Scotland. Total revenues for those years – from the taxes on laity and clergy, the cynical debasement of the currency, revenues from dissolved monastic lands via the Court of Augmenta-tion and the like – came to £594,925 (£210 million at 2004 prices) and £620,246 (£201 million) respectively, reflecting the impact of both rampant inflation and devaluation. The wars cost more than £740,000 each year for 1544 and 1545 (£260 million and £242 million) and after adding other expenditure (the king's works, diplomatic missions and servicing the large loans taken out with the Fuggers banking family and others) there were overspends of £329,706 (£115 million) and £311,451 (£102 million) for those two years.[27] In addition to reducing the proportion of gold and silver in everyone's money, in May 1544, England's currency was devalued and two new coins introduced: the sovereign, worth £1 (or £350 in today's spending power), and the half-sovereign. Inflation over the previous decade, fuelled by government spending and the debasement, amounted to 100 per cent. No wonder the Privy Council and Henry's administrators were keen to end the war with France: England was bankrupt.

The exchequer painfully clambered into the black in 1546, showing a surplus of around £180,000 for that year, prompting Henry to continue his shopping sprees, as shown by Denny's accounts. The king had always liked nice things around him:[28] thirteen items in gold and silver gilt – bowls, cups, flagons – were ordered from Morgan Wolf, the royal goldsmith, in March that year alone.[29] Then, as now, there is nothing like a little retail therapy to distract one's mind from every trouble and ailment. Petty cash was kept in coffers inside the 'withdrawing chamber' at his Palace of Westminster and topped up to meet the king's most immediate needs:

April 1: Delivered out of his majesty's removing coffers in his great withdrawing chamber, by the hands of Sir Thomas Cawarden,[30] the sum of £518 8s 4d.

April 2: Delivered by the king his majesty out of his said removing coffers, £2,000 thereof being brought to his said majesty by ... merchants for non performance of a bargain of bringing in wines made by them to the king, the sum of £1,536 5s 8d.

April 3: Received out of the king, his majesty's own hands, lately brought to his highness by Sir Edmund Peckham,[31] the sum of £2,000.

April 7: Delivered out of his majesty's removing coffers by the hands of Sir Thomas Cawarden, the sum of £57 6s 8d.[32]

Each section of the voluminous accounts was signed by Nicholas Bristow, clerk, and countersigned by his master, Anthony Denny.

Henry's eyesight was also failing and his accounts from 1544 onwards show purchases of spectacles, ten pairs at a time, from Germany.[33] These would be clipped on to the nose and the repeated orders perhaps indicate the king's proclivity for losing them. His poor sight, combined with his traditional distaste and impatience for signing official papers, created the need in his last years for a new, less irksome method of indicating his approval for actions or decisions on the mountain of letters, dispatches, petitions, grants, accounts and bills that came into his Privy Chamber for administrative processing.

As a solution, the so-called 'dry stamp' was used in lieu of the royal autograph or 'sign manual' from September 1545. This was a small carved wooden block that was impressed on paper – probably with a special hand press[34] – to leave a dry imprinted facsimile of Henry's signature. This would later be inked in by William Clerk, one of the clerks of the Privy Seal serving under Sir Anthony Denny and his brother-in-law John Gates of the Privy Chamber, who always witnessed the deployment of this signature block. All transactions involving the dry stamp were specially recorded in a separate book, which was supposed to be regularly reviewed by the king[35] because of the obvious dangers of abuse and misuse that the process invited. Initially the wooden block, kept within a small, locked black leather casket, was held securely by the king himself. But as the months went by and his melancholy increased, he gave up custody of the stamp to Gates and so handed over the reins of power to those closely surrounding him.[36]

Of course, forging the royal signature would normally be a treasonable offence, so to ensure that the procedure did not transgress the law, those wielding the dry stamp had to be formally and retrospectively pardoned as well as licensed, as an administrative convenience, in its use for a limited period in the future. Thus, in August 1546, Denny was officially pardoned 'for all treasons concerning the counterfeiting, impression and writing of the king's sign manual since September 20 last'[37] and the same pardon was issued immediately to William Clerk and John Gates. Furthermore, Denny, Gates and Clerk were authorised to use the dry stamp until 10 May 1547 in a document approved at Hampton Court on 31 August 1546. They were permitted

> to sign on the king's behalf and name during his pleasure; warrants, bills, gifts, grants, leases, pardons, letters and minutes ... in form following; namely, two of them with a stamp, called a 'dry stamp' shall at the King's command make an impression without blackening and afterwards the said Clerk or else the said Anthony and John shall blacken the same, provided that all such warrants and other writings are entered in a book or certain schedules to be signed by the king's own hand monthly.[38]

The certificate was examined by the law officers, led by Henry Bradshaw, Chief Baron of the Exchequer, who countersigned it, together with a bevy of officials and courtiers led by Wriothesley.

Those who had custody of the dry stamp now held the keys to the exchequer, the power of royal patronage and the means finally to destroy their political enemies. In the months to come, some of the greatest figures in the land were to feel the devastating effects of that small wooden block, simply pressed down on state papers, and to pay dearly for Henry's rapidly deteriorating medical condition.

The sands of time had almost run out for the grumbling, gargantuan monarch. The last great state occasion of Henry's reign was staged in August 1546, when the French admiral Claud d'Annebaut, with a glittering train of 200 nobles and their liveried followers, came to London aboard the *Great Zachary* of Dieppe and fourteen galleys to ratify the new peace treaty ending the war between England and France. The king was infirm and the eight-year-old Prince Edward deputised for him, riding out on 23 August to welcome the French formally at Hounslow, Middlesex, with 700 gentlemen and nobles in attendance, escorted by eighty yeomen of the guard. It was a glorious, dazzling spectacle. The admiral and his party rode down two lines of 500 mounted English yeomen, all wearing 'new liveries', before halting in front of the young prince, who was mounted on horseback with the rest of his party, all dressed in rich velvet coats. The precocious Edward impressed the French with his Latin speech of welcome, which displayed 'great wit and audacity', and with his skilled horsemanship.[39] Afterwards, one of the French party, Monsieur de Morette, told Dr Nicholas Wotton that he 'rejoiced very much to have seen my lord prince's grace, of whose praises, he can not speak [highly] enough'.[40] The party moved on to Hampton Court where Wriothesley and senior members of the Privy Council greeted the French party. Four days were then spent hunting in pleasant pastime between the two former enemies. Each night there were lavish banquets and masques in two specially erected marquees, complete with boarded walls and windows of painted horn, decorated inside with rich hangings and filled with cupboards holding gold plate,

sumptuously decorated with jewels and pearls 'which shone richly'.[41]
The visitors were accommodated in a village of tents made of cloth of
gold, pitched in the palace gardens.[42]

On the first evening, after the feasting, Henry, with his lame legs, was
being supported by both Archbishop Cranmer and the French admiral.
To the utter surprise of d'Annebaut, Henry suddenly came out with far-
reaching proposals for the 'establishment of sincere religion' in both
England and France. They should 'change the Mass in both the realms
into a [Protestant] communion', said the king, and after Francis I had
publicly repudiated the supremacy of the pope, he and Henry should
demand that the Imperial Emperor Charles V should do the same 'or
else they would break off with him'.[43] Was Henry being devious, provoca-
tive or was he really now prepared to embrace Protestantism totally,
foreshadowing what would happen in England a few years later during
his son's short, iconoclastic reign? Was Henry, so often the instrument
of mass destruction in his own realm, now bent on a policy of destruction of the Mass? The Chantries Act, designed to seize the wealth of
religious charities, could possibly be construed as the opening shot in a
state attack on the Mass, although more likely it was designed solely
for fiscal benefit. The conversation, recounted later by Cranmer, has
caused debate and controversy ever since, particularly as it comes from
(and was reported by) such an obviously militant Protestant source.
Certainly, the evangelical party was now becoming more powerful at
court and increasingly had Henry's ear. Whilst this was probably not a
deliberate, rational policy on the king's part, perhaps it was a portent
that the religious conservatives were sometime soon to lose their authority and influence in the dark, sequestered little world of Henry's secret
royal apartments.

CHAPTER SEVEN

The Plot to Burn the Queen

'They curse and ban my words everyday
and all of their thoughts be set to do me
harm ... They watch my steps, how they may
take my soul in a trap ... They do beset my
way, that I should not escape.'

KATHERINE PARR, *PSALMS OR PRAYERS TAKEN OUT*
OF HOLY SCRIPTURE, MAY 1544.[1]

On the morning of Christmas Eve, 24 December 1545, Henry made what was to be his last speech to Parliament, during its prorogation,[2] until 4 November the following year, a task normally undertaken by Lord Chancellor Wriothesley. Given his declining health, many then believed that Henry might be making his final appearance in the House of Lords at Westminster. Henry was never a great public orator, far from the eloquent rabble-rouser that his daughter Elizabeth was to become. But his speech that cold day was surprisingly both measured and compelling, although apparently delivered without notes. He wanted to impart a stern message, not just for the ears of his legislators, but also for the far wider audience beyond the walls of Parliament. All his subjects were intended to hear and obey his words.

The king began by thanking his MPs for passing the cash-raising Chantries Bill into law – although this had earlier only narrowly escaped defeat at the last minute.[3] Henry sought to reassure any doubters amongst them about his planned sequestration of the ecclesiastical chantries and colleges. He solemnly pledged that he would not suffer the ministries of the Church to decay, education to be diminished or the needs of the poor to go unrelieved. No prince in the world, he said pompously, 'more favours his subjects than I do you, nor no subjects or commons more love and obey their sovereign lord than I perceive you do me.'

The polite niceties over, the king – standing painfully, and only with the aid of some Gentlemen of his Privy Chamber – moved on to the real reason for his being there: to deliver an articulate, sobering, chastising speech to his Lords spiritual and temporal and the Commons about the continuingly vexed issue of religion. Like a testy Victorian schoolmaster, he appealed for better order in the festering debate between devout conservative and radical evangelical reformer:

> My loving subjects: Study and take pains to amend one thing which surely is amiss and far out of order, to the which I most heartily require you which is that charity and concord is not amongst you but discord and dissensions beareth rule in every place.
>
> What love and charity is amongst you when the one calls the other heretic and Anabaptist and he calls him again papist, hypocrite and Pharisee?[4] Are these tokens of charity amongst you? Are these the signs of fraternal love between you?

Perhaps by now more than weary of the ceaseless wrangling between the religious factions within his court and the doctrinal conflicts and controversies throughout the realm, he moved his regal sights on to the bishops:

> I see and hear daily of you of the clergy who preach one against another; teach contrary to [one] another; inveigh one against another, without charity or discretion ... All men almost be in variety and discord and few or none preach truly and sincerely the word of God, according as they ought to. Alas! How can the poor souls live in concord when you preachers sow amongst them in your sermons

debate and discord? To you, they look for light and you bring them darkness.

Amend these crimes, I exhort you, and set forth God's word both by true preaching and good example giving.

Henry went on to add an ominous 'or else' – he was, after all, the supreme head of the Church of England and wherever and whenever he had seized power, he was never afraid to exercise it, remorselessly and pitilessly. It was time for a firm reminder to them all of the true and unchanging realities of the state they lived in:

I, whom God hath appointed his vicar and high minister here, will see these divisions extinct and those enormities corrected, according to my very duty, or else I shall be accounted an unprofitable servant and untrue officer.

The secular lords and MPs were also singled out for similar criticism:

You of the temporality be not clean and unspotted of malice and envy, for you rail on bishops, speak slanderously of priests and rebuke and taunt preachers, both contrary to good order and Christian fraternity.

If you know surely that a bishop or preacher ... teaches perverse doctrine, come and declare it to some of our Council or to us, to whom is committed by God the high authority to reform and order such causes and behaviour and be not judges of your own fantastical opinions and vain expositions for in such high cases you may lightly err.

Although you are permitted to read Holy Scripture, and to have the Word of God in your mother tongue, you must understand that you have this licence only to inform your own conscience and to instruct your children and family and not to dispute and make Scripture a railing and a taunting stock against priests and preachers as many light persons do.

The king was also deeply shocked by the way in which the Word of God was being misused by all and sundry:

I am very sorry to know and hear how irreverently that most precious jewel, the Word of God is disputed, rhymed, sung and jangled in every alehouse and tavern, contrary to the true meaning and doctrine of the same.

It was really time for Parliament and realm finally to forget their religious differences:

For of this I am sure: that charity was never so faint amongst you and virtuous and godly living was never less used nor God himself amongst Christians never less reverenced, honoured or served.

Therefore, as I said before, be in charity one with another, like brother and brother. Love, dread and serve God (to which I, as your supreme head and sovereign lord, exhort and require you) and then I doubt not the love and league ... shall never be dissolved or broken between us.[5]

Even the king's own officials were taken aback by his articulacy and passion, which reportedly reduced many to tears, although some at least were comforted by the session ending shortly before noon, allowing time for many members to ride home in time for the Christmas celebrations. Sir William Petre, appointed Privy Councillor and secretary the year before, wrote enthusiastically about the speech to his colleague Sir William Paget, Henry's other secretary of state, then away on diplomatic duties in France. It was given, he said, with gravity,

so sententiously, so kingly, or rather fatherly, as peradventure[6] to you that have been used to his daily talks should have been no great wonder ... but to us, that have not heard him so often, was such a joy and marvellous comfort as I reckon this day one of the happiest of my life.

The toadying Paget thanked him for sending him a copy of 'the most godly, wise and kingly oration', which he would have given anything to hear personally – even eating fish every day for a year, the food he hated so much.[7] Emotion would have overcome him, too, if he had been present: 'I am sure my eyes would largely have uttered the affections of my heart.' He adds: 'Our Lord save him, good king, and make his subjects good.'

Prosaically, the always businesslike Paget ends his letter with the postscript: 'If we come not home shortly, you must help us with more money.'

The leader of the conservative faction in Henry's council, Gardiner, Bishop of Winchester, was abroad in January 1546 on diplomatic duties, tasked with cementing England's rickety alliance with the imperial emperor, Charles V. Cranmer, after some discussions with Henry, had decided to take advantage of Gardiner's absence to sweep away some of the last vestiges of ritual surviving from the unreformed religion – the giant veil that shrouded church chancels during Lent, the congregation's creeping to the cross on Good Fridays and the pealing of church bells during the nocturnal vigil of All-Hallows. He carefully drafted a letter for the king to send to Gardiner, describing the new policy, which was read out to Henry in his Privy Chamber late one afternoon by Sir Anthony Denny. The king abruptly stopped him with a sharp, 'I am now otherwise resolved.' Henry then brusquely ordered:

Send my lord of Canterbury word that since I spoke with him about these matters, I have received letters from my lord of Winchester ... and he writes plainly to us that the league [with Spain] will not prosper nor go forward if we make any other innovation, change or alteration, either in religion or ceremonies.[8]

There could be no gainsaying, no argument against this sudden change of Henry's mind. Gardiner, although overseas, was still clearly well informed about events at court. He had cleverly stymied Cranmer, playing the diplomatic card to halt further reforms. The king's mercurial decision heralded a period of six months when Gardiner's party held almost total sway in the desperate infighting for supremacy amongst Henry's Council.

The religious conservatives had reached the zenith of their power within the court when they hatched an audacious plot to strike at the very heart of the king's world: his loving wife and companion, Queen Katherine Parr, who by January 1546 was leaning more and more towards the reformist religion. In July of that year, van der Delft reported conversations he had had with Gardiner and Paget,

> whom I found very favourable to the public good and to the interests of his majesty [Charles V]. As these are the councillors most in favour with the king, I doubt not that they will be good instruments for maintaining the existing friendship and for preventing the protestants [sic] from gaining footing or favour here. [The bishop and Paget] have confidently promised this.[9]

The queen, her Privy Chamber full of women with voluble and dangerous evangelical opinions, became the target of a conspiracy, probably stage-managed by the Bishop of Winchester and involving Norfolk, Paget, Wriothesley and the perjured Sir Richard Rich. Katherine's ladies had long been perpetual thorns in the sides of the conservatives. The lively and irrepressible Katherine, Duchess of Suffolk, the last wife of the late Charles Brandon, even kept a pet dog at court mischievously named 'Gardiner', which she teased and taunted outrageously in public. This time, sexual misconduct was not a viable means by which to entrap the queen, a lady of well-known propriety and impeccable morals. Heresy looked to be the best bet – and as a possible 'plan B', they also sought to use Norfolk's daughter, the Duchess of Richmond, as another *femme fatale* to seduce the king's affections away from Katherine. But first the conspirators had to soften up their prime target.

Their plot initially manifested itself as a widespread whispering campaign against Henry's consort. On 27 February, van der Delft wrote to Charles V:

> I hesitate to report that here are rumours of a new queen. Some attribute it to the sterility of the present Queen while others say there will be no change during the present war.
>
> Madame Suffolk is much talked about and in great favour but the king shows no alteration in his demeanour to the queen although she is said to be annoyed at the rumours.[10]

On 7 March, Stephen Vaughan, Henry's financial agent in Antwerp, wrote to Wriothesley and Paget that

> This day came to my lodging a High Dutch, a merchant of this town, saying he had dined with certain friends, one of whom offered to lay a wager with him that the king's majesty would have another wife and he prayed me to show him the truth.
>
> He would not tell who offered the wager and I said; 'that I never heard of any such thing and that I was sure that there was no such thing.'
>
> Many folks talk of this matter and from whence it comes I cannot learn.[11]

Gardiner, perhaps significantly, was in Antwerp that day[12] on his way back from diplomatic discussions with the emperor in Utrecht. The rumours were spreading like wildfire. Cornelius Sceppurus, a member of the emperor's Council, coyly wrote to Dr Louis Schore, President of the Council of Flanders, from London on 6 April:

> I dare not write the rumours current here with regard to the feminine sex. Some change is suspected to be pending.[13]

Katherine felt increasingly under threat: in February, she ordered secure coffers and boxes for her private apartments with new locks to prevent any unauthorised prying into her papers.[14] Some of her more controversial religious books were hidden in her garderobe (toilet) and others smuggled out of the palace and into the safekeeping of her uncle at his house in Horton, Northamptonshire.[15] She was prudent: the conspirators' net was drawing in around her. A later Protestant writer claimed that the hunt for heretics within the court that summer 'grew exceeding hot. [As there were] many men and women that stood well affected to religion, it was thought expedient for a terror to the rest to begin with them'.[16]

One of the first to be ensnared was Norfolk's second son, the reformist Lord Thomas Howard. He was dragged before the Privy Council on 7 May, charged with 'disputing indiscreetly of Scripture with other young gentlemen of the court'[17] and offered mercy if 'he would confess what he said in disproof of sermons preached in court last Lent and his other talk in the Queen's chamber.' He escaped with a stern adjuration to reform his ways.

Gardiner's pack was in full cry by the early summer of 1546, still spreading rumours of the queen's imminent downfall. Richard Worley, a page of the pallet chamber, was sent to prison for his 'unseemly reasoning of the Scripture' and the hunt cornered the fashionable preacher Dr Edward Crome in June. He had given a sermon at the Mercers' Chapel in London two months before in which he denied the reality of Purgatory and had been ordered to recant at Paul's Cross. This he refused but later faced the agonies of indecision. The London merchant Otwell Johnson sarcastically wrote to his brother in Calais:

> Our news here [is] of Dr Crome's canting, recanting, decanting or rather double canting.[18]

Dr William Huicke, probably a relation of Henry's physician Robert Huicke, was arrested for his support of Crome, as was John Lassels, a sewer of the Privy Chamber who, five years earlier, had provided the damning information to Cranmer about Katherine Howard's teenage depravity.

The minor poet and evangelical Sir George Blagge, one of Henry's cronies, was also detained in Newgate and sentenced at the Guildhall to be burnt after being accused of heresy by Sir Hugh Caverley and a man called Littleton. But Blagge was freed through the personal intervention of the outraged king. Henry remonstrated with Wriothesley over his arrest – 'for coming so near to him, even to his Privy Chamber'. The Lord Chancellor then quickly pardoned Blagge, who laboured under the king's nickname of 'my pig'. When Henry next saw him, he called out: 'Ah, my pig! Are you safe again?' Blagge, bowing low, replied: 'Yes, sire. And if your majesty had not been better to me than your bishops, your pig had been roasted ere this time.'[19]

On 18 June, Henry Hobberthorne, Lord Mayor of London, arraigned Anne Askew, or Ascough, for preaching against the 'Real Presence' in the wafers and wine of the Mass. She had already been in trouble in London the previous year over the same issue, when she lived in The Temple, on the city's western edge. The then mayor, Sir Martin Bowes (who, as one of the sheriffs, had wretchedly presided over the execution of Robert Barnes in 1540), had questioned her but had been confounded by her wit and knowledge:

> *The Mayor*: You foolish woman. Do you say that the priests cannot make the Body of Christ?
>
> *Anne Askew*: I say so, my lord, for I have read 'God made man,' but that man can make God I [have] never yet read, nor, I suppose, ever shall read it.
>
> *Mayor*: After the words of consecration is it not the Lord's body?
>
> *Askew*: No, it is but consecrated bread or sacramental bread.
>
> *Mayor*: What if a mouse eat it after the consecration? What shall become of the mouse? What say you, you foolish woman? I say that mouse is damned.
>
> *Askew*: Alack, poor mouse![20]

She had been set free then, but was now again accused of heresy after the interception of a letter she had written.[21] Anne, aged twenty-five and an 'elegant beauty and rare wit', had been thrown out of her Lincolnshire home by her incompatible older husband Thomas Kyme for her vocal and unorthodox religious views. The Jesuit Robert Parsons wrote four decades later that she 'was a coy dame and of very evil fame for wantonness' and had

> gad[ded] up and down the country, gospelling and gossiping where she might and ought not. This for diverse years before her imprisonment; but especially she delighted to be in London near the court.[22]

In the Tower, her investigation began on 29 June, conducted by Wriothesley, Rich and Sir John Baker, now Chancellor of the Exchequer, with questions about Queen Katherine's ladies-in-waiting. In papers smuggled out of prison, Anne described the interrogation:

'They asked me [about] my lady of Suffolk, my lady of Sussex,[23] my lady of Hertford,[24] my lady Denny and my lady Fitzwilliams.'[25]

Being further pressed to state from whom she had received relief whilst in prison, on their saying there were diverse ladies who had sent her money, she admitted 'that there was a man in a blue coat which delivered me ten shillings and said that my lady of Hertford sent it me and another in a violet coat gave me eight shillings and said my lady Denny sent it me.

'Whether it were true or no, I cannot tell, for I am not sure who sent it to me, but as the men did say.'

Then they asked, 'Were there [any] of the [Privy] Council that did maintain me?' And I said, 'No.'[26]

She deftly sidestepped their questions or bravely refused point blank to answer. In desperate frustration, Wriothesley and Rich sent for Sir Anthony Knyvett, Lieutenant of the Tower, and ordered him to put her on the rack to be tortured to extract the truth. Very unwillingly, Knyvett had her strapped to the machine and told his men just to 'pinch' her, as a sharp warning to tell all. The questions still went unanswered and he was told to use the machine to stretch her body agonisingly further. Knyvett refused, maintaining rightly that racking a woman was illegal even under Henry's harsh penal laws.

Angrily, Wriothesley and Rich stripped off their gowns and them-selves turned the windlasses controlling the ropes of the rack, tearing her muscles and sinews and cracking her bones. Anne's account of her torture is both graphic and horrific:

Because I confessed no ladies nor gentlewomen to be of my opinion, they kept me [on the rack] a long time. And because I lay still and did not cry, my Lord Chancellor and master Rich took pains to rack me [with] their own hands till I was nigh dead.

Knyvett insisted that she should be released.

I immediately swooned and then they recovered me again. After that, I sat two long hours reasoning with my Lord Chancellor upon the bare floor, where he with many flattering words, persuaded me to leave my opinion. But my Lord God gave me grace to persevere and will do (I hope) to the very end.

The Lieutenant of the Tower, disgusted at her treatment, took a boat to Westminster and informed the king of the woman's torture. 'When the king had understood, he seemed not very well to like their extreme handling of the woman' and pardoned Knyvett.[27] (The Jesuit Parsons, however, later claimed that the king himself had caused Anne Askew to be racked to find out if she had talked with his queen and 'corrupted' the Duchess of Suffolk.)

Henry, always interested in theology, frequently had conversations with his wife about religious matters. In late June or early July, she went too far in her disputation and her arguments irritated the king, who was already feeling depressed and too unwell to go to Mass or to limp too often around the Privy Gardens of his Palace of Westminster. After she retired to bed, Henry turned to Gardiner, who was conveniently present, and snapped crossly:

A good hearing it is when women become such clerks [scholars] and a thing much to my comfort to come in my old days to be taught by a woman![28]

Here was the bishop's chance to strike. He murmured in the king's ear that the queen's views were heresy under law and that

he with others of his faithful councillors, could, within a short time, disclose such treasons cloaked with this heresy that his majesty would easily perceive how perilous a matter it is to cherish a serpent within his own bosom.[29]

Henry himself must have signed the warrant for Katherine's arrest. Probably by 4 July, the charges against her had been drawn up. On 8 July, a proclamation was issued prohibiting the possession of heretical books, to provide some legal basis for the jaws of the trap about to snap shut on Katherine.

Then the king's innate cunning came into play.

He confided details of the planned arrest to one of his doctors, probably Thomas Wendy. A copy of the arrest warrant was conveniently dropped by one of his Councillors in a corridor of the queen's apartments. Katherine, who had taken to her bed ill, knew quickly about the plot against her.

Her naked panic can only be imagined.

Was she to follow Anne Boleyn and Katherine Howard to become yet another of Henry's slaughtered queens? Only this time, her end would come on top of her own funeral pyre, at the stake. When the king came to see her,

> she uttered her grief, fearing lest his majesty had taken displeasure with her and had utterly forsaken her. He, like a loving husband, with sweet and comfortable words, so refreshed and appeased her careful mind that she began to recover.[30]

Despite his soothing words, Katherine knew full well after the fatal experiences of her unhappy predecessors as royal consort that simply throwing herself on Henry's mercy would not save her from execution. To Henry, an abject apology or appeals for clemency were tantamount to complete surrender – an admission of legal culpability. That evening, probably 13 July, she went to the king's bedchamber, accompanied by her sister Anne Herbert and preceded by the nine-year-old Lady Jane Grey, carrying a candle.

Henry deliberately began to talk again about religion. She snatched her chance. The queen said she was 'but a poor silly woman, accompanied by all the imperfections natural to the weakness of her sex'. She would defer her judgement 'in this, in all other cases, to your majesty's wisdom, as my only anchor, supreme head and governor here on earth, next unto God, to lean unto'.

Henry maliciously toyed with her. 'Not so, by St Mary,' he said pointedly. 'You are become a doctor, Kate, to instruct us (as we take it) and not to be instructed or directed by us.' Shrewdly, she recognised this as the all-important test. She both flattered him and humbled herself:

If your majesty take it so, then has your majesty very much mistaken me, for I have always held it preposterous for a woman to instruct her lord. If I have presumed to differ with your highness on religion it was partly to obtain information for my own comfort regarding nice points on which I stood in doubt.[31]

Katherine discussed such matters

not only to the end your majesty might with less grief pass over this painful time of your infirmity, being attentive to our talk and hoping that your majesty should reap some ease thereby. Also that, hearing your majesty's learned discourse, might receive to myself some profit thereby.

A grimace, masquerading as a smile, spread across Henry's bloated features. 'And is it even [so] sweetheart? And tended your arguments to no worse end? Then perfect friends are we now, as ever any time heretofore.'[32] With that, he pulled her into his arms and tenderly kissed her.

She was safe.

But one last scene remained to be played out in this tight little human drama. The next afternoon, Henry and Katherine were sitting in the Privy Gardens with three of her ladies – Anne Herbert, Lady Tyrwhitt and Lady Jane Grey. He appeared 'as pleasant as ever he was in all his life before' but his mood changed swiftly as Wriothesley, with an escort of forty halberdiers, entered the gardens and marched up to the royal party. The Lord Chancellor had come at the appointed hour to arrest the queen and her ladies. Henry pulled Wriothesley aside and he fell on his knees before the king and reminded him of the arrangements he had previously agreed. An angry Henry shouted: 'Arrant knave! Beast and fool!' and some later reports said he cuffed the Lord Chancellor around the head. With an imperious sweep of his hand, he ordered him to 'avaunt [leave] my sight'. He turned his back on the thoroughly confused Wriothesley, who was forced to make an embarrassed exit, accompanied by the steady tread of his guards following him. Katherine, watching the scene with some relief, tried to calm the still angry king. 'Ah my poor soul,' said Henry, 'you little know how evil he deserves this grace at your hands. Oh, my word, sweetheart. He has been towards thee, an arrant knave and so let him go.'[33]

During the remainder of the year Henry showered gifts of jewellery, furs and clothes upon Katherine, 'his dearest wife', in an attempt to reassure her of his continuing fondness and high regard.

On 16 July, Anne Askew was executed at Smithfield, together with Lassels, Nicholas Belenian – a priest from Shropshire, and John Adams – a tailor, all accused of heresy. She had to be taken there in a chair, carried by two sergeants, as she could not walk because of the 'great torments ... she suffered on the rack'. She had to sit in the chair, bound to the stake. A small gunpowder charge hidden within the faggots exploded after the fire was lit, bringing her sufferings to an end.

CHAPTER EIGHT

Protestants Ascendant

'As long as King Henry lived, no man could do me hurt.'

LETTER FROM STEPHEN GARDINER
TO THE DUKE OF SOMERSET, JUNE 1547.[1]

The collapse of the devious and audacious plot against the queen left the conservative faction at Henry's court in disarray and only too vulnerable to royal retribution. Gardiner himself was shortly to taste the king's displeasure. Henry had always mistrusted this egotistical but talented churchman and might have 'used extremity against him' if his own life had not been rapidly running out. But Henry believed he could always exercise a degree of power over the testy bishop because he possessed secret, and probably damning, information that held the key to Gardiner's obedience or, more likely, would justify a timely charge of treason against him. Perhaps to reassure himself of that hold, the king several times asked Paget 'for a certain writing touching the said bishop, commanding him to keep it safe, that he might have it when he called for it'.[2] What this weapon was can only be a matter of prurient conjecture, as no such document has yet been discovered.

Gardiner was born around 1483 in Bury St Edmunds, Suffolk, educated at Trinity Hall, Cambridge, and subsequently trained as a lawyer. He started his long career in government as secretary to Wolsey, but after the cardinal's downfall he faithfully served the king up to 1534 in the same capacity and thereafter was employed on important diplomatic missions overseas. Although Gardiner had supported the difficult question of Henry's supremacy over the Church in England – writing a lengthy oration, *De verá Obedientiá* (The True Obedience), in favour of secular or princely control of religion in 1535 – the latest evangelical reforms in doctrine led him into direct and successful conflict with Cromwell and Cranmer and, later – disastrously for him – the Seymours and John Dudley, Viscount Lisle.

A portrait of the bishop at Hardwick Hall, near Chesterfield, Derbyshire, shows an image of a man with a double chin and full, almost sensual lips, the eyes staring out of the painting directly and inquisitively. His quick anger – his 'sanguinary temper' – was notorious for its vitriol and fire. Gardiner's successor at the see of Winchester, the staunchly Protestant John Ponet who was Cranmer's chaplain before 1547 and thus clearly no friend to Gardiner, described him as having frowning brows, deep-set eyes, a 'nose hooked like a buzzard' and 'great paws (like the devil)'.[3] Certainly, in Catholic Mary's reign when he became Lord Chancellor, Gardiner showed little mercy for those he saw as enemies of the state, whether political or religious. The seventeenth-century divine Thomas Fuller wrote of Gardiner: 'His malice was like ... white [gun] powder, which surely discharged the bullet, yet made no report, being secret in all his acts of cruelty.' Thomas Mowntayne, Protestant rector of St Michael Tower Royal in London, described a public bout of Gardiner's anger later on during Mary's reign. Mowntayne saw Gardiner riding with the queen and her husband King Philip through Cheapside on 26 August 1555, resplendent all in scarlet, blessing bystanders as he passed:

> He was greatly laughed to scorn. Gardiner [was] sore offended ... because the people did not put off their caps and make curtsey to the cross that was carried before ...
>
> [He said] to his servants: 'Mark that house,' 'Take this knave and have him ...'
>
> Such a sort of heretics he [n]ever saw that will neither

reverence the cross of Christ, no[r] yet once say so much as 'God save the king and queen.'

'I will teach them to do both, [as] I live.'[4]

That night, one of Gardiner's spies reported seeing Mowntayne watching the procession. 'Here he fell into a great rage, as was told to me by one of his own men, as was unseemly for a bishop, and with great speed sent for the knight marshal.' When he arrived, Gardiner asked him how he

handled himself in his office? Did I not send you one Mowntayne that was both a traitor and a heretic to this end that he should have suffered death? This day, the villain knave was not ashamed to stand openly in the street, looking the Prince [Philip] in the face. I would counsel you to look him up and that there be diligent search made for him this night in the city, as you will answer before the Council.

In his book *A Detection of the Devil's Sophistry*, first published in 1546, the bishop railed against the Anabaptists and the Sacramentarians who

have with devilish pertinacity manifested their heresies, whose wilful death in obstinacy, if it could serve as an argument to prove the truth of their opinion, the truth of God's Scripture should be brought into much perplexity.

If such as lately suffered ... there may appear tokens sufficient ... to declare their zeal not to have proceeded of the spirit of God, but of arrogant pride and presumption and the spirit of the devil.[5]

Later in the book, Gardiner recalls with some nostalgia the days when the realm lived in 'faith, charity and devotion, when God's word dwelt in men's hearts and never came abroad to walk in men's tongues'. Now, says the bishop scornfully, 'jesters, railers, rhymers, players, jugglers, prattlers and simpering parrots take upon them to be the administrators and officers to set forth God's word'. We shall see later that Gardiner did not have much patience with actors anyway, but his book was widely circulated 'and received in many places more reverently than the blessed Bible' amongst the still largely conservative population.

One letter the bishop wrote later, on the evening of 11 February 1554 to Sir William Petre, graphically illustrates his ruthless and uncompromising determination to root out treason. In the immediate aftermath of Sir Thomas Wyatt's failed uprising against Mary that month, a number of prisoners were captured and interrogated. Gardiner writes from Southwark:

> Tomorrow at the Tower be earnest with little [Edward] Wyatt,[6] prisoner there, who may tell all.
>
> He is a bastard and has little substance.
>
> It might stand with the Queen's pleasure were no account made whether you pressed him by sharp punishment or promise of life.

These words would send a chill down anyone's spine. 'Sharp punishment' is a phrase that leaves little to the imagination regarding what Gardiner was urging Wyatt to be subjected to in the dark, sweat-soaked rooms beneath the Tower. The words resound coldly like a metal torture instrument dropped on the stone-flagged floor.

But for Gardiner, possession of such life-or-death power lay some years in the future, after the return of England to Catholicism under Mary. Now he and his fellow conservatives faced the reformers' determination to seize political supremacy as Henry's life drew inexorably to a close.

To his great chagrin, Sir Thomas Heneage, Chief Gentleman of the Privy Chamber and Groom of the Stool, was suddenly ousted in October 1546 after a decade in the post and twenty years' faithful service to the king. Denny succeeded him and William Herbert, brother-in-law to the queen, took over the number-two position in the Privy Chamber. The reformist party had now grasped all the levers of power within the court.

Gardiner's own sudden, catastrophic fall came as a result of a simple misunderstanding about an exchange of episcopal land, which was quickly exploited by his waiting enemies. Henry, always obsessively keen to acquire choice lands, wanted the property to tidy up the boundaries of one of his many royal estates but was refused. In this unwise decision, Gardiner was too confident of his good standing with the king, but later scented a strong whiff of royal displeasure in the unexpected denial to him of access to the Privy Chamber. A probably apocryphal story relates how the king spotted Gardiner lurking amongst his fellow Councillors at Windsor.

When Henry saw him, he turned to Wriothesley [and said:] 'Did I not command you that he should come no more among you?'

[The Lord Chancellor replied:] 'My lord of Winchester has come to wait upon your highness with the offer of a benevolence [a voluntary tax] for the clergy.'

Mollified by the prospect of cash flowing into his coffers, the king accepted the offer.[7] But still the bishop was excluded from court. Gardiner wrote respectfully to the king from London on 2 December 1546:

having had no opportunity to make humble suit to your highness' presence as the trouble of my mind enforces me, I am so bold to molest your majesty with these my letters.

Gardiner desired 'a continuance of favour' and had always valued the benefits given to him by the king:

If for want of circumspection, my doings or sayings be otherwise taken in this matter of lands wherein I was spoken with, I must and will lament my own infelicity and most humbly, on my knees, desire your majesty to pardon it.

I never said 'nay' ... to resist your highness' pleasure, but only ... to be a suitor to your highness' goodness, as emboldened by the abundance of your majesty's favour heretofore shown to me.[8]

He adds:

Because I have no access to your majesty, no hearing of late any more of this matter, I cannot forebear to open truly my heart to your highness with a most humble request to take the same in the most gratuitous part.

Suspecting that this letter would inevitably be intercepted by his reformist enemies in the Privy Chamber, he also wrote to Paget, begging him to deliver his letters personally to Henry and seeking permission to come to court to see the king himself, as 'I have no access' to the Privy Chamber:

I hear no speciality of the king's majesty's discontentment in this matter of lands but confusedly, that my doings are not well taken and [I] am sorry, for I care only for this, that it should be thought I wanted discretion, to neglect the king's majesty's goodness towards me, which, as you know, I ever esteemed only and thereupon made my worldly foundation. I pray you send me some word.[9]

It is clear that the king did safely receive Gardiner's letters, but his earnest pleas did him no good. Unknown to him, Paget, his erstwhile ally, had suddenly turned against him. Henry, then staying at Otelands, was swift and brutal in his response on 4 December:

Had your doings ... been agreeable to such fair words as you have now written in your letters of the 2nd., you should neither [have] had cause to write this excuse nor we to answer it.

But we marvel at your writing that you never said 'nay' to any request for those lands, considering that to our chancellor [Wriothesley], secretary [?Petre] and chancellor of our court of augmentations [Sir Edward North], both jointly and apart, you utterly refused any conformity, saying that you would make your answer to our own person.[10]

A Henry thwarted in his designs, particularly over his relentless acquisition of property, was a dangerous, malevolent king. He did not mince his words: 'We see no cause why you should molest us further' – a phrase that has a note of awful finality. Significantly, perhaps, his letter was signed by means of the royal dry stamp, duly witnessed by Denny and Gates, and thus the bishop, rightly or wrongly, detected a plot against him by his enemies, spelt out in the letter's sharp, uncompromising words of rejection.

But proud Gardiner could not bring himself to quit the precincts of the Palace of Westminster. To do so would be to admit that he had fallen from the king's grace. Shamefaced, he loitered miserably in the outer chambers near the king's secret apartments, waiting for the summons into the royal presence that never came. He listened to the whispers and the gossip of the court as he impotently watched the comings and goings of those on official business. He made a point of leaving the palace in the company of more favoured courtiers in a pathetic attempt to maintain the public image of his continued power and influence. The bishop could not acknowledge that he had been out-manoeuvred and effectively neutralised, probably by Hertford and Dudley.

The tensions between the two factions in the king's Council had been rising throughout 1546, culminating a few weeks before with Dudley angrily striking Gardiner full in the face during a torrid, ill-tempered Privy Council meeting,[11] a blow that caused the admiral 'trouble and danger' from the king, who always condemned violence within his court precincts.[12] However, the tide of royal disfavour had turned and Dudley 'now seemed well received'. Shortly afterwards, there were also 'violent and injurious words' exchanged again between Dudley and Gardiner and by Hertford to Wriothesley.

Those who sought a Protestant succession – and with it the power, status and wealth attached to regency governing a malleable young boy on the throne – also had their sights firmly fixed on the powerful house of Howard, led by Gardiner's ally, the Duke of Norfolk. His sudden downfall was also not long in coming.

Norfolk's son Henry Howard, Earl of Surrey, is, like his father, an unattractive character to modern eyes. Surrey was arrogant, vain, impetuous, resentful of the merest slight discerned by him and, most of all, contemptuous of any who lived in, or came from, a lower station in life. He was an extraordinary paradox: a distinguished, sensitive, very talented poet, but also a rowdy hooligan and a proud coxcomb whose conceited behaviour and beliefs easily nettled those around him. The king, however, loved this 'most foolish proud boy [in all] England'[13] for in his youth, Surrey had spent two very happy years at Windsor at his lessons with Henry Fitzroy, Duke of Richmond, the king's bastard son, who later married Surrey's sister, Mary.[14] The two youths became great friends there, a relationship that later flourished during their further studies together in France. Surrey wrote a poem about one of their tennis matches, which were continually disrupted as they were distracted by the charms of young ladies watching them near by:

> The palm-play [15] where, despoiled for the game
> With dazzled eyes oft we by gleams of love
> Have missed the ball ...[16]

This hothead was inevitably often in trouble, even after his arranged marriage in 1532 to Frances de Vere, daughter of the Earl of Oxford, and the birth of a son, Thomas, on 10 March 1536.[17] Later that year, the nineteen-year-old was imprisoned at Windsor Castle for two weeks for striking Edward Seymour, then Viscount Beauchamp, in the face within the precincts of the royal court after Seymour rashly suggested that Surrey was sympathetic to the cause of the Pilgrimage of Grace rebels in the North. An intervention by Cromwell prevented a worse punishment under court ordinances. That was not, however, the end of the earl's hot-tempered escapades. In July 1542, he recklessly challenged a member of the royal household, Sir John Leigh, to a duel and was again jailed, this time in the Fleet Prison, but was accompanied by two servants to look after him. He wrote to the Privy Council:

> I have of late severally required [from] each of you, by my servant
> Pickering, [indications] of your favour, from whom as yet I have
> received no other comfort than my past folly has deserved. I have yet
> thought it my duty again, as well as [to] renew my suit, as humbly

to require you rather to impute this error to the fury of reckless youth than to a will not conformable and contented of the just reward of my folly.[18]

He asked the Councillors to help restore the king's esteem for him, so that he could be freed

from this noisome prison, whose pestilent airs are not unlike to bring some alteration of health. If your good lordships judge me not a member rather to be clean cut away, than reformed; it may please you to be suitors to the king's majesty on my behalf, or else, at the least, if his pleasure be to punish this oversight with the forbearing of his pleasure (which unto every loving subject, specially unto me, from a prince cannot be less counted than a living death), yet it would please him to command me into the country, to some place of open air, with like restraint of liberty, there to abide his grace's pleasure.[19]

Surrey's flowing, honeyed words resulted in his freedom on 7 August, but only after his payment of the huge sum of £6,666 as a surety for future good behaviour ('to bridle my heady will') – more than £2,400,000 at today's prices. The 'grave heads' of the council were not fooled by his fluent, graceful phrases. Nor should they have been. After military service in Scotland, his next brush with royal authority came in February 1543, when he and a party of young, rich bucks, including Thomas Wyatt the Younger[20] and William Pickering, took part in 'a riot' in the City of London.

Armed with hunting crossbows firing pebbles, they drunkenly broke the windows of houses (including those of Sir Richard Gresham's home) and those of churches. From a rowing boat on the Thames, they amused themselves hugely by firing at the prostitutes plying their trade outside the brothels on seedy Bankside, in Southwark. Lord, what a lark! But it was a lark that once again brought Surrey, now aged twenty-six, to the attentions of the Privy Council following a complaint from the Lord Mayor of London, and they diligently rooted out a Mistress Millicent

Arundell of St Lawrence Lane, Cheapside, at whose house Surrey and his friends had spent the night of the riot. She testified

> that the earl of Surrey and other young noblemen frequented her house, eating meat in Lent and committing other improprieties. At Candlemas, they went out with stone bows at nine o'clock at night and did not come back till past midnight. The next day there was a great clamour [about] the breaking of many glass windows both of houses and churches and shooting at men that night in the street. And the voice [word] was these hurts were done by my lord and his company ...
>
> That night, or the night before, they used the same stone bows, rowing on the Thames and Thomas Clere told how they shot at the queans [whores] on the Bankside.[21]

Appropriately on 1 April, Surrey was hauled up before the Council at St James's Palace and charged with eating flesh during Lent and on Fridays and walking about the streets in a 'lewd and unseemly manner', firing the crossbows. In his defence, Surrey told them that he had a special licence to eat meat during the religious fast, but pleaded guilty to the second charge, saying lamely in mitigation that he only broke the windows of papists. Furthermore, he said, he was astonished at the licentious behaviour of the London citizens, which 'resembled the manners of Papal Rome in her corrupted state'. Typically, it was a justification of extraordinarily arrogant bravura but it did not wash with the Privy Council. Surrey found himself back in the Fleet Prison, where he passed the long hours by writing a poem, *A Satire Against the Citizens of London*, in which he reiterates that his unruly behaviour was designed purely to punish them for their many crimes:

> From justice rod no fault is free
> But that all such as work unright
> In most quiet, are next ill rest [sleeping]
> In secret silence of the night.
> This made me, with a reckless breast

Henry VIII portrayed in all his majesty, painted by Hans Holbein the Younger *c.*1537. A magnificent propaganda image with the monarch staring at us out of the canvas, daring us not to be humbled by his imperial presence. *www.bridgeman.co.uk / Walker Art Gallery, Liverpool*

RIGHT Henry VIII painted by an unknown artist, *c.*1542. Gone is the spry gallantry of Henry's youth and the splendour of Holbein's swaggering and domineering monarch. The king grasps a staff to help him walk, as he suffers from 'the worst legs in the world'. His weight has vastly increased as disease takes a firm grip on his body. *National Portrait Gallery, London*

OPPOSITE RIGHT Henry VIII and Will Somers, from the *King's Psalter*, written by John Mallard around 1540. The king sits in his chamber, playing the harp, melancholy and thoughtful. Old age, infirmity, pain and his bulk are sapping the royal strength and patience. Note the appearance of a hump on his back. *www.bridgeman.co.uk/ British Library /Roy 2 A XVI f.63v*

LEFT *Family of Henry VIII*, painted in 1545 by an unknown artist. The king is flanked by his heir, Edward, and the boy's mother, Jane Seymour, with the Princesses Mary and Elizabeth on each side. The two archways provide glimpses of the ornate Privy Gardens outside and frame the jester Will Somers, with a monkey on his shoulder, and a female figure, probably Jane, Mary's own fool. *The Royal Collection © 2004, Her Majesty Queen Elizabeth II*

patri **S** icut erat.

Dixit insipiẽs in corde suo nõ est Deꝰ or= rupti sũt

ABOVE Henry VIII in old age, engraved by Peter Isselburg in 1646, after an unknown sixteenth-century artist. This telling portrait shows Henry with a 'moon face', his shoulders hunched, his eyes cast left, suspicious and often doubtful of the loyalty and motives of those around him. *National Portrait Gallery, London*

OPPOSITE Edward VI as a boy, after William Scrots. The precocious nine-year-old was swiftly snatched and brought to London to be proclaimed king by Edward Seymour, leader of the small government of self-seeking men whom Henry left behind when he died. *www.bridgeman.co.uk/Richard Philp, London*

ABOVE Princess Elizabeth, aged thirteen and holding a book of devotions, painted by an unknown Flemish artist in 1546. She was unwittingly dragged into Thomas Seymour's plot to seize power in Edward's reign. There were unfounded rumours that she was 'in the Tower and with child by my Lord Admiral'. *The Royal Collection © 2004, Her Majesty Queen Elizabeth II*

OPPOSITE Princess Mary and Will Somers, holding a small dog, painted by Holbein *c.*1536. Mary was recalled to act as hostess at her father's palaces after the shameful scandal and death of Katherine Howard. *© Hulton Archive*

Anne of Cleves, painted in 1539 by Holbein. His demure portrait fooled
Henry into a wedding and even after their humiliating marriage and divorce,
Anne still nourished impossible hopes of reconciliation.
www.bridgeman.co.uk/Louvre

KATHARINE PARRE

Katherine Parr, by an unknown artist, *c.*1545. Her personal motto – 'To be useful in all I do' – has the ring of a sensible and practical Girl Guide captain, and made her the ideal candidate for Henry's sixth wife. But she was to fall foul of the plots and intrigues within the court and narrowly escaped arrest and probable execution for her religious beliefs. *National Portrait Gallery, London*

Of perfect rare sitens limbs a manly shape,
of nature framed to serve on sea or land,
of Trinities firm in every state, in ill hap
in peace faithe and in warre skill great bold hand
on horse on fote in peril or in playe
none coulde excel though many did essaye
A subiects true to Kinge in words and dede,
frind to Gods truth enimye to romes decree
surpluse aborad for honnor of the lande
temperate at home yet keepe great state in all
and gave more notable were meate
then some adwansd one higher state to stand
yet enmy nelwe rekon so iust leawes
his blood was spilt iustly without iust cauf

ABOVE Sir Thomas Seymour, later Lord High Admiral, by an
unknown artist. Henry's roguish rival for Katherine Parr's hand, he
married her within months of the king's death. The poem inscribed
on the portrait describes him as a rare person 'with strong limbs
and manly shape' who in war displayed 'skill great, bold hand on
horse, on foot in peril or in play, [which] none could excel...' No
wonder the matronly Katherine fell for his glamour, piratical good
looks and charm! *National Portrait Gallery, London*

OPPOSITE Thomas Howard, 3rd Duke of Norfolk, by Holbein.
Norfolk is holding the white staff of office as Lord High Treasurer of
England. A bluff, devious and ambitious man, he had the misfortune
of having two nieces beheaded after they became Henry's queens.
Henry's death saved him from the executioner's axe on charges of
treason. *The Royal Collection © 2004, Her Majesty Queen Elizabeth II*

LEFT Sir Anthony Denny, later Chief Gentleman of the Privy Chamber, painted at the age of twenty-nine in 1541. Denny was Henry's 'fixer' and later controlled all access to the monarch, as well as organising his personal finances. Truly, he was the power behind the throne. *Private Collection. Photograph: Photographic Survey, Courtauld Institute of Art*

ABOVE LEFT Archbishop Thomas Cranmer, painted in 1546 by Gerlach Flicke. On Henry's death, at two o'clock in the morning on 28 January 1547, he clambered up onto the great walnut bed to seek a sign that the king died in grace, secure in the faith of Christ. Henry was only able to squeeze his hand. Afterwards, Cranmer grew a beard as a mark of mourning for his dead king. *www.bridgeman.co.uk/National Portrait Gallery*

ABOVE RIGHT Stephen Gardiner, Bishop of Winchester, implacable opponent of many religious reforms. His successor as bishop, the staunch Protestant John Ponet, described him as having frowning brows, deep-set eyes, a 'nose hooked like a buzzard' and 'great paws (like the devil)'. His temper was notorious for its vitriol and fire. *National Trust Photographic Library/J.Whitaker*

To wake thy sluggards with my bow
A figure of the Lord's behest
Whose scourge for sin the Scriptures show
That as the fearful thunder's clap
By sudden flame at hand we know
Of pebble stones the soundless rap
The dreadful plague might make thee see
Of God's wrath, that doth thee enwrap.[22]

By May he was free again. His father, Norfolk, no doubt wanting him both out of the way and to dissipate his energies in more useful directions, in October sent him off to the wars in Europe to join the English and Spanish operations in the Low Countries. The Spanish Emperor Charles V was much taken with the poet-soldier, writing to Henry:

> As to what we have written in commendation of the son of our cousin the duke of Norfolk for his eagerness in learning the arts of war, he is shown such an excellent example of your men that he cannot fail to profit thereby.
>
> All of our side respect ... his person and deservedly so, the courage of the father and the noble nature of the son.[23]

He also distinguished himself during Henry's campaign in France, being badly wounded in an assault, under artillery fire, during the siege of Montreuil in 1544[24] and after convalescence in England, in September 1545 he succeeded his father as commander-in-chief of the English land and naval forces in France and captain of the captured town of Boulogne. His frequent, overly optimistic dispatches home impressed Henry, now back in England, with his courage and continually nurtured the king's hopes of both military glory and victory in France.

But Boulogne was an expensive place to defend, the exchequer was rapidly running out of money and Henry's hard-pressed Council in London were now anxiously seeking any method to abandon the town without losing face – or, more pertinently, without antagonising the glory-seeking king. Wily Norfolk warned his son:

Have yourself in await [beware] that you animate not the king too much for the keeping of Boulogne, for who so doth at length shall get small thanks. Look well to what answer you make to the letter from us of the council. Confirm not the enterprises contained in them.[25]

Surrey's martial fame was short-lived, however. On 7 January 1546, he intercepted a large French resupply force of 3,000 foot soldiers and 600 cavalry at St Etienne, near Boulogne, and was roundly defeated, largely through his own incompetence and impetuosity, losing fourteen of his captains amongst the 205 English dead (including his own second-in-command) and, shamefully, a number of standards or flags.[26] He instantly fell out of Henry's favour and two months later, when he wrote seeking permission for his wife to join him on campaign, he received a peremptory 'no' – the king pointing out, with some asperity, that 'time of service, which will bring some trouble and disquiet, [and] not meet for women's imbecilities, [now] approaches'.[27] On 21 March, he was relieved of his command as lieutenant-general and Captain of Boulogne, being replaced by the Earl of Hertford (the former Viscount Beauchamp) of all people. Sir William Paget, the king's secretary, wrote helpfully to Surrey:

The latter part of your letter, touching the intended enterprise of the enemy, gives me occasion to write to you, frankly, my poor opinion; trusting your lordship will take the same in no worse part than I mean it.

As your lordship wishes, so his majesty wants to do something for the damaging of the enemy and for that purpose has appointed to send over an army shortly and that my lord of Hertford shall be his highness' lieutenant general ... whereby I fear your authority ... shall be touched.[28]

Wise Paget urged Surrey to seek another appointment to regain Henry's favour:

In my opinion, you should do well to make sure by times to his majesty to appoint you to some place of service in the army, as to the captainship of the forward or rearward [forces] or to such place of honour as should be meet for you, for so should you be where knowledge and experience may be gotten. Whereby you should be better able hereafter to serve and also to have ... occasion to do some notable service in revenge of your men, at the last encounter with the enemies, which should be to your reputation in the world.[29]

The choice of Hertford as the new military supremo could not have been more unfortunate. Surrey had long nurtured a deep grudge against the Seymours, whom he regarded as hardly of noble blood and mere loud upstarts. This disdain had not prevented his earlier foolhardy attempts to woo, despite her vigorous objections, Anne Stanhope, wife of Sir Edward Seymour, then Viscount Beauchamp, now Earl of Hertford and a brother of the dead queen. This incident, which lay behind the unseemly fisticuffs at Windsor described earlier in this chapter, merely poured fuel on the fire of hatred burning deep within Surrey's heart, flames that were again fanned by Hertford's brother Thomas urging harsh punishment upon him when he came up before the Privy Council in 1543 for his nocturnal jolly japes in the streets and alleys of the City of London. To cap it all, after Hertford's appointment in France displacing Surrey, Hertford announced allegations against Surrey of corrupt misuse of office in Boulogne and immediately purged many of his appointees.[30] 'There are in Boulogne,' Surrey wrote, angrily denying the claims, 'too many witnesses that Henry of Surrey was never corrupted by personal considerations and that his hand never close[d] upon a bribe.' Those slights and prejudices were still uppermost in Surrey's mind and he rejected Paget's helpful advice and returned home in June 1546, vengeful and full of angry spleen.

But the Seymours struck first. Now or never, they had to make their bid for absolute power and finally eliminate the threat posed by the conservative faction at court, led by Norfolk and Surrey since Gardiner had been neutralised. It was the earl's scarcely suppressed ambition to become protector of Prince Edward after Henry's approaching death and to restore the nobility of England to its rightful place next to the throne that had to be smothered. With Henry ailing and his end clearly not far off, it was time to make a move, but still utilising the king's failing power and ruthlessness. As reformers, they were unlikely to use the charge of heresy to silence Surrey. The means was found in Sir Richard Southwell, an MP for Norfolk and former crony of Cromwell's, who told the Privy Council on 2 December that he had information about Surrey 'that touched his fidelity to the king'.

Why Henry acted so suddenly now against Surrey and Norfolk remains something of a mystery. A seventeenth-century writer pointed out that 'it was notorious how the king had not only withdrawn much of his wonted favour, but promised immunity to such as would discover anything concerning [Surrey]'.[31] Henry's desire to destroy him had become passionate and despite his deteriorating health, he took an avid personal interest in the proceedings against father and son (if not direct- ing them), sometimes from his sickbed. Possibly it was a combination of the veiled threat posed to the Tudor succession by the Howards' royal ancestors and the allegations that they would seek the regency of the kingdom after his death that stirred Henry's dark suspicions, awakened fears about what his young son would face after ascending to the throne and led him to listen attentively as the poisonous rumours were whis- pered in his sometimes fevered ear.

The inevitable arrest came a few days later. Henry 'very secretly' ordered Sir Anthony Wingfield, Captain of the Royal Guard, to seize Surrey as he was coming to the Palace of Westminster:

> The next day, after dinner, [Wingfield] saw the earl coming into the palace whilst he was walking in the great hall downstairs.
>
> He had a dozen halberdiers waiting in an adjoining corridor and approaching the earl, said: 'Welcome, my lord, I wish to ask you to intercede for me with the duke your father in a matter in which I need his favour, if you will deign to listen to me.'
>
> So he led him to the corridor and the halberdiers took him and without attracting notice put him into a boat.[32]

Surrey was taken to Ely Place, Wriothesley's house in Holborn, on the western edge of the city, for interrogation, initially about a letter written by him to a gentleman that was 'full of threats', according to Francis van der Delft, the Spanish ambassador. Southwell was also being held there – the hot-headed earl said he would fight him 'in his shirt' over his accusations – before Surrey was moved publicly through the streets, under close guard, to the Tower of London on Sunday 12 December. During that painful journey, his escort pushing aside the crowds, he was reported – understandably – to be 'much downcast'. Norfolk, who was out of London when Surrey was arrested, hastily wrote letters to Westminster to establish why his son had been taken into custody. These were naturally intercepted and closely scanned for possible evidence against him. He did not have long to wait for an answer. A death warrant was plainly writ large on the walls of the Tower for him, too.

Norfolk was duly summoned to court and later that Sunday also committed to the grim fortress on the eastern side of London. He was taken by river, after suffering the humiliation of his Garter insignia and white staff, or wand of office, as Lord High Treasurer being ceremoniously removed – ironically the same disgrace he had inflicted on Thomas Cromwell more than six years earlier. The duke 'both in the barge and on entering the Tower' publicly declared 'no person had ever been carried thither before who was a more loyal servant [of the king] than he was and always had been'. His vociferous pleas were politely noted but pointedly ignored.

The fall of the house of Howard had been very carefully planned, timed and executed. That same Sunday, between three and four in the afternoon, Henry's trusted courtiers – the brutish John Gates of the Privy Chamber and his brother-in-law Sir Wymond Carew – tellingly joined by a released Southwell, had departed London post-haste for Norfolk. Their mission was firstly to seek out damning evidence against father and son, and secondly the securing and careful listing of their possessions for later seizure by the crown. They arrived at Kenninghall, Norfolk's richly furnished home set in 700 acres of deer park, at daybreak on the Tuesday morning after a ride of about eighty miles via Thetford. Gestapo-like, they hammered on the doors of the sleeping household to gain admission to the great house. Their dawn arrival and their harsh, barked orders came as a terrible shock to the occupants: news of the incarcerations in the Tower had not yet reached Kenninghall. Gates reported to Henry that night:

> As the steward was absent taking musters, we called the almoner and first taking order for the gates and back doors, desired to speak with the Duchess of Richmond and Elizabeth Holland who were only just risen but came to us without delay in the dining chamber.

We can easily guess the horrified reaction of Surrey's sleepy sister and Norfolk's tousled, blowsy mistress at the sight of the mud-stained and armed men standing breathless before them in this dawn raid, determined to extract incriminating information.

> On hearing how the matter stood, the duchess was sore perplexed, trembling and like to fall down, but recovering, she reverently upon her knees humbled herself to the king, saying that although constrained by nature to love her father ... and her brother, which she noted to be a rash man, she would conceal nothing but declare in writing all she could remember.

Gates advised her to use truth and frankness in her answers and, rather disingenuously, not to despair. The three men then examined her coffers and closet 'but found nothing worth sending, all very bare and her jewels sold to pay her debts'. Norfolk's long-time mistress was a different matter, however.

> We then searched Elizabeth Holland and found girdles, beads, buttons of gold, pearls and rings set with many stones, whereof they are making a book [inventory].

'Trusty men' were sent on to other houses owned by the family in Norfolk and Suffolk 'to prevent embezzlement' and were told not to forget 'Elizabeth Holland's house, newly made'. The steward and almoner at

Kenninghall were made responsible for all the plate and 'such money as remains of his last account'.[33] In his next letter, Gates promised the king, he would report 'further of these matters and also of the duke's jewels and lands'. Tudor royal investigations were nothing if not thorough and searching.

Back in his room in the Constable's lodgings at the Tower, a puzzled, frightened and lonely Norfolk wrote a grovelling letter to Henry the day after his incarceration, on 13 December. He complained:

> Some great enemy has informed the king untruly, for God knows, he [Norfolk] never had one untrue thought against the king or his succession and can no more guess the charge against him than a child born that night.

The duke did not know against whom he had offended, 'unless it were such as are angry with me for being quick against such as have been accused for sacramentaries' (the religious radicals). And, whilst on the subject of religion,

> I have told your majesty and many others that knowing your virtue and knowledge, I shall stick to whatever laws you make and for this cause many have borne me ill will, as do appear by casting libels abroad against me.

Significantly, then, he believed that his sudden incarceration stemmed from his conservative religious beliefs.[34] Pathetically, Norfolk also begged that he should recover Henry's favour – the king could now take all his lands and possessions – and asked to be told of the charges he faced.

His early suspicions must have been confirmed by his initial inter-rogation, which focused on politico-religious issues. As for the pope, declared Norfolk,

> if I had twenty lives, I would rather have spent them all than he should have any power in this realm ... And since he has been the king's enemy, no man has felt and spoken more against him both here and in France and also to many Scottish gentlemen.[35]

The ghost of Cromwell and his horrible fate haunted the duke, sitting alone in the heart of the forbidding Tower: 'My lords, I trust you think Cromwell's service and mine are not [to] be like ... He was a false man and surely I am a true poor gentleman,' he told the Council. Time and again, Norfolk desperately repeated his plea to meet and face down his still unknown accusers, 'for I will hide nothing. Never gold was tried better than [by] fire and water than I have been'.

He conjured up in his lugubrious mind the faces of all his many enemies during the long, turbulent reign of Henry Tudor. There was Wolsey, who '[for] fourteen years [sought] to destroy me'; Cromwell, of course, his great adversary; Edward, Third Duke of Buckingham,[36] 'of all men living, he hated me the most'; Thomas Boleyn, Earl of Wiltshire, husband of his sister, who 'confessed the same and wished he had found means to thrust his dagger in me'. Then there was the 'malice borne me by both my nieces whom it pleased the king to marry', a malice remembered by those still in authority in the Tower.[37]

In a hastily scribbled letter, he plaintively protested his past loyalty to the crown:

Who tried out the falsehood of the Lord Darcy,[38] Sir Robert Constable,[39] Sir John Bulmer,[40] Aske[41] and many others – but only I?

Who showed his majesty the words of my mother-in-law[42] for which she was attainted of misprision – but I?

I have always shown myself a true man to my sovereign and, since these things done, have received more profits of his highness than before.

Who could now think that I should now be false?

Poor man as I am yet, I am his near kinsman. For whose sake should I be untrue?[43]

These are the frantic ramblings of a man still in shock and petrified by his numbing fear of the unknown – again, what exactly were the charges made against him? Who was accusing him? What was the evidence?

Unknown to Norfolk at this stage, it was not heresy that had undone him: treason was the steely weapon of choice for his determined enemies, the Seymours, uncles to young Prince Edward. Surrey, for his part, was still naïvely unaware of the seriousness of the conspiracy against him. In a letter to the Privy Council written from the Tower, he protested about 'mine old father brought in[to] question by any stir between South-well and me'. Norfolk's arrest, he complained, 'sore enfeebled me'.[44]

Henry's case against the Howards became clear when Wriothesley sent a message to van der Delft on 16 December, disclosing that the cause of Norfolk and his son's imprisonment 'was that they planned by sinister means to obtain the government of the king, who was too old now to allow himself to be governed' and

> their intention was to usurp authority by means of the murder of all members of the council and the control of the prince [Edward] by them alone.[45]

The government's propaganda machine grew still more vocal. Nicholas Wotton, the English ambassador to the court of the French king, told Francis I of the 'most execrable and abominable intent and enterprise' of Norfolk and Surrey. Francis replied simply that if their guilt was clearly proved, they should both be put to death.[46] The courts of Europe were stunned by news of the arrests. Thomas Thirlby, Bishop of West-minster, on a diplomatic mission at the court of Charles V, wrote to Paget on 25 December of

> those two ungracious and inhuman *non homines*,[47] the Duke of Norfolk and his son, of whom I did confess that I did love, for I ever supposed him a true servant to his master. Before God, I am so amazed.[48]

There is a romantic story, from only one source, of Surrey attempt-ing an escape from the Tower, involving a break-out from his privy window, arming himself with a dagger smuggled to him by his servant Martin and climbing out of the window of a room overlooking the Thames, where a boat was waiting in St Katherine's Dock. But accord-ing to the writer – Antonio de Guaras, a Spanish merchant in London at the time – the earl was surprised by his guards and recaptured.[49]

The legal proceedings for Surrey's downfall gathered momentum.[50] Lord Chancellor Wriothesley was once a staunch ally of Norfolk but, like Paget, after sensing the shift in political power at court, had almost overnight become a resolute enemy. He changed and counter-changed the main thrust of the indictments as the evidence was pieced together, much of it mere hearsay hardly worthy of the name. But there was still plenty of damning information to be garnered and evaluated. Mistress Arundell, a central character in Surrey's drunken escapades of 1543, had told of conversations in her household when the earl stayed there that now seemed very incriminating indeed:

> Once, when my lord of Surrey was displeased about buying of cloth, she told her maids in the kitchen how he fumed and added, 'I marvel they will thus mock a prince.'
>
> 'Why,' said Alice, her maid, 'is he a prince?'
>
> 'Yes, marry he is, and if aught should come at the king but good, his father should stand for king.'
>
> Another maid, Joan Whetnall, 'talking with her fellow touching my lord of Surrey's bed, she said the arms were very like the king's.'[51]

No doubt this testimony was triumphantly retrieved from the Privy Council's files and added to the pile of evidence lying before Wriothesley.

Surrey's embittered sister also recounted how he had vilified the Seymours and 'these new men [who] loved no nobility and if God called away the king, they should smart for it'. Norfolk's mistress 'Bess' Holland also related how her lover had complained that few on the Privy Council loved him 'because they were no noblemen born themselves' and how he had forecast the demise of the ailing Henry. Sir Gawen Carew described a very public row between Surrey and his sister in the Long Gallery of the Palace of Westminster over his violent opposition to her planned marriage to Thomas Seymour, which he objected to because of Seymour's supposed low birth. Surrey suggested, said the witness, that she should come to court to 'delight the king' with her body, so that she could control him as Madame d'Estampes, Francis I's mistress, governed the French king, which should not only be a means to help herself but all her friends should receive a commodity by the same. Whereupon she defied her brother and said that they all should perish and she would cut her own throat rather than she would consent to such a villainy.[52]

Edward Rogers told the investigators of an argument between the earl and his friend George Blagge, one of Henry's favourites and a notorious religious reformer, about a regency to govern England during Prince Edward's minority, after the king's death:

The earl held that his father was meetest, both for good services done and for estate.

Blagge replied that then the prince should be but evil taught and in multiplying words, said, 'Rather than it should come to pass that the prince should be under the government of your father or you, I would bide the adventure to thrust this dagger into you.'

The earl said he was very hasty.[53]

Sir Edmund Knyvett[54] was another eager witness. He had told Surrey that 'because of his father's and his unkindness I would go from my country and dwell there and wait, so unable to bear their malice'. The earl had contemptuously replied: 'No, no, cousin Knyvett, I malice not so low; my malice is higher – my malice climbs higher.' He repeated: 'These new erected men would, by their wills, leave no noble man in life.'

Surrey himself was interrogated in the Tower, and the list of twenty-three sharp questions that were put to him by the Privy Council still survives. The devious Wriothesley drafted the 'interrogatories' personally and their content shows that the royal hounds were firmly on the scent of their hapless quarry, based on the evidence already gathered. These questions included: 'If the king should die in my lord prince's tender age, whether you have devised who should govern him and the realm?' This had been amended from the original: 'Who ought, within the realm, to be protector and governor of him during nonage [minority]?' More pointedly: 'Whether you have said that in such case you or your father would have the rule and governance of him, or words to that effect?' Another – 'whether you procured any person ... with the intent the same might grow [in the king's] favour for the better encompassing of your purposes' – had been altered from 'procuring your sister or any other woman to be the king's concubine'. In those long, hard days for Surrey, such euphemistic niceties seem out of place. The questions also home in on the issue of his wilfully bearing the royal arms of King Edward the Confessor and 'whether you are next heir or kin to St Edward and if so, how?' And: 'To what intent do you put the arms of St Edward in your coat?' Finally, the 'killer' questions of his interrogators: 'Do you acknowledge yourself the king's true subject?' and 'Have you at any time determined to fly out of the realm?'[55] One can almost hear proud Surrey's angry denials and bluster when questioned repeatedly by his enemies.

As the Privy Council scurried about taking witness statements, the draft charges against both Norfolk and Surrey were drawn up and presented to the king who read them carefully, despite his rapidly deteriorating medical condition, his spectacles on the end of his nose. He was taking a great personal interest in the case: 'he is deeply engaged and much perplexed in the consideration of this affair,' reported van der Delft.

> It is understood that he will thus be occupied during the holidays and some days in addition, the queen and all the courtiers having gone to Greenwich, though she has never been known before to leave him on solemn occasions like this. I do not know what to think or suspect.

The king was 'keeping himself very secluded at court, all persons but his councillors and three or four gentlemen of his chamber being denied entrance'.[56]

Henry made copious handwritten notes in the margins of the charge sheets. They demonstrate great clarity of thought, despite his poor state of health, and must indicate his grim single-mindedness to see his noble prisoners brought safely to the block. He may have been physically weak, but he was as cold-blooded as ever. The king's annotations show that he reinforced the case against both men for heraldic misdemeanours. Some of the evidence may have triggered painful echoes of the past and two unfortunate marriages into the old king's mind. He wrote:

> If a man compassing with himself to govern this realm, do actually go about to rule the king and should, for that purpose advise his daughter or sister to become his harlot, thinking thereby to bring it to pass and so would rule both father and son, as by this next article doth more appear; what this importeth?

Then, putting his finger on the crux of the issue, Henry asked pointedly:

> If a man says these words: 'If the King dies, who should have the rule of the Prince but my father or I' – What it importeth?[57]

The cynical van der Delft strongly suspected that the Council's feverish investigations were a cunning stratagem to hide yet another relapse in the king's health, so he sent one of his men to see John Dudley, the Lord Great Admiral, at Westminster:

> Whilst he was at court, where he slept that night, he learnt from a friend that the king was not at all well, though he had seen him dressed on the previous day.[58]

The astute ambassador pointed out in a dispatch to Charles V on Christmas Eve 1546 that

> four or five months ago, great inquiries and prosecutions were carried out against the heretics and sacramentarians, but they have now ceased, since the earl of Hertford [Seymour] and the Lord Admiral have resided at court. The publicly expressed opinion, therefore, [is] that these two nobles have obtained such influence over the king as to lead him according to their fancy.[59]

Van der Delft had warned of 'the evils and dangers threatened by these sects' in conversations with some of the leading councillors and they asked him to pass on his opinions to Henry.

I find them [the councillors] now of a different aspect and much inclined to please and entertain the earl and the Admiral ...

As regards the diversity of religion, the people at large are to a great extent on their side, the majority being of these perverse sects and in favour of getting rid of the bishops.

They do not indeed conceal their wish to see the Bishop of Winchester and other adherents of the ancient faith sent to the Tower to keep company with the Duke of Norfolk.[60]

Norfolk made his confession on 12 January 1547 in the Tower of London, signing it, of course, 'without compulsion or counsel'. Despite that preposterously unlikely disclaimer, the statement would certainly have been written for him by his accusers, as every 'i' is dotted, every 't' crossed:

I, Thomas duke of Norfolk do confess and acknowledge myself to have offended the king in opening his secret counsels at diverse times to sundry persons to the peril of his highness and disappointing of his affairs.

Likewise I have concealed high treason in keeping secret the false acts of my son, Henry, Earl of Surrey, in using the arms of St Edward the Confessor which pertain only to kings of this realm, whereto the said earl could make no claim.

Also I have without authority borne in the first and principal quarter of my arms, ever since the death of my father, the arms of England with a difference of three labels of silver, which are the proper arms of my lord the prince.

I confess my crime no less than high treason and although I do not deserve it, humbly beg his highness to have pity upon me. I shall daily pray to God for the preservation of his noble succession.[61]

The usual suspects in such circumstances signed the confession as witnesses, amongst them Wriothesley, Lord St John – Lord President of the Council, the Earl of Hertford – Lord Great Chamberlain, Dudley – Lord High Admiral, Secretary Paget and Sir Anthony Browne, Master of the King's Horse. It was too late to expect mercy from Henry, the Seymours or Dudley.

If there were ever any futile, lingering doubts about the foregone conclusion to Surrey's trial at the Guildhall the next day, Thursday 13 January, they were destroyed by his father's craven and prejudicial confession.

Surrey was popular in London, despite his previous hooligan escapades, and his downfall was to damage irretrievably the public perception of the Seymours. The Spanish merchant de Guaras, who recounted the story of the earl's escape attempt, reported that 'it was fearful to see the enormous number of people in the streets' watching as Surrey was escorted,[62] under guard by 300 halberdiers, by the Constable of the Tower Sir John Gage, who was responsible for delivering him safely to his trial. Always a dandy, the prisoner wore a new coat of satin purchased especially for the occasion, paid for by Walter Stonor, the new Lieutenant of the Tower.[63]

The servile twelve-man jury, made up of Norfolk knights and squires, had been handpicked to include some of his enemies. Surrey pleaded 'not guilty' to the indictment, which ran as follows:

Whosoever, by words, writings, printing or other external act, maliciously shall procure anything to the peril of the king's person or give occasion whereby the king or his successors might be disturbed in their possession of the crown, shall be guilty of treason.[64]

And whereas Henry VIII is true King of England and Edward, formerly king of England, commonly called Saint Edward the Confessor in right of the said realm of England used certain arms and ensigns, namely, *azure, a cross fleury*[65] *between five merletts*[66] *gold*, belonging to the said king Edward and his progenitors in right of the crown of England, which arms and ensigns are therefore appropriate to the king and no other person.

And whereas Edward, now prince of England, the king's son and heir apparent, bears ... the said arms and ensigns with three labels called *three labels*[67] *silver*.

Nevertheless, one Henry Howard, late of Kenninghall, knight of the Garter, otherwise called Henry Howard, earl of Surrey, on October 7, 1546, at Kenninghall, in the house of Thomas duke of Norfolk, his father, openly used and traitorously caused to be depicted, mixed and conjoined with his own arms and ensigns, the said arms and ensigns of the king, with *three labels silver*.[68]

The earl stood defiantly at the bar facing his justices, three of them the very architects of his downfall: alongside Lord Mayor Hobberthorne sat Wriothesley, Hertford and Dudley. Their number also included the Earls of Arundel and Essex and professional judges like Sir William Shelley, there to lend legal verisimilitude to the proceedings. Paget and Sir Anthony Browne were also present as commissioners.

The king's lawyer opened his prosecution:

My lords, for either of the offences the earl has committed he deserves death. First for usurping the royal arms which gives rise to suspicion that he hoped to become king and the other for escaping from prison, whereby he showed his guilt.[69]

Surrey, 'with manly courage', interrupted:

You are false and to earn a piece of gold, would condemn your father. I never sought to usurp the king's arms, for everybody knows that my ancestors bore them. Go to the church in Norfolk and you will see them there, for they have been ours' for five hundred years.[70]

Paget, fearing Surrey's eloquence and the impact on public opinion of what was rapidly becoming a strong defence, shouted at Surrey:

Hold your peace, my lord! Your idea was to commit treason and as the king is old, you thought to become king.

The earl snapped back:

And thou catchpole! What hast thou to do with it? Thou had better hold *thy* tongue, for the kingdom has never been well since the king put mean creatures like you into government.

The jibe was born out of Surrey's uncontrollable contempt for the *nouveau riche* who had come to power, displacing the rightful role of the nobility. 'Catchpole' was street slang at the time for a bailiff and the stinging insult was hurled at Paget because his father was said to have been a humble constable. Whatever the truth of his parentage, Paget was now suddenly silenced, 'very much abashed'. Dudley then questioned Surrey about why he had attempted to escape from the Tower. Surrey replied:

I tried to get out to prevent myself from coming to the pass in which I am now and you my lord know well that however right a man may be, they always find the fallen one guilty.[71]

Hard, realistic words from a man despairing of his certain terrible fate. Surrey was also accused of possessing a painting of himself that demonstrated 'malicious thoughts' and that he proposed his father to be Lord Protector of the young king after Henry's death. His sister, the Duchess of Richmond, also signed one of the depositions, or witness statements. After her husband's death, which left her a penniless widow, she had harboured deep resentment against both father and brother for her painful impecuniosity. Now she told how Surrey had altered his arms and placed over them the cap of maintenance,[72] with the royal crown with the king's cipher 'H. R.' for *Henricus Rex* beneath. When this was read out in court, Surrey burst out: 'Must I then be condemned on the word of a wretched woman?'[73]

After six hours of hearing the depositions, Paget hurriedly left the court to see the king at Westminster. When he returned hotfoot, probably with the royal order for Surrey's condemnation tucked safely inside his doublet, the jury dutifully retired to consider their verdict. One wonders what they talked about. After a decent interval – the niceties had to be observed – they returned and Hertford stood up to speak for them all.

Asked whether they found Surrey guilty or not guilty, Hertford replied in a loud voice: 'Guilty' – a brief pause – 'And he should die.'[74]

He hardly finished speaking before the court erupted in a tumult 'and it was a long while' before the people in the court could be silenced.

Even with death staring him in the face, Surrey's irrepressible prejudices burst out. The prisoner at the bar spat out:

> Of what have you found me guilty? Surely you will find no law that justifies you! But I know the king wants to get rid of the noble blood around him and employ none but low people.[75]

Wriothesley, his voice rising above the excited babble, then pronounced sentence: that Surrey was to be 'taken back to the Tower and thence led through the city of London to the gallows of Tyburn and hanged and disembowelled' and his body quartered, the traitor's usual ignominious death. He was led out of the Guildhall under heavy guard, with the axe turned towards him as a sinister sign of his condemnation. It was, commented the Spanish merchant de Guaras, 'shocking to hear the things that he kept saying and to see the grief of the people'.

The Bill of Attainder against Norfolk and Surrey was introduced into Parliament on Tuesday 18 January, presaging their deaths and, as usual, forfeiting their lands and fortunes to the crown, backdated to 7 October 1546. No details of their high treason were mentioned within the Bill.

There were many at Westminster who cast envious eyes on the Howards' ample estates, vastly augmented by the proceeds of dissolved religious houses, and no doubt the vultures were already circling, waiting for the rich pickings to be distributed after the deaths of Surrey and Norfolk. Henry promised Paget that these assets would be 'liberally disposed and given to his good servants', no doubt with the Seymour clan at the front of the line of those waiting to be enriched. The king said he had drawn up a list of beneficiaries, which he had put 'in the pocket of his nightgown'. Ironically, it was not found after his death, despite frantic searches by those self-seeking men at Westminster who surrounded the king during his last hours. This may have been Henry's last laugh at his senior courtiers.

Surrey's downfall was predicated on a heraldic technicality, a dubious charge at best. His father's confession was vague and tenuous, much of the substance being only the swift abandonment of his son to the axeman. What truly destroyed the Howards was the testimony of the Duchess of Richmond – Norfolk's daughter and Surrey's sister – and Norfolk's mistress 'Bess' Holland. The family was a house divided against itself. Both women harboured grudges, even hatred, against one or other of the men and it was these volcanic domestic tensions that enabled the destruction of probably the richest, the proudest and, at times, the most powerful noble family in England.

On 19 January 1547, Henry having generously commuted the sentence of his 'foolish proud boy' to mere beheading, Surrey was executed on Tower Hill and was buried immediately in the Church of All Hallows, Barking, close by in Upper Thames Street.[76] On the scaffold 'he spoke a great deal but said he never meant to commit treason. They would not let him talk any more.'[77]

Just over a week later, on 27 January, Wriothesley presided over a joint session of both Houses of Parliament and announced the Royal Assent to the Bill of Attainder, as Henry was too ill to attend in person. The last legal hurdles before the father's execution had been jumped. For Norfolk, still in the Tower, it seemed only a matter of hours or days before his own lonely march to the scaffold. At least he was relatively comfortable, lodged in the Constable's apartments. The accounts of Walter Stonor, the Lieutenant of the Tower, for 12 December to 6 February show £210 (£56,000 in today's money) spent on the board and lodging of the duke and his attendants, including the cost of coals and candles.[78]

Away from the drama and excitements of this intense jockeying for power and position within the court, as the king's health slowly worsened, at least a public face of normality was being maintained by other members of the royal family.

Edward dutifully wrote to his father from Hertford on 10 January, thanking him for his New Year's gift and promising to follow his example in 'virtue, wisdom and piety'.[79] He also politely wrote to the queen and to Princess Mary, thanking them for their presents – Katherine's was a miniature portrait of Henry and herself. She was

> gratified by his appreciation of her little ... gift, hoping that he will meditate upon the distinguished deeds of his father, whose portrait he is so pleased to have, and to consider [Henry's] rare virtues, whenever he should examine it, with rare attention.[80]

Edward also wrote belatedly (on 24 January) to Archbishop Cranmer, thanking him for his present of a cup, which bore testimony 'that his loving godfather wishes him many happy years' and for his letters exhorting him to the study of good, no doubt Protestant, literature 'which may be useful to him in manhood'.[81]

CHAPTER NINE

The Mystery of the Royal Will

'His Majesty ... being by God's sufferance born
by just and most certain title and succession
to such a kingdom as knows no superior,
his crown being close and his progenitors before
him emperors in their own realm and
dominions, doubts not but, with God's help, he
will so prepare himself as he shall be able to
leave it in as good case to his son as his father
before left it to him – and better.'

HENRY VIII IN A LETTER TO THE DUKE OF NORFOLK, 1540.[1]

Prince Edward was probably unaware just how serious his father's decline was. Henry's health had been steadily growing worse during the course of 1546, confining him more and more to his secret apartments. In March that year, the king was 'indisposed with a slight fever for two or three days'[2] and he passed the listless hours of convalescence playing cards with Dudley and his other court intimates. The imperial ambassador van der Delft reported to Charles V: 'I do not know what will come of it, as his principal medical man, Dr Butts, died this [last] winter. I will inquire daily and will report to your majesty.'[3] Three months later, Henry was again ill, this time with colic, and was taking his prescribed medicine.

The frustration resulting from his immobility and the pain from his legs worsened his temper and he grew 'exceedingly perverse and intractable'. He could still ride, with some difficulty, and during the summer of 1546 he spent much time hunting at Chobham, Guildford, and elsewhere in Surrey, with most of the kills probably stage-managed by his huntsmen. A ramp had been constructed in the grounds of Otelands, one of his houses in that county, to help him climb into his horse's saddle.[4] However, by September he was physically exhausted and the delights of the chase had to be curtailed. Henry journeyed to Windsor to recover, accompanied by Queen Katherine.

Once there, he was again taken ill, but Wriothesley said reassuringly on 17 September that he had 'only a cold and was now cured'.[5] Van der Delft heard differently and believed that Henry had been very sick indeed – that his life had been in great danger and his physicians had given up all hope of his recovery. But recover he did, and within three weeks he was back in the saddle in the hunting field. The king returned to London in November 'for certain baths which he usually has at this season' and then moved back to Otelands. The Spanish ambassador saw him there on 5 December, when Henry told him he had suffered a 'sharp attack of the fever, which lasted in the burning stage for thirty hours, but now he was quite restored'. But the ambassador had his doubts: 'his colour does not bear out [this] statement and he looks to me greatly fallen away.'[6] Henry's last feeble foray into the hunting field came on 7 December. Three days later, he was due to see the French envoy Odet de Selve, but the audience was postponed because of a royal cold. However, the king was able to meet Scottish ambassadors three times in mid-December, after the 16th of that month, and de Selve and van der Delft on the 17th.

Some vital clues to Henry's condition and its treatment come from the apothecaries' bills submitted for the drugs and medicines supplied and approved by his doctors, George Owen and Thomas Wendy. Thomas Alsop, chief apothecary to the court, had been joined at Michaelmas 1546 by another called Patrick Reynolds.

Alsop's bill for the last five months of the king's life jumped in value as potions and medicines were increasingly prescribed by the royal physicians: from £5 in August (£1,247 in today's values) to £25 for December (£6,239). But this was not all for Henry's medicinal needs. Alsop also had to supply a huge range of different products for various uses by the court – including liquorice and barley sugar for the king's hounds; horehound water, sugar candy and rhubarb for his hunting hawks; and perfumes and fragrances to sweeten the atmosphere of the royal apartments and banquets. (The king's apothecary also had to deliver disposable pottery urinals for use during Privy Council meetings at 3d a time, so that calls of nature did not interrupt the important proceedings. The bill for Hampton Court in August alone for these very personal items was two shillings.)[7]

The king's medicines included fomentations, glisters, plasters and sponges for the stomach and anus and eyebright water for bathing the eyes. The bewildering array of balms and potions, listed in dog Latin, yield few clues to the modern pharmacist about what Henry was prescribed to ease his sufferings, apart from the increasing use of the phrase *ut patet*, which implies that the prescription or formula was a new one and that it had been copied into a book, available for inspection by court officials.[8]

His physicians were becoming desperate and were willing to try anything new in the hope of keeping Henry alive. It was not just his legs that were sapping his stamina and casting a cloud of depression over him – the king was suffering from something far more insidious. The symptoms today seem clear enough: that huge royal bulk was probably a victim of an endocrine abnormality called Cushing's syndrome,[9] a rare affliction that still affects ten to fifteen people per million of today's population.

The symptoms of untreated Cushing's syndrome vary, but most sufferers have gross obesity in the body's trunk, increased fat around their necks and sometimes a buffalo hump to the back. The face becomes distressingly swollen with substantial fat deposits on the lower half beneath the eyes, creating the so-called 'moon face' characteristic of the condition. The victim's skin becomes fragile and thin, not only bruising easily but also exhibiting slow, poor healing of wounds or lesions. It also takes on a deepening in pigmentation. The sufferer's bones are weakened and any exercise, even something as simple as standing up from a chair, causes severe backaches, even fractures of the ribs. The muscles around the hips become wasted. Blood pressure is increased, as are blood sugar levels. There may be mild diabetes as a side effect, causing frequent thirst. Irritability, depression, anxiety, insomnia and sudden mood swings become commonplace in around twenty per cent of cases. The sufferer also becomes psychotic, exhibiting a paranoia that drives a deep suspicion of everything and everyone around them. Sometimes they become emotionally detached from their loved ones, or from those close to them. The victim, afflicted with recurrent headaches and chronic fatigue, is quarrelsome and frequently unnaturally aggressive. Men suffer reduced fertility and their desire for sex disappears entirely.

Of course, after the passage of nearly five centuries, no diagnosis on the basis of purely anecdotal reports from his courtiers and inquisitive foreign ambassadors can be 100 per cent certain; only in the unlikely event of a forensic examination of Henry's bones could a more decisive conclusion be derived. Even then, most signs and symptoms of the syndrome are to be found in the body's soft tissues, which would have long ago disappeared. All these symptoms, however, fit very well the descriptions that have come down to us of Henry's condition in the last four or five years of his life. He did have gross obesity in his trunk and lower face; he did suffer prolonged periods of melancholy and severe headaches. He was psychotic, displaying irrational anger and aggression. He was sometimes detached from those he was fond of – as demonstrated by the death warrants he signed for Cranmer and Queen Katherine Parr. He did experience mood swings and sudden changes of mind – such as his subsequent decisions to inform them of the threats they faced. He even had the hump on his back, as suggested by the illustration of him in his *Psalter*. Add the agony of his ulcerated legs to the debilitation of the disease and you have a king suffering an exhausting purgatory of pain on earth.

Abnormally excessive levels of the hormone cortisol, secreted by the adrenal glands (located above the kidneys) over long periods of time, cause the disease. The hormone's normal purpose is to help maintain blood pressure and cardiovascular functions and to reduce the body's immune system's inflammatory response. It balances the effects of insulin in breaking down sugar for energy and regulates the metabolism of proteins, fats and carbohydrates. It also helps to reduce stress.

Today, Cushing's syndrome is treated by hormone-inhibiting drugs or, more drastically, chemotherapy or radiation treatment. In some cases, surgery may have to be performed to remove adrenal tumours. None of these recourses were available to Henry's physicians, Doctors Wendy, Cromer and Owen, or to his apothecary Thomas Alsop, with the very basic medical science available to them in the mid-sixteenth century.

Thus we have before us the image of a remorselessly cruel monarch, totally ruthless in his hold on the reins of power; careless of the lives of his friends and subjects; always determined to get his own way; and rapacious in the accumulation of wealth, almost always at the expense of others. He was a psychotic, paranoid bully, perilously enjoying absolute authority. But if he did suffer from Cushing's syndrome, perhaps somewhere even in the coldest of hearts we may find a few shreds of sympathy for the old ogre.

Henry's life was patently drawing to an end and the thoughts and schemes of those around him became ever more focused on the future governance of the realm of England after his death.

The reformist party now held complete sway at court and some of the remainder of the Council were scrambling to realign to their new loyalties. Hertford and Dudley, reported van der Delft in December 1546,

have entirely obtained the favour and authority of the king.

A proof of this is, that nothing is now done at court without their intervention and the meetings of the Council are mostly held in the earl of Hertford's house.

It is even asserted here that the custody of the prince and the government of the realm will be entrusted to them and the misfortunes that have befallen the house of Norfolk may well have come from the same quarter.[10]

Henry had returned to Westminster via his huge new Palace of Nonsuch near Ewell, Surrey, towards the end of December, still suffering from 'some grief of his leg' and the fever that it had caused. By now, he could hardly walk more than a few steps by himself.[11] Van der Delft wrote on Christmas Eve:

> The king is so unwell that considering his age and corpulence, fears are entertained that he will be unable to survive further attacks, such as he recently suffered at Windsor. God preserve him! If he should succumb there is but slight hope of the change for the better.[12]

The Council deferred the ambassador's planned interview with Henry 'for two or three days on the pretext that they were very busy, but said they would send me word when they could see me'. The queen was banished to Greenwich Palace for Christmas. Van der Delft thought it was 'an innovation for them to be separated during the festivities'.

The king himself must have suspected that the hour of his death was approaching. Henry wanted his queen out of the way whilst he made arrangements for the government of his young son. He had already been irritated by Katherine's attempts to counsel him on religious reform; he did not want her to claim the regency of England until Edward came of age. On the evening of 26 December, he summoned his now most favoured courtiers and officials – Hertford, Dudley, Paget and Denny – to his bedchamber. He ordered Sir Anthony Denny to fetch the latest copy of his will, drawn up in early 1544 before he went off to the French wars. The wrong one was produced, an error quickly spotted by the king when Paget began to read its terms: 'That is not it, there is another of a later making, written with the hand of Lord Wriothesley, being secretary,' came the sharp words from the heavily pillowed great bed. The correct one was eventually brought to his bedside and Henry wanted to make some changes to the list of executors, some 'he meant to have in and some he meant to have out'. Paget was ordered to make the amendments, to 'put in some that were not named before and to put out the Bishop of Winchester ... a wilful man, not meet to be about his son, nor trouble his [Privy] Council any more'.[13]

Gardiner, then, was still firmly in disgrace. Henry also had the name of Thomas Thirlby, Bishop of Westminster,[14] deleted because 'he was schooled by the Bishop of Winchester'.[15] The next day, the king was said to be feeling better and planned an interview with the French ambassador Odet de Selve, who had been insisting on seeing him.[16] That respite was short, however. On 9 January 1547, van der Delft reported that his access to Henry was still denied 'owing to his indisposition'.[17]

Several days later, Gardiner's ally Sir Anthony Browne[18] knelt down by the side of the king's bed and hesitantly suggested that the bishop's name had been omitted by mistake from the will:

> My lord of Winchester, I think by negligence is left out of your majesty's will, who hath done your highness most painful, long and notable service and one without whom the rest shall not be able to overcome your great and weighty affairs committed unto them.

Henry, feeble and weak though he now was, and probably lapsing in and out of a pained sleep, snapped:

> Hold your peace! I remembered him well enough and of good purpose have left him out.
>
> For surely, if he were in my testament and one of you, he would encumber you all and you would never rule him, he is so troublesome a nature.
>
> Marry, I myself could use him and rule him to all manner of purposes, as it seemed good to me – but so shall you never do.[19]

When Browne tried to raise the issue again, the king angrily told him: 'If you do not cease to trouble me, by the faith of God, I will surely despatch you out of my will also.' Gardiner's last ally was effectively silenced.

Paget had completed writing the new will[20] by 30 December and, significantly, delivered it to Hertford. In the document, Henry expressed the hope that his final testament would be acceptable to 'God, Christ and the whole company of heaven and satisfactory to all godly brethren on earth'. Reference to his sins, unsurprisingly for God's deputy on earth, is pretty thin, merely that he repents 'his old life' and talks of his resolve never to return to its ways. In truth, he now had neither the time left to him, nor the strength, for any such wicked actions. The king, however, humbly bequeathed his soul to God, whose Son 'left here with us in his Church Militant, the consecration and administration of his precious Body and Blood'. With predictable self-confidence, he desired the Blessed Virgin and the holy company of Heaven to pray for him while he lived and at his passing that he might 'the sooner attain everlasting life'.

After instructions for his burial at St George's Chapel, Windsor, alongside Queen Jane Seymour and for the pious embellishment of the tombs there of Henry VI and Edward IV, he directed that 1,000 marks[21] be paid in alms to the poor (though not to 'common beggars, as much as may be avoided') with injunctions for them to pray for his soul. The chantry chapel was to be endowed with lands worth £600 annually[22] to pay for two priests to say Mass at the altar attached to his tomb and to keep four solemn obits every year, when £10 should be distributed to the poor. The thirteen Poor Knights of Windsor – a long-established charity for old soldiers – were each to be given 12d a day and a new gown of white cloth every year, together with the annual sum of £3 6s 8d.[23]

The meat of the will comes in the following section. The crown and the realms of England, Ireland and the title of France followed the Act of Succession of 1544.[24] These would go directly to Prince Edward and any lawful heirs of his body and, in default, to Henry's daughter Mary and her heirs, 'upon condition that she shall not marry without the written and sealed consent of a majority' of Edward's surviving Privy Council. In the event of her childless death, the crown would pass to Elizabeth with a similar condition as to marriage. Finally, if none of this was applicable or went unfulfilled, the succession would be settled on the heirs of Lady Frances, eldest daughter of Henry's late sister, Mary, or to the fifth in line, Lady Frances' sister, Lady Eleanor.

Together with the crown, Edward was left all Henry's plate, 'household stuff', artillery and other ordnance, ships, money and jewels – a very substantial legacy indeed, valued at an estimated £1,200,000[25] in the prices of the day, or nearly £325 million in 2004. Henry's inventory of military equipment was also considerable: a total of 2,250 artillery pieces were located in the crown's fortresses around the realm's coastline and borders and a further 600 guns and 6,500 handguns were held at the Tower of London. The navy, which Henry had so patiently (and expensively) built up, now numbered seventy ships, displacing a total of 11,620 tons,[26] a formidable fighting force and the forerunners of Elizabeth's warships that defeated the mighty Spanish Armada four decades later.

Henry appointed sixteen executors to oversee his will: Archbishop Cranmer; Lord Chancellor Wriothesley; Lord St John (Lord Steward of the Royal Household); Hertford (then Great Chamberlain of England); Lord Russell (Lord Privy Seal); John Dudley, Viscount Lisle (Lord Great Admiral); Cuthbert Tunstall (Bishop of Durham); Sir Anthony Browne (Master of the King's Horse); Sir Edward Montague (Chief Judge of the Common Pleas); Sir Thomas Bromley (Puisne Justice of the King's Bench); Sir Edward North (Chancellor of Augmentations); Sir William Paget (Chief Secretary); Sir Anthony Denny and Sir William Herbert (Chief Gentlemen of the Privy Chamber); Sir Edward Wotton (Treasurer of Calais); and his brother Dr Nicholas Wotton (Dean of York and ambassador to France).

Debts – and Henry knew of none – were to be their first duty to settle after his burial. All grants and payments that he had made or promised but not undertaken were to be honoured generously. But, ever jealous of the Tudors' dynastic wealth, he firmly instructed his executors not 'to presume to meddle with our treasure'.

More importantly, these members of the 'great and good' were to form the new Privy Council that would operate the regency until Edward completed his eighteenth year. Knowing well the proclivity for dissension amongst his advisers, the king firmly stipulated: 'None of them shall do anything appointed by this will alone but only with the written consent of the majority.'

He bequeathed £10,000 in money and plate to each of his daughters for their marriages 'or more at the executors' discretion' and both would have £3,000 a year to live on from the hour of his death. His wife Katherine was to have £3,000 in plate, jewels and household stuff and to take what she liked of what she already possessed. She would further receive £1,000 in cash in addition to the enjoyment of her jointure – the estate settled on her during her lifetime after the king's death.

Henry then left a raft of personal bequests to his favourites: 500 marks (about £650) to Cranmer; £500 each to Wriothesley, St John, Russell, Hertford and Lisle; and £300 each to Denny, Herbert, Sir Anthony Browne, Paget, Sir Edward North, Nicholas Wotton and four others. Paget had left blank spaces for the amounts in the draft, but he later filled these in, most likely after more discussion with the king. Further, smaller bequests 'in token of special love and favour' went to a host of royal household courtiers and servants, including Sir Thomas Seymour, John Gates and Sir Richard Rich. His doctors – Wendy, Owen and 'the Scot' Cromer – each received £100 and the apothecaries Thomas Alsop and Patrick Reynolds, 100 marks (£130) apiece.[27]

The eleven witnesses included John Gates and, in true royal tradition, three doctors – Wendy, Owen and Huicke – presumably to enable them to testify that the king was of sound mind when the testament was drawn up. The final signatory was the ubiquitous Privy Chamber clerk, William Clerk.

The will, contained in a small book, was signed 'with our hand, in our palace of Westminster, the 30th day of December' 1546. It all looked clear cut and unequivocal. But it wasn't – far from it – and the circumstances in which the will was drawn up and signed have caused considerable controversy amongst historians over nearly five centuries since.[28]

In reality, Henry did not sign the will.

The dry stamp was deployed for the facsimile signatures at its beginning and end, use of the stamp witnessed by Hertford, Paget, Denny and Herbert and 'also in the presence of certain other witnesses to the same'.

William Clerk noted in his monthly record of the stamp's employment:

> Which testament, your majesty delivered in our sights with your
> own hand to the said earl of Hertford as your own deed, last will
> and testament, revoking and annulling all your highness' former
> wills and testaments.[29]

It was then placed in a locked 'round box or bag of black velvet' for
safekeeping.

The date of the will is something of a mystery. It refers to Thomas
Seymour as a Privy Councillor – but he was not admitted to the Council
until 23 January 1547.[30] Years later, Dudley was to testify that Seymour's
name had been included against the king's wishes. Henry, 'on his
deathbed', on hearing the name read, cried out: 'No, no!' even 'as his
breath was failing'. Was this because of Henry's old jealousy of him
over his wife's affections?

Moreover, the will appears as the penultimate item in Clerk's register
for January 1547 recording all stamped documents. He must have already
prepared the schedule for January when it became necessary to add a
note of the will and the Howard attainder to the document. An extra
piece of parchment, 100 mm in depth, was stuck on at the last minute,
containing the entries for the will and the attainder, as well as Clerk's signature.[31] Was the will in fact signed (or rather dry-stamped) just a few
days or even hours before Henry's death – and not on 30 December?
The conspiracy theorist will point out that the king would have been in
no fit state to inspect this register of the dry stamp's use in late January,
when it would have been offered up for his close inspection. In fact, he
did not live long enough to inspect it.[32] Or was this merely honest for-
getfulness – or, frankly, incompetence – on Clerk's part and there really
was no conspiracy? From such happenstance was spawned a thousand
doctoral dissertations.

There were other issues that those around Henry were keen for
him to settle before his demise.

Paget was later to tell the Privy Council how the king

> being remembered in his deathbed that he promised great things
> to diverse men ... willed in his testament that whatever should in any
> wise appear to his Council to have been promised by him, the same
> should be performed.

This mirrors the so-called 'unfulfilled gifts' clause in the will that has sparked speculation that this section was drawn up later in January and inserted after the dry stamping.[33] Indeed, a judicious, if not suspicious, individual may conclude that the will was not stamped until Henry was near death, or dead already. It may be, of course, that Henry, anxious to maintain his grasp on his court's loyalties, postponed signing the will until he was too ill to physically lift a pen and write legibly. To maintain stable governance of the realm, his Councillors may have then felt impelled to wield the dry stamp themselves and backdated the will to a point when Henry would have been well enough to approve it himself. But would not the threat of a last-minute, last-gasp codicil have kept them in line?

Paget, now a loyal ally of Hertford, was 'privy in the beginning, proceeding and ending of the will' and is the only one who truly knew what went on during those last anxious days – and he took his secrets to the grave.

During the final month of Henry's life, his robust spirit struggled manfully against approaching death. On some days, he seemed much better; on others, his health suffered setbacks, slowly sapping his strength and resilience. Clues to his physical and mental state come in diplomatic dispatches written by ambassadors who constantly tapped their sources at court for news of what was happening behind the closely guarded doors of the king's Privy Chamber. Odet de Selve told the French ambassador in Flanders on 8 January that Henry had

> been so ill for the past fifteen days that he was reported dead. Many
> people here still believe him so, seeing that whatever amendment
> is announced, few persons have access to his lodging and his
> chamber.[34]

Two days later, he wrote to Francis I that he had learnt

> from several good quarters that the king's health is much better
> ... he seems to have been very ill and in great danger owing to his
> legs which have had to be cauterised. Neither the Queen nor
> the Lady Mary could see him, nor do we know that they will now
> do so.[35]

The ambassador ended with a prediction: he had 'great reason to conjecture that whatever his health, it can only be bad and [he] will not last long'.

Poor Henry – now his legs were being cauterised, seared with hot irons by his doctors. He at least seems to have remained *compos mentis* until around mid-January.

Henry may still have retained a feeble hand on the tiller of state affairs. At the Privy Council at Ely Palace on 27 December, harsh things were said about the failure of the English administration in Boulogne to provide details of the strength of the garrison, food stocks and the amount of cash available to them. The king 'marvelled not a little that they had hitherto been so remiss in neglecting so special a point, [as] these three months past, they had reported [to London] nothing touching these matters'. And two days later, the Privy Council sent a letter to the Council of the North indicating that Henry had pardoned two Sacramentarians 'as they were now penitent'.[36] Even confronting death, the king summoned energy enough to attend to the minutiae of palace life: two documents that received the dry stamp, probably in early January, were concerned with a batch of apple trees that the royal gardener, the priest Sir John de Leu, was to collect from France for the Privy Gardens.[37] Knowing Henry's dislike of talk of his mortality, perhaps he was in a state of denial.

On 17 January, Henry briefly saw the Spanish and French ambassadors, who had been warned not to tire him with lengthy conversation. This was the last time the king was seen by outsiders and he seemed 'fairly well' and talked of diplomacy and military issues, although at times he sought help from the attentive Paget on matters of detail. Two days later, he was reported to be planning the investiture of Edward as Prince of Wales.

As the days went by, the condition of the king, lying propped up in bed, worsened. He began to drift in and out of consciousness. There were those around him who saw this as an opportunity to grab their last chance of enrichment or advancement before his long reign ended. John Gates had already received some choice grants from the Court of Augmentations on 30 December: Keeper of Suffolk's mansion in Southwark and Chief Steward of the lands of St Mary Overy in the same parish.[38] During that pain-wracked, hazy January, the dry stamp was deployed by William Clerk on eighty-six documents, all dutifully recorded on a parchment roll of four membranes, or pages. In all cases, the stamp was used in the presence of Sir Anthony Denny and John Gates.

Amongst the documents were:

A bill to pass by Act of Parliament for the better assurance of your majesty's grant in fee simple to Sir William Paget, chief of your majesty's two principal secretaries, of certain lordships, manors, parks etc which the bishops of Coventry, Lichfield and Chester lately gave and rendered to your highness. (Preferred by secretary Paget.)

Gift in fee simple of the manors of Berwick, North Newton etc., Wiltshire, parcel of the late monastery of Wilton and other lands, yearly value £119 4s 9d, for Sir William Herbert [Gentleman of the Privy Chamber] who pays George Howard £800 for them.

Custody of the manors of Magna Raveley and Moynes in Upwood parish and a messuage [a dwelling house with outbuildings] with a close and pasture in Raveley, Huntingdonshire, and the lands called Goldings, Hunts and Drapers, in Ashwell, Hertfordshire, in the king's hands by minority of William Sewster, son and heir of John Sewster esq., to William Clerk, the king's servant.

Wardship [no name of minor given] granted to William Clerk.

John Roberts, yeoman extraordinary of the privy chamber, to have the portership of the fortress of Falmouth in Cornwall which he has long exercised.[39]

There was also a special mandate to Wriothesley, Lord St John, Russell and Hertford to deliver the king's consent to the Act of Attainder of Thomas, Duke of Norfolk, and Henry, late Earl of Surrey. The document was dated January, but the day of the month was left blank.[40] The last document in the collection was the commission to Hertford instructing him to 'pronounce in the Parliament House your majesty's assent to the attainder of the Duke of Norfolk by Act of Parliament'.

At mid-morning of Thursday 27 January, Henry had received communion from his confessor (possibly John Boole[41]) and afterwards he was conscious enough to discuss matters of state with a few of his Councillors. But as the day wore on, it was apparent to all who saw him that he was rapidly losing his last battle with Death.

All in that silent Palace of Westminster knew full well that by law it was foul treason to predict the king's death. Some had been brutally executed for unwisely uttering such thoughts. Outside the doors of his bedchamber, there was apprehension about what was now inevitable. Would anyone have the courage to tell the old man that his end was approaching? All still feared the king's power to exact terrible vengeance; everyone, including his doctors, was still wary of his violent temper. They knew of his repugnance to any mention of his mortality. The dangerous duty predictably fell to Denny.

He entered the king's silent chamber that evening and knelt quietly beside the bed. The king was conscious and stared down at him as the courtier strove to summon the courage to utter the unspeakable. Henry's skin had probably taken on a yellow colour as a result of his condition; he may have found it difficult to breathe evenly. Denny finally warned Henry that in 'man's judgement you are not like to live' and therefore exhorted him to prepare himself for death. There was a silence. Denny hurried on, urging the king to remember his sins 'as becomes every good Christian man to do'.

The king said he believed 'the mercy of Christ is able to pardon me all my sins, yes, though they were greater than they be'. Denny, delicately hedging around the issue of bringing in a priest to say the Last Rites, asked if Henry wanted to see 'any learned man to confer withal and open his mind unto'. The king nodded, but, as ever, avoided taking the final decision: 'If I had any, it should be Dr Cranmer but I will first take a little sleep. And then, as I feel myself, I will advise [you] upon on the matter.'[42] These were his last known words: shortly afterwards, Henry lost the power of speech and later probably passed into a uraemic coma.[43]

A message was quickly dispatched by courier to Archbishop Cranmer, who was staying at his palace at Croydon. The weather was very cold that night and the frozen roads delayed his arrival at Westminster. By the time he arrived, chilled and out of breath, sometime shortly after midnight, Henry was probably still unconscious. His old friend clambered awkwardly on to the great bed and, speaking close to the king's ear, urged him to make some sign or token that he put his trust in the mercy of Christ: a nod, a mere flicker of the eyelids or a small gesture by his hand was all that was required. There was no response in the silence apart from the laboured breathing of the dying monarch. But Cranmer grasped the king's hand and Henry 'did wring [it] as hard as he could'.[44] All present in the room took it to be the conclusive sign that he still dwelt firmly in the faith of Christ.

Henry died shortly afterwards, probably from renal and liver failure, coupled with the effects of his obesity.[45]

Queen Katherine, who had returned to Westminster from Greenwich on 10 January, thus became a widow for the third time. All her jewels were sent to the Tower of London and she changed into her widow's weeds again, acquiring special mourning jewellery, including a gold ring with a death's head for her finger.

CHAPTER TEN

'Dogs Should Lick His Blood'

'He was evermore too good for us all.'

ARCHBISHOP THOMAS CRANMER,

AFTER HENRY VIII'S DEATH.[1]

For three days, Henry's body lay within his secret apartments in the Palace of Westminster while the power brokers in his Council fashioned the shape of the government of the new young king, Edward VI. They also debated long and hard about whether to execute Norfolk, who was doubtless still anxiously pacing up and down in his lodgings in the Tower of London, expecting, every minute, the dreaded knock on his door that would summon him to the last short walk to the scaffold. The bureaucrats also needed many days to complete the complicated arrangements for the king's funeral, which was to be a suitably impressive affair despite the state of the royal exchequer, still only slowly recovering from the bankruptcy caused by the war in 1544–5.[2]

Elaborate hearses had to be constructed – not vehicles in the modern sense but temporary structures fitted with a myriad of mounted candles – beneath which the coffin would rest while Masses, *diriges*[3] and other religious services were said. One was required for the palace chapel, another for Syon, the midway resting point on Henry's last journey, and a third within St George's Chapel inside Windsor Castle. Almost 33,000 yards of black cloth and 8,085 yards of black cotton had to be found and purchased from London merchants at a cost of around £12,000,[4] or more than £3.2 million at today's prices – urgency and instant demand carried the penalty of an inflated cost. These massive quantities of cloth were used to hang in the chapels and to drape the cortège, as well as to make the hooded cloaks and other apparel for the mourners and official guests at the funeral.

Between eight and nine o'clock in the evening of 2 February – the feast of Candlemas – Henry's bulky coffin was moved to the palace chapel, escorted by the officers of his household, the esquires of the body and other noblemen and gentlemen 'both spiritual and temporal, and placed in their degrees' or order of precedence. The coffin was positioned beneath a hearse supported by six pillars, which was festooned with eighty-two foot-long square wax tapers, heraldic pensils (small pennons) and escutcheons of arms. At the four corners stood banners depicting saints, their images woven in fine gold thread upon damask, and over all hung a huge canopy of rich cloth of gold. In total, 1,800 lb. of wax were used to adorn the hearse. It must have been a magnificent, bright, colourful spectacle in the candlelight, made sombre only by the black cloth draping the interior of the chapel. A wooden rail surrounded the hearse, containing seats for the twelve chief mourners, led by Henry Grey, Third Marquis of Dorset. At its foot stood

> an altar, covered with black velvet, adorned with all manner of plate and jewels of the vestry, upon which … there was said mass continually during the time the corpse was there remaining.[5]

The next day, between nine and ten in the morning, the herald Gilbert Dethicke, Norroy King of Arms,[6] resplendent in his richly embroidered tabard, stood at the choir door facing the people and cried out in a loud voice:

> You shall of your charity, pray for the soul of the most famous Prince, King Henry VIII, our late most gracious King and Master.[7]

So began a series of Requiem Masses held night and day, the clouds of incense billowing towards the chapel's vaulted ceiling, each celebrated by three out of nine nominated bishops, all splendid in mitre and full pontifical vestments. Ironically, the irascible and devious Gardiner, only recently banned from the precincts of the Palace of Westminster during one of Henry's last, violent explosions of temper, was to lead all the services, as he was prelate of the Order of the Garter. Daily, before each Mass, *placebo*[8] and *dirige*, Norroy repeated the late king's style of address.

Amid the mourning, Gardiner found time to write an outraged letter to Paget on 5 February, complaining about plans to stage a play by John de Vere in Southwark, to be performed by the Earl of Oxford's actors – 'lewd fellows', he called them – just before Henry's state funeral. Piously, the bishop wrote that the next day the parishioners of Southwark

> and I have agreed to have solemn dirige for our late sovereign lord and master, as becomes us, and tomorrow certain players of my lord of Oxford, as they say, extend on the other side, within this borough of Southwark, to have a solemn play to try who shall have most resort, they in game or I in earnest ...
>
> I follow the common determination in sorrow till our late master be buried. And what the lewd fellows should mean in the contrary, I cannot tell or cannot reform it and therefore write to you ...
>
> I have spoken with Master Acton, justice of peace, whom the players [hold in] small regard and press him to a peremptory answer, whither he dare let them play or not.
>
> Where unto, he answers neither yes nor no as to the playing; but as to the assembly of people in this borough, in this time, neither the burial finished nor the coronation done, he does not plead with the players until he has a commandment to the contrary.
>
> But his 'no' is not much regarded, and mine less, as party to players ...[9]

The actors' plans were incomprehensible to the wrathful bishop, and symptomatic, he believed, of the moral decline in London, a city notoriously infected with the new evangelism. Although he still dwelt out in the cold as far as the Privy Council was concerned, no doubt they quickly discovered that he was very much in earnest and the play was cancelled.

On 7 February, more than 21,000 poor Londoners crowded into Leadenhall and the nearby churchyard of St Michael's Cornhill, to be each handed a groat, a silver coin worth 4d (or just under £5 in twenty-first-century purchasing power) as a dole, or alms, to encourage them to pray for the king's soul. Such was the clamorous press of the great unwashed that the distribution that day lasted from noon until six in the evening, from two separate doorways.[10] The next night they got their chance to fulfil their side of the bargain: every parish church in the city kept a solemn *dirige* for the departed despot, with all the bells ringing a knell, followed the next day by a Requiem Mass said in all the churches of England.

Meanwhile, work was continuing on the massive gilded chariot that was to convey Henry's body to Windsor and on a life-size effigy of the king that was to lie atop the coffin, beneath a canopy. The face was probably fashioned in wax, but the body was stuffed like a common tailor's dummy beneath its sumptuous robes, garments specially made for the funeral. The carver responsible was almost certainly Nicholas Bellin of Modena, who had been working on Henry's tomb, still lying partially completed at Westminster and Windsor, after components from the disgraced Cardinal Wolsey's grandiose monument were appropriated by the king seventeen years before. The Florentine serjeant painter Antonio Toto also decorated the escutcheons bearing the king's and other royal arms for the chariot and hearses, as he had for the funeral of Jane Seymour on 12 November 1537.[11] Joiners, blacksmiths and other artisans were hard at work constructing the chariot, the frame for its canopy of estate and the metal sockets for the fourteen banners to be fixed to its sides and ends.[12]

There were other important tasks to complete before the funeral could take place. An order was issued for the

> clearing and mending of all the highways between Westminster and Windsor whereas the corpse should pass: and the noisome boughs cut down [on] every side [of] the way [to prevent] prejudicing of the standards, banners and bannerols.[13]

And where the ways were narrow, there were hedges opened

[cut down] on either side so as the footmen might have free passage, without tarrying or disturbing of their orders.[14]

Bridges along the route were also checked in case they required repairs. At Windsor, the cortège's destination, the route from the castle bridge to the west door of St George's Chapel was lined with timber railings, all hung with black cloth and emblazoned with the king's arms, to hold back the crowds of spectators. Lord Worcester, the king's almoner, broke off from his now daily distribution of alms, given 'to the great relief and comfort of the poor people' at Leadenhall and at the Palace of Westminster, to arrange for two laden carts to deliver boards painted with heraldic arms to the forty-one parishes in Middlesex, Buckinghamshire and Berkshire through which the funeral procession would pass, or those near the route. His deputies also distributed dole money and torches to the priests at each church.

Concurrently, the arrangements for Edward's coronation were also being made. On 8 and 12 February, Hertford delivered gold and gemstones from Henry's secret jewel house at Westminster to be made into a new crown for the boy king.[15] The coronation ceremonies were also redrafted 'lest their tedious length should weary the king, being yet of tender age'.[16]

On Sunday 13 February, three solemn Masses were said over the old king's coffin, which was still resting within its hearse in the chapel of the Palace of Westminster. The first was a Mass of Our Lady, conducted by two bishops dressed in white vestments; the second was a Mass of the Trinity, with the bishops in blue pontificals; and the third was a Requiem Mass, said by Gardiner himself, dressed in black. Throughout, the Marquis of Dorset, as chief mourner, 'with all the rest of the lords ... were [seated] and kneeled within the hearse, the chapel and all the people keeping silence'. At the end, the bishops liberally blessed the corpse with incense before withdrawing into the vestry, the choir singing '*Libera me, Domine*'.

All men wearing black livery were ordered to gather at Charing Cross by five o'clock the next morning for the first stage of the funeral procession to Syon, on the banks of the River Thames in Middlesex. The destination was the former Bridgettine house surrendered to the crown in 1539 during the Dissolution of the Monasteries. With typical Henrician efficiency, part of it had been used in 1545 as a factory for manufacturing munitions for the wars against France and Scotland.[17]

The procession took some time to assemble, for once on the move it would stretch out for four miles and include more than 1,000 horsemen, as well as many hundreds on foot, all carrying torches. The now completed chariot, drawn by eight great horses draped in black,[18] six of them ridden by 'a child of honour' carrying a banner of the dead king's arms, moved to the door of the chapel:

> The corpse with great reverence [was escorted] from the hearse ... by mitred prelates ... two and two in order, saying their prayers; torches plenty on every side, the corpse born [sic] by sixteen yeomen of the guard under a rich canopy of blue velvet fringed with silk and gold ... [held] up by six blue staves with [knots] of gold [carried] by the Lords Burgavenny, Conyers, Latimer, Fitzwater, Bray and Cromwell.[19]

Henry's vain need for the trappings of majesty had survived beyond his death. The coffin was slid on to the chariot and covered with a pall of rich cloth of gold. On top was placed the funeral effigy of the dead king – 'a goodly image like to the King's person in all points, wonderfully richly apparelled in velvet, gold and precious stones of all sorts'. The Spanish chronicler, apparently an eyewitness, also wrote: 'The figure looked exactly like that of the king himself and he seemed just as if he were alive.'[20] Upon the head of the 'picture', or effigy, which wore a black satin nightcap, was placed 'a crown imperial of inestimable value, a collar of the Garter about his neck and a garter of gold about his leg'.[21] On the feet were crimson velvet shoes, specially made.[22] Two gold bracelets set with pearls and jewels had been slipped on to the effigy's wrists, a 'fair arming sword' laid by its side and a sceptre placed in the right hand, an orb[23] in the left. Sir Anthony Denny and Sir William Herbert scrambled up on to the chariot to take their seats at the head and foot of the coffin as the effigy was secured to the pillars, or uprights, of the chariot's superstructure with silken ribbons.

The chariot remained stationary for two hours while the heralds and marshals ensured that everyone took their correct places in the procession.

> About eight of the clock, the weather being very fair, and the people very desirous to see the sights, the nobles mounted their horses and marched forward with the noble corpse.[24]

At the head rode John Herd and Thomas Mervyn, two porters of the king's household, carrying black staves and acting as 'conductors' to clear the way 'that neither cart, horse nor man should trouble or cumber them in this passage'.[25] Behind them walked the choir and priests of the Chapel Royal, singing orations and prayers, led by a crucifier. They were flanked by 250 'bedesmen' – 'poor men in long mourning gowns and hoods with badges on their left shoulders, the red and white cross in a sun shining, [with] a crown imperial over that'. Each one carried a burning torch as the cortège passed through the towns and villages, and two carts, filled with fresh supplies of torches to replenish those that had burnt out, accompanied their straggling lines.

The procession was ordered according to rank and status. Behind the choristers and bedesmen came Thomas Bruges, carrying a banner bearing a dragon, the badge of Owen Tudor; then came Sir Nicholas Sturley, carrying a banner blazoned with the Lancastrian emblem of a greyhound, accompanied by twelve London aldermen, followed by Lord Windsor with Henry VIII's own lion banner. Behind him followed – two by two – lords and barons, viscounts, earls and bishops, in strict order of precedence, then the foreign ambassadors 'accompanied with such lords as best could entertain and understand their language'. Francis van der Delft, as the representative of an emperor, was accorded a special place of status, mounted alongside the Archbishop of Canterbury. Cranmer now was unshaven, in fulfilment of a solemn vow made at Henry's death to grow a beard in remembrance. Four heralds were assigned to ride about this section of dignitaries, 'to keep order'.

Lord Talbot came next, carrying a banner embroidered with Henry's arms, leading a section of heralds carrying the king's helmet, shield and sword. Chief amongst them was Christopher Barker, Garter King at Arms, bearing the dead monarch's 'rich coat of arms, curiously embroidered'. Then came the twelve 'banners of descent' showing the arms of the king's favoured marriages and ancestors, led by two displaying his arms impaling those of Queen Jane Seymour and Queen Katherine Parr.

Next came the chariot bearing the coffin, a knight riding at each corner bearing banners depicting saints or deities – St Edward, the Trinity, Our Lady and St George – in a conscious display of the King's piety.[26] Flanking it were six hooded assistants and behind rode the chief mourner and the twelve other mourners, followed by the King's Champion with his staff and Sir Anthony Browne, bare-headed, leading Henry's charger, trapped 'in cloth of gold down to the ground'. Behind, Sir Anthony Wingfield, captain of the guard, led his men, who marched three abreast, dressed all in black, their halberds resting on their shoulders, point down.

Other places were filled by the innumerable members of Henry's household – the gentlemen, yeomen, grooms and pages of the bakehouse, pantry, cellars, buttery, confectionery, laundry, kitchen, boilinghouse, poultry yard and wood yard, all wearing the black mourning provided. There were his cupbearers, his trumpeters, caretakers and the Keeper of Marylebone Park. Amongst the legion of retainers on the royal payroll in the procession were members of the king's extensive medical staff: the four physicians – Doctors Chambre, Owen, Cromer and Wendy, his five surgeons, led by John Ayliffe, and two of his apothecaries, Alsop and Reynolds. Listed amongst the queen's household was Henry's faithful fool and long-time companion, Will Somers.[27]

The procession left the palace 'in goodly order' and, via Charing Cross, Knightsbridge, Chelsea, Kensington, Fulham, Hammersmith, Chiswick and Brentford, slowly made its way to Syon, some eight miles from Westminster, along the route of today's Great West Road, the A4, attracting 'the great admiration of them that beheld it, which was an innumerable people'. As it wended its way through each village, the priests dutifully came out of their churches, wearing their best vestments, and offered prayers for their dead sovereign, devoutly censing and sprinkling the cortège with holy water as it trundled by.

Shortly after leaving Brentford, the head of the procession reached Syon at about two o'clock in the afternoon, passing through lines of London aldermen and nobility mounted on horseback on either side of the road. The chariot was brought to the west door of the huge 260-ft.-long double-aisled church and the coffin placed on trestles within another gilded hearse inside. The standards and banners were raised on each side along the choir. The effigy was solemnly removed to the vestry.

After further Masses were said by the Bishops of London, Bristol and Gloucester, Paulet, Lord Steward of the Household, set an overnight watch about the king's corpse 'done with great reverence and devotion'.

Herein lies a curious legend. During the night, it was reported later, putrid matter leaked from the coffin and, in apparent fulfilment of a sermon delivered to Henry at Greenwich by a friar back in 1534 predicting that 'the dogs should lick his blood as they had done Ahab's',[28] stray curs wandered into the church and did just that. According to another version, the coffin's huge weight caused it to fall, fracturing its outer casing and cracking the lead anthropoid shell within. A third account, by Agnes Strickland in the nineteenth century and quoting 'a contemporary document', tells of the leaden coffin

> being cleft by the shaking of the carriage, [and] the pavement of the church was wetted with Henry's blood.
>
> In the morning came plumbers to solder the coffin under whose feet was suddenly seen a dog creeping and licking up the king's blood. If you ask me how I know this, I answer William Greville, who could scarcely drive away the dog, told me and so did the plumber also.[29]

It is possible that a soldered joint may have sprung open. Certainly, the king's body would have been in an advanced state of putrefaction by this time, more than two weeks after his death. If these accounts were true, any damage or hasty repairs could have been hidden beneath the pall.

Between six and seven o'clock that Tuesday morning, after three blasts on the trumpets,[30] the procession resumed its slow progress to Windsor amid funereal knells rung in the towers of churches they passed, reaching the royal town at about one o'clock in the afternoon. It was greeted by Eton scholars kneeling bare-headed in white surplices, carrying tapers and singing psalms.

> At the bridge foot, the mayor and most substantial men stood on the one side, and on the other, priests and clerks, and by them the corpse passed through the castle gate.[31]

Within the chapel, another painted and gilded hearse had been constructed, this time 35 ft. high, of two storeys, fringed with black silk, with thirteen pillars bearing candles – the candles made up, it was estimated, of 4,000 lb. of the finest wax. The coffin was placed inside, with the effigy on top of a black velvet pall. Looking down from above, from the queen's closet, was Katherine Parr, wearing the blue velvet robes, lined with sarsenet, and a purple bodice on her 'kirtle' made for the funeral. Below her, the ambassadors and other noblemen watched the splendour and pageantry from the choir, as yet another Mass and *dirige* were conducted.

The next morning, 16 February, after a number of Masses had been said, Gardiner, assisted by Thomas Goodrich, Bishop of Ely, and Edmund Bonner, Bishop of London, began the Requiem. Henry's coat of arms, his shield, sword and helmet were reverently laid upon the altar.

> And with that, the man of arms, which was Chidock Paulet, came to the choir floor upon his horse in complete harness [armour] all save his head-piece, and a pole-axe in his hand, with the point downward.[32]

This weapon was also laid on the altar. After the offering of various palls, Gardiner climbed into the pulpit before the high altar and preached a sermon on the text 'Blessed are the dead that die in the Lord'. This was a late change of plan: Henry Holbeach, Bishop of Rochester, was originally scheduled to preach.[33] Gardiner spoke of the frailty of man and the 'community of death' involving both rich and poor, great and lowly, who had suffered such a 'dolorous loss' from the death of so gracious a king. But he also comforted them by speaking of 'the resurrection in the life to come and exhorted everyone to rejoice and give thanks to Almighty God, having sent us so toward and virtuous a prince to reign over us'.[34] Six knights removed the effigy to the vestry as the archbishop and the bishops came down to the hearse, singing '*Circumdederunt me*'[35] and the rest of the funeral canticle.

The vault in the floor of the choir where Henry had asked to be temporarily buried, alongside Jane Seymour, was then uncovered. Sixteen 'tall yeomen of the guard' using five strong linen towels then slowly lowered the great coffin into the vault, with Gardiner standing at the head of the grave, reciting the burial service, and the officers of the household crowding around him in the candlelight. As the bishop threw handfuls of earth into the vault, declaiming '*Pulverem, pulveri et cinerem cineri*',[36] Paget, Sir Thomas Cheyney – Treasurer, Sir John Gage – Comptroller, Sir Edmund Knyvett – Serjeant Porter, and the four gentlemen ushers broke their white wands of office over their heads and hurled the fragments into the grave 'with exceeding sorrow and heaviness, not without grievous sighs and tears'. The trappings of Henry's power and authority had followed him into the vault.

The grave was covered with planks and Christopher Barker, Garter King at Arms, dressed magnificently in his tabard, took up his position in the centre of the choir, surrounded by the other heralds. In a loud voice, he cried out:

> Almighty God of his infinite goodness, give good life and long to the most high and mighty Prince, our sovereign lord King Edward VI, by the grace of God, King of England, France and Ireland, Defender

of the Faith and on earth, under God, of the Church of England and Ireland, the supreme head and Sovereign, of the most noble order of the Garter.[37]

Then he shouted, '*Vive le noble roy Edward*' – a cry echoed three times by the officers of arms about him. Above them, in the rood loft, the trumpets sounded 'with great melody and courage to the comfort of all that were there present'.[38]

Various items used in the funeral were later handed over to officials as gifts or fees. These included the cloth of estate of blue velvet, which was given to the Grooms of the Privy Chamber, and an iron chair, covered with purple velvet and fringed with purple silk, and three blue cushions which provided the fee to Hertford as Chamberlain.[39]

After dinner, the Lords of the Privy Council took to horse and rode speedily to London. The old king was dead. Another, a young, impressionable boy, was on the throne and his ceremonial entry into the capital was planned for Saturday 19 February – with the coronation the next day, Shrove Sunday, in Westminster Abbey.

A new reign had dawned on an anxious England.

Epilogue

*'Under Henry VIII, all men feared to speak
though the meaning were not evil. Now every man
has the liberty to speak without danger.'*

SIR WILLIAM PAGET TO EDWARD SEYMOUR, DUKE OF SOMERSET,

LORD PROTECTOR, 25 DECEMBER 1548.[1]

On 31 January 1547, Edward had been publicly proclaimed king, his
courtiers 'tempering their sorrow for the death of their late master with
the joy of his son's happy succeeding [of] him'.[2] The salvoes of guns
firing triumphantly along the battlements of the Tower of London and
the strident, clarion notes of the trumpets sounding that afternoon
must have startled the Duke of Norfolk, still imprisoned within its walls
and tremulously awaiting his grim fate. But those guns signified his
reprieve, despite reports to the contrary.[3]

Norfolk was scheduled to die on the block the very morning Henry
died. The legal formalities were all in place; it was simply a question of
Hertford and his allies delivering the signed death warrant to the Constable of the Tower. That order was never issued, probably because of
their preoccupations with forming a new regency government under
Hertford, as Lord Protector of the realm. Perhaps even Hertford
wondered whether he could dare to press ahead with the execution. In
the event, he took no chances: the Duke of Norfolk remained in the
Tower throughout the six years of Edward's reign and was only released

on Mary's accession in 1553. The Act of Attainder against him was then reversed and his estates and title restored to him on 3 August of that year. As Earl Marshal, he presided over Mary's coronation[4] and the following year, at the age of eighty-one, he was appointed lieutenant-general of government forces to put down the Kentish rebellion (Wyatt's Rebellion), caused primarily by Mary's decision to marry Philip of Spain. But he hardly covered himself with military glory, being panicked into a humiliating retreat back to London with his small force of white-coated royal troops.[5] Norfolk died in his own bed at Kenninghall on 25 August 1554[6] and was later buried in his new mortuary chapel at Framlingham, Suffolk. His beautifully carved Renaissance tomb was erected five years later.[7]

Back in 1547, the French king, Francis I, ordered a solemn Mass to be said for Henry's soul at the Cathedral of Notre Dame in Paris.[8] He was dead himself in March. The Emperor Charles V renounced his throne in favour of his son Philip in 1555 and died, after living the pious life of a monk, three years later. The three monarchs who had dominated Europe for more than three decades had all gone in the space of eight years.

A week after ascending to the English throne, Edward – still closely guarded inside the Tower – wrote a dutiful letter of condolence, in his best schoolroom Latin, to his stepmother. 'Since it has seemed good to God, the best and greatest, that my father, your spouse, the most famous king, has now ended this life, the two of us share one common grief,' he wrote pompously, if not precociously. He continued:

> This indeed brings us consolation: he is now in heaven [and] that he has departed this wretched life [and entered] fortunate and eternal bliss.
>
> For whosoever lives a fortunate life here and well governs the commonwealth, as my most noble sire has done, who has promoted all religion and driven forth all superstition, shall have a most sure way into Heaven.
>
> Though nature bids me weep and shed much tears for the loss

of him that has departed; nevertheless scripture and wisdom bids me restrain these sentiments, lest we seem void of all hope in the resurrection of the dead and life eternal.

Since your highness has conferred so much good on me, it is meet I should hasten to bestow upon you what advantage I may. I pray for your highness. Farewell revered queen.

The letter was signed: 'Edward the king.'[9]

One of the first actions of his councillors was to award themselves new titles and generous grants of lands, in addition to confirming Hertford as Lord Protector and Governor of the King's Person. He was also called the 'Lord Great Master' – a title with the Stalinist ring of a modern-day North Korean leader.

Secretary Paget swore before the Privy Council a deposition of Henry's unfulfilled intentions – 'to have such things paid and performed as was partly owing to them and partly promised'. According to Paget, all these royal good intentions were contained in a book that Henry had slipped into the pocket of his nightshirt. Sadly, the book had now gone missing and 'ere [these plans] could be achieved, God took him from us', said the official solemnly. But all was not lost. *Mirabile dictu!*[10] Paget, like any efficient civil servant, was of course blessed with a remarkable photographic memory and his vivid, detailed and wholly convenient recollections were naturally fully supported by Sir Anthony Denny and Sir William Herbert, his master's confidants – and subsequent beneficiaries.

The old king, Paget testified, considered that 'the nobility of this realm was greatly decayed, some by attainders, some by their own misgovernance and riotous wasting and some by sickness and sundry other means'. Therefore, even whilst facing the forbidding prospect of death, Henry had discussed with his secretary the advancement of some of his courtiers 'to higher places of honour' and Paget had duly noted down the names of the candidates.

The names on his list will hardly come as a surprise. To the victors and survivors in the great struggle for power went the spoils. Hertford was to be made Duke of Somerset and Earl Marshal, and Dudley, Viscount Lisle, Earl of Warwick[11] and Great Chamberlain. William Parr was elevated to Marquis of Northampton, while Russell, Wriothesley and Lord St John were also to be made earls. Amongst the barons to be created were Sir Thomas Seymour, now Lord High Admiral, and that notorious weathercock Sir Richard Rich, ever swinging with the political wind. Incomes from the estates of Norfolk and Surrey were also available for distribution. Paget said that he had suggested to Henry that as he had advanced these true and faithful servants

> it might please him to bestow liberally upon such as should please him. Whereunto, he accorded and willed me to bring him [the titles] of the lordships and valuations.
>
> But he liked it not and in my presence called Master Gates and bad him fetch such books as he had of the duke of Norfolk and earl of Surrey's lands, which he did.[12]

The king's first attempt at sharing out the spoils was not satisfactory. The secretary, no doubt with an eye to bestowing favours that would have to be repaid in the future, said this 'was too little' and discussed it further with Henry. 'He bade me speak with them [the intended recipients of the king's munificence] and know their dispositions and he would after tell me more.' The faithful and manipulative Denny was also not to be forgotten:

> And then considering what painful service Master Denny did take daily with him [the king], and also moved of honesty for that Mr Denny had diverse times been a suitor for me and I never for him, I beseeched his majesty to be [a] good lord unto him and to give him [the manor of] Bungay [Suffolk] which I had heard he much desired.
>
> His majesty much commended my suit and said he had thought before to be good to him and to Mr [William] Herbert and Mr Gates also ... [13]

Henry, ever avaricious, finally decided to keep Norfolk's lands in his own hands, with the exception of some in Sussex and Hampshire.

Thus, at a stroke and by very dubious practice, members of the new government considerably enriched themselves. If you have the power, why not flaunt it? Who was going to argue with them or dispute this largesse?

Hertford received lands worth £800 a year, with a further £300 annually from 'the next bishop's lands that shall fall void'. Lisle and Wriothesley were to get revenues of £300 a year and Sir Thomas Seymour lands worth £500 per annum. Rich was awarded the very precise income of £66 13s 4d a year. Denny got Bungay and lands worth £200; Herbert, lands worth 400 marks ('to help get him out of debt withal'); and Gates, 100 marks.

Straight-faced, Paget pledged that all this being 'remembered on his deathbed' by Henry 'that he had promised great things to diverse men, he willed in his testament that whatsoever should in any wise appear to his Council to have been promised by him, the same should be performed'.[14]

Herbert attested that one name was missing from the long list of beneficiaries of Henry's munificence – Paget himself. According to Herbert, they had pointed this out to the dying king and had praised the secretary's faithful service. Yes, said Henry, he remembered him well enough and 'he must needs be helped'.[15] So Paget, too, was given lands worth 400 marks a year.

Hertford, or Somerset as he now was, and his colleagues on the Council agreed that these bountiful gifts 'had been determined' by 'our late sovereign lord' and therefore after his death, 'partly for the conservation of our own honesty and specially for the honour and surety of our sovereign lord that now is, [we] take upon us the degrees of honour and enter into the charge of attendance and service in the great and weighty affairs' of Edward VI. Moreover, they thought that 'we cannot otherwise discharge ourselves towards God and the world then if we paid [back] that which was given or promised'.[16] So that was all right, then. There are few things in life more comforting than feeling morally justified in accepting great honours and wealth.

Paget had delivered fully: not only, at best, a doubtful will, but also a cynical distribution of royal gifts to those who had conspired to provide absolute power to Somerset. Only Wriothesley objected to Somerset's *coup d'état*, and he was quickly to pay the price of opposition. He was accused of acting illegally in his use of the Great Seal of the realm in appointing four colleagues to hear Chancery cases on his behalf. On 6 March, Wriothesley was fired as Lord Chancellor, kicked off the Privy Council, fined £4,000 and put under house arrest in London[17] to prevent any chance of him fomenting trouble in his home county of Hampshire. He was, however, readmitted to the Council sometime in 1548, but in the internecine struggles for power that followed two years later he was again struck off and banished from court after an abortive conspiracy against the government leaders. He died, supposedly of grief over his expulsion from court, on 30 July 1550.

Somerset turned out to be a good soldier but a hopeless administrator. He was arrogant, headstrong and impetuous, and ruled by his imperious second wife, Anne Stanhope. Paget tried desperately to make him both more amenable to the differing views within the Council and more flexible in the implementation of government:

> Of late, your grace is grown into great choleric fashions when so ever you are contraried [to] that [which] you have conceived in your head.
>
> A subject in great authority, as your grace is, using such fashion is like to fall into great danger and peril of his own person besides that to the commonwealth.
>
> I beseech you: when the whole Council shall move you or give you advice in a matter ... to follow the same and relent some time from your own opinions.[18]

No wonder Paget later wrote to the Lord Protector on 7 July 1549:

> Remember what you promised me in the gallery at Westminster before the breath was out of the body of the king ... Remember

what you promised me immediately after, devising with me concerning the place which you now occupy. And that was to follow my advice in all your proceedings, more than any man's.[19]

Paget also felt it necessary later to send Somerset very sensible advice about the practice of good governance, laying down his 'manifesto' in a letter to the Lord Protector on 2 January 1549: 'I pray your grace accept this token in good part which very hearty love and great carefulness of your grace's well doings has moved me to send [you], to whom I wish as well as I do to my own soul.' Always, he counselled:

Deliberate maturely in all things.

Execute quickly the deliberations.

Do justice without respect.[20]

Make assured and staid wise men ministers under you. Maintain the ministers in their offices.

Punish the disobedient according to their deserts.

Reward the king's worthy servants liberally and quickly. Give your own to your own and the king's to the king's frankly.

Dispatch suitors shortly. Be affable to the good and stern to the evil.

Follow advice in Council.

Take fee or reward of the king only.

Keep your ministers about you uncorrupt.

Paget added: 'Thus God will prosper you, the king favour you and all men love you.'[21] It is good advice that some governments could do worse than follow closely today.

What of Katherine, now the dowager queen? In his will, Henry repaid her devoted care of him and her compassion for his children with substantial legacies granted in praise of her virtues of 'great love, obedience, chastity of life and wisdom'.[22]

She was angry that the role of regent had been taken away from her and protested to the new government, but it ignored her appeals. At least she was not going to starve. The cash and goods left to her, worth just over £1 million at today's prices, were not overgenerous, but the dower and jointure made Katherine very wealthy indeed. Her income and her matronly good looks rendered her an attractive catch for anyone audacious enough to woo the king's widow.

Within just a month after Henry's death, she was again smitten with her old sweetheart, the roguish Thomas Seymour. Nine love letters exchanged between them over a period of seventeen months survive in various private and public archives to this day. By March 1547, Katherine had probably accepted the Lord High Admiral's offer of marriage but, as with Henry, told him that there had to be a decent period of public mourning before a wedding could be staged.

In one letter, Seymour writes playfully of a supper with Katherine's sister Anne Herbert and her husband, Sir William, later to be created Earl of Pembroke.

> She waded further with me touching my lodging with your highness at Chelsea, which I denied ... but that indeed, I went by the garden as I went to the bishop of London's house and at this point stood with her a long time.
>
> Till at last, she told me further tokens, which made me change my colours, who, like a false wench, took me [in] with the manner.
>
> Then remembering what she was and knowing how well you trusted her, examined whether those things came from your highness or were feigned. She answered that they came from your highness ... for which I render unto your highness my most humble and hearty thanks.
>
> For by her company, in default of yours, I shall shorten the weeks in these parts, which heretofore were four days longer in everyone of them than they were under the plummet [featherbed] at Chelsea.[23]

He writes of Katherine's 'goodness to me, showed at our last lodging together' and asks to receive her letters – even just 'three lines in a letter from you'[24] – and for her to send him 'one of your small pictures, if you have any left, who with his silence,[25] shall give me occasion to think on the friendly cheer that I shall receive when my suit shall be at an end'.

The Herberts acted as a discreet post office for the lovers' letters, but chief amongst the couple's concerns was what the new boy king, let alone the Lord Protector, would think of their plans for marriage so soon after Henry's death. Katherine wrote to Seymour from her palace in Chelsea regarding his attempts to win approval from his brother:

> My lord: As I gather from your letter, delivered to my brother Herbert, you are in some fear how to frame my lord your brother [the Lord Protector] to speak in your favour. The denial of your request shall make his folly more manifest to the world, which will grieve me more than the want of his speaking.
>
> I would not wish you to importune for his goodwill, if it come not frankly at the first ...
>
> I would desire you might obtain the king's letters in your favour and also the aid and furtherance of the most notable of the Council ... which thing obtained shall be no such small shame to your brother and loving sister.[26]

Seymour was obviously in a hurry to arrange the wedding ceremony, which worried her:

> My lord, whereas you charge me with a promise, written with mine own hand, to change the two years into two months, I think you have no such plain sentence written in my hand.
>
> I know not whether you be a paraphraser or not.
>
> If you be learned in that science, it is possible you may of one word make a whole sentence, and yet not at all times alter the true meaning of the writer; as it appears by this your exposition upon my writing.

Katherine was keen to keep up good appearances and to avoid the risk of scandal:

> When it shall be your pleasure to repair hither, you must take some pain to come early in the morning that you may be gone again by seven o'clock and so I suppose you may come without suspect [suspicion].
>
> I pray you let me have knowledge overnight at what hour you will come, that your portress may wait at the gate to the fields for you.

She signs herself: 'By her that is, and shall be, your humble, true and loving wife during her life, Katherine the Queen.'

Another of her letters sought reassurance that her lover was not offended by her slowness in writing, 'for my promise was but once in a fortnight'. The letter also contains the first signs of a rift between Katherine and her prospective brother-in-law, the Lord Protector, and his feisty wife Anne. Katherine, as dowager queen, felt very slighted at being edged away from the court and the centre of attention:

> My lord, your brother, has deferred answer concerning such requests as I made to him till his coming here, which he said shall be immediately after the term.
>
> This is not his first promise I have received of his coming and yet under-performed.
>
> I think my lady has taught him this lesson: for it is her custom to promise many comings to her friends and to perform none. I trust in greater matters, she is more circumspect.[27]

Seymour, in his thin, spindly, spider-like scrawl, replied in haste from St James's Palace:

> Yesterday in the morning, I had written a letter to your highness upon occasion I met with a man of my Lord Marquis [Katherine's brother William Parr, Marquis of Northampton] as I came to Chelsea, whom I knew not, who told Nicholas Throgmorton[28] that

I was in Chelsea fields with other circumstances which I defer till at more leisure.

Which letter being finished ... I remembered your commandment [29] to me, wherewith I threw it into the fire, be minding to keep your requests and desires, and for that it hath pleased you to be the first breaker of your appointment, I shall desire your highness to reserve my thanks of the same ...

As touching on my lord's promise, I trust to make you friends, assuring you that I wait as well on him as any man he has, to creep into his favour to bring our matters well to pass.

My lady of Somerset told me on Friday night that she would [go] to Sheen the next day and at her return on Tuesday (which is tomorrow) she would see your highness, but I think it will be Wednesday ere she comes for that my lord will be tomorrow all day in the Star Chamber.[30]

He adds: 'I never over-read it after it was written, [therefore] if any faults be I pray you hold me excused.'

Katherine received another of Seymour's letters, delivered by one of her sister's servants. She wrote back that beforehand, she was hell bent on writing to Somerset so that

he might well and manifestly perceive my fantasy to be more towards you for marriage than any other.

Notwithstanding I am determined to add thereto a full determination never to marry and to break it when I have done, if I live two years. I think to see the king one day this week at which time I would be glad to see you, though I scarce dare ask in speech.

She promises to write letters to him once every three days and that she had

sent in haste to the painters for one of my little pictures which is very perfect by the judgement of as many as has seen the same. The last I had myself I bestowed ... upon my lady of Suffolk.

Katherine adds plaintively:

I dare not desire to see you for fear of suspicion. I wish the world was as well pleased with our meaning as I am well assured the goodness of God's but the world is so wicked that it cannot be contented with good things.[31]

Both official and family approval for the marriage was essential. After being approached by Seymour, Princess Mary, on 3 June, firmly declined to become involved:

[I have] received your letter wherein (I think) I perceive strange news concerning a suit you have in hand to the Queen for marriage.

My lord ... it stands less without my poor honour to be a meddler in this matter, considering whose wife her grace was of late.

Besides, if she be minded to grant you your suit my letters shall do you but small pleasure. On the other side, if the remembrance of the king's majesty, my father (whose soul God pardon) will not suffer her to grant your suit, I am nothing able to persuade her to forget the loss of him who is as yet very ripe in my remembrance.

Wherefore, I shall most earnestly require you to think no unkindness in me though I refuse to be a meddler anyways in this matter (wooing matters set apart, wherein I being a maid, am nothing cunning).[32]

Seymour then tried the young king. He employed John Fowler, a member of the Privy Chamber, to suggest the idea that Edward's uncle should marry his stepmother. After several embarrassing false starts – including the king's bright but inconvenient idea of Seymour marrying Anne of Cleves – on 25 June, Edward wrote to Katherine blessing the union:

Proceed therefore in your good course. Continue to love my father and show the great kindness to me, which I have ever perceived in you.

Cease not to love and read the Scriptures but persevere in always reading them.[33]

The couple may have signed the written marriage contracts and exchanged rings within thirty-four days of Henry's death. They were probably not married at Chelsea until early June, although it may even have been later by a few weeks, as van der Delft reported on 10 July 1547 that

> the Queen [dowager] was married a few days ago since to the Lord Admiral, the brother of the Protector and still causes herself to be served ceremoniously as queen, which, it appears, is the custom here.
>
> Nevertheless, when she went lately to dine at the house of her new husband she was not served with the royal state, from which it is presumed that she will eventually live according to her new condition.[34]

Somerset was sorely offended by the marriage and disputed the ownership of the jewels given to the dowager queen by Henry. Katherine vented her anger to her new husband at the cavalier treatment accorded her by Somerset:

> My lord: This shall be to advertise you that my lord your brother has this afternoon a little made me warm.
>
> It was fortunate we were so much distant for I suppose else I should have bitten him.
>
> What cause have they to fear [you] having such a wife? It is requisite for them to continually pray for a short dispatch of that hell.
>
> Tomorrow or else upon Saturday at afternoon about three o'clock I will see the king where I intend to utter all my choler to my lord your brother, if you do not give me advice to the contrary: for I would be loath to do anything to hinder your matter.
>
> I will declare unto you how my lord has used me concerning Fausterne,[35] and after I shall most humbly desire to direct mine answer to him in that behalf ... My lord, I beseech you send me word with speed how I shall use myself to my new brother.[36]

It was a testing time for her, made worse by the insistence of precedence over her at court by Somerset's wife. Katherine wrote to Seymour:

> How is this that through my marriage to you, the wife of your brother
> is treating me with contempt and presumes to go before me.
>
> I will never allow it, for I am Queen and shall be called so all my
> life and I promise you if she does again what she did yesterday I
> will pull her back myself.[37]

Somerset was unsympathetic. He wrote to Seymour: 'Brother, are you not my younger brother and am I not Protector? Do you not know that your wife, before she married the king, was of lower rank than my wife?'

The next day, in the chapel either at Westminster or St James's Palace, the Protector's wife 'came and thrust herself forward and sat in the Queen's place. As soon as the Queen saw it, she could not bear it and took hold of her arm and said: "I deserve this for degrading myself from a queen to marrying the admiral." The other ladies that were there would not allow the quarrel to go further.'

The duchess was brimming over with fury about Katherine's behaviour, refused to bear her train and told all and sundry about her contempt for the dowager queen:

> Did not Henry VIII marry Katherine Parr in his doting days when
> he brought himself so low by his lust and cruelty that no lady that
> stood on her honour would venture on him?
>
> And shall I now give place to her who in her former estate was
> but Latimer's widow and is now fain to cast herself on a younger
> brother.
>
> If master admiral teaches his wife no better manners, I am
> she that will.[38]

Aside from court jealousies and the row over ownership of her jewels, Katherine was still dutifully concerned about the welfare of her stepchildren. A letter to her from Elizabeth, written from Cheshunt, Hertfordshire, sometime in 1547 talks fondly of the queen dowager's friendship:

Truly I was replete with sorrow to depart from your highness, especially leaving you undoubtful of health. Although I answered little,
I weighed it more deeper when you said you would warn me of all
evils that you should hear of me.

For if your grace had not a good opinion of me, you would not
have offered friendship to me that way, that all men judge the
contrary.

But what may I more say than thank God for providing such
friends to me; desiring God to enrich me with their long life and
[grant] me grace to be in heart no less thankful to receive it than I
now am glad in writing to show it.

Although I have plenty of matter, here I will stay for I know
you are not quiet to read.[39]

Elizabeth, now aged thirteen, came to live with Katherine at Chelsea
very soon after Henry's death and was to spend seventeen months with
her stepmother and her new husband. Therein lay great danger: the
boisterous Seymour was fond of fun and games with the princess, and
she, in the first flush of puberty, enjoyed his flirtations. Her governess
Catherine, or 'Cat', Ashley later testified:

At Chelsea, after he was married to the Queen, he would come
many mornings into Lady Elizabeth's chamber before she was
ready and sometimes before she had risen and if she were up he
would bid her good morrow and would ask her how she did and
strike her on the back or on the buttocks familiarly ...

And if she were in bed, he would put open the curtains and
make as though he would come at her and one morning he strove
to have kissed her in bed.

That one morning at Hanworth, the Queen came with him
and she and the Lord Admiral tickled the Lady Elizabeth in the bed.

Another time at Hanworth, he romped with her in the garden
and cut her gown, being black cloth, into a hundred pieces, and
when this deponent came up and chided Lady Elizabeth, she

answered that she could not strive withal, for the Queen held her
while the Lord Admiral cut her dress.[40]

There is evidence that Katherine grew uneasy and angry at this flirting:
'The Lord Admiral came sometimes [to Elizabeth's chamber] without
the Queen, which some misliked.'[41] Shortly after Whitsun 1548, Katherine put her foot down and sent Elizabeth back to Cheshunt.

Then, astonishingly, the dowager queen, at the age of around thirty-
five, became pregnant. She retreated from Chelsea to her manor of
Hanworth in Middlesex because of the spread of the plague. One of her
letters from there, on 9 June 1548, talks of her unborn child stirring in
her womb:

> I gave your little knave your blessing who like an honest man stirred
> apace after and before. For Mary Odell, being abed with me, had
> laid her hand upon my belly to feel it stir.
>
> It has stirred these three days every morning and evening so
> that I trust when you come, it will make you some pastime.
>
> And thus I end, bidding my sweetheart and loving husband
> better to fare than myself.[42]

Katherine was hoping that Seymour would escort her from Hanworth to
their home at Sudeley Castle, near Winchcombe, Gloucestershire, where
she was planning to spend her confinement. But a threatened attack by
the French fleet on Pevensey Castle, Sussex, could have summoned the
admiral to duty at any time. 'I am very sorry for the news of the Frenchmen,'
she wrote to him. 'I pray God it not be a let [hindrance] to our journey. As
soon as you know what they will do, good my lord, I beseech you to let
me hear from you, for I shall not be quiet till I know.'

Her husband replied from Westminster the same day, saying that her
letter revived his spirits 'partly for that I do perceive you be armed with
patience' but 'chiefest, that I hear my little man doth shake his poll',
referring to the unborn child's movements, probably of its head. Seymour
had spoken to the Lord Protector about taking a leave of absence from
his duties:

I spoke to him of your going down into the country on Wednesday, who was sorry thereof, trusting that I would be here all tomorrow to hear what the Frenchmen will do.

And on Monday dinner, I trust to be with you. As for the Frenchmen, I have no mistrust that they shall be any let of my going with you on this journey or of any continuance [at Sudeley] there with your highness.[43]

He adds: 'I do desire your highness to keep the little knave so lean and gaunt with your good diet and walking, that he may be so small that he may creep out of a mouse hole.' Seymour took his wife and Lady Jane Grey – the young daughter of the Marquis of Dorset and Seymour's ward – to Sudeley on 13 June, for the last three months of Katherine's pregnancy. She was clearly having a difficult time. Elizabeth wrote to Katherine as her confinement drew near:

Although your highness's letters be most joyful to me in absence, yet considering what pain it is for you to write, your grace being so great with child and so sickly ...

I much rejoice at your health, with the well liking of the country, with my humble thanks that your grace wished me with you ... [Seymour] shall be diligent to give me knowledge from time to time how his busy child doth and if I were at his birth, no doubt I would see him beaten for the trouble he hath put to you.

Master [Sir Anthony] Denny and my lady [his wife, Joan] with humble thanks pray most entirely for your grace, praying the almighty God to send you a most lucky deliverance ...

Written, with very little leisure, this last day of July.

Your humble daughter, Elizabeth.[44]

Mary also wrote, rather stiffly, on 9 August:

I trust to hear great success of your grace's great belly and in the meantime shall desire much to hear of your health, which I pray almighty God to continue and increase to his pleasure as much as your own heart can desire.[45]

Katherine, attended by Henry's former physician Dr Robert Huicke, gave birth to a healthy daughter on 30 August. She was named Mary, after the princess, her stepsister. Seymour's brother, the Lord Protector, wrote to congratulate him from Syon on 1 September:

> We are right glad to understand by your letters that the Queen your bedfellow has had a happy hour and escaping all danger, has made you the father of so pretty a daughter.
>
> Although (if it so pleased God) it would have been both to us and we suppose to you, a more joy and comfort if it had been this the first a son, yet the escape of danger and the prophecy and good promise of this to a great sort of happy sons, the which as you write, we trust no less than to be true.[46]

But all was not well. Like Jane Seymour, Katherine contracted an infection and became delirious. She died of puerperal fever between two and three in the morning of 5 September 1548. Lady Elizabeth Tyrwhit said that two days before her death, Katherine told her that 'she did fear such things in herself' and 'that she was sure she could not live'. Katherine had held Seymour's hand and said: 'My lady Tyrwhitt, I am not well handled, for those that be about me care not for me, but stand laughing at my grief and the more good I will them, the less good they will to me.' The admiral answered: 'Why sweetheart, I would do you no hurt.' But she replied: 'No, my lord, I think so,' and whispered in his ear, 'But my lord, you have given me many shrewd taunts.' She went on: 'My lord, I would have given a thousand marks to have had my full talk with Huicke the first day I was delivered but I dared not for [fear of] displeasing you.'[47]

Although sounding sinister, these are likely to be the murmurings of a woman in delirium. She recovered her reason to dictate her will, 'being persuaded of the approach of death', leaving everything to her husband. It remained unsigned but was attested as a true record of her wishes by her doctor, Huicke, and her chaplain, John Parkhurst.

Seymour was devastated. He told the Marquis of Dorset that he was 'so amazed [by] my great loss' that he would break up and dissolve 'my whole house'.[48] But it was not long before he saw an end to his grief and his ambitions remained unchecked. In January 1549, Pigott, his servant, told his sister that he had overheard the admiral saying that 'he would wear black for a year and then knew where to have a wife'.[49]

In May 1782, Katherine's grave was found by one of those strange parties of eighteenth-century tourists, part day-trippers, part antiquarians, always with an active morbid curiosity. Some ladies were examining Sudeley Castle's ruined chapel of St Mary,[50] then used to house rabbits, and after noting a large alabaster slab fixed in the north wall, they began digging in the ground not far away:

> Not much more than a foot from the surface, they found a leaden envelope[51] which they opened in two places, on the face and breast, and found it to contain a human body wrapped in cerecloth.
>
> Upon removing what covered the face, they discovered the features and particularly the eyes in perfect preservation.
>
> Alarmed at this sight and with the smell, which came principally from the cerecloth, they ordered the ground to be thrown in immediately without judiciously closing up the cerecloth and lead, which covered the face.[52]

Written on a label attached to the lead coffin was an inscription identifying the body within: Katherine – 'wife to King Henry the VIII and the wife of Thomas Lord of Sudeley, high admiral of England and uncle to King Edward VI'. Two years later, another party disturbed her remains and found that decomposition had 'reduced the face to bone'. In 1786, an antiquary recovered samples of the clothes worn by the corpse, its hair and a tooth, which are preserved still at Sudeley Castle. The queen was reburied in a new monument, including a life-size effigy of her, designed by that architect of high Victorian gothic taste, Sir George Gilbert Scott, in 1863.[53]

Katherine's daughter Mary went to live with her mother's old friend and lady-in-waiting, Katherine, Duchess of Suffolk, but died probably before the age of two.

Just over a month after being chief mourner at Katherine's funeral,[54]

Lady Jane Grey, then a child of eleven, wrote a letter in her careful handwriting to the Lord Admiral:

> Thinking myself so much bound to your lordship for your great goodness towards me from time to time, that I cannot by any means be able to recompense the least part thereof, I purposed to write a few rude words to your lordship rather as a token to show how much worth I think your lordship's goodness than to give worthy thanks for the same.
>
> These my letters shall testify to you that like as you have become towards me a loving and kind father, so I shall be always most ready to obey your godly monitions and good instructions as becomes one upon whom you have heaped so many benefits.[55]

Thomas Seymour, always jealous of his brother, the Protector, had long nourished plans to snatch power and control the king. He had tried to win influence by giving Edward presents and pocket money. In addition, he had other grievances against Somerset. The admiral showed his brother-in-law William Parr, Marquis of Northampton, 'the suits to the Protector touching the Queen's servants, jewels and other things which he claimed to be hers'.[56] All these had been denied her since Henry's death. He also harboured dreams of marrying one of the two princesses, ideas firmly quashed by members of the Privy Council. He was, as in most things, rather obvious, and was arrested on 17 January 1549 for treason. Rumours swept London about what had happened. The Spanish ambassador van der Delft reported to his imperial master on 27 January:

> Sire, I have heard that the Admiral of England, with the help of some people about the court, attempted to outrage the person of the young king by night and has been taken to the Tower.
>
> The alarm was given by the gentleman who sleeps in the king's chamber, who awakened by the barking of the dog that lies before the king's door, cried out: 'Help! Murder!'

Everybody rushed in but the only thing they found was the lifeless corpse of the dog.

Suspicion points to the Admiral because he had scattered the watch that night on several errands and because it has been noticed that he has some secret plot on hand, hoping to marry ... the lady Elizabeth who is also under grave suspicion.[57]

John Fowler, Groom of the Privy Chamber, told the Council how, early one morning, Seymour had arrived at St James's Palace and was surprised at the lack of guards there. He said there was 'slender company about the king' – no one in the presence chamber and 'not a dozen in the whole house. A man might steal away the king now for I came with more men than is in all the house besides'.[58]

Paget told van der Delft later: 'He [Seymour] has been a great rascal,'[59] which may serve as a suitable epitaph on his life. Somerset signed his brother's death warrant and the admiral was executed on 20 March 1549.

Elizabeth had been unwittingly dragged into Seymour's plot and was now facing some embarrassing questions. She wrote in her careful, clear hand to Somerset that she had never contemplated marriage 'without the Council's consent thereto'. Moreover, she had heard that there were

rumours abroad which be greatly both against my honour and honesty which above all other things I esteem, which be these that I am in the Tower and with child by my Lord Admiral.

Elizabeth ends:

My Lord, these are shameful slanders for the which besides the great desire I have to see the king's majesty, I shall most heartily desire your lordship that I may come to the court after your first determination that I may show myself there as I am. Written in haste from Hatfield, this 28 of January. Your assured friend to my little power, Elizabeth.[60]

Somerset himself was toppled from power after openly quarrelling with his old ally John Dudley, Earl of Warwick. His influence and authority had also been damaged by his brother's disgrace. In the government crisis of 1549, when rebellions broke out in the West, East Anglia and the Midlands and were threatened elsewhere, Somerset had acted hesitantly and incompetently. On 6 October, he had moved the king for his safety to Windsor Castle, but his colleagues in the Council in London arrested him on 14 October and he confessed to twenty-nine charges on 24 October. He was released in February 1550, freely pardoned and restored to membership of the Privy Council on 10 April, only to be arrested again in October 1551 on trumped-up charges of high treason and felony. He was convicted only of felony (for inciting a riot) but none the less was executed on 22 January 1552. The king, in his personal chronicle, recorded his uncle's death merely as: 'The Duke of Somerset had his head cut off upon Tower Hill between eight and nine o'clock in the morning.'

The energetic Warwick, later created Duke of Northumberland, had triumphed in the power struggle for control of king and realm, becoming president of Edward's Council. When the king fell ill, probably with tuberculosis, in the early summer of 1553, the prospect of staunchly Catholic Mary succeeding loomed large in his and other Protestant minds. The king, sometime in early April, drew up his plan for the succession, which excluded both his half-sisters, who had been laid down as his successors by the Third Act of Succession passed in Henry VIII's reign. Edward's document created a brand-new succession path, beginning with the male heirs of Frances, Duchess of Suffolk, daughter of Mary, Henry's younger sister. It continued with the male heirs of Frances' daughters, Jane, Catherine and Mary Grey. The major problem was that none had any sons when Edward's 'devise for the succession' was written.[61] The solution for the Privy Councillors was easy: to make the succession far more viable by ensuring that it went directly to Lady Jane Grey and her male heirs. The alteration was open and above board: the judges, led by Lord Chief Justice Montague, were asked to deploy their legal brains on the issues raised. Unsurprisingly, they declined to become involved 'for the danger of treason' and Northumberland

> fell into a great anger and rage and called [Montague] traitor before all the Council and said that in the quarrel of that matter, he would fight in his shirt with any man living.[62]

Edward summoned the judges to his presence on 15 June and told them in no uncertain terms 'with sharp words and angry countenance' to help him draw up the royal will. The legal opposition collapsed and letters patent, implementing the succession, were drawn up within the next few days.

Edward died, 'thin and wasted', on 6 July, in his sixteenth year. Lady Jane Grey was duly named as his successor and was proclaimed queen of England in London on 10 July 1553. Princess Mary had fled to East Anglia and, after mustering forces loyal to her cause and to a Catholic accession, marched on the capital where the Council named her as queen nine days later. Jane, who had married one of the sons of Dudley, now Duke of Northumberland, was beheaded on 12 February 1554, aged just seventeen. Northumberland was also doomed. At his trial, he questioned whether his actions, under the authority of the Great Seal of the realm, could be treason, but his judges told him that the Seal was not that of the lawful queen but of an usurper,[63] the unhappy and unwilling Lady Jane Grey. On the Tower Hill scaffold, on 22 August 1553, he paid the penalty for it.

One of his confederates involved in the fiasco of Lady Jane Grey's abortive succession was the ubiquitous John Gates. While he undoubtedly was a religious reformer, his upwardly mobile progression through the Edwardine government was more motivated by personal ambition and greed. He was, however, a notorious and enthusiastic despoiler of churches. As Sheriff of Essex, he was ordered to enforce the injunctions of 1550 to destroy 'superstitious altars'. The Essex historian Philip Morant later wrote of him:

This covetous man pulled the chancel [of Chelmsford Church] down for the sake of making money out of the materials, notwithstanding so many noble persons had chosen it for their resting place, namely Humfrey Stafford, duke of Buckingham, Anne, his wife and three of the sons, including Sir Henry, who had married Margaret, countess of Richmond, grandmother of Henry VIII.[64]

Gates also played a role in preventing the planned clandestine flight of Princess Mary to Antwerp in July 1550. In April 1551, he was made Vice-Chamberlain and Captain of the King's Guard, with a seat on the Privy Council, and granted further lands worth £120 a year.[65] On 7 July 1552, he was made Chancellor of the Duchy of Lancaster. He was also executed for treason on 22 August 1553, shortly after Mary's accession, the axeman requiring three blows to bloodily sever his head.[66]

Anthony Denny served in William Parr's expedition to put down the Norfolk insurgents in Kett's Rebellion in 1549, but died in September that year, probably on the 10th, at his home at Cheshunt, Hertfordshire.[67]

Paget was created Baron Paget of Beaudesert in 1549 and remained faithful to his troublesome leader, Somerset. After the Protector's downfall, Paget was arrested in 1551 on suspicion of plotting against Dudley and the following year was degraded from the Order of the Garter and fined £6,000 over allegations that he exploited his offices for private gain. After Edward's death, he joined Queen Jane's Council, but quickly changed sides and sanctioned the proclamation declaring Mary queen. He was rewarded by being appointed a Privy Councillor and was made her Lord Privy Seal in 1556. On Elizabeth's accession, he quit all his offices and died in 1563.

Stephen Gardiner quickly fell foul of the new Protestant government of Edward VI following its introduction of doctrinal changes and was held in the Fleet Prison from September 1547, to which 'he had been as well used as if it had been his house'.[68] He was released after promising to conform but

forgetful of his promises, he had raised much strife and contention and had caused all his servants to be secretly armed and harnessed[69] and had put public affronts on those whom the Council sent down to preach in his diocese.

In some places, to disgrace them, he went into the pulpit before them and warned the people to beware of such teachers and to receive no other doctrine but what he had taught them.

He was placed under house arrest at his home in Southwark and, after preaching a 'seditious' sermon before Edward, was sent to the Tower 'and the door of his closet sealed up'. In April 1551, he was deprived of his bishopric, but after the accession of the Catholic Mary Tudor in 1553, he was swiftly freed on 9 August, the day after Edward's funeral, and was given the Great Seal of England, as Lord Chancellor, four days later. But his glory days were short-lived: on 13 November 1555, he died at the Palace of Westminster between noon and one o'clock. His body was brought by water to his home in Southwark and elaborate obsequies followed, before he was buried at Winchester.[70]

As for Cranmer, the *Book of Common Prayer*, with its wonderful, rolling English words and phrases, is his lasting memorial.[71] The first version appeared in 1549 and a revised edition in 1552. As if his Protestant views were not damning enough in Mary's eyes, he was persuaded to sign the document naming Lady Jane Grey queen and consequently, after her succession, he quickly ended up in the Tower, accused of treason and sedition. He was taken to Oxford and confronted with charges of heresy. In the face of death, the old man's resolve weakened and he signed a number of papers acknowledging the supremacy of the Pope and the truth of Catholic doctrine. In the end, he withdrew these recantations and was burnt at the stake on 21 March 1556.

Anne of Cleves died in 1557 and was buried in Westminster Abbey in a tomb now scarcely visible on the south side of the high altar. At least in death she had attained the status of being amongst the kings and queens, a place so long denied her.

Finally, there is Will Somers, Henry's fool. After the old king's death, he went into honourable retirement in apartments at Hampton Court, occasionally appearing in plays, masques and entertainments at Edward's court. Amongst these popular guest appearances was one at Christmastime 1551, at Greenwich, when he appeared in cardboard armour for personal mock-combat with the young king. Five shillings were also paid for other costumes for him of 'white-banded blue brocaded silk, guarded [edged] with red satin' and 'a frock of tawny silk striped with gold [and] furred about the neck'.[72] He also appeared in 'interludes' for Mary and was present at the coronation of Elizabeth in January 1559. He died on 15 June 1560,[73] his laughter and merry jibes at last silenced, and was buried in the church of St Leonard's, Shoreditch, London.

'Tombs of Brass are Spent'

*'Our own body be buried and interred in the
choir of our College of Windsor, midway
between the stalls and the high altar and there to
be made and set ... an honourable tomb
for our bones to rest in, which is well onward and
almost made therefore ready with a fair
grate about it ... in which we will also [that] the
bones of our true and loving wife Queen
Jane be put also.'*

WILL OF HENRY VIII, 30 DECEMBER 1546.[1]

In the sixteenth century, there were two very important motivations in
the erection of tombs, aside from merely marking the graves of the
dead for posterity. The first was visual impact – the monument should
always reflect the deceased's power, status and wealth, real or imagined.
The second, before the religious changes of the Reformation, was a
continuation of the medieval need to persuade worshippers or passers-
by to pray for the soul of the departed, trapped in purgatory. Sometimes,
tombs were constructed during the lifetime of those commemorated, not
only as a constant pious reminder of inevitable mortality, but also to
ensure that their wishes and tastes were precisely fulfilled – very much
a case of 'if you want something done well, you have to do it yourself'. So
it was for Henry VIII, with his strong desire to demonstrate, in perpetuity,

the importance and prestige not only of the Tudor dynasty, but also his role as a Renaissance king astride the European political stage. Moreover, he was, despite his break with Rome and consequent excommunication and his largely politically motivated dalliances with the German Lutherans, still a devout and passionate adherent of the traditional beliefs of the Holy Catholic Church.

Paradoxically, despite his all-consuming vanity and his careful planning, history was to deal a series of very cruel blows to his sepulchral ambitions. The story of this monument to one of England's greatest sovereigns is a sad saga of greed, penny-pinching, sacrilegious desecration and neglect. What is left to us now from the king's grandiose plans is only a large, imposing black marble sarcophagus, inevitably commandeered from another's tomb by Henry, and, irony of ironies, later reused itself, cavalierly, 260 years later by a parsimonious Georgian government for the monument to England's fallen hero Admiral Lord Nelson, in the crypt of St Paul's Cathedral in London.

Henry's plans for an ambitious monument looked ill-fated from the very start. Work began on a tomb for the king and his first wife, Catherine of Aragon, in 1518 – only nine years after he ascended the throne, while he was still a hale and hearty twenty-seven-year-old with a full and active life ahead of him. A contract to design a grandiose monument was signed with the distinguished Florentine sculptor Pietro Torrigiano, who three years earlier had completed the magnificent Renaissance tomb for the king's parents, Henry VII and his wife, Elizabeth of York, in Westminster Abbey, for £1,500, or £805,000 in 2004 values.[2] The new monument was to be of white marble and black touchstone, like that of the king's father, but 'more greater by the fourth part [twenty-five per cent bigger]'.[3] The tomb had to be 'so fully and cleverly [constructed] and sightly' and also 'to be made and finished in beauty, fairness, costs and adornments'. It was to cost no more than £2,000 and be finished in four years.[4] A model was to be completed within a set period, but this was never settled.

As an indication of its importance, the king's Chief Minister Thomas Wolsey was put in charge of the project, with the choice of the place of the burial site left to Henry. He had apparently already made up his mind: at a meeting of the Chapter of the Order of the Garter at Greenwich in 1517, the king had announced 'that when the Most High God called him out of this world, he would have his corpse interred at Windsor and no where else'.[5] There was some discussion about payment – Torrigiano wanted negotiable Florentine merchants' bonds rather than English ready money, perhaps a reflection of his distrust of the value of Henry's coinage – but the agreement was never pursued and the Italian left England in disgust, without official permission, sometime before June 1519.

Henry was not discouraged by this abortive start of the project. There are some grounds for belief that he later sought new designs elsewhere. In 1527, the Venetian architect and sculptor Jacopo Sansovino was reported to be considering a commission from the English king for an unspecified but ambitious project worth the astonishingly high fee of 75,000 ducats[6] or £18,750.[7] It has been argued[8] that this project was the design and construction of the tomb shown in a drawing owned by Nicholas Charles, Lancaster Herald, and described a century later by John Speed in his *History of Britain*[9] and which was perhaps based on one originally produced for Pope Leo X (who died in December 1521) by Baccio Bandinelli.

This monument was to be 28 ft. high, 15 ft. long and topped by an effigy of the king on horseback in grand Italian Renaissance style. Beneath this high canopy were to lie the effigies of the king and queen. In its sheer megalomaniac scale, it was deliberately intended to be a monument to outshine that of any pope or monarch found within the churches and abbeys of Europe. The famous sculptor John Flaxman, nearly three centuries later, was full of enthusiasm, saying that the tomb would have been 'one of the most magnificent sepulchral monuments ever conceived and surpassing everything of the kind in the modern world'.[10] But this design was also never created.

The butcher's son Wolsey was also a creature of his times, desiring an equally impressive monument to preserve his memory and speak volubly of his achievements as a statesman. The cardinal recruited another Italian sculptor, Benedetto da Rovezzano,[11] to design and build him a tomb in the chapel built by Edward IV located at the east end of St George's, the Chapel Royal, Windsor.[12] Work began in 1524 and continued for five years. It was to be a stupendous edifice, with a black marble sarcophagus 7 ft. long and 4 ft. wide supporting a massive effigy of the cardinal made of gilded bronze, with two griffins recumbent at its feet. This figure and tomb-chest, complete with a facsimile cardinal's hat, were to rest on a platform of black marble with four bronze pillars at the corners, each 9 ft. high. Angels, each more than 3 ft. tall and holding candlesticks, were to be placed on top of each pillar. There were also to be twelve small images of saints, a cross and two pillars – symbols of the cardinal's and papal authority, and two shields, or escutcheons, bearing Wolsey's arms.

Included in the project costings was the sum of £800 for gilding portions of the monument, which should be compared with the £200 paid out for Henry VII's tomb at Westminster. Lord Herbert of Cherbury, in his *Life of Wolsey* published in 1622, pointed out that its 'design ... [was] so glorious that it exceeded far that of Henry VII'. Vanity of vanities: Wolsey, always conscious of his status, was now equating himself with royalty, if not surpassing it in grandeur. The point was probably not lost on Henry VIII.

This tomb was also never completed. Wolsey suddenly fell from royal favour in the autumn of 1529, victim of Anne Boleyn's hatred and Henry's fury at Wolsey's failure to secure his divorce from Catherine of Aragon. Crippled by ill health and facing charges of treason, the disgraced cardinal pathetically petitioned for the effigy portraying him to be sent to him in York for a new tomb for him there. His request was peremptorily denied.[13]

Henry, ever rapacious and undoubtedly savouring a delicious sense of piquancy, seized components of Wolsey's tomb for his own use, employing Rovezzano and his assistant Giovanni de Maiano[14] to complete it to revised designs for a dynastic monument. The bronze effigy of Wolsey was discarded (no doubt ignominiously consigned to the melting pot) and the sarcophagus appropriated. In the new design, a gilded bronze life-size figure of the king was to lie upon it. The podium of Wolsey's tomb was to be raised about 5 ft. and bronze friezes inserted into its walls. The cardinal's four corner pillars were replaced by eight or ten taller versions, capped by figures of the Apostles – Matthew, Mark, Luke and John. Between the pillars were bronze candlesticks 9 ft. tall.[15] These may have formed part of Torrigiano's original design, as Rovezzano talks of the

> four pillars ... which were not sufficient ... to stand the weight of the said altar which Master Peter Torrigiano had made of the said pillars which appertain to the King's most noble grace.[16]

An altar was to be set up to the east of the tomb, surmounted by a canopy with four kneeling figures of angels on top and supported by four pillars 'on stilted bases' decorated with figures. At the base were to be sixteen effigies of children, all holding candlesticks.[17] Both tomb and altar were to be surrounded by a 4 ft.-high bronze and black marble enclosure to form a separate chantry in the centre of the chapel, where priests would pray for the royal soul.

Cromwell efficiently made a number of payments to the Italians and the English metal founders who were their assistants during the years 1530–6[18] 'for labour and expenses' connected with the tomb, the last in August of the latter year. It may be that the events of the northern rebellion, the 'Pilgrimage of Grace', distracted both Henry and Cromwell's attentions after that. In addition, it is known that Rovezzano was in poor health and suffering with his eyesight, possibly caused by the choking chemical fumes of the metal furnaces used to melt the copper and bronze for casting parts of the tomb, and had to return to Italy[19] around 1543, but not before the effigy of the king had been cast and polished. The work passed to another Italian, Giovanni Portinari, an engineer and probably the same man who had been employed by Cromwell in the rapid, ruthless demolition of Lewes Priory during the Dissolution of the Monasteries. In December 1543, Portinari was paid £37 9s 2d for copper and other charges incurred in work on the tomb that month.[20]

The level of work must have fallen off to only sporadic activity during the final years of the last decade of the king's reign, probably because of the heavy demands of the campaigns in France and Scotland on government income, which had pushed the royal balance sheet into the red. The tomb was still unfinished by the time Henry made his will, in which he asks that

> as soon as conveniently may be done after our decease, by our executors at our costs and charges an honourable tomb for our bones to rest in which is well onward and almost made therefore already with a fair grate about it, in which we will also [that] the bones of our true and loving wife Queen Jane be put also.[21]

The tombs of Henry VI and Edward IV in St George's, located to the left and right of St George's high altar, were also to be embellished and made 'more princely in the same places where they now be' as part of Henry's clear design to revive Edward IV's plans make Windsor the royal mausoleum – the house of kings – in the years to come. When referring to his own monument, he also uses the phrase 'if it be not done by us in our lifetime', presumably meaning completed. Henry must have been fully conscious of his impending death and he could not realistically have expected to finish the tomb in such a short time span, after so long a delay. His words may also imply that he was being misled by the Gentlemen of his Privy Chamber regarding the true state of the progress of the work, who may not have wanted to worry the old man as he neared the hour of meeting his Maker. Alternatively, this phraseology may be symptomatic of the king's well-known aversion to thoughts or talk of his own mortality. The grating or enclosure of brass or bronze around the tomb was already in place in Edward IV's chapel, however, with this proud inscription in brass inlaid upon it:

HENRICVS OCTAVVS REX ANGLIAE FRANCIAE
DOMINVS HIBERNIAE FIDEI DEFENSOR [22]

After Henry's death, it fell to the filial responsibility of Edward VI to complete his parents' tomb. Portinari was still employed in March 1547[23] but was obviously labouring under the task. By 1551, another Italian had been brought in to work on the monument – the painter, carver and moulder Nicholas Bellin of Modena,[24] who was living within the precincts of Westminster Abbey in an area called 'the Tomb House',[25] where some components of Henry's monument were still being stored. Edward's Privy Council wrote to the Dean and Chapter of Westminster on 2 August 1551, licensing them to repair 'their house where His Highness's father's tomb is a making and where Modena dwells' and to take down part of the structure 'without hindering of the making of the same tomb and Modena's habitation'.[26] Life must have been fraught for the carver in the Abbey, as the Italian fell out with the Dean and Chapter. The Privy Council wrote on 5 October 1551 to Sir Richard Sackville,[27] Chancellor of Augmentations, urging him to ensure that Modena was 'restored to his house, which the priests of Westminster had expelled him out of'. What is more, the Chancellor was told to investigate 'what spoil has been made of things belonging to King Henry VII's [sic] tomb which by Modena has informed to be of the value of 900 crowns': this, then, was the cause of the angry rift between the Dean and Chapter and the Italian sculptor.[28]

Within two years, Edward was dead. Despite a plea in the minutes drafted for his will by his secretary, Sir William Petre, that 'the King, my father's tomb to be made up', nothing was done. Modena's carving skills were diverted into the urgent task of making a wax effigy of Edward VI to lie atop his coffin.[29] Even the chantry priests intended to pray for Henry and Jane Seymour's souls were denied by Edward's government's Protestant policies after just one year.[30]

His half-sister Mary, on her accession to the throne, also nurtured the good intention to complete her father's tomb, but reportedly 'dared not for fear a Catholic should seem to countenance the memory of one dying in schism with the Church of Rome'.[31] She therefore took no action. Or did she? There is an intriguing account that one of her Privy Councillors, Sir Francis Englefield, had witnessed the opening of the vault by Henry's arch-enemy Cardinal Reginald Pole,[32] now Mary's Archbishop of Canterbury. According to the account, the king's body was removed and ignominiously consigned to the flames – on her orders.[33] Whether this was Catholic propaganda, or merely wishful thinking, remains a matter of conjecture. But, as we will see, Henry's body remained safely in his grave.

Five years after Elizabeth became queen, her conscience must have prodded her about the king's tomb. Her Lord Treasurer William Paulet, Marquis of Winchester, wrote to Sir William Cecil from Chelsea about Henry's monument, listing the parts still needed to complete it[34] after a through survey had been made of the components still lying at Westminster and Windsor.[35] These included three bronze figures, each 4.5 ft. in height, two pillars, eight friezes, twenty-five small statues intended to stand on the pillars and four metal doors, or gates, to the enclosure.

> More[over] there doth lack a number of small things [such] as leaves, small dragons and lions and other small beasts with diverse and sundry things, the which is overmuch to trouble your Lordship with ...

However, it confirms that Henry's effigy was finished, weighing eight hundredweight[36] in gilt-bronze of the total twenty hundredweight[37] of metal already used in the tomb.

Paulet was clearly drawing up a revised design for the queen to approve, based on the completed components and incorporating new pillars. With an eye on economy, the Lord Treasurer trusted that Elizabeth would like the design, to avoid seeking an expensive 'workman' or sculptor from Europe to draw up another version.

She did not like it. Two years later, in 1565, Richard Rowlands[38] had prepared new plans and a model of the tomb, at a cost of £13 6s 8d.[39] Lewis Stockett, Surveyor of the Queen's Works, transported the remaining parts from Westminster to Windsor and work started again on completion of the monument in the centre of the eastern chapel at St George's. There was still more discussion about its final design, however, and more plans were sent to Cecil by Paulet in 1567 – the debate was no doubt motivated by the pressing need to save money.[40] In 1573–4, the Dutch Protestant refugee sculptor Cornelius Cure was called in to make yet another plan of the monument at a cost of £4 and Rowlands was also paid for carving figures, presumably for the pedestals.[41] Elizabeth was being finicky and had in her mind a grand plan for the erection of a sumptuous tomb for her half-brother as well.[42] But after Paulet's death in 1572, other pressing issues of state distracted Elizabeth and all idea of these dynastic monuments disappeared from her mind and those of her advisers. The stock of white marble purchased for these tombs and stored in Scotland Yard was later used up by Cure, by 1586–7, for other more prosaic purposes, such as the great fountain at Hampton Court.[43]

A German cleric, Canon Paul Hentzner, visited St George's in 1598 and saw the partially completed tomb in 'the quire or appendage of this chapel'. He counted

> about eight great pillars of brass: nearer the tomb, four made in the form of candlesticks. The tomb itself is of white and black marble. All which things, it is reported, are being reserved for the burial of Queen Elizabeth. The expenses already made in this matter are reckoned at over £60,000.[44]

Disputes followed between the government and the Dean and Chapter of St George's as to who was responsible for the chapel, its keys and the unfinished tomb.[45] Clearly, the structure had become a tourist attraction and whoever held the keys no doubt had access to an enviable income from visitors like Hentzner wishing entry to view the interior. A Chapter meeting in May 1613 rather sniffily declared that they had nothing to do with the chapel[46] and in 1618, William Herbert, Third Earl of Pembroke, Lord Chamberlain, wrote to them, saying:

> Whereas the keeping of the keys of the tombhouse by his Majesty's free chapel of St. George in Windsor Castle where the tomb of King Henry the Eight lies has usually been in the hands or keeping of the verger of the same free chapel.
>
> These are therefore to require you, the Dean and Canons of the same free chapel, to command those who have the keeping of

the same keys of the Tombhouse aforesaid to deliver to this bearer, John Darknall, now verger there, the said keys that he may have the keeping and custody thereof and these shall be your sufficient warrant and discharge in that behalf.[47]

The official injunction to allow Darknall, a gentleman, to 'freely and quietly enjoy the said keys together with the custody of the said Tombhouse in as free and beneficial manner as he or any other of his predecessors have ever enjoyed' had to be sternly repeated on 21 March 1626 in another missive from Whitehall.

With the arrival in power at Westminster of the Commonwealth, even the incomplete tomb of Henry VIII was not safe. It seems apparent that Parliamentary soldiers had already damaged the tomb when 'scandalous monuments and pictures' were removed from the churches and chapels of Eton and Windsor in accordance with a Commons ordinance of 20 December 1643. Worse was to come. The *Journal* of the House of Commons for 19 September 1645 records the appointment of a three-man committee to consider 'a statue of brass at Windsor and its condition, and to report their opinions concerning it to the House'. That gilt-bronze statue was Henry's effigy, still lying on its black marble sarcophagus, and the MPs' intention was to sell it to raise much-needed cash. Their requirement was urgent and only two days later, the House resolved

that the brass statue at Windsor Castle and the images there defaced and the other broken pieces of brass be forthwith sold to the best advantage of the State and that the committee formerly appointed do take care of the sale thereof.

On 7 April 1646, the Commons decided that they would be seeking a price of £400 in cash for Henry's effigy, which would be paid to 'Colonel [Christopher] Whichcot, governor of Windsor Castle, to be by him employed for the pay of that garrison'.[48] The Lords agreed with the plan three days later, and both Houses resolved that the purchasers of the metal from Henry's tomb should 'have the liberty to transport them beyond the seas for making their best advantage of them'. A keen buyer must have been found who wanted to export the despoiled metal. Probably more than the required sum had been offered, perhaps as much as £600.[49]

Four candlesticks from the tomb, bearing Henry's royal arms supported by dragons and greyhounds, found their way to the Cathedral of St Bavo in the city of Ghent, Belgium, apparently presented by Anthony Triest, Bishop of Ghent from 1622 to 1657.[50] They remain there today.[51] Of the great gilt-bronze effigy of the king there is now tragically no trace, but there seems every reason to suppose that his sarcophagus and its base remained in position for another 150 years.

After the Restoration of the monarchy in 1660, Charles II and his Attorney-General were keen to repair the monument and recover some of the lost statues and there was an agreement for 'Robert Clarke (of Blackman Street in Southwark, next door to the Woolsack) and John Gerard (brasier at the Frying Pan in Basinghall Street)'[52] to undertake some work, although this is likely to have been more tidying up than restoration. The remains of the tomb are marked on a plan of St George's Chapel published in 1672.[53]

But the chapel containing the monument was in a state of decay in James II's reign and its ruinous condition continued for some decades to come. In 1749, it was stated:

> Pity it is that this chapel which might be an ornament, should be suffered to run to ruin and stand a work of publick Resentment for being once employed in a service disagreeable to a Protestant people but certain it is since that Prince's [James II] reign, it has been entirely neglected, though the care and repair of it is peculiar to the Crown, being no appendage to the Collegiate Church.[54]

More than a half a century later, the final act of destruction was to be wreaked on Henry's hopes and plans for a monument reflecting his imperial status. In 1804, plans were announced for the construction of a huge new royal mausoleum or catacombs beneath the chapel and work began under the fashionable architect James Wyatt. This involved the destruction of the chapel floor in order to construct the new vault beneath, and the last remnants of the king's empty tomb were removed and put into storage. The black sarcophagus and its base were sent to London in 1808 for re-use in the huge monument to Lord Nelson in St Paul's, where it remains today – commemorating its third person after Wolsey and Henry VIII.[55]

Henry and his beloved Jane Seymour were also not allowed to rest in peace: their unmarked burial chamber in the middle of the choir was opened up several times over the centuries.

The first occasion was during the burial of Charles I in February 1649, after his execution by Parliament outside the Banqueting House in Whitehall. Colonel Whichcot, Governor of Windsor Castle, had prepared a shallow grave on the south side of the chancel of St George's, but Charles' faithful courtiers wanted to bury the body in a royal vault.[56] A resident of Windsor told them of the existence of Henry's vault, which they found by stamping on the pavement and listening out for the hollow sound reverberating back. A slab was levered up with crowbars and in the gloom beneath they could see the velvet palls still covering the coffins of Henry and Jane Seymour. These 'seemed fresh, though they had laid there above 100 years'.[57] Puddifant, the sexton, was ordered to lock the chapel while Charles' grave was prepared, but Isaac, the sexton's man, reported

> that a foot soldier had hid himself, so as he was not discovered, and being greedy of prey, crept into the vault and cut so much away of the velvet pall that covered the great body as he judged would hardly be missed and wimbled a hole through the said coffin that was largest, probably fancying that there was something well worth his adventure.
>
> The sexton at his opening the door espied the sacrilegious person who being searched, a bone was found about him with which he said he would haft a knife.
>
> The governor being ... informed, he gave him [the sexton] his reward and the lords and others present were convinced that a real body was in the said great coffin which some before had scrupled.[58]

This was obviously Henry's coffin and the soldier had stolen one of his bones.

According to manuscript notes held in the archives of St George's Chapel, the vault was examined when the pavement was broken up for re-laying with squares of new black and white marble on 7 February 1686:

> The vault … is about eight or nine feet wide, encompassed on all sides with brick and a brick arch turned over the top of it. It is about seven or eight feet deep, neither is there any passage by steps or otherwise as some do conjecture.
>
> On the North side of it lies the body of the Lady Jane Seymour and next to her the body of King Henry VIII, both of them lying in coffins of lead and standing upon wooden trestles.
>
> On the south side of the vault lyeth the body of King Charles the first in a coffin of lead …[59]

The vault was again opened at the end of the seventeenth century for the interment of the body of a stillborn child of Princess George of Denmark (later Queen Anne), whose tiny mahogany coffin was laid diagonally across the lower end of King Charles'.[60] Another opening was made on 1 April 1813, in the presence of the Prince Regent, later George IV, and the Duke of Cumberland.[61] After examining Charles' coffin, they turned to those of Henry and Jane Seymour. Henry's coffin was made of lead, enclosed in an elm shell one or two inches thick.

> But this was decayed and lay in small fragments near it.
>
> The leaden coffin appeared to have been beaten in by violence about the middle and a considerable opening of it exposed a mere skeleton of the king. Some beard remained on the chin but there was nothing to discriminate the personage contained in it.
>
> The smaller coffin, understood to be that of queen Jane Seymour was not touched, mere curiosity not being considered by the Prince Regent, as sufficient motive for disturbing these remains.[62]

The witness, Sir Henry Halford, physician to both George III and his son, the Prince Regent, said the damage to Henry's coffin could have been caused 'by the precipitate introduction of the coffin of King Charles' after a funeral 'without any words or other ceremonies than the tears and sighs of the few beholders'.[63]

Other notes, written in 1888 when the then Prince of Wales deposited some relics of Charles I in a small casket in the vault through an 18 in.-wide hole in the floor, discount this theory. A light, lowered into the vault, disclosed that

> the large leaden coffin of King Henry VIII lies in the centre ... in a condition of great dilapidation.
>
> The king's skull, with its very broad frontal, his thigh bones, ribs and other portions of the skeleton are exposed to view as the lead has been extensively ripped open, apparently, to judge by the fractured edges, owing to the action of internal forces outward.[64]

It seems chemically highly unlikely that after more than three centuries, in the words of one later report, Henry's coffin had been 'split open by the fumes of decomposition',[65] particularly as the king's bowels had been removed during the embalming process. And dropping Charles' coffin into the vault probably did not cause the buckling and breaches, as it had been laid on trestles. Perhaps the leaden coffin was damaged when its own supporting trestle collapsed. Or maybe this damage confirms the grisly tradition of it breaking open at Syon in fulfilment of the monk's fateful prophecy. Alternatively, did the coffin's fall there cause a fatal weakness in its lead casing?

Today a brass-letter inscription marks the black marble slab, measuring 42 in. by 76 in., that covers the vault. Such an epitaph had been requested by the Prince Regent on 21 March 1818 and the Dean and Chapter 'dispensed with the former order of Chapter dated November 4 1789' banning new inscriptions and agreed to the proposal.[66] Strangely, however, the grave remained unmarked until 1837. It reads, simply and starkly:

IN A VAULT

BENEATH THIS MARBLE SLAB

ARE DEPOSITED THE REMAINS

OF

JANE SEYMOUR QUEEN OF KING HENRY VIII

1537

KING HENRY VIII

1547

KING CHARLES I

1648

AND

AN INFANT CHILD OF QUEEN ANNE

THIS MEMORIAL WAS PLACED HERE

BY COMMAND OF

KING WILLIAM IV. 1837.

Many visitors to the chapel today casually walk over the slab, unaware of the vault's regal contents as they stand mesmerised by the sight of the wonderful carved woodwork of the stalls behind them and the colourful banners and heraldic plates of the Garter Knights.

Truly, how are the mighty fallen!

For all his power and might, for all his pride and vanity, for all his grandiose plans, Henry is now commemorated only by the plain, bare essentials – his name and date of death – in humble brass letters set into a slab in the pavement of the choir, walked over heedlessly by thousands of tourists every year.

Henry's vainglorious ambitions for his tomb have been thwarted by history. In the end, it all seems rather sad.

Notes

Prologue

1 LP Spanish, Edward VI, Vol. IX, p.36.

2 The title was defined by statute, 35 Henry VIII cap.3, 1543. See C. H. Williams, pp.474–5.

3 The time of death is provided by a letter of 31 January 1547 written to his wife by Henry Ratcliffe, Earl of Sussex, quoted in Strype, 'Ecclesiastic Memorials', Vol. II, pt.i, p.118, from BL Cotton MS Titus B ii 25, fol.51.

4 Extrapolated from reports of executions from available county assizes throughout the reign and those who were killed for treason or heresy, or who died during insurrection and other civil disturbances. The population of England and Wales in 1547 was 2.7 million. The chronicler John Stow believed that the total was 72,000 and has been accused of hopeless exaggeration. See also: BL Add. MS 27,402, fol.47 – 'A list of such were executed in Henry VIII's time' – for some state executions.

5 The average male life expectancy during this period was around forty years.

6 He apparently liked the liquor 'marvellously well'. Chamberlin, p.379.

7 Ellis, 'Eminent Men', p.14. Letter from Ascham in Brussels to Sir William Cecil, 23 March 1553, in which he reported Denny's comment, made several years before.

8 Jordan, p.4. Tytler, Vol. I, pp.15–16.

9 NA SP 10/1/1.

10 LP Spanish, Edward VI, Vol. IX, p.4. Van der Delft added: 'I should like to have conveyed this intelligence to your Majesty before this, but that all the roads have been and still are, closed; so that in order to send the present letter a passport has been necessary.' The ports were reopened by order of the Privy Council on 2 February. (APC, n. s., Vol. II, 1547–50, p.11.)

11 'Ordo de exeguiis regalibus' in Legg, Vol. II, pp.734–5.

12 There has always been some debate as to whether both of the king's legs were afflicted by fistulas. Henry mentions 'a humour ... fallen unto our legs' in a letter to the Duke of Norfolk in 1537. See LP, Vol. XII, pt.ii, p.27.

13 Strype, 'Ecclesiastic Memorials', Vol. II, pt.ii, p.289.

14 Bayles, p.795.

15 Dale, p.30.

16 Strype, 'Ecclesiastic Memorials', Vol. II, pt.ii, p.290. For a more detailed description, see Litten, pp.39–40.

17 Strype, 'Ecclesiastic Memorials', Vol. II, pt.i, p.17.

18 The mural, by Hans Holbein the Younger, is recorded as still being in the presence chamber in 1586. A smaller copy by Remigius van Leemput of 1667 is now in the Royal Collection at Hampton Court Palace. The original was lost when the palace was burnt in January 1698 after a maid left her washing to dry before an open fire.

CHAPTER 1 A Dangerous Honour

1 LP, Vol. XVIII, pt.i, p.490.

2 Neville Williams, p.171. The following verses, translated from the Latin, were inscribed on her tomb, now lost:

> Here a Phoenix Lieth, whose death
> To another Phoenix gave breath.
> It is to be lamented much
> The world at once ne'er knew two such.

See Tighe and Davis, Vol. I, p.509.

3 LP, Vol. XII, pt.ii, p.449.

4 She married him in May 1538.

5 His comment to the French ambassador Castillon at the end of December 1537.

6 Kaulek, pp.48 and 51–3.

7 LP, Vol. XIII, pt.ii, p.111.

8 LP, Vol. XIII, pt.ii pp.110–11.

9 Kaulek, pp.80–1, and LP, Vol. XIII, pt.ii, p.28.

10 LP, Vol. XIII, pt.ii, p.28.

11 Letter from John Hutton, the English ambassador in Brussels, to Cromwell, 9 December 1537. See SP, Vol. VIII, p.67.

12 LP, Vol. III, pt.ii, p.1188.

13 SP, Vol. VIII, p.146.

14 These words were reported in Wriothesley's letter to the king, so high levels of sycophancy should be expected.

15 Neville Williams, p.172.

16 LP Spanish, Vol. VI, pt.i, p.99.

17 Strickland, Vol. III, p.170.

18 Henry was impressed by the drummers and trumpeters – probably the only thing connected with Anne of Cleves that did impress him.

19 Strype, 'Ecclesiastic Memorials', Vol. I, pt.ii, p.454.

20 As Henry was called by the Protestant reformer Philip Melanchthon.

21 Strype, 'Ecclesiastic Memorials', Vol. I, pt.ii, p.455.

22 Ibid., Vol. I, pt.ii, p.457.

23 Later, the Greek traveller Nicander Nucius described her as 'masculine'. See Revd J. A. Cramer (ed.), *The Second Book of Travels*, Camden Society, London, 1841, p.48.

24 Strype, 'Ecclesiastic Memorials', Vol. I, pt.ii, p.457.

25 Ibid., Vol. I, pt.ii, p.455. Sun-tanned complexions were far from fashionable for women in the Tudor period.

26 Fraser, p.309.

27 Burnet, Vol. II, p.lxxxv.

28 Strype, 'Ecclesiastic Memorials', Vol. I, pt.ii, p.452. The promise was never fulfilled. Such papers that were sent 'not being authentic' put the issue of the pre-contract 'in much more doubt'.

29 Hall, p.836.

30 Strype, 'Ecclesiastic Memorials', Vol. I, pt.ii, p.458.

31 Burnet, Vol. II, p.lxxxvi.

32 Goldsmid and Goldsmid, p.8.

33 Goldsmid and Goldsmid, p.10.

34 Burnet, Vol. II, p.lxxxvi.

35 Strype, 'Ecclesiastic Memorials', Vol. I, pt.ii, p.458.

36 Ibid., Vol. I, pt.ii, p.459.

37 Ibid., Vol. I, pt.ii, p.461.

38 Ibid., Vol. I, pt.ii, p.461. Butts' deposition to the commission is in Cecil Papers 1/22 at Hatfield House. Henry's own account is in Cecil Papers 1/23.

39 Strype, 'Ecclesiastic Memorials', Vol. I, pt.ii, p.462.

40 Ibid., Vol. I, pt.ii, p.460.

41 'Spanish Chronicle', pp.98–9.

42 Robinson, p.32.

43 Burnet, Vol. II, p.lxxxvii.

44 Questions to be asked of Cromwell relating to the marriage are laid out in BL Cotton MS Otho C x, fols.241 and 246. The establishment of the commission inquiring into the marriage is at fol.236.

45 Burnet, Vol. I, pt.i, p.206.

46 Burnet, Vol. I, pt.i p.203. LP, Vol. XV, p.364.

47 LP, Vol. XV, p.377.

48 Richard Rugeley and David Phinsent of the king's Department of Wardrobe of Beds and Nicholas Bristowe, its clerk, were paid for stripping Cromwell's 'stuff' from his house in June 1540. Their charges were for conveying the loot 'to the king's wardrobe, [then] to the Tower of London, to Hampton Court, eleven miles with one cart, with two carts, four miles and two carts to the Tower and for bed ropes to the beds, and for all the charges by the space of six days at twenty pence a day each, on the vice chamberlain's bill, 35s 5d'. See LP, Vol. XVI, p.187.

49 32 Henry VIII cap.62.

50 Burnet, Vol. I, pt.i, p.204.

51 The commissioners' report, signifying her full assent to the terms and conditions, is in BL Cotton MS Otho C x, fol.247.

52 SP, Vol. VIII, p.395.

53 BL Cotton MS Otho C x, fol.240.

54 Smith, 'A Tudor Tragedy', p.121.

55 LP Spanish, Vol. VI, pt.i, p.305.

56 Nichols, 'Narratives', p.259.

57 Henry chose a rose for her arms. See Strickland, Vol. III, p.122, note 2.

58 LP Spanish, Vol. VI, p.37.

59 His father destroyed the Scots army with the power of English artillery at Flodden Field in September 1513, killing the Scottish king, James IV, and many of his nobility. As a result, the title of Duke of Norfolk was restored to him in 1514 after losing it by attainder early in Henry VII's reign.

60 Cited by Robinson, p.25.

61 Smith, 'A Tudor Tragedy', p.121.

62 A broadsheet issued after Cromwell's death, now in the Society of Antiquaries of London Library (no.4, although a later copy), perhaps illustrates some of the crude propaganda of the time. The sheet carries sixteen verses of three lines each plus a refrain, beginning (in the original spelling):

> Both man and child is glad to hear tell
> Of that false Traytour Thomas Cromwell
> Now that he is set to learne to spell
> Sing trolle on away.

and ending

> God save King Henry with all his power
> And Prince Edward that goodly flower
> With all his lordes of great honour
> Sing trolle on away, Sing trolle on away
> Here and how, rombelowe, trolle on away.

See Robert Lemon, *Catalogue of Printed Broadsheets in Possession of Society of Antiquaries of London*, London, 1866, and also LP, Vol. XVI, p.541. In his speech on the scaffold, Cromwell sought to deny the accusations of heresy against him. He said that he died in 'the Catholic faith, not doubting any article of my faith, no, nor doubting in any sacrament of the Church'. Many had slandered him 'and reported that I have been a bearer of such as have maintained evil opinions, which is untrue but I confess that like God by his Holy Spirit, so the devil is ready to seduce us and I have been seduced'. See Hall, p.839; Scarisbrook, pp.378–80.

63 He was also accused of employing magicians to predict the date of Henry's death and of employing a chaplain who sympathised with the Pilgrimage of Grace. See Ridley, *Henry VIII*, p.342, and Foxe, 'Acts', Vol. V, pp.402–3. Hungerford was said to be 'very unquiet in his mind and rather in a frenzy' at his execution. Who can blame him? The account may be more suggestive of his insanity. See Hall, p.840.

64 LP, Vol. XXI, pt.ii, p.282. The reference to 'a staff' means an Act of Attainder.

65 Cited by Smith, 'A Tudor Tragedy', p.123.

66 LP, Vol. XVI, p.148.

67 Kaulek, pp.236–7. This was not unusual practice by a king terrified by the plague. In 1532, during a visit to Calais, Henry similarly ordered that all plague victims should be dragged out of their houses, taken to a field outside the town and left to die. See Ridley, *The Tudor Age*, p.195.

68 LP, Vol. XVI, p.450.

69 Marble Arch in London, on the edge of Hyde Park, is the site of Tyburn.

70 Dacre was even more cruelly treated by hopes of a last-minute reprieve. As he left the Tower on foot, escorted by the two sheriffs of London, on his way to Tyburn, 'Mr Heyre, controller of the Lord Chancellor's [Lord Audley of Walden] house came and commanded, in the king's name, to stay the execution till two of the clock, which caused the people to hope that the king would pardon him' (Wriothesley, Vol. I, p.126). The prisoners waited hopelessly until three o'clock and then were taken to the gallows where they were 'strangled as common murderers' (Hall, p.842). Dacre was buried in St Sepulchre's Church, near Newgate.

71 LP, Vol. XVI, p.466.

72 Wriothesley, Vol. I, p.73.

73 LP, Vol. XVI, p.608.

74 A story recounted by a London merchant in a letter to Germany after Culpeper's execution. See 'Original Letters', Vol. I, pp.226–7.

75 The rack was named after the fifteenth-century duke who introduced this method of extracting information into England during the reign of Henry VI. It was also known as 'the brake'.

76 LP, Vol. XVI, p.620.

77 LP, Vol. XVI, p.616.

78 LP, Vol. XVI, p.649.

79 LP, Vol. XVI, p.611.

80 Scarisbrook, p.430.

81 LP, Vol. XVI, pp.665–6.

82 Smith, 'A Tudor Tragedy', pp.178 ff.

83 LP, Vol. XVI, pp.670–2.

84 LP, Vol. XVI, p.610.

85 Ibid.

86 Ibid.

87 Burnet, Vol. II, p.cccxci.

88 Ominously, he was also vice-chamberlain to Anne Boleyn at the time of her disgrace.

89 LP, Vol. XVI, p.610.

90 Wriothesley, Vol. I, pp.130–1.

91 LP, Vol. XVI, p.620.

92 LP, Vol. XVI, p.628.

93 LP, Vol. XVI, p.613.

94 LP, Vol. XVII, p.44.

95 LP, Vol. XVI, p.534.

96 LP, Vol. XVI, p.628.

97 LP, Vol. XVI, p.646. The pre-contract would have rendered any children she had with Henry illegitimate.

98 Smith, 'A Tudor Tragedy', pp.166–7.

99 Their heads were set on spikes on one of the turrets of London Bridge and were still there in 1546 when they were seen by the Greek traveller Nicander Nucius. See Revd J. A. Cramer (ed.), *The Second Book of Travels*, Camden Society, London, 1841, p.48: 'The skulls are even at this time to be seen, denuded of flesh,' he observed. See also Wriothesley, Vol. I, p.32. Culpeper was buried in St Sepulchre's Church, Newgate, near the Old Bailey.

100 LP, Vol. XVI, p.677.

101 Concealment of knowledge of treason or treasonable intent.

102 LP Spanish, Vol. VI, pt.i, p.409.

103 33 Henry VIII cap.21.

104 Lehmberg, pp.146–7.

105 LP Spanish, Vol. VI, pt.i, p.472.

106 Ibid.

107 Ibid.

108 Passed on 4 February. 33 Henry VIII cap.21.

109 Seven attended, absentees being the Duke of Suffolk, who was 'indisposed', and,

significantly, the Duke of Norfolk. Norfolk's son, the Earl of Surrey, was, however, amongst the crowd of noble spectators.

110 LP Spanish, Vol. VI, pt.i, p.473.

111 Strickland, Vol. III, pp.84–5. They were reprimanded for their indelicate words. See also LP, Vol. XVI, p.655.

112 LP Spanish, Vol. VI, pt.i, p.409.

113 LP, Vol. XVI, pp.678–9, and SP, Vol. I, p.716.

114 Mary of Guise.

115 LP Spanish, Vol. VI, pt.ii, p.31.

116 Twenty-four Scottish guns were captured in the battle. Seventeen 'Scottish guns of brass' of various types were listed at the Tower of London in the inventory of Henry's possessions made after his death. See Starkey, 'Inventory', p.102.

117 LP Spanish, Vol. VI, pt.ii, p.223.

118 LP Spanish, Vol. VI, pt.ii, p.224.

119 Her orthodox Catholic stepfather Lord Lisle, who had spent twenty months imprisoned in the Tower, had just been released and pardoned. He died shortly afterwards. His wife had gone mad in his absence. See Ridley, *Henry VIII*, p.363.

120 Herbert had the reputation of being a rough, rowdy soldier. In 1533, he was involved in a brawl and the murder of John Thomas, 'one honest man', in Newport, South Wales. See LP, Vol. VI, p.670. On 23 February 1533, while George ap Morgan was 'uncoupling his hound ... Herbert struck him in the arm [and] into the body so that he would have been in great danger had he not got into a house to save himself'. Four days later, Herbert, with 'an inordinate company', made a second assault on ap Morgan. During the mêlée, Thomas was murdered.

121 John Weever, *Ancient Funerall Monuments*, London, 1631, p.371. Sir William Dugdale, in his *History of St Paul's Cathedral*, 2nd ed., London, 1716, p.48, records Latimer's tomb as having been destroyed during the reign of Edward VI or Elizabeth. Probably it was a monumental brass.

122 It is also possible that she had been pregnant during one of her previous marriages. See James, 'Kateryn Parr', p.113.

123 An estimate based on the length of her coffin discovered in the ruins of the chapel of Sudeley Castle in 1782. See Nash, p.2.

124 LP, Vol. XV, p.243.

125 Dent-Brocklehurst Papers, D2579, Gloucester Record Office.

126 LP, Vol. XVIII, pt.i. p.418.

127 NA E 30/1,472/6.

128 This was an élite force of, initially, fifty mounted troops called 'the spears', founded in December 1539 by Cromwell and normally drawn from good families. They were responsible for the king's personal security and with typical Tudor parsimony were expected to provide their own weapons – the 'noble' pole-axe and a sword. Their strength was later

expanded to 150. On Sir Anthony Browne's death in 1548, the Marquis of Northampton became captain.

129 Meaning yielding, polite and gentle.

130 LP, Vol. XVIII, pt.i, p.483.

131 See Flugel, p.277.

132 LP, Vol. XVIII, pt.ii, p.18.

133 LP Spanish, Vol. VI, pt.ii, p.436.

134 The plague was so bad in London that the law courts were moved to St Albans in Hertfordshire for the Michaelmas Term. See Hall, p.859.

135 LP, Vol. XVIII, pt.i, p.498.

136 LP Spanish, Vol. VI, pt.ii, p.447.

137 'Spanish Chronicle', p.108.

138 LP Spanish, Vol. VI, pt.ii, p.447.

139 BL Add. MS 46,348, fol.206. Inventory of jewels and plate of Henry VIII.

140 BL Add. MS 46,348, fol.168b

141 Ibid.

142 BL Add. MS 46,348, fol.169a.

143 Listed in Starkey, 'Inventory', pp.77–80.

144 James, 'Kateryn Parr', p.24.

CHAPTER 2 God's Imp

1 'Imp' is used in the sense of 'outcome'. See Tanner, p.49, fn.

2 Burnet, Vol. II, p.lxxxvi.

3 Kaulek, pp.350–4, and LP, Vol. XVI, p.598.

4 Modern historians have rejected this version of a delicate child. See Hester Chapman, *The Last Tudor King: A Study of Edward VI*, Bath, 1958, and Loach, *Edward VI*.

5 Kaulek, p.302, and LP, Vol. XVI, p.396.

6 LP, Vol. XVI, p.598.

7 Kaulek, pp.408–10.

8 Cited by Loach, *Edward VI*, p.11.

9 Wriothesley, Vol. I, pp.66–7.

10 Margaret, Marchioness of Dorset, was due to have the honour of carrying the prince at the ceremony. She wrote to the king thanking him for her appointment to 'bear my lord prince' but apologising for being 'banished from court by the sickness here [at Croydon]'. Clearly, that sickness – it was the plague – put paid to her role. See LP, Vol. XII, pt.ii, p.317.

Gertrude, a devout Catholic, was imprisoned in the Tower in 1538 and attainted in July the following year. Her husband Henry was beheaded as an aspirant to the crown on 9 December 1538.

11 Great care was taken to guard the royal baby from dangerous draughts. Temporary barriers, draped with rich hangings, were erected along the route of the procession where there were no protective walls.

12 Strype, 'Ecclesiastic Memorials', Vol. II, pt.i, p.4.

13 The robe was still displayed at Hampton Court in 1600. See Thurley, 'Hampton Court', p.69.

14 The number attending was severely restricted by the household because of the risk of infection from the plague then raging in the City of London and the suburbs. The proclamation limiting the size of the nobility's entourages warns of the king's 'most high indignation and displeasure' for any breach of the stipulated numbers. The text of the proclamation is at BL Harleian MS 442, fol.149.

15 Strype, 'Ecclesiastic Memorials', Vol. II, pt.i, p.6.

16 On the day of the christening, Mary received £100 from Mr Heneage of the king's Privy Chamber, probably to recompense her for expenditure on her gift.

17 LP, Vol. XII, pt.ii, p.319. See also BL Add. MS 45,716 A, fols.112–15, and BL Egerton MS 985, fol.33, for sixteenth-century accounts of the ceremonial for the christening.

18 They had been firm friends since Brandon was appointed an esquire of the body to Henry in 1509.

19 The debate continues as to whether or not Edward was born by caesarean section. No contemporary source mentions any such operation, let alone the conversation reported by Nicholas Sanders in 1581 that Henry, asked by his doctors whether the mother or child should be saved, chose the boy because he 'could easily provide himself with other wives'. (See R. L. de Molen, 'The Birth of Edward VI and the Death of Queen Jane: Arguments for and Against Caesarean Section' in *Renaissance Studies*, 4 (1990), pp.359–91.) The story's veracity is undermined by the sex of the child being known before birth, which would have been impossible in the sixteenth century. Indeed, Jane is believed to have come through the birth relatively well: John Husee (Lisle's agent in London) wrote to Lord Lisle expressing the hope that the king would have many more sons (see 'Lisle Letters', Vol. IV, p.425). Loach (*Edward VI*, p.5) believes delivery by caesarean cannot totally be eliminated but that it 'seems very implausible'.

20 BL Cotton MS Nero C x, fol.1. The document was sealed rather than signed.

21 The word 'tyrant' is used advisedly. Henry was the head of, in modern terms, a totalitarian state. Only the previous July, he had admonished the Justices of the Peace in Cornwall for their laxness in prosecutions, threatening to correct the 'lewdness of the offenders' himself. He especially instructed the JPs to search out all those 'who in spite of the usurped powers of Rome having been with great travail and labour expelled from the kingdom, retain their old fond fantasies and superstitions, muttering in corners as they dare'. They also had to arrest all spreaders of rumours against the king and the state of the realm; punish all vagabonds and valiant beggars; and have 'special regard' that no man be involved in unlawful games, but instead should 'apply himself to use the longbow, as the laws require'. Religion, propaganda, law and order and defence were Henry's concerns in this missive. See BL Stowe MS 142, fol.14.

22 Rebuilt in 1886 after the fire in Chapel Court.

23 A sweet liqueur wine from Smyrna, flavoured with aromatic spices and then filtered.

24 LP, Vol. XII, pt.ii, p.325.

25 LP, Vol. XII, pt.ii, p.342.

26 LP, Vol. XII, pt.ii, p.339. Signed: '[Your] sorrowful friend T Norfolk.'

27 LP, Vol. XII, pt.ii, p.348, and SP, Vol. VIII, p.1. Cromwell had received a report from Thomas Rutland and five other doctors regarding Jane's 'extreme illness' dated 17 October. See BL Cotton MS Nero C x, fol.2.

28 LP, Vol. XII, pt.ii, p.339.

29 LP, Vol. XII, pt.ii, p.360.

30 BL Cotton MS Vitellius C i, fol.65B.

31 LP, Vol. XIII, pt.ii, pp.360 and 505.

32 Simon Thurley, 'Henry VIII and the Building of Hampton Court: A Reconstruction of the Tudor Palace', *Architectural History*, 31 (1988), pp.1–58.

33 Thurley, 'Hampton Court', pp.68–9.

34 BL Cotton MS Vitellius C i, fol.65. A modern copy. The original draft had corrections and additions in Cromwell's hand. Sir John Cornwallis died at Ashridge, while the prince was in residence there, in 1544. Sir William Sidney succeeded him as steward and Sir Richard Page became chamberlain.

35 Neville Williams, p.165.

36 LP, Vol. XVI, pp.179 and 699. Joan was the wife of Peter Mewtes, a member of Henry's Privy Chamber and Controller of the Mint.

37 LP, Vol. XIII, pt.ii, p.120.

38 LP, Vol. XIII, pt.ii, p.373.

39 In comparison, the Civil List spending by Queen Elizabeth II in 2002–3 (the latest figures available at the time of writing) amounted to £8,153,000. This represents the contribution by the taxpayer in funding the queen's royal duties and the costs of her official household.

40 LP, Vol. XII, pt.ii, p.348.

41 They were still receiving pensions of £10 each in 1553, at the end of Edward's reign.

42 LP, Vol. XIII, pt.i, p.474.

43 LP, Vol. XIII, pt.i, p.372.

44 BL Royal MS Appendix 89, fol.41.

45 She was married to John Penn, barber-surgeon to Henry VIII, who died in 1557. In 1538, she wrote to Cromwell seeking employment in the prince's household for her brother-in-law Griffith Richards, 'the bearer' of the letter. See LP, Vol. XIII, pt.ii, p.519.

46 Jordan, p.3.

47 Muller, 'Letters', pp.161–2, and Loach, *Edward VI*, p.10.

48 Butts (?1485–1545) was born in Norfolk and became a physician to the king in 1524. He was a member of the Royal College of Physicians in 1529. He attended both Anne Boleyn and Jane Seymour while they were queens and also treated Henry's illegitimate son, Henry Fitzroy, Duke of Richmond, as well as Princess Mary and the Duke of Norfolk. He was paid the then fabulous salary of £100 a year, or £40,000 in today's money, with an additional £20 for his attendance on Fitzroy. See MacNalty, pp.144–5.

49 A stool. See *Middle English Dictionary*, Ann Arbor, Michigan, 1986.

50 LP *Addenda*, Vol. I, pt.ii, p.523.

51 In 1551, there were extensive but abortive negotiations with the French for a marriage between Edward and Elizabeth – the daughter of the new French king, Henry II. Elizabeth's portrait had been sent to London the previous year. Agreement on a dowry was reached in July and Edward sent her a New Year's gift of a 'fair diamond' from Katherine Parr's collection of jewels. Cited by Loach, *Edward VI*, p.108.

52 Cheke (1514–57) was knighted by Edward in 1552 and became his secretary of state the following year. He was imprisoned in the Tower of London by Mary in 1554 before exile in Switzerland and Italy and was again imprisoned in London in 1556. Quotations from his homily on St Chrysostom, delivered in August 1543, are contained as article three in the two volumes of controversial theological works traditionally known as *Archbishop Cranmer's Commonplace Books*, now in the British Library as Royal MS 7B xi–xii.

53 Cox (1500–81), a former headmaster of Eton, was a favourite of Cranmer. He was imprisoned in 1553 before being exiled in Frankfurt. After Elizabeth's accession he became Bishop of Norwich and shortly afterwards transferred to the see of Ely.

54 Ascham (1515–68), although a Protestant, became Latin secretary to Queen Mary in 1553. His unfinished book, *The Schoolmaster*, a practical treatise on education, was published in 1570.

55 The Frenchman John Belmaine taught him French, at a quarterly salary of £6 12s 4d. He was a follower of the religious reformer John Calvin.

56 Nichols, 'Literary Remains', Vol. I, p.lxxvii.

57 BL Add. MS 4,724.

58 Nichols, 'Literary Remains', Vol. I, p.6.

59 Later owned by Sir William Cecil, First Baron Burghley, who married Cheke's sister in 1541 and noted the dates of his marriages and other family details for the period 1541–5. Now BL Add. MS 6,059.

60 Now in the British Library.

61 See Judith Blezzard and Frances Palmer, 'King Henry VIII: Performer, Connoisseur and Composer of Music', *Antiquaries Journal*, 80 (2000), pp.251–2, citing BL Cotton MS Vitellius C i, fol.246.

62 Nichols, 'Literary Remains', Vol. I, p.liv.

63 Blezzard and Palmer, op. cit., p.252. He was also Princess Mary's lute teacher and later during Edward's reign became master of the 'King's singing children'. Edward, after

succeeding to the crown, learnt to play the virginals, using some of the money given him by Thomas Seymour to pay John Ashley for the lessons. See Loach, *Edward VI*, p.15.

64 LP, Vol. XXI, pt.i, p.400, and Nichols, 'Literary Remains', Vol. I, p.9.

65 BL Harleian MS 5,087, no.17. Written on 12 August 1546.

66 BL Royal MS 7 D xx. The donor was appointed a minister of the Dutch Church in London in 1550.

67 BL Royal MS 2 D iii.

68 Nichols, 'Narratives', p.317.

69 Scarisbrook, p.457, who suggests that this Grindal was probably a relative of the Elizabethan Archbishop of Canterbury.

70 Used for hunting game.

71 NA SP 1/217 and E 101/424/12.

72 Cited by Weir, p.469.

73 See BL Cotton MS Nero C x 4, fol.3, from Hertford on 10 January 1547 and BL Cotton MS Vespasian F iii, fol.18, from Hunsdon on 24 May 1546.

74 BL Harleian MS 5,087, no.17.

75 BL Cotton MS Vespasian F iii, fol.18.

76 Nichols, 'Literary Remains', Vol. I, Letters, p.16.

77 Nichols, 'Literary Remains', Vol. I, p.33.

78 NA E 101/424/8.

79 See Blezzard and Palmer, op. cit., p.252.

80 35 Henry VIII cap.1. The preamble mentions the marriage of Henry and Katherine Parr and adds, rather hopefully, 'by whom yet his majesty hath none issue but may full well when it shall please God'.

81 Nichols, 'Literary Remains', Vol. I, p.xxxix.

82 LP, Vol. XIX, pt.i, p.606.

83 Mary's work was abandoned because of her ill health.

84 Elizabeth wrote in a letter to Katherine that she had joined the sentences together 'as well as the capacity of my simple wit and small learning could extend themselves' and that the work was imperfect and that she hoped the queen would 'rub out, polish and mend the words ... which I know in many places to be rude'. Cited by Neville Williams, p.239.

85 A copy (in Latin) given as a New Year's gift to Henry Fitzalan, Earl of Arundel, by the translator, Sir John Ratcliffe, is in the British Library as Royal MS 7 D ix. This was probably published after 1548, as Katherine is described as *quondam Regina* – 'once queen'.

86 Martienssen, p.199.

87 BL Royal MS 7 D x.

88 He received this epithet because of his frequent resort to corporal punishment of his scholars.

89 He was also the author, in 1553–4, of the earliest English comedy, *Ralph Roister Doister*, printed in 1566.

90 Cited by Neville Williams, p.233.

CHAPTER 3 The Hunt for Heretics

1 Eighty-one heretics were burnt during Henry VIII's reign, compared with twenty-four in his father's; two in the short reign of his son, Edward VI; 280 in Mary's; and four in Elizabeth's. See Ridley, *The Tudor Age*, p.77.

2 One of the last public burnings of books in London during Henry's reign was on 26 September 1546. See Wriothesley, Vol. I, p.175.

3 Later, after the break with Rome, Henry explained his embarrassing change of heart by claiming that he was forced to write the book by Wolsey and some of the bishops.

4 26 Henry VIII cap.i.

5 28 Henry VIII cap.io.

6 Anglo, pp.269–70.

7 Tanner, pp.93–4.

8 Tanner, p.94. A similar instruction was included in early drafts of the 1536 Injunctions but was omitted before they were published.

9 Both presses and type were smuggled out of Paris to London.

10 This was the second edition of *Matthew's Bible*, comprising the translations from the Latin of the New Testament completed by William Tyndale in 1525 and of the Old Testament based on the work of John Rogers and Miles Coverdale, which was the first English text to be freely available. Its title page showed Henry handing down copies to his bishops, kneeling in cope and mitre before him, and the nobility in ermine robes and coronets.

11 34 and 35 Henry VIII cap.i.

12 Anabaptists believed that those baptised as infants should be rebaptised as adults.

13 Hall, p.827.

14 Foxe, 'Acts', Vol. V, pp.229ff.

15 Later almoner to Katherine Parr. He was appointed Bishop of Chichester in 1543 and assisted in drawing up the first English Prayer Book in 1548, but voted against its use the following year.

16 Burnet, Vol. I, pt.i, book iii, p.186.

17 Ibid.

18 Foxe, 'Acts', Vol. V, pp.181–234.

19 Foxe, 'Acts', Vol. V, p.236; Wriothesley, Vol. I, p.80; Burnet, Vol. I, pt.i, book iii, p.187.

20 LP, Vol. XIII, pt.ii, pp.384–5.

21 'Lisle Letters', Vol. V, p.291 (Letter 1273).

22 Wriothesley, Vol. I, p.80.

23 Cited by Wilson, p.436.

24 Writing in code.

25 31 Henry VIII cap.14.

26 He married Margaret, niece of the Lutheran divine Andreas Osiander, during his time in Germany as ambassador to Charles V's court in 1530, before becoming Archbishop of Canterbury in 1533. Clerical marriage was still illegal then.

27 Mori and Vivis, Book I, letter 28, cols.22–9.

28 See Scarisbrook, p.421, fn.

29 A light, shallow-draft rowing boat, designed to convey passengers.

30 Burnet, Vol. I, pt.i, book iii, p.195. The bearward was employed by Princess Elizabeth. See Nichols, 'Narratives', p.237.

31 Burnet, Vol. I, pt.i, book iii, p.195.

32 Burnet, Vol. I, pt.i, book iii, p.201.

33 Burnet, Vol. I, pt.i, book iii, p.204.

34 Vicar of Stepney in East London.

35 Garret had escaped execution for heresy in Oxford in 1532. He did penance 'carrying a faggot in open procession from St Mary's Church to St Friswides, Garret having his red hood on his shoulders like a master of arts'. See Nichols, 'Narratives', p.294.

36 Burnet, Vol. I, pt.i, book iii, p.216.

37 Cited by Neville Williams, p.193.

38 Said by Hilles (see 'Original Letters', Vol. I, p.211) 'to have been kept in a most filthy prison [and] almost eaten up by vermin'.

39 Foxe, 'Acts', Vol. V, pp.434–8.

40 'Spanish Chronicle', p.196.

41 Hall, p.840.

42 Foxe, 'Acts', Vol. V, pp.434–6.

43 Hall, p.836.

44 Burnet, Vol. I, pt.i, p.219.

45 Hall, p.841.

46 LP, Vol. XVI, p.270.

47 Foxe, 'Acts', Vol. V, p.251, and Wriothesley, Vol. I, p.119.

48 Rich, then Solicitor General and acting on Cromwell's behalf, interviewed More (Henry's former Lord Chancellor) in the Tower in June 1535, and trapped him into discussing hypothetical issues surrounding the royal supremacy. Rich, in his testimony at More's trial in Westminster Hall, claimed that More had said that Parliament did not have the authority to make Henry the head of the Church of England. This was the only evidence against More, and he was beheaded on 6 July 1535.

49 He recovered and was later exonerated after his accusers were found guilty of perjury.

50 Foxe, 'Acts', Vol. V, pp.486–92.

51 Nichols, 'Narratives', p.252.

52 Brigden, p.78.

53 Nichols, 'Narratives', pp.255–8.

54 'Original Letters', Vol. I, p.211.

55 22 Henry VIII cap.9.

56 Tanner, p.381.

57 Wriothesley, Vol. I, pp.134–5.

CHAPTER 4 The Final Quest for Military Glory

1 See Claude Blair, 'A Royal Swordsmith and a Damascener: Diego de Çaias', *Metropolitan Museum Journal*, 3 (1970), p.168. The symbolism of the inscription is both subtle and telling. It refers to the dominant roses of the Tudor dynasty and the French lilies crushed by the English military victory in capturing the town of Boulogne. The original Latin text also has a punning play on the word '*gallus*', which could mean both 'cock' and 'Gaul' – the former being the French national motif, and the latter the ancient name for France. My grateful thanks to Claude Blair for drawing the significance of this sword to my attention and for supplying this information.

2 Information kindly supplied by Claude Blair. Herbert had been made a Gentleman of the Privy Chamber and principal esquire to the king on the day of the journey from Calais to Boulogne.

3 The last date he is known to have worn armour was at a tournament in 1540, though it is not known whether he took part. There are references to enlarging of the protective clothing worn under armour in the Wardrobe accounts for September 1543 to September 1544 because of the huge increase in his girth.

4 'Item. One harness for the king's majesty all graven and parcel gilt both for the field and tilt [joust] complete which was commanded to be translated [altered] at the king's going to Boulogne which lies in pieces part translated and part untranslated by a contrary commandment by the king's majesty.' See Starkey, 'Inventory', p.161, no.8384. The armour remained in the tiltyard at Greenwich, in the custody of Sir Thomas Paston.

5 It lacks armour to protect the lower legs and feet.

6 See Blair and Phyrr, pp.95–143. The armour remains in the collection of the Metropolitan Museum, New York.

7 LP, Vol. XIX, pt.i, p.537.

8 Meaning in the sense of establishing a quorum or check in the process of raising money.

9 LP, Vol. XIX, pt.i, p.552.

10 LP, Vol. XIX, pt.i, p.553.

11 Oyer and terminer comes from Norman French, meaning 'to hear and determine'. It describes the commissions, or assizes, in which a travelling judge tries cases alleging felonies and misdemeanours that have been committed in the specified counties. Now an obsolete legal term, replaced by Crown Courts in England and Wales.

12 BL Add. MS 32,655, fol.100.

13 LP, Vol. XIX, pt.i, p.572.

14 LP, Vol. XIX, pt.i, p.573.

15 LP, Vol. XIX, pt.i, p.606.

16 LP, Vol. XIX, pt.ii, p.18.

17 LP, Vol. XIX, pt.ii, p.113.

18 LP, Vol. XIX, pt.ii, p.127.

19 BL Add. MS 32,655, fol.168.

20 BL Lansdowne MS 1,236, fol.9. Also see Strype, 'Ecclesiastic Memorials', Vol. II, p.33, appendix.

21 *Chronicles of England, Scotland and Ireland*, new edn., Vol. II, London, 1586, p.964. A painting of the siege of Boulogne was at Cowdray House, Sussex, until it was destroyed by fire in 1793. See 'An Account of Some Ancient English Historical Paintings at Cowdray, Sussex', *Archaeologia*, III (1786), pp.251–61. An engraving of this painting, published by the Society of Antiquaries of London in 1788, clearly shows the angled artillery mount towering over the Boulogne defences, buttressed with gabions, or earth-filled basketwork, to add strength and protection against counter-battery fire. Henry, wearing a broad-brimmed hat, can be seen directing operations from his command post.

22 A method used to bring down the walls of fortifications. The besiegers employed miners to dig under the foundations, propping up the tunnel roof with wood. Combustible material would then be packed into the mine and set alight. The roof would then fall in, bringing down the wall above.

23 Lady Margaret Douglas.

24 LP, Vol. XIX, pt.ii, p.110.

25 Hall, p.861.

26 LP, Vol. XIX, pt.ii, p.119.

27 Hall, pp.861–2. Henry spent the next two days riding around the town and arranging for its future defence. He commanded that the Church of Our Lady of Boulogne should be defaced and 'plucked down' and an earthwork thrown up on its site 'for the great force and strength of the town'.

28 A beautiful sword, especially made for Henry and now at Windsor, had an illustration of the siege of Boulogne and a poem about the victory inscribed on its blade. See Claude Blair, 'A Royal Swordsmith and a Damascener: Diego de Çaias', *Metropolitan Museum Journal*, 3 (1970), pp.149–98.

29 Muller, 'Letters', pp.185–6.

30 Wriothesley, Vol. I, p.156.

31 50 metric tons.

32 The English Admiral Lord Lisle had 160 ships and 12,000 men at sea.

33 The accidental firing of a gun on board ignited a firkin of gunpowder, killing three sailors instantly, burning four others who later died, while another drowned after he jumped into the river. See Wriothesley, Vol. I, p.157.

34 LP, Vol. XX, pt.i, p.7

35 LP, Vol. XX, pt.i, p.516.

36 2,000 French soldiers did arrive in Scotland.

37 LP Spanish, Vol. VIII, p.104.

38 LP Spanish, Vol. VIII, p.106.

39 LP Spanish, Vol. VIII, p.109. These incidents may figure in a letter, dated 23 June, from the Bishop of Ajaccio in Caen, in which he reports that the Chevalier de'Ans, 'captain of the galleys which have been made here, was lately at anchor off Boulogne when six English ships, aided by the tide, came upon him so unexpectedly that he was forced to cut his cables with great difficulty'. See LP, Vol. XX, pt.i, p.492.

40 They had been alerted of the French approach by English fishermen.

41 The ship, technically a four-masted carrack, was the first purpose-built warship and was named after Henry's sister, then aged thirteen. Laid down at Portsmouth in 1509 with a sister ship, the *Peter Pomegranate*, she fought against the French off Brest in 1512. The *Mary Rose* was refitted in 1536 to carry a greater load of ordnance and so increase firepower. After her loss, two Venetian sailors were immediately hired to salvage the ship but the unsuccessful operation was abandoned about a month after the sinking. The hulk was raised in the autumn of 1982 and is now on display in Portsmouth Historic Dockyard, together with a host of recovered artefacts revealing what life and combat were like aboard a Tudor warship.

42 Pollard, p.279.

43 Wriothesley, Vol. I, p.158. The main propulsion method of the French galleys was oars, so they could manoeuvre without the wind. Each galley had a small gun mounted in the bows.

44 New forts were afterwards built at Sandown and Yarmouth to protect against a repeat of the incursion.

45 Hastily gathered forces of English levies and gentlemen drove off the French. At Seaford, the invaders fled to their boats after a skirmish with militia led by a local magnate, Sir Nicholas Pelham (d.1559), whose monument in St Michael's Church, Lewes, contains this tortuous pun:

> What time ye French sought to sack Seaford
> This PELHAM did repel 'em back aboard.

46 He was buried in the south choir aisle. The present inscription was carved in 1947–8. Elias Ashmole, in his *Antiquities of Berkshire*, London, 1719, Vol. III, p.131, reported that the duke's achievements – his coat of arms, shield, helmet and crest – hung within the fifth arch of the aisle in the seventeenth century. The first inscription over Brandon's grave had

disappeared by 1749 and a second was laid down in 1797 that survived until the latest addition was made. See Bond, p.23.

47 LP, Vol. XX, pt.i, pp.372, 464, 517 and 561, and LP, Vol. XX, pt.ii, pp.130, 168, 243–4, 250, 254, 263, 269–70, 278–9, 292–3, 304–5, 307–8, 331–2, 334, 358 and 431–2.

48 Cited by Ridley, *Henry VIII*, p. 388.

49 LP, Vol. XX, pt.i, p.372.

50 LP, Vol. XX, pt.ii, p.334.

51 £12,500, or £4.5 million in 2004 spending power.

52 Reiffenberg was last heard of in the defence of Augsburg against the imperial forces in January 1547. See LP, Vol. XXI, pt.ii, p.374.

53 LP, Vol. XX, pt.ii, pp.304–5.

54 LP, Vol. XX, pt.i, p.489.

55 Wriothesley, Vol. I, pp.159–60. Each coat cost 4s and each man was paid 2s 6d in 'conduct money' to fund the journey to Dover, where they would join the king's payroll.

56 LP, Vol. XX, pt.i, p.43.

57 Wriothesley, Vol. I, p.156.

58 Wriothesley, Vol. I, p.157. The tempest was so vehement and terrible that the Parisians 'thought the day of doom had come'.

59 LP, Vol. XX, pt.ii, p.71.

60 Cited by Scarisbrook, p.453. See: F. Dietz, 'English Public Finance 1485–1558', *University of Illinois Studies in Social Sciences*, 9 (1920), p.149.

61 Lehmberg, p.201.

62 LP, Vol. XX, pt.i, pp.44–5.

63 LP, Vol. XX, pt.ii, p.471. Beaton was assassinated by sixteen Scottish Protestant gentlemen on 29 May 1546 at his castle of St Andrew's.

64 SP, Vol. I, p.840, and LP, Vol. XX, pt.ii, pp.338–9.

65 Cited by Lehmberg, p.232.

66 LP, Vol. XXI, pt.i, p.374.

67 LP, Vol. XXI, pt.ii, pp.462–3.

68 Now called Campagne-les-Guisnes.

69 The Treaty of Ardres was ratified by Francis I at Fontainebleu on 1 August 1546; Francis even styled Henry 'Defender of the Faith and Supreme Head of the Church of England'. Diplomacy can sometimes mask many differences. See Scarisbrook, pp.463–4.

CHAPTER 5 'Anger Short and Sweat Abundant'

1 LP, Vol. XIII, pt.ii, p.317. Under the Treasons Act of 1534, it was high treason 'maliciously to wish, will, or desire by words or writing' or to 'imagine, invent, practise or attempt any bodily harm' to the king, queen or their heirs apparent. Montague was executed for these words. See Tanner, p.379.

2 Moriarty, p.13.

3 Although recent research has revealed the purchase of a pair of boots for playing football early on in his reign.

4 Kybett, p.22.

5 Moriarty, p.13.

6 Brewer, p.120.

7 MacNalty, p.67. Vicary, who died in 1561, was a member of the Barber's Company in 1525, becoming master in 1530. He was appointed a governor of St Bartholomew's Hospital in London in 1548, living in a house provided by that institution, and that year published his *Anatomy of the Body of Man*. Vicary is seen receiving the charter of the new Barber Surgeons' Company from Henry in the cartoon by Holbein. See Furdell, p.33.

8 First suggested by the obstetrician A. S. Currie. See his 'Notes on the Obstetric Histories of Catherine of Aragon and Anne Boleyn', *Edinburgh Medical Journal*, 1 (1888), 34pp. The syphilis theory was also propounded by the gynaecologist and surgeon C. MacLaurin in 'The Tragedy of the Tudors' in *Post Mortems of Mere Mortals*, 1930, pp.50–102. He writes of Henry and his court (p.68): 'The general atmosphere of lust, obscenity, grandiose ideas ... and violence combined with cowardice especially about disease, is all very typical of syphilis, one might almost call it diagnostic.'

9 Born 1519. Died in 1536 of tuberculosis, a disease particularly fatal to the Tudors, which also claimed the king's eldest brother, Prince Arthur, in 1502 and his father, Henry VII, in 1509. Henry's legitimate son, Edward VI, died in 1553 from a suppurating pulmonary infection and generalised septicaemia with renal failure, although Brewer (p.130) strongly suggests that the cause of death was pulmonary tuberculosis, aggravated by an attack of measles. See Moriarty, p.12, and Loach, *Edward VI*, pp.160–2.

10 For example, see Brinch.

11 Park, p.36.

12 MacNalty, p.161.

13 A letter from Augustine to the Duke of Norfolk, dated Ghent, 3 June 1531, reporting several audiences with Charles V and the discussions about religion at the English court, is in BL Cotton MS Galba, B x, fol.8.

14 MacNalty, p.161.

15 Brewer, p.129.

16 LP, Vol. XII, pt.ii, p.27. Henry was explaining his reasons for postponing a visit to the restive North of England after the Pilgrimage of Grace had been brutally put down.

17 3 Henry VIII cap.11. See Bloom and James, p.1.

18 BL Sloane MS 1,047, a book containing 230 prescriptions in ninety-four pages, including contributions by Drs Chambre, Butts, Cromer and Augustine. See Blaxland Stubbs, 'Royal Recipes for Plasters, Ointments and other Medicants', *Chemist & Druggist*, 114 (1931), pp.792–4.

19 A brown-flowered plant of the genus *Sanguisorba* or *Poterium*.

20 A feathery-leaved herb, *Chrysanthemum parthenium*.

21 An evergreen shrubby plant, *Ruta graveolens*, used in herbal medicine as a cure for coughs, colic and flatulence. It is strongly anti-spasmodic and stimulating.

22 Juice or resin of the dragon tree, *Dracaena draco*.

23 A vessel holding two quarts or four pints of liquid.

24 'Medicine for the pestilence of King Henry VIII which has helped diverse persons.' Ellis, 'History', Vol. I, p.292.

25 See MacNalty, p.126.

26 Roberts, p.221.

27 Copeman, p.117.

28 32 Henry VIII cap.42.

29 Copeman, p.131.

30 Copeman, p.148.

31 Copeman, p.149.

32 Furdell, p.24. His accepted biography is William Osler's *Thomas Linacre*, Cambridge, 1908.

33 Dugdale, p.56.

34 Furdell, p.25.

35 He was sent to the Tower in April 1534, but his crime is not known. His imprisonment may have been a result of his sympathies with Catherine of Aragon and Princess Mary. He retained friends in high places, however. Sir William Paulet, then Comptroller of the Household, wrote to Cromwell a few weeks later seeking Augustine's release: 'Be good to Mr Augustine that he may be relieved of his charge.' See Hammond, p. 234.

36 LP, Vol. XII, pt.ii, p.340.

37 The Lord Privy Seal was now Sir William Fitzwilliam, Earl of Southampton, appointed in June 1540 in succession to Cromwell.

38 LP Spanish, Vol. VI, pt.i, p.285.

39 LP, Vol. XXI, pt.ii, pp.285–6.

40 For a detailed account of Augustine's mysterious life, see Hammond, pp.215–49, who suggests that permission was sought for Augustine to carry weapons with which to defend himself in Venice.

41 Butts' tomb was an altar monument made from Purbeck marble close against the south wall of the chancel of Fulham Church, with a effigy in brass on top and his arms – *azure*,

three lozenges gules on a chevron or between three etoils or – and a scroll inscribed: 'Mine Advantage.' The inscription was three elegiac Latin verses written by Sir John Cheke, tutor to Prince Edward. The lost brass is engraved in Faulkner, p.78, and the inscription transcribed in BL Redgrave Hall Papers 40,061, fol.8. A small alabaster and black marble tablet was erected in the north aisle of the church in 1627 by a descendant, Leonard Butts.

42 CPR, *Philip & Mary*, Vol. IV, pp.450–1. Wendy's funeral in Cambridge on 27 May 1560 was a grand affair, recorded by the merchant tailor and undertaker Henry Machyn, with 'a great dole' provided for the poor: '500 people had great plenty of meat and drink … Great store has been seen for a middle-rank gentleman and a great moan made.' Machyn, pp.235–6.

43 His inscription fulfilled the Protestant requirement for just factual information: 'Here lieth/ THOMAS WENDYE Doctor in Phesicke/ and was buried the xxvij daye of Maye 1560.' See Munk, Vol. I, p.50.

44 Munk, Vol. 1, p.37.

45 MacNalty, p.149.

46 Cited by Weir, p.457 and Furdell, p.28.

47 He died in 1556 and was buried in St Michael, Bassishaw, Basinghall Ward, London, where his epitaph, now lost, read:

> In surgery brought up in youth
> A knight here lieth dead
> A knight and also a surgeon such
> As England seld[om] hath bred
> For which so sovereign gift of God
> Wherein he did excel
> King Henry VIII called him to court
> Who loved him dearly well.

48 MacNalty, pp.69–70.

49 Henry had grown a beard a number of times during his reign: Catherine of Aragon persuaded him to shave it off, and the golden beard familiar from his portraits appeared only after 1535 when he ordered his courtiers to grow whiskers and cut their hair short.

50 Furdell, p.35.

51 Furdell, p.30.

52 LP, Vol. X, p.71. The writer Chapuys pondered whether he should ask destiny for 'what greater misfortune' was reserved for Henry 'like the other tyrant who escaped from the fall of the house in which all the rest were smothered and soon after died'.

53 Scarisbrook, p.485, suggests that the headaches may have been due to persistent catarrh.

54 Park, p.44.

55 LP, Vol. XII, pt.i, p.486.

56 LP, Vol. XIII, pt.i, p.368.

57 LP, Vol. XIII, pt.ii, p.313.

58 'Lisle Letters', Vol. V, p.1415. This demonstrates Henry's adherence to Catholic liturgy: 'On Holy Thursday, his Grace went [on] procession about the Court at Westminster. And the high altar in the chapel [Royal] was [decorated] with all the apostles and [there was] mass by note and the organs playing with as much honour to God [as] might be devised to be done. Upon Good Friday last, the King's grace crept to the cross from the chapel door upward, devoutly, and so served the priest to mass that same day, his own person kneeling on his grace['s] knees.'

59 Boned and pressed white meat, served cold in aspic.

60 Cited by Neville Williams, p.186.

61 Copeman, pp.156–7. Potatoes were not eaten in England until the vegetable was introduced from the West Indies by Hawkins in 1564.

62 *Portulaca oleracea.*

63 See Kybett, pp.19–25.

64 LP, Vol. XIV, pt.ii, p.45. 12 September 1539, 'between 10 and 11 am'.

65 Faced with the prospect of the thrill of the chase, Henry sometimes woke up at four o'clock in the morning to go hunting.

66 LP, Vol. XVI, p.284. 3 March 1541.

67 Ibid.

68 Ibid.

69 LP, Vol. XVI, p.285.

70 Now in Liverpool's Walker Art Gallery, the Museo Thyssen, Madrid, and elsewhere.

71 The Walker Art Gallery portrait, by Hans Holbein the Younger, was painted when the king was forty-six and was probably derived, like the portrait at Petworth House, Sussex, from the mural painted in the Palace of Westminster. Holbein employed considerable artistic licence to create an imposing figure: by lengthening the figure's legs, for example, he created a slimmer image.

72 LP, Vol. X, p.117.

73 An oil on panel painted by an unknown artist. National Portrait Gallery 496. Now on display at Montacute House, Somerset. Other versions are at Castle Howard, Yorkshire, St Bartholomew's Hospital, London, and Hever Castle, Kent.

74 MacNalty, p.126.

75 Printed and published in London, 1608. Armin is listed amongst the actors in the Folio Edition of Shakespeare's plays. He was a comic player, probably performing the roles of Touchstone in *As You Like It*, Feste in *Twelfth Night* and the Fool in *King Lear*.

76 The source for this is a reference in the Revd James Granger's *Biographical History* of 1779. Fermer gained some influence at court as a result and was appointed Sheriff of Bedfordshire and Buckinghamshire in 1532–3. However, he incurred royal displeasure in 1540 for his determination to comfort his former chaplain and confessor, Nicholas Thayne, then a close prisoner in Buckingham Gaol for denying the king's religious supremacy, although nothing was proved except Fermer's provision of a paltry 8d and several clean shirts. Fermer was briefly jailed in the Marshalsea Prison, Southwark, and his extensive estates were confiscated for the king's use (his lands are listed in BL Royal MS Appendix 89, fol.158) but he recovered them after Henry's death in 1549, possibly after an intervention by Somers with Edward VI. See Robert Hutchinson and Bryan Egan, *Transactions of the Monumental Brass Society*, 16 (1999), pp.247–8, and NA E 318, Court of Augmentations, Particular of Grants, Edward VI.

77 The Protestant John Bale takes Somers' name in vain in an attack on an unreformed priest who performed a service 'with no small strutting and stammering, turning his arse to the people after the old popish manner ... More apish toys and gawdy feats [were showed] at the communion. He turned and tossed, lurked and licked, snored and snorted, gaped and gasped, kneeled and knocked ... with both his thumbs at his ears and other tricks more that he made me twenty times to remember Will Somer[s]'. Nichols, 'Narratives', p.318.

78 Doran, p.137.

79 Ibid.

80 LP, Vol. XXI, pt.ii, p.401. The ferryman was paid at the rate of 1d per horse. The accounts were marked '1546' but probably refer to the previous year, as they also talk of Henry moving from Westminster to Hampton Court. The king remained at Westminster for Christmas 1546.

81 BL Royal MS 2A xvi, fol.63b.

82 He is mentioned in the household accounts as 'orator in the French tongue' in 1540–1.

83 BL Royal MS 2A xvi, fol.3, illustrating Psalm 1.

84 Cited by Weir, p.483.

85 LP, Vol. VIII, pp.366–7.

86 Now in the Royal Collection.

87 Queen Katherine Parr provided three geese and hens for Jane to look after in the Privy Garden. See Southworth, p.103. A skin infection contracted in 1543 necessitated a barber shaving her hair every month. Another school of thought believes the figure is 'Mistress Jak', Edward's wet nurse, but given the iconography of the picture, this seems unlikely.

88 A picture of Henry painted towards the end of his life, showing him wearing a jewelled cap and holding a staff in his right hand, with his three children and Will Somers in the background, was in the possession of the Earl of Bessborough in 1800. See Nichols, 'Literary Remains', Vol. I, p.cccliii.

89 LP *Addenda*, Vol. I, pt.ii, p.618.

90 It was a healing power believed to be possessed by later Tudor and Stuart monarchs as well, acquired from God through the holy oil used to anoint kings and queens at their coronations.

91 Starkey, 'Inventory', p.75, item 2524.

92 A small upholstered area.

93 NA E 315/160, fol.133v. Virtually the same descriptions appear in the inventory of Henry's goods made after his death. They were listed under 'Refuse Stuff at Westminster in the charge of James Ruffoth'. See Starkey, 'Inventory', p.263.

94 She was the daughter of Norfolk's steward at Kenninghall. When the duke separated from his wife during Lent 1534 to live with his mistress, Bess, the duchess moved to Redbourne, Hertfordshire, constantly complaining about her husband's behaviour. On 24 October 1537, she wrote: 'I have been his wife twenty-five years and borne him five children and because I would suffer the bawd and the harlots that bound me to be still in the house, they pinnacled [manacled] me and sat on my breast till I spat blood, all for speaking against the woman in the court, Bess Holland. It is four years come Tuesday in Passion week since he came riding all night and locked me up in a chamber and took away my jewels and apparel and left me with but £50 a quarter ... to keep twenty persons in a hard country.' On another occasion she wrote: 'I reckon if I come home I shall be poisoned.' See LP, Vol. XII, pt.ii, p.342. Her complaints about 'hard usage' by Norfolk are contained in a letter to his enemy, Cromwell, in BL Cotton MS Titus B i, fol.388.

95 See Robinson, p.26.

96 LP, Vol. XXI, pt.ii, p.110.

97 NA E 315/160, fol.135.

98 LP, Vol. XXI, pt.ii, p.325. Slanning was paid on 11 January 1547, receipting the document with her mark.

99 LP, Vol. XXIII; *Addenda*, Vol. II, p.610.

CHAPTER 6 The New Levers of Power

1 *Ordinances of the Royal Household*, Society of Antiquaries, London, 1790, p.159.

2 He died in 1553. His tomb, which re-uses stonework from older monuments, is at Hainton, Lincolnshire. Its iconography clearly reflects Heneage's adherence to the old faith.

3 See David Starkey, *The King's Privy Chamber 1485–1547*, unpublished Ph.D. thesis, Cambridge University, 1973, and Starkey, *The Reign of Henry VIII*, pp.109–12.

4 Thynne Correspondence TH/VOL/II, at Longleat House, Wiltshire, dated Westminster, 8 August 1549. This was a premature report of his death, as an addition to Denny's will is dated 7 September (written while he was 'lying sick, but of good mind and memory'). He probably died on 10 September.

5 Sir Edmund married three times and had eighteen children. Of the sons, only two survived.

6 His father left him £160 in his will to purchase land and the income from a property in Kent to fund his 'exhibition and learning' at Cambridge.

7 The letter directed the Sheriff to elect Denny – 'one of our privy chamber' – as Burgess to fill the vacancy caused by the death of Thomas Alvred. The year is not indicated. See Ipswich Borough Correspondence HD36/A, Suffolk Record Office, Ipswich.

8 Shakespeare has Denny as one of his characters in his play *King Henry the Eighth*. During its first performance, on 29 June 1613, the Globe theatre was burnt to the ground.

9 Another sister, Joyce, first married William Walsingham and was mother to Francis, who would go on to become Elizabeth's Secretary of State and spymaster. She later married Sir John Carey of Pleshy, Essex.

10 This handled the exchequer revenues from the Church, including the Oxford and Cambridge colleges, after the break with Rome and following the passing of the Act annexing papal revenues in 1534 (26 Henry VIII cap.3).

11 The Court of Requests, established in 1483, was a kind of 'small-claims court' of the time, intended specifically for legal cases brought by the poor and by women. Its judges were called 'Masters'.

12 Sil, p.191.

13 Ellis, 'Eminent Men', p.14. Ascham's letter to William Cecil, dated 23 March 1553.

14 Cited by Neville Williams, p.171.

15 Strype, 'Cheke', p.168.

16 A copy of the painting is in the Courtauld Institute in London.

17 Holbein also designed the combined clock and table salt given by Denny to Henry as a New Year's present in 1544, but now sadly lost. Holbein's clever design in a Renaissance style also included a compass and two sundials. His drawing of the object survives in the British Museum. Holbein died in London in 1543 of the plague.

18 Martienssen, p.113.

19 Foxe, 'Acts', Vol. V, p.562.

20 He was represented by a deputy.

21 See Robert E. Brook, *Early Tudor Courtiers in Society, Illustrated from Select Examples*, unpublished Ph.D. thesis, University of London, 1963, pp.271–3.

22 LP *Addenda*, Vol. I, pt.ii, pp.588–9.

23 LP, Vol. XVIII, pt.i, pp.334 and 406.

24 LP *Addenda*, Vol. I, pt.ii, p.593.

25 Three card tables are recorded in the Inventory of Henry's goods, together with gaming dice and chessboards. See, for example, Starkey, 'Inventory', items nos. 2613, 10480, 15842 and 16672.

26 Sil, p.194.

27 See Cunich, 'Revolution and Crisis in English State Finance 1534–47', and tables.

28 In 1542, Henry ordered wardrobes full of new clothes such as: 'A gown of purple satin furred with the sleeves and border set with 130 diamonds and 131 clusters of pearls ... set in gold, and in every cluster is four green pearls.' Then there was a new mantle for Parliament: 'crimson velvet partly furred with powdered ermine and a cap; three mantles for the order of St George; two of blue velvet, the other of purple velvet, lined.' And there were precious, sacred objects: 'An image of Our Lady standing upon an angel, St Edward having an arrow in his hand, weighing 33 ozs; an image of St Peter in gilt standing upon a base of silver and gilt with a book and two keys in his hands, weighing 124 ozs. An image of St Paul standing upon a base with a sword and a book in his hands, weighing 135 ozs.' And so the purchases went on. See NA PRO 31/17/40.

29 NA E 315/160, fol.136r.

30 Master of the Revels at Henry's court from 1544.

31 Appointed Treasurer and Master of the Mint in 1546.

32 NA E 315/160, fol.265v.

33 For example, the accounts for 1554–5 have 'ten pair of spectacles at 4d the pair, 3s. 4d'. See LP, Vol. XXI, pt.ii, p.400.

34 See Starkey, *The Reign of Henry VIII*, p.112.

35 NA SP 4. Signatures by stamp, Henry VIII, 1545–7, 1 vol.

36 The dry-stamp system was revived in the last months of Mary's reign in 1558 when she became too sick to cope with signing the amount of paper laid before her 'without distress and peril of her body'. In her case, licensees to ink in her signature 'as surely as [the documents] had been signed with the queen's own hand' were John Boxall, Dean of St George's Chapel, Windsor (her secretary), Anthony Kempe (one of the Gentlemen of her Privy Chamber), Barnard Hampton (a clerk of the Privy Council) and John Clyff (one of the Clerks of Signet). The stamp was to be used in the presence of Mary and any two of her Councillors, which number would include Sir William Petre, who would also authenticate the use of the dry stamp by signing in a special book. See CPR, *Philip & Mary*, Vol. IV, pp.453–4.

37 LP, Vol. XXI, pt.i, p.767.

38 Ibid.

39 Hall, p.867. Edward had written to the queen on 12 August enquiring in advance about the admiral's skill in Latin. 'If he is so skilled, I should rather learn better how to speak with him, when I come into his presence.' See BL Harleian MS 5,087, no.17.

40 Nichols, 'Literary Remains', Vol. I, p.lxxviii.

41 Wriothesley, Vol. I, p.173.

42 LP, Vol. XXI, pt.i, pp.694–5.

43 Foxe, 'Acts', Vol. V, p.568.

CHAPTER 7 The Plot to Burn the Queen

1 Convincingly ascribed to her by James, 'Devotional Writings', pp.137–8.

2 End of the session, with dissolution of Parliament.

3 LP, Vol. XX, pt.ii, p.513. Petre said that the bill had been 'driven to the last hour and yet then passed only by division of the House'.

4 A jibe based on the ancient Jewish sect that strictly adhered to traditional laws and had pretensions to superior sanctity.

5 Hall, pp.864–6. The chronicler wrote it down 'word for word as near as I was able to report it'.

6 Meaning 'perhaps'.

7 LP, Vol. XX, pt.ii, pp.513 and 522.

8 Foxe, 'Acts', Vol.V, p.562.

9 LP Spanish, Vol. VIII, p.425.

10 LP, Vol. XXI, pt.i, p.135.

11 LP, Vol. XXI, pt.i, p.169.

12 Martienssen, p.210.

13 LP, Vol. XXI, pt.i, p.271.

14 NA E 314/22, fol.44.

15 James, 'Kateryn Parr', p.268.

16 Strype, 'Ecclesiastic Memorials', Vol. I, pt.ii, pp.597–8.

17 APC, Vol. I, 1542–7, p.400.

18 Ellis, 'History', Vol. II, p.176.

19 Nichols, 'Narratives', p.42, fn.

20 Strype, 'Ecclesiastic Memorials', Vol. I, pt.ii, p.599.

21 According to her nephew, Edward Ascu, in his *History Containing the Wars*, London, 1607, p.308.

22 Nichols, 'Narratives', p.309.

23 Anne, second wife of Henry Ratcliffe, Second Earl of Sussex. She separated from her husband between May 1547 and June 1549 and was charged with wanting to marry Sir Edmund Knyvett. She was imprisoned in the Tower in 1552 on charges of sorcery.

24 Anne Stanhope, wife of Hertford, afterwards Duchess of Somerset.

25 Jane Fitzwilliam, third wife of the London Alderman Sir William.

26 Nichols, 'Narratives', p.311.

27 Nichols, 'Narratives'., p.304, fn.

28 Foxe, 'Acts', Vol. V, pp.553 ff.

29 Ibid.

30 Cited by Martienssen, p.218.

31 Strickland, Vol. III, p.246.

32 Foxe, 'Acts', Vol. V, pp.559–60.

33 Cited by Martienssen, p.220.

CHAPTER 8 Protestants Ascendant

1 Foxe, 'Acts', Vol. VI, p.36.

2 Foxe, 'Acts', Vol. VI, p.163.

3 Ponet, Book XLVI, p.78.

4 Nichols, 'Narratives', pp.209–10.

5 Muller, *Stephen Gardiner and Tudor Reaction*, p.133.

6 He may have been a bastard son or brother of Sir Thomas Wyatt. After the defeat of the rebellion, Sir Thomas was executed on 11 April 1554, when the French ambassador reported that people crowded the scaffold to dip their handkerchiefs in his blood. See Anthony Fletcher and Diarmaid MacCulloch, *Tudor Rebellions*, London, 1997, p.90. There is no record of the fate of Edward Wyatt.

7 Strickland, Vol. III, p.247.

8 LP, Vol. XXI, pt.ii, p.252, and Muller, 'Letters', pp.246–7.

9 Muller, 'Letters', p.248.

10 Foxe, 'Acts', Vol. VI, p.138.

11 LP, Vol. XXI, pt.ii, p.173. Letter from the French ambassador Odet de Selve to the Admiral of France, 24 November 1546.

12 An Act for Murder and Malicious Bloodshed within the Court was passed in 1542 (33 Henry VIII cap. 12), imposing a mandatory punishment of amputation of a hand for drawing blood within the precincts of the court, although noble courtiers were not liable to such penalties if they had merely struck their servants for the purposes of chastisement.

13 Surrey was called thus in 1539 by Constantine Barlow, Dean of Westbury. See *Archaeologia*, Vol. XXIII, p.62.

14 It turned out to be an unconsummated union, probably because of the Duke of Richmond's contraction of tuberculosis, and he died, aged seventeen, in 1536.

15 A tennis court.

16 *Poems of Henry Howard, Earl of Surrey*, Aldine edn, London, n.d., p.19.

17 He was to succeed his grandfather as the Fourth Duke of Norfolk on 25 August 1554. He was executed on 2 June 1572 and attainted for his attempt to marry Mary, Queen of Scots.

18 *Poems of Henry Howard*, op. cit., pp.xxvii–xxviii.

19 *Poems of Henry Howard*, p.xxix.

20 Son of the poet Sir Thomas Wyatt, who died in 1542. Wyatt the Younger was later the leader of the rebellion in Kent against Mary in 1554.

21 *Poems of Henry Howard*, op. cit., p.xxxi, fn.

22 *Poems of Henry Howard*, pp.68–9.

23 Brenan and Statham, Vol. II, p.383.

24 His squire Thomas Clere saved his life but later died from his wounds, Robinson, p.46. He was buried in the Howard Chapel of St Mary's Lambeth, Surrey, under a monumental

brass depicting him in armour. Surrey wrote a poetical epitaph to him, once displayed on the wall above the slab in the north chapel, now lost:

> At Montreuil gates, hopeless of all recure [recovery]
> Thine Earl, half dead, gave in thy hand his will
> Which cause did thee this pining death procure.

25 Nott, Vol. I, p.178, fn.1.

26 LP, Vol. XXI, pt.i, p.16.

27 LP, Vol. XXI, pt.i, p.175.

28 *Poems of Henry Howard*, op. cit., pp.xlv–xlvii.

29 Ibid.

30 Robinson, p.47.

31 Lord Edward Herbert of Cherbury, *Life and Reign of King Henry VIII*, London, 1649, p.562.

32 'Spanish Chronicle', p.144.

33 LP, Vol. XXI, pt.ii, p.277.

34 LP, Vol. XXI, pt.ii, p.273.

35 BL Cotton MS Titus B i, fol.94.

36 Executed by Henry in 1521 on trumped-up charges of disloyalty.

37 BL Cotton MS Titus B i, fol.94.

38 Thomas Darcy, Baron Darcy, who surrendered Pontefract Castle to the rebels during the Pilgrimage of Grace in 1536 and who was betrayed by an intercepted letter to one of the rebel leaders. Beheaded for treason 1537.

39 One of the leaders of the Pilgrimage of Grace who seized Hull but was pardoned. He refused to come to London and was executed in Hull in 1537.

40 Another rebel in the Pilgrimage of Grace. He was hanged, drawn and quartered at Tyburn as a traitor in 1537. His wife, 'a very fair creature and beautiful' according to the herald and chronicler Wriothesley, was burnt at Smithfield in London after being dragged through the streets on a hurdle.

41 Robert Aske, attorney and fellow of Gray's Inn who led the Pilgrimage of Grace insurrection in Yorkshire, was hanged in chains in York in 1537 after apparently being pardoned by Henry.

42 His stepmother Agnes, Dowager Duchess of Norfolk, implicated in the downfall of Queen Katherine Howard.

43 LP, Vol. XXI, pt.ii, no.554.

44 LP, Vol. XXI, pt.ii, p.273. Norfolk was then aged seventy-three and suffered regularly from indigestion and chronic rheumatism, the latter probably not helped by his imprisonment in the dank, damp Tower, fronting the River Thames.

45 LP Spanish, Vol. VIII, p.533.

46 LP, Vol. XXI, pt.ii, p.310.

47 He was questioning their humanity.

48 LP, Vol. XXI, pt.ii, p.313.

49 'Spanish Chronicle', pp.145–6.

50 The charges, dated 10 January 1547, in Latin, are contained in the roll NA KB 8/14.

51 Robinson, p.49.

52 LP, Vol. XXI, pt.ii, p.285.

53 LP, Vol. XXI, pt.ii, pp.284–5.

54 Knyvett was no friend of Surrey's. He was threatened with amputation of his right hand as a punishment for striking the earl's squire, Thomas Clere, and drawing Surrey's blood on the tennis court at Greenwich in February 1541. He was pardoned as he faced the block and the serjeant surgeon.

55 LP, Vol. XXI, pt.ii, p.287.

56 LP Spanish, Vol. VIII, p.533.

57 Byrne, pp.422–3.

58 LP Spanish, Vol. VIII, p.533.

59 LP Spanish, Vol. VIII, pp.533–4.

60 Ibid.

61 BL Harleian MS 297, fol.256. See also Herbert, p.567.

62 'Spanish Chronicle', p.146.

63 NA E 101/60/22 contains details of the cash owing on Surrey's board at the Tower, including attendants, candles, coals and an allowance for hangings and plate in his room, totalling £24. The cost of the new coat 'against his arraignment' is also included.

64 Under 28 Henry VIII cap.7.

65 Decorated with fleur-de-lis at the terminations of each arm of the cross.

66 A 'merlett' or 'merlion' is a heraldic bird. This is an old term for martlet, or swallow, often displayed in arms without legs or feet, in the belief that the bird could not perch on the ground. Edward the Confessor's arms actually had doves. See J. P. Brooke-Little, *Boutell's Heraldry*, London, 1970, p.206.

67 The label is a heraldic device similar to a riband, with several shorter ribands hanging down, which overlays arms to indicate those of an eldest son.

68 LP, Vol. XXI, pt.ii, p.365.

69 'Spanish Chronicle', p.146, a reference to the merchant's earlier account of Surrey's attempted escape.

70 Probably East Winch, near King's Lynn, which housed a monument to the Howards that bore the arms of Edward the Confessor. See discussion in Moore.

71 'Spanish Chronicle', p.147.

72 A cap of crimson velvet and ermine, generally belonging to a duke but in this sense clearly signifying that part of royal regalia carried before the monarch at coronations.

73 LP Spanish, Vol. IX, p.4.

74 'Spanish Chronicle', p.147.

75 'Spanish Chronicle'. p.148.

76 Surrey's body was removed to the Howard Chapel in Framlingham Church, Suffolk, in 1614 and reburied there. The monument to him and his wife includes his coronet, which is not worn on the effigy's head but rather laid separately on a cushion by his legs to indicate his attainder. See Robinson, p.52. Construction of the mortuary chapel was begun by his father after 1545 but the work was not completed until a few years later.

77 'Spanish Chronicle', p.148.

78 NA E 101/60/22.

79 BL Harleian MS 5,087, no.31, and LP, Vol. XXI, pt.ii, p.360.

80 BL Cotton MS Nero C x, fol.6. A rough draft in Latin.

81 BL Harleian MS 5,087, no.32.

CHAPTER 9 The Mystery of the Royal Will

1 Byrne, p.418.

2 LP Spanish, Vol. VIII, p.320.

3 Ibid.

4 Cited by Weir, p.495.

5 LP, Vol. XXI, pt.ii, p.52.

6 LP Spanish, Vol. VIII, p.533.

7 See: LP, Vol. XXI, pt.ii, pp.394–9; Matthews, pp.172–3; and Bayles, pp.794–6.

8 Bayles, p.796.

9 First suggested by Brewer, pp.123–4.

10 LP Spanish, Vol. VIII, p.534.

11 Dale, p.31.

12 LP Spanish, Vol. VIII, p.535.

13 Foxe, 'Acts', Vol. VI, p.163.

14 Burnet describes Thirlby as a 'learned and modest man' but 'of so fickle and cowardly a temper that he turned always with the stream in every change that was made'.

15 Foxe, 'Acts', Vol. VI, p.163.

16 LP Spanish, Vol. VIII, p.537.

17 LP Spanish, Vol. VIII, p.542.

18 Some accounts say it was Sir Anthony Denny. This seems highly unlikely.

19 Foxe, 'Acts', Vol. V, pp.691ff., and Burnet, Vol. I, book iii, p.255.

20 NA E 23/4/1.

21 About £1,300 in the money of the time, or £324,450 in today's values.

22 The bequest is worth around £165,000 in 2004 spending power.

23 The 'Poor Knights' was a charitable foundation created by Edward III for those of his followers captured during the French wars and bankrupted by ransom fees. It exists today as 'the Military Knights' and is open to any British army officer under the age of sixty-five. They are still provided with grace and favour accommodation in the lower ward of Windsor Castle and every year take part in the ceremonials of many state occasions. They claim to be the oldest military establishment on the *Army List*.

24 35 Henry VIII cap.1.

25 Starkey, 'Inventory', p.xi.

26 Starkey, *Henry VIII: A European Court*, p.131. Details of the ordnance, weapons, armour and munitions are provided in Starkey, 'Inventory', pp.102–63.

27 Some of the minor legatees waited a long time to receive their bequests; some indeed died before the bequests were paid.

28 See, for example, Smith, 'Last Will', pp.20ff.; Levine, pp.471–85; Ives, 'A Forensic Conundrum'; and Houlbrooke.

29 LP, Vol. XXI, pt.ii, p.408.

30 Wriothesley administered the 'accustomed oath' of allegiance to Seymour on that date at Westminster. See APC, n.s., Vol. I, 1542–7, p.566.

31 Ives, 'A Forensic Conundrum', p.786.

32 Ives, 'A Forensic Conundrum', p.784.

33 See H. Miller, 'Henry VIII's Unwritten Will: Grants of Lands and Honours in 1547' in E. W. Ives, R. J. Knecht and J. J. Scarisbrook (eds.), *Wealth and Power in Tudor England: Essays Presented to S. T. Bindoff*, London, 1978, pp.87–106.

34 LP, Vol. XXI, pt.ii, p.356.

35 LP, Vol. XXI, pt.ii, p.360.

36 APC, Vol. I, 1542–7, pp.558, 562.

37 LP, Vol. XXI, pt.ii, p.407.

38 LP, Vol. XXI, pt.ii, p.434. On 27 January, he received another grant as Under-Steward and Clerk of the Forest and Clerk of the Swaincote Courts of Waltham Forest, Essex.

39 LP, Vol. XXI, pt.ii, pp.406–8, and NA SP 4.

40 LP, Vol. XXI, pt.ii, p.420.

41 Identified by a grant of the rectory of Grayingham, Lincolnshire, on 30 April 1546.

42 Foxe, 'Acts', Vol. V, p.689, and Burnet, Vol. I, book iii, p.255.

43 Brewer, p.121.

44 Foxe, 'Acts', Vol. V, p.689.

45 Brewer, p.124.

CHAPTER 10 'Dogs Should Lick His Blood'

1 Foxe, 'Acts', Vol. V, p.697.

2 See Cunich, 'Revolution and Crisis in English State Finance 1534–47', and tables at www.le.ac.uk/ni/bon/ESFDB.

3 Derived from the opening words of the antiphon of the first nocturn of the Office for Matins: '*Dirige, Domine, Deus Meus, in conspectu tuo vitam meam*' – 'Direct me, O God ...' – one of the three parts of the Office for the Dead. The origin of the modern word 'dirge'. See Paul Binski, *Medieval Death: Ritual and Representation*, London, 1996, p.53.

4 NA LC 2/2, fol.87. See also Loach, 'Function and Ceremonial ...', p.58. The Privy Council, meeting at the Tower on 2 February, approved payments of some of the bills. Warrants were addressed to Sir Edmund Peckham, Cofferer of the Household, and John Hales, Treasurer of the Privy Chamber.

5 Strype, 'Ecclesiastic Memorials', Vol. II, pt.ii, p.290.

6 Dethicke was promoted from Richmond Herald to Norroy in January 1547 before Henry died and succeeded Christopher Barker as Garter King of Arms on 29 April 1550. (SPD, *Edward VI, 1547–53*, p.7.)

7 Sandford, p.493. Strype ('Ecclesiastic Memorials') gives a slightly different version.

8 The Vespers of the Dead, so called for the opening antiphon: '*Placebo Domino in regione vivorum*' – 'I will walk before the Lord in the land of the living ...'

9 Muller, 'Letters', p.254.

10 Wriothesley, Vol. I, p.181.

11 Toto came to London in 1519 and received a £25 annuity in 1530–53. He was appointed serjeant painter in 1544. He was a resident of St Bride's Parish in Fleet Street, dying intestate in 1554. See Auerbach, pp.56 and 145.

12 NA LC 2/2, fol.7.

13 Bannerols were banners of greater width used to display the arms of the ancestors of the deceased and their marriages.

14 Strype, 'Ecclesiastic Memorials', Vol. II, pt.ii, p.296.

15 NA SP 10/3/7.

16 SP 10/1/9, 13 February 1547.

17 A few months later, it was to be granted to Edward Seymour, by then created Duke of Somerset and Lord Protector of the realm. The coffin of Edward IV had rested at Syon overnight *en route* to his burial place at Windsor in 1483.

18 There are reports of only seven horses, but Sandford, John Stow in his *Annals* and the 'Spanish Chronicle' all talk of eight. See 'Spanish Chronicle', p.154.

19 Strype, 'Ecclesiastic Memorials', Vol. II, pt.ii, p.298.

20 'Spanish Chronicle', p.154.

21 John Bruges, now the king's tailor, was paid 13s 4d for making the robe of estate in blue velvet, lined with white sarsenet (a soft, silky material), for the effigy and John Benyns was

paid 4s for making a doublet of blue satin 'lined with sarcenet and flamed and edged with velvet'. NA LC 2/2, fol.3.

22 Sandford, p.493.

23 The jewellery was supplied from the Jewel House in the Tower of London. See NA E 101/426/5.

24 Strype, 'Ecclesiastic Memorials', Vol. II, pt.ii, p.299. It was more likely to be later: Sandford says the procession left at about ten o'clock, which would accord with the two-hour delay incurred while the procession was assembled.

25 There had been orders issued 'to all men with baggage or carriage to remain at the appointed place out of the way'. SPD, *Edward VI, 1547–53*, p.5.

26 Eight banners used in the funeral were still hanging in St George's Chapel in the seventeenth century. They are drawn in a collection of epitaphs and arms in BL Lansdowne MS 874, fol.49. The Chapel inventory, compiled later in 1547, lists 'a hearse cloth of king Harry the viiith of cloth of tissue with black satin of Bruges'. See Maurice F. Bond: *Inventories of St George's Chapel, Windsor Castle, 1384–1667*, Windsor, 1947, p.185.

27 NA LC 2/2, fol.45. Missing from the procession were the senior judges. They were originally included but 'the chief justices and master of the rolls' were deleted from the list of attendees because they were 'spared for the law in the term time'. See SPD, *Edward VI, 1547–53*, p.5.

28 Related by Burnet, Vol. I, pt.ii, p.298. The prophecy was made by Friar (later Cardinal) Peto, who escaped with only a rebuke from the Privy Council for his insolence. The incident was apparently seen as a divine judgement upon Henry for having ousted the Brigantines from their religious sanctuary at Syon. Burnet adds: 'Having met with this observation in a MS written nearer that time, I would not envy the world the pleasure of it.' Aungier (p.92) repeats the legend.

29 Strickland, Vol. III, p.255.

30 Pote, p.361.

31 Strype, 'Ecclesiastic Memorials', Vol. II, pt.ii, pp.304–5.

32 Ibid., p.308.

33 NA SP 10/1/17.

34 Muller, *Stephen Gardiner and the Tudor Reaction*, p.143.

35 'Surround me with your protection.'

36 'Dust to dust, ashes to ashes ...'

37 Strype, 'Ecclesiastic Memorials, Vol. II, pt.ii, p.310.

38 Henry's funeral was the first for which heralds were paid an attendance fee. It was £40 for the whole office in 1547 and it remains the same today. See Wagner, p.113.

39 Starkey, 'Inventory', pp.197–8.

Epilogue

1 Paget, 'Letters', p.19.

2 Burnet, Vol. I, p.291.

3 The French ambassador Odet de Selve told Francis I of the heralds' proclamation of Edward as king and wrongly 'that yesterday Norfolk was secretly beheaded in the Tower'.

4 Machyn (p.45) reported that the duke 'rode up and down' Westminster Hall as part of the ceremony of Mary's coronation dinner.

5 See Anthony Fletcher and Diarmaid MacCulloch, *Tudor Rebellions*, 4th edn, London, 1997, p.85.

6 Robinson, p.35. He was succeeded as Fourth Duke by his grandson.

7 His ornate tomb chest carries the last major display of overt religious imagery in sixteenth-century English monumental art. His funeral is recorded by Machyn on 2 October as having been marked by an extravagant dinner: 'For the furnishing ... were killed forty great oxen and a hundred sheep and sixty calves besides venison, swans, cranes, capons, rabbits, pigeons, pikes and other provisions, both flesh and fish. There was also great plenty of wine and of bread and beer ... both for rich and poor; all the country came thither.' (Machyn, p.70.)

8 A later account is in BL Add. MS 30,536, Vol. 1, fol.194b.

9 BL Harleian MS 5,087, no.35, dated 8 February 1547.

10 Wonderful to report!

11 The title was to be Earl of Leicester, but this was deleted in the list of dignitaries drawn up on 15 February 1547. NA SP 10/1/11.

12 APC, n.s., Vol. II, 1547–50, p.16.

13 APC, n.s., Vol. II, 1547–50, p.17. 'Painful' in this context means 'painstaking'.

14 APC, n.s., Vol. II, 1547–50, p.19.

15 APC, n.s., Vol. II, 1547–50, pp.14–22.

16 APC, n.s., Vol. II, 1547–50, p.20.

17 For a more sympathetic discussion of Wriothesley's actions, see Slavin, pp.268–85.

18 Gammon, p.151.

19 H. Miller, 'Henry VIII's Unwritten Will', in E. W. Ives (ed.), in *Wealth and Power in Tudor England*, London, 1978, p.87.

20 Paget probably meant the administration of justice without regard to rank or privilege.

21 Paget, 'Letters', pp.19–20.

22 NA E 23/4/1.

23 NA SP 10/1, fol.41.

24 Seymour is indicating how much he would value even a short letter from Katherine.

25 Seymour's convoluted words of love indicate that the imagery of the picture would

increase his eager anticipation of his marriage with the dowager queen.

26 Bodleian Library, Ashmolean MS 1729, fol.4.

27 Dent-Brocklehurst Papers, D2579, Gloucester Record Office.

28 Nicholas Throckmorton, cupbearer in Katherine's household.

29 Katherine had clearly instructed Seymour to burn all letters to avoid the risk of discovery of their affair.

30 NA SP 46/1, fol.14.

31 Bodleian Library, Rawlinson MS D.1070.4.

32 BL Lansdowne MS 1,236, fol.26.

33 Strickland, Vol. III, p.264.

34 LP Spanish, Edward VI, Vol. IX, p.123.

35 Somerset had let this property, belonging to Katherine, to a Mr Long.

36 Cecil Papers 133/2.

37 'Spanish Chronicle', p.160.

38 Strickland, Vol. III, p.260.

39 Tytler, Vol. I, p.70.

40 Cecil Papers 150/85. NA SP 10/6/21.

41 Cecil Papers 150/74.

42 Cecil Papers 133/3.

43 NA SP 10/4/14.

44 G. B. Harrison, *Letters of Queen Elizabeth I*, New York, 1968, pp.8–9, and Strickland, Vol. III, p.275.

45 Thomas Hearne (ed.), *Sylloge Epistolarum*, Oxford, 1716, p.151.

46 NA SP 10/5/2.

47 Tytler, Vol. I, p.140.

48 Cited by James, 'Kateryn Parr', p.333.

49 NA SP 10/6/9.

50 Damaged by Parliamentary forces in 1649.

51 An anthropoid lead coffin.

52 Nash, p.2.

53 It was carved by the sculptor John Birnie Philip (1824–74) and was exhibited at the Royal Academy in London in 1859. The work was paid for by J. C. Dent, then owner of the castle.

54 Her obsequies were the first royal funeral solemnized according to Protestant rites.

55 Tytler, Vol. I, p.133.

56 SPD, *Edward VI, 1547–53*, p.88.

57 SPD, *Edward VI, 1547–53*, Vol. IX, p.332.

58 NA SP 10/6/10.

59 SPD, *Edward VI, 1547–53*, Vol. IX, p.340.

60 Cecil Papers 133/4/2.

61 Loach, *Edward VI*, p.163.

62 'Montague Papers', p.4.

63 NA SP 11/1, fols.16–17v.

64 Morant, Vol. II, pp.450–4.

65 One of the first suits to be presented to Mary after she became queen was from one of her yeomen of the guard, Philip Gerrard, who sought a review of rents. He had made a similar plea in Edward's reign, but Gates, his captain, 'nothing at all favouring the effects thereof, would not deliver it'. See BL Royal MS 17B xl.

66 The inventory of his possessions is in NA E 154/2/45.

67 His will is NA PCC PROB 11/32 F 37 Populwell, dated 7 September 1549.

68 Burnet, Vol. I, pt.i, p.339.

69 Clad in armour.

70 Described by Machyn, pp.97 and 100–1.

71 For an interesting discussion of the legacy of Cranmer, see MacCulloch.

72 Feuilleist, pp.xii and 73–7.

73 Southworth, p.78.

Sequel: 'Tombs of Brass are Spent'

1 NA E 23/4/1.

2 LP, Vol. III, pt.i, p.2. Torrigiano was still living in the precincts of St Peter's Westminster, Westminster Abbey. He completed Henry VII's tomb sometime around 1515. Margaret Whinney (*Sculpture in Britain: 1530–1830*, Harmondsworth, 1964, p.4) calls it '*the* major Renaissance work created in England'. (An earlier design, in 1506 by Guido Mazzoni, for Henry VII's tomb was for a gilt-bronze kneeling figure on a monument to be located at Windsor; see B. M. Meyer, 'The First Tomb of Henry VII of England', *Art Bulletin*, 58 (1976), pp.358–67.) Torrigiano also designed and erected a monument with a gothic-style effigy to Margaret Beaufort, Henry VIII's grandmother, in the south aisle of the Henry VII Chapel at Westminster. See Philip Lindley, 'Sculptural Functions and Forms in Henry VII's Chapel', in Tatton-Brown and Mortimer, p.268.

3 Alfred Higgins, 'On the Work of Florentine Sculptors in England in the Early Part of the Sixteenth Century with Special Reference to the Tombs of Cardinal Wolsey and King Henry VIII', *Archaeological Journal*, 51 (1894), p.143.

4 *Archaeologia*, 16 (1812), pp.84–8.

5 *Annual Report of Friends of St George's*, 5, 1 (1970), p.35.

6 Colvin *et al*, Vol. IV, p.24.

7 £7,896,763 in 2004 cash terms.

8 Margaret Mitchell, *Journal of the Warburg and Courtauld Institute*, 34 (1971), pp.189–90.

9 London, 1623, pp.796–7. See also *Walpole Society*, 18 (1930), pp.40–1.

10 John Flaxman, *Lectures on Sculpture ... as Delivered before the President and Members of the Royal Academy*, 2nd edn, London, 1838, p.47.

11 Born 1474, died *c*.1554 in Florence. He had been working on the base of the monument to the Dukes of Orléans in France in 1502.

12 Known thereafter as 'Wolsey's Tombhouse'. Now the Albert Memorial Chapel.

13 He died in Leicester and was buried in the Augustinian abbey there 'before day' on 30 November 1530. At the burial, 'such a tempest with such a stench arose that all the torches went out and so he was thrown into the tomb and there laid'. See Foxe, 'Acts', Vol. IV, p.616.

14 Maiano was also responsible for ten terracotta medallions fitted to the exterior walls of Hampton Court. See Colvin *et al*, Vol. IV, pt.ii, p.25.

15 Hope, Vol. II, pp.483–6.

16 Hope, Vol. II, p.483.

17 See Higgins. A conjectural drawing of this canopy forms plate VII, facing p.172. Higgins' drawing of the whole tomb is to be found facing p.190.

18 Higgins, p.164. Privy Purse accounts for the tomb for 1531 are reprinted in full on pp.207–19 and for 1534–5 on pp.214–15.

19 Higgins, p.164.

20 NA E 336/27. Portinari later went abroad. On 7 September 1552, the Duke of Northumberland wrote to Sir William Cecil of the high estimation in which Portinari was held at the French court. The Italian, however, was ready to return to England as he 'is at the king's command' and spoke of 'the devotion he bears ... this realm'. NA SP 10/15/3, and SPD, *Edward VI 1547–53*, p.257.

21 NA E 23/4/1.

22 'Henry the Eighth, King of England and France, Lord of Ireland. Defender of the Faith.'

23 NA E 315/256, fol.90. Allowance for expenses 'about the tomb', 1547. See also Biddle, p.115.

24 He was working in England as early as 1537, as there are records of payments of an annual salary of £10 a year to him and for the provision of a livery gown.

25 This was located in the area of today's Dean's Yard.

26 APC, n. s., Vol. III, p.347.

27 He was called 'Fill Sack' by his contemporaries for his propensity for accumulating wealth.

28 APC, n.s., Vol. III, p.380. On p.347 are details of a warrant, dated 9 July 1551, to Sir Raffe Sadler for eight yards of damask to make a gown for Modena, four yards of velvet for a coat and three yards of satin to make him a doublet.

29 *Archaeologia*, 39 (1863), p.37.

30 A deputation of Edward's councillors, led by Richard Rich, met Princess Mary at the end of August 1551 and told her that the young king wished to 'forbid her chaplains to say mass or any other unlawful service'. A defiant Mary replied that 'she would rather die on the block than use any services other than those in use at her father's death' and that she would obey Edward's instructions on religion 'only when he was old enough to judge'. See NA SP 10/13/35.

31 Thomas Fuller, *Church History of Britain*, London, 1655, p.254.

32 Cardinal Reginald Pole (1500–58). Nominated papal legate to England in 1537, but while he was *en route*, Henry urged Francis I to arrest him as a rebel. Pole returned safely to Rome and accepted a mission from Pope Paul III to form an alliance of Christian princes against Henry. Pole's mother and eldest brother were executed in England on charges of treason. On Mary's accession, he was consecrated Archbishop of Canterbury in March 1556.

33 Cited by Scarisbrook, p.497, quoting the Jesuit Robert Parsons, *Certamen Ecclesiae Anglicanae*, Joseph Simons (ed.), Assen, 1965, p.273.

34 BL Lansdowne MS 6, no.31, 12 September 1563. See also Colvin *et al*, Vol. IV, p.321. Higgins has the letter wrongly addressed to Burghley.

35 BL Lansdowne MS 116, no.13.

36 406.4 kg.

37 1,016 kg.

38 *Alias* Verstegen, fl. 1565–1620.

39 NA E 351/3,203.

40 NA SP 12/43, fol.73.

41 NA E 351/3,209.

42 A drawing, probably by Cure, for Edward's tomb survives in the Bodleian Library in Gough Maps 45, 17,554, no.63. It was never built.

43 NA E 351/3,221. See also Colvin *et al*, Vol. IV, p.321.

44 Paul Hentzner, *Itinerarium, etc.*, Breslau, 1617, p.148. Translated from the Latin.

45 It was, of course, a mere cenotaph as Henry's body lay alongside that of Jane Seymour in the vault in the centre of the choir of St George's Chapel.

46 St George's Chapter Acts VI B:2, fol.31b.

47 St George's Chapter Acts XI F:6. Darknall was appointed verger on 28 January 1618 and later signed a number of property transactions involving the Chapter as a witness.

48 *Journal* of the House of Commons, 7 April 1646.

49 William Sanderson, *Complete History of the Life and Reign of King Charles*, London, 1658, p.888.

50 Higgins, pp.177–80. The original casting, from moulds, of the candlesticks was not well done: several patches have been inserted to cover defects. See fn. p.180.

51 There is a cast in the Victoria and Albert Museum.

52 St George's Chapter Acts VI B:3, p.11, and Bond, p.111.

53 Elias Ashmole, *The Institution, Laws and Ceremonies of the Most Noble Order of the Garter*, London, 1672.

54 Pote, p.62.

55 Queen Victoria restored the chapel in memory of the Prince Consort. The cost of the sarcophagus and its transportation was not to exceed £1,000.

56 C. V. Wedgwood, *The Trial of Charles I*, London, 1964, p.204.

57 Anthony Wood, *Athenae Oxonienses*, Vol. II, London, 1721, p.703.

58 Ibid. The last statement about the contents of the great coffin is a reference to the story that Henry VIII's body had been removed and destroyed in Mary I's reign.

59 On p.362 of the hand-foliated and heavily annotated copy of Pote's *History and Antiquities of Windsor Castle*, given to the Chapter by Dr Joseph Goodall, Provost of Eton, in 1814. It was previously owned by a G. Wingfield; the MS notes are by a Capt. Wingfield. (Pote, a Windsor bookseller, is traditionally believed to have written the *History*; this copy is signed by the true author, John Stapletoft.) The cost of the re-laying of the choir was met by William Childe, organist.

60 Pote, p.362.

61 They were seeking to prove that Charles I was buried there.

62 Halford, p.10. The wall at the west end of the vault had been partly pulled down and repaired again 'not by regular masonry but by fragments of stones and bricks, put rudely and hastily together without cement'.

63 Edward Hyde, Earl of Clarendon, *History of the Rebellion and Civil Wars in England*, Oxford, 1807, Vol. III, pt.i, p.393.

64 Bound at the back of the copy of Halford in the Chapter Archives of St George's Chapel, Windsor.

65 *Annual Reports of the Friends of St George's 1933–1950*, p.10.

66 St George's Chapter Acts VI B:9, p.109.

Bibliography

PRIMARY SOURCES

Manuscript Sources

BRITISH LIBRARY

Add. MS 4,724 – *Orationes* or Declamations in Latin and Greek written by Edward VI, 1548–52.

Add. MS 6,059 – Astronomical calendar in Latin, owned by Sir John Cheke and later by William Cecil, First Baron Burghley.

Add. MS 27,402, fol.47 – 'A list of such were executed in Henry VIII's time.'

Add. MS 30,536, Vol. 1, fol.194b – Account of obsequies observed in Paris after Henry VIII's death (in French in an eighteenth-century hand).

Add. MS 32,655, fols.98 and 100 – Letter from Francis Talbot, Lord Shrewsbury, and others to Queen Katherine Parr and the Council relating to Scottish Border issues, 14 and 18 July 1544; fol.168 – Letter from Queen Katherine Parr to the Wardens of the [Scottish] East and West Marches, 2 September 1544.

Add. MS 45,368 – Inventory of jewels and plate belonging to Henry VIII.

Add. MS 45,716 A – *Book of New Ordering of the King's Most Honourable Household*, fols. 12–15 – Details of the ceremonial for the christening of Prince Edward, 15 October 1537.

Add. MS 46,348, fols.168b–171b – Inventory of Queen Katherine Parr's jewels; fol.206 – Details of pet dog's collar.

Cotton MS Galba B x, fol.8 – Letter from August de Augustini to the Duke of Norfolk reporting several audiences with Charles V, Ghent, 3 June 1531.

Cotton MS Nero C x, fol.6 – Rough draft of a letter from Queen Katherine Parr to Prince Edward, January 1546.

Cotton MS Nero C x 4, fol.3 – Prince Edward to Henry VIII, from Hatfield, 27 September 1546, and to Katherine Parr from Hertford, 10 January 1547.

Cotton MS Otho C x – Matters relating to the annulment of Henry's marriage to Queen Anne of Cleves.

Cotton MS Titus B i, fol.94 – Letter from Thomas, Duke of Norfolk, to the Privy Council from the Tower of London.

Cotton MS Titus B i, fol.388 – Letter from the Duke of Norfolk's wife to Thomas Cromwell, complaining of her 'hard usage' by him.

Cotton MS Titus B ii 25, fol.51 – Letter, 31 January 1547, from Henry Ratcliff, Earl of Sussex, to his wife, announcing the death of Henry VIII.

Cotton MS Vespasian F iii, fol.18 – Letter from Prince Edward to Queen Katherine Parr, from Hunsdon, 24 May 1546.

Cotton MS Vitellius C i, fol.65B – Instructions from Henry VIII to Sir William Sidney and Sir John Cornwallis for the arrangements of Prince Edward's household.

Egerton MS 985, fol.33 – Ceremonial for the christening of Prince Edward.

Harleian MS 297, fol.256 – Confession of the Duke of Norfolk in the Tower of London, 12 January 1547.

Harleian MS 5,087, no.17 – Letter from Prince Edward to Queen Katherine Parr, from The More, Rickmansworth, Hertfordshire, 12 August 1546.

Harleian MS 5,087, no.31 – Letter from Prince Edward to Henry VIII from Hertford, 10 January 1547, thanking him for his New Year's gift.

Harleian MS 5,087, no.35 – Letter from Edward, now king, to Dowager Queen Katherine Parr, written from the Tower of London, 8 February 1547.

Lansdowne MS 6, no.31 – Letter from the Lord Treasurer to Sir William Cecil, dated 12 September 1563, regarding Henry VIII's tomb.

Lansdowne MS 116, no.13 – Certificate to the Lord Treasurer on the state of the tombs of Henry VII at Westminster and Henry VIII at Windsor.

Lansdowne MS 874, fol.49 – Collection of epitaphs and arms in various churches and chapels, showing eight banners used in Henry's funeral, still hanging in St George's Chapel, Windsor.

Lansdowne MS 1,236, fol.9 – Letter from Queen Katherine (Parr) to Henry VIII, Greenwich, 1544, 'full of duty and respect'; fol.26 – Letter from the Lady Mary (afterwards Mary I) to Lord Admiral (Seymour) declining to become involved in his suit for marriage to the dowager queen, dated 3 June 1547.

Royal MS 2A xvi – Psalter in Latin with three canticles from St Luke's Gospel, *c*.1540.

Royal MS 2D iii – *Ecclesiastes* and *Song of Solomon* translated into Latin elegiac verses by Martinus Briannaeus.

Royal MS 7B xi–xii – Archbishop Cranmer's so-called *Commonplace Book*.

Royal MS 7C xvi, fol.92 – 'The names of such officers in ordinary of the chamber of the late king's majesty as are now discharged,' *c*.1547.

Royal MS 7C xvi, fol.94 – 'Such gentlemen, yeomen, grooms and others that remain unplaced and served the king's majesty being prince,' *c*.1547.

Royal MS 7C xvi, fol.96 – 'The names of such of the king's majesty's servants as are newly placed in ordinary of the chamber,' *c*.1547.

Royal MS 7D ix – *Prayers and Meditations* composed by Queen Katherine Parr, published after 1548.

Royal MS 7D x – Queen Katherine Parr's *Prayers and Meditations* translated into French, Latin and Italian by Princess Elizabeth, with a dedicatory letter to Henry VIII, dated 20 December 1545.

Royal MS 7D xx – Lectures in Latin on the first three chapters of the *Book of Genesis* – a New Year's gift to Edward VI from Glaterus Doloenus.

Royal MS 17B xl – Exhortation to Queen Mary for reformation of rents from Philip Gerrard, yeoman of the guard.

Sloane MS 1,047 – Book of recipes for medicines and balms.

Stowe MS 142, fol.14 – Henry VIII's admonishment of Sir Thomas Arundell and the other Justices of the Peace in Cornwall for remissness and threatening to 'correct the lewdness of the offenders in this behalf'.

Stowe MS 396, fol.8 – Report of the trial of Henry Howard, Earl of Surrey, 1546.

Stowe MS 492 – Register of the Acts of the Privy Council, 31 January 1547 to 4 October 1549. [Copy of the original. Bought *c*.1748 from a cheesemonger's shop, where it was used for waste paper.]

NATIONAL ARCHIVES (AT THE FORMER PUBLIC RECORD OFFICE)

'NA' prefix National Archives.

'E' series records of the exchequer and related bodies, including the Office of First Fruits and the Court of Augmentations.

'KB' series records of the Court of King's Bench.

'LC' series records of the Lord Chamberlain and officers of the Royal Household.

'LR' series records created by the Court of Augmentations/Office of Auditors, Land Revenue.

'PCC/PROB' series Prerogative Court of Canterbury, responsible for probate and granting administrations from 1383 onwards.

'PRO' series notes and transcripts created within the Public Record Office.

'SP' series State Papers.

NOTE: Some documents were created and are catalogued by regnal year rather than calendar year.

E 23/4/1 – Henry VIII's will, dated 30 December 1546.

E 30/1,472/6 – Licence by Thomas Cranmer, Archbishop of Canterbury, for the marriage between Henry VIII and Katherine Latymer, *née* Parr, issued at Lambeth, 29 July 1540.

E 101/60/22 – Account of Sir Walter Stonor, Lieutenant of the Tower of London, for expenses incurred in boarding the Earl of Surrey and Duke of Norfolk as prisoners.

E 101/424/5 – Expenses of the queen's household, 38 Henry VIII and 1 Edward VI.

E 101/424/8 – Allowances for a child named Ralfe Lyons, who was given to Henry VIII.

E 154/2/45 – Inventories of goods of attainted persons: Sir John Gates, Andrew Dudley, Francis Jobson and Thomas Palmer, knights, 1553.

E 314/22 – Vouchers of expenses for the household of Queen Katherine Parr, 37–38 Henry VIII.

E 315/160 – Household book of Sir Anthony Denny, Keeper of the Palace of Westminster, 34 Henry VII to 2 Edward VI. PRO 31/17/40 is a nineteenth-century transcription of fols.1–40 of this book.

E 315/256 – Book of payments ... made within the office of Sir John Williams, 1547.

E 315/340 – Book of receipts and payments from Comptroller to Queen Katherine Parr, including rewards and payments made by her command, 1547.

E 315/384/16 – Book of the receipts of the lands of the queen (Katherine Parr) and of Lord Seymour of Sudeley, Gloucestershire, Oxfordshire and Hereford, 2 Edward VI.

E 328/131/1 – Indenture of agreement between Henry VIII, Sir Anthony Denny and Sir William Herbert, granting custody and marriage of Margaret and Mary Audley, daughters and co-heiresses of Sir Thomas Audley, 7 January 1545.

E 336/27 – Court of First Fruits and Tenths, and Exchequer, Office of First Fruits and Tenths.

E 351/3,203 – Works and buildings payments, 1565.

E 351/3,209 – Works and buildings payments, 1573–4.

E 351/3,221 – Works and buildings payments 1586–7.

KB 8/14 – Special Commission of Oyer and Terminer with charges against Henry Howard, Earl of Surrey, 10 January 1538 (roll in Latin).

KB 8/22 – Special Oyer and Terminer roll and file, principal defendants and charges: Sir John Gate and others, levying war against Queen Mary and proclaiming Lady Jane Grey queen in Hertfordshire, Suffolk and Cambridgeshire.

LC 2/2 – Wardrobe accounts for the funeral of Henry VIII.

LR 2/115 – Inventory of the goods of the Duke of Norfolk at Kenninghall and Castle Rising, Norfolk, and of Henry, Earl of Surrey, at St Leonard's by Norwich, as at December 1546.

PCC PROB 11/32 F 37 Populwell – Will of Sir Anthony Denny, 7 September 1549.

PCC PROB 11/34 F 13 Bucke – Will of Thomas Wriothesley, Earl of Southampton, 1551.

PCC PROB 11/36 F 11 Tashe – Will of Dame Joan Denny, 1553.

PCC PROB 11/40 – Will of Stephen Gardiner, Bishop of Winchester.

PRO 31/17/40 – Nineteenth-century transcript of fols.1–40 of E 315/160.

SC 12/14/10 – Brief valor [list and valuation] of lands of Thomas Seymour, Lord Seymour of Sudeley, in Wiltshire, Gloucestershire and Berkshire.

SP 1/217 – Letters and state papers, April–May 1546.

SP 4 – Documents issued under Henry VIII's 'dry stamp', 1545–7, in one volume.

SP 10/1, fol.41 – Letter from Thomas Seymour, Lord Admiral, to Katherine Parr, 1547.

SP 10/1/1 – Letter from Hertford to Paget, 29 January 1547.

SP 10/1/9 – Planned order of service for the coronation of Edward VI.

SP 10/1/11 – 'List of promotions to dignities' dated 15 February 1547 but probably drawn up at the end of December 1546 and later amended by Secretary Paget.

SP 10/1/17 – Instructions for Henry VIII's funeral.

SP 10/3/7 – Account of gold, rings and precious stones removed from the king's secret jewel house at Westminster, 12 February 1547.

SP 10/4/14 – Letter from Thomas Seymour to his wife, the dowager queen, about travelling with her to her confinement at Sudeley Castle.

SP 10/5/2 – Letter from the Lord Protector to his brother, Thomas Seymour, Syon, Middlesex, 1 September 1548.

SP 10/6/9 – 'Deposition of Sir Richard Cotton', ?January 1549.

SP 10/6/10 – State Papers, January–April 1549. Testimony of John Fowler.

SP 10/6/21 – 'Deposition of Catherine "Cat" Ashley', 4 February 1549.

SP 10/13/35 – State Letters and Papers, 1551.

SP 10/15/3 – State Letters and Papers, September–December 1552.

SP 11/1, fols.16–17v – Questions posed by the Duke of Northumberland at his trial, 18 August 1553.

SP 12/43, fol.73 – Letter from the Marquis of Winchester to Sir William Cecil dated 20 July 1567 including new plans for Henry VIII's tomb for consideration.

SP 46/1, fol.14 – Thomas Lord Seymour, letter to the queen (Katherine Parr) on their love affair.

SP 46/2, fol.101 – Commission under seal of Court of Augmentations to require Lady Jane Denny, relict of Sir Anthony Denny, to account for stuff late in his charge at the Palace of Westminster.

BODLEIAN LIBRARY, OXFORD

Ashmolean MS 1729 – Letter from Katherine Parr to Thomas Seymour, 1547.

Gough Maps 45, 17,554, no.63 – A drawing, probably by Cornelius Cure, for Edward VI's tomb (never constructed).

Rawlinson MS D.1070.4 – Letter from Katherine Parr to Thomas Seymour, 1547.

GLOUCESTERSHIRE RECORD OFFICE

Dent-Brocklehurst Papers, D2579, 'Z' box.

ST GEORGE'S CHAPEL, WINDSOR, CHAPTER ARCHIVES AND LIBRARY

Chapter Acts VI B:2, fol.31b.

Chapter Acts VI B:3, p.11, 31 May 1661.

Chapter Acts VI B:9, p.109.

Chapter Acts XI F:6.

Chapter Acts XIV, Bundle for 1883.

HATFIELD HOUSE

Cecil Papers 1/22 – Deposition of Dr William Butts, one of Henry VIII's doctors, to the commission inquiring into the validity of Henry's marriage to Anne of Cleves.

Cecil Papers 1/23 – Deposition of the king to the commission inquiring into the validity of his marriage to Anne of Cleves.

Cecil Papers 133/2 and 133/3 – Two letters written by Katherine Parr to her husband, Lord Seymour of Sudeley.

Cecil Papers 133/4/2 – Letter by Princess Elizabeth denying that she was pregnant by Lord Seymour.

Cecil Papers 150/74 – Confession of J. Harrington concerning the Lord High Admiral.

Cecil Papers 150/85 – Deposition of Catherine Ashley, governess to Princess Elizabeth.

Printed Sources

APC – Acts of the Privy Council, new series:

>   Vol. I, 1542–7, John Roche Dasent (ed.), London, 1890.

>   Vol. II, 1547–50, John Roche Dasent (ed.), London, 1890.

>   Vol. III, 1550–2, John Roche Dasent (ed.), London, 1891.

Brigden, Susan (ed.), 'Letters of Richard Scudamore to Sir Philip Hoby', *Camden Miscellany*, Camden Society 4th series, 39 (1990), pp.67–148.

CPR – Calendar Patent Rolls:

Philip & Mary, 1554–5, Vol. II, London, 1936.

Philip & Mary, 1555–7, Vol. III, London, 1938.

Philip & Mary, 1557–8, Vol. IV, London 1939.

Ellis, Henry (ed.), 'Eminent Men' – *Original Letters of Eminent Literary Men of the Sixteenth, Seventeenth and Eighteenth Centuries*, London, 1843.

—— 'History' – *Original Letters Illustrative of English History*, 2nd series, 3 vols., London, 1825–7.

Feuilleist, Albert, *Documents Relating to the Revels at Court in the time of Edward VI and Queen Mary*, Louvain, 1914, reprinted 1963.

Foxe, John, 'Acts' – *Acts and Monuments*, J. Pratt (ed.), 8 vols., London, 1874.

—— 'Narratives' – *Narratives of the Days of the Reformation*, John Gough Nichols (ed.), Camden Society, Westminster, 1859.

Gardiner, Bishop Stephen, *A Detection of the Devil's Sophistry, Wherewith he Robbeth the Unlearned People of the True Belief in the Most Blessed Sacrament of the Altar*, London, 1546.

Goldsmid, E. and G. Goldsmid (eds.), *A Collection of Eighteen Rare & Curious Historical Tracts & Pamphlets*, Edinburgh, 1886.

Hall, Edward, *Chronicle*, London, 1809.

Haynes, Samuel (ed.), *A Collection of State Papers ... left by William Cecil, Lord Burghley*, London, 1740.

Jordan, W. K., *Chronicle and Political Papers of Edward VI*, London, 1966.

Kaulek, J. (ed.), *Correspondance Politique de MM de Castillon et de Marillac*, Paris, 1885.

Legg, J. Wickham, *Missale ad usum ecclesie Westmonasteriensis*, 3 vols., London, 1891–7.

'Lisle Letters' – *The Lisle Letters*, Muriel St Clare Byrne (ed.), 6 vols., Chicago and London, 1981.

LP – *Letters and Papers, Foreign and Domestic, of the Reign of Henry VIII*, J. S. Brewer, James Gairdner and R. H. Brodie (eds.), 21 vols., London, 1862–1910. *Addenda*, 2 vols., London, 1932.

LP Spanish – Letters, Dispatches and State Papers, Spanish:

    Henry VIII, Vol. VI, pt.i, 1538–42, Pascualde Gaynagos (ed.), London, 1890; pt.ii, Pascualde Gaynagos (ed.), London, 1895.

    Henry VIII, Vol. VIII, 1545–6, Martin A. S. Hume (ed.), London, 1904.

    Edward VI, Vol. IX, Martin A. S. Hume and Royall Taylor (eds.), London, 1912.

Machyn, Henry, *The Diary of Henry Machyn, Citizen and Merchant Taylor of London, 1550–1563*, John Gough Nichols (ed.), Camden Society, London, 1848.

'Montague Papers' – *Historic Manuscripts Commission Report on the MSS of Lord Montague of Beaulieu*, London, 1900.

Muller, James (ed.), 'Letters' – *Letters of Stephen Gardiner*, Cambridge, 1931.

Nichols, John Gough (ed.), 'Literary Remains' – *Literary Remains of King Edward the Sixth*, Roxburghe Club, Vol. I, no.75, London, 1857.

—— 'Narratives' – *Narratives of the Days of the Reformation*, Camden Society, London, 1859.

'Original Letters' – *Original Letters Relative to the English Reformation*, H. Robinson (ed.), 3 vols., Cambridge, 1846–7.

Paget, William Lord – 'Letters' – *Letters of William Lord Paget of Beaudesert, 1547–63*, Barrett L. Beer and Sybil Jack (eds.), Camden Society, 4th series, XIII (1974).

Ponet, John, *A Short Treatise of Political Power and of the True Obedience which Subjects owe to Kings and other Civil Governors*, 1556. Reprinted in facsimile by Scholar Press, Menston, 1970, and Theatrum Orbis Terrarum, Amsterdam, 1972.

'Salisbury Manuscripts' – *Historic Manuscripts Commission Catalogue of the MSS of the Marquis of Salisbury ... at Hatfield House*, London, 1883.

SP – *State Papers*, Vol. I, London, 1830; Vol. VIII, London, 1849.

'Spanish Chronicle' – *Chronicle of King Henry VIII of England ... Written in Spanish by an unknown hand*, Martin A. Hume (ed.), London, 1889.

SPD – State Papers Domestic:

>*Calendar State Papers Domestic, Edward VI, 1547–53*, C. S. Knightley (ed.), London, 1992.

>*Calendar State Papers Domestic, Edward VI, Mary & Elizabeth, 1547–80*, Robert Lemon (ed.), London, 1856.

>*Calendar State Papers Domestic, Mary, 1553–58*, C. S. Knightley (ed.), London, 1998.

SP Foreign – *Calendar State Papers Foreign, Edward VI*, William Turnbill (ed.), London, 1861.

SP Venice – *Calendar State Papers: MS Relating to English Affairs in Archives and Collections of Venice*, Vol. V, 1534–54, Rawden Brown (ed.), London, 1873.

Starkey, David (ed.), 'Inventory' – *The Inventory of King Henry VIII: The*

Transcript, London, 1998. (From Society of Antiquaries MS 129 and BL Harleian MS 1,419.)

Stow, John, *The Annals of England collected out of the most Authentic Authors, Records and other Monuments of Antiquity*, London, 1605.

Strype, John, 'Ecclesiastic Memorials' – *Ecclesiastic Memorials Relating Chiefly to Religion ...*, 6 vols., Oxford, 1832.

Tanner, J. R., *Tudor Constitutional Documents 1485–1603*, Cambridge, 1951.

Tytler, Patrick, *England Under the Reigns of Edward VI and Mary*, 2 vols., London, 1839.

Williams, C. H. (ed.), *English Historical Documents 1485–1558*, London, 1967.

Wriothesley, Charles (Windsor Herald), *Chronicle of England During the Reign of the Tudors, 1485–1559*, Vol. I, William Douglas Hamilton (ed.), Camden Society, London, 1875.

SECONDARY SOURCES

Calculations of modern monetary values were derived from McCusker, John, 'Comparing the Purchasing Power of Money in Great Britain ...', Economic History Services, 2001, www.eh.net/hmit/ppowerbp.

Anglo, S., *Spectacle, Pageantry and Early Tudor Policy*, Oxford, 1969.

Auerbach, Erna, *Tudor Artists: A Study of Painters in the Royal Service ... from the Accession of Henry VIII to the Death of Elizabeth I*, London, 1954.

Aungier, George, *History and Antiquities of Syon Monastery*, London, 1848.

Bayles, Howard, 'Notes on Accounts paid to the Royal Apothecaries in 1546 and 1547', *Chemist and Druggist*, 114 (27 June 1931), pp.794–7.

Biddle, M., 'Nicholas of Modena', *British Archaeological Association Journal*, 3rd series, 29 (1966).

Blair, Claude and Stuart Phyrr, 'The Wilton "Montmorency" Armor: An Italian Armor for Henry VIII', *Metropolitan Museum of New York Journal*, 38 (2003), pp.95–143.

Bezzard, Judith and Frances Palmer, 'King Henry VIII: Performer Connoisseur and Composer of Music', *Antiquaries Journal*, 80 (2000), pp.249–72.

Bloom, James and Robert James, *Medical Practitioners in the Diocese of London, Licensed Under the Act of 3 Henry VIII, An Annotated List, 1529–1725*, Cambridge, 1935.

Bond, Shelagh M. (ed.), *Monuments of St George's Chapel, Windsor Castle*, Windsor, 1958.

Brenan, Gerald and Edward Statham, *The House of Howard*, 2 vols., London, 1907.

Brewer, Clifford, *The Death of Kings*, London, 2000.

Brinch, Ove, 'The Medical Problems of Henry VIII', *Centaurus*, 5 (1958).

Burnet, Gilbert, *History of the Reformation of the Church of England*, 2 vols., London, 1841.

Byrne, Muriel St Clare, *The Letters of King Henry VIII: A Selection*, London, 1968.

Chamberlin, Frederick, *The Private Character of Henry the Eighth*, London, 1932.

Colvin, H. M. *et al*, *History of the King's Works 1485–1660*, Vols. III–IV, London, 1975–82.

Copeman, W. S. C., *Doctors and Disease in Tudor Times*, London, 1960.

Cunich, Dr Peter, *Administration and Alienation of ex-Monastic Lands by the Crown, 1536–47*, unpublished Ph.D. thesis, Cambridge University, 1990, pp.38–50.

— 'Revolution and Crisis in English State Finance 1534–47' in W. M. Ormrod, M. M. Bonney and R. J. Bonney (eds.), *Crises, Revolutions and Self-Sustained Growth: Essays in European Fiscal History 1130–1830*, Stamford, UK, 1999, pp.118–39. For tables of revenue and expenditure from the European State Finance Database, see also the website www.le.ac.uk/ni/bon/ESFDB.

Dale, Philip Marshal, *Medical Biographies*, Norman, Oklahoma, 1987.

Doran, John, *History of Court Fools*, London, 1858.

Dugdale, Sir William, *History of St Paul's Cathedral, London*, 2nd edn, London, 1716.

Emmison, Fred, *Tudor Secretary: Sir William Petre at Court and at Home*, London, 1961.

Faulkner, T., *History & Topography of Fulham*, London, 1828.

Fletcher, Benton, *Royal Homes Near London*, London, 1930.

Flugel, J. C., *Men and their Motives: Psycho-analytical Studies*, London, 1934.

Fraser, Antonia, *Six Wives of Henry VIII*, New York, 1992.

Furdell, Elizabeth Lane, *The Royal Doctors 1485–1714: Medical Personnel at the Tudor and Stuart Courts*, Rochester, New York, 2001.

Gammon, S. R., *Statesman and Schemer: William, First Lord Paget, Tudor Minister*, Newton Abbot, 1973.

Granger, Revd James, *Biographical History of England*, 3rd edn, London, 1779.

Halford, Sir Henry, *An Account of What Happened on Opening the Coffin of King Charles the First in the Vault of King Henry the Eighth in St George's Chapel, Windsor*, London, 1813.

Hammond, E. A., 'Dr Augustine, Physician to Cardinal Wolsey and King Henry VIII', *Medical History*, 29 (1975), pp.215–49.

Herbert, Lord Edward of Cherbury, *Life and Reign of King Henry VIII*, London, 1649.

Higgins, Alfred, 'On the Work of Florentine Sculptors in England in the Early Part of the Sixteenth Century, with Special Reference to the Tombs of Cardinal Wolsey and King Henry VIII', *Archaeological Journal*, 51 (1894).

Hope, Sir William St John, *Windsor Castle: An Architectural History*, 3 vols., London, 1913.

Houlbrooke, R. A., 'Henry VIII's Wills: A Comment', *Historical Journal*, 37, 4 (1994), pp.891–9.

Ives, E. W., 'Henry VIII's Will: A Forensic Conundrum', *Historical Journal*, 35, 4 (1992), pp.779–804.

— 'Henry VIII's Will: The Protectorate Provisions of 1546–7', *Historical Journal*, 37, 4 (1994), pp.901–14.

James, Susan E., 'Devotional Writings' – 'The Devotional Writings of Queen Katherine Parr', *Transactions of the Cumberland and Westmorland Archaeological Society*, 82 (1982).

— 'Kateryn Parr' – *Kateryn Parr: The Making of a Queen*, Aldershot, 1999.

Knight, Charles, *Guide to Windsor*, Windsor, c.1811.

Kybett, Susan M., 'Henry VIII: A Malnourished King?', *History Today*, 39 (September 1979), pp.19–25.

Lamont-Brown, Raymond, *Royal Poxes and Potions: The Lives of Court Physicians, Surgeons and Apothecaries*, Stroud, 2001.

Lehmberg, Stanford, *Later Parliaments of Henry VIII, 1536–1547*, Cambridge, 1977.

Levine, Mortimer, 'The Last Will and Testament of Henry VIII: A Reappraisal Reappraised', *Historian*, 26, 4 (August 1964).

Litten, Julian, *The English Way of Death*, London, 1991.

Loach, Jennifer, 'Function of Ceremonial in the Reign of Henry VIII', *Past and Present*, 142 (February 1994), pp.56–66.

— *Edward VI*, Newhaven and London, 1999.

MacCulloch, Diarmaid, 'Cranmer's Ambiguous Legacy', *History Today* (June 1996).

MacLaurin, C., *Mere Mortals: Medico-Historical Essays*, 2nd series, London, 1925.

MacNalty, Sir Arthur S., *Henry VIII: A Difficult Patient*, London, 1952.

Martienssen, Anthony, *Queen Katherine Parr*, London, 1973.

Matthews, Leslie G., 'Royal Apothecaries of the Tudor Period', *Medical History*, 3 (1964).

Moore, Peter R., 'The Heraldic Charge Against the Earl of Surrey, 1546–7', *English Historical Review* (June 2001).

Morant, Philip, *History & Antiquities of the County of Essex*, 2 vols., Chelmsford, 1816.

Mori, Thomas and Ludovic Vivis, *Epistolae Phillipi Melanchthonis*, London, 1652.

Moriarty, Dr E. J., 'Henry VIII, Medically Speaking', *Historical Bulletin*, Calgary Associate Clinic, 20 (1955–6).

Muller, James, *Stephen Gardiner and the Tudor Reaction*, New York, 1926.

Munk, William, *Roll of the Royal College of Physicians of London ...*, 2nd edn, 2 vols., London, 1878.

Nash, The Revd Treadway, 'Observations on the Time of Death and Burial of Queen Katherine Parr', *Archaeologia*, 9 (1789).

Nott, G. F. (ed.), *Works of Henry Howard, Earl of Surrey and of Sir Thomas Wyatt the Elder*, 3 vols., London, 1815–16.

Park, Bert, *Ailing, Aging, Addicted: Studies of Compromised Leadership*, Lexington, Kentucky, 1993.

Pollard, A. F., *Henry VIII*, London and Paris, 1902.

Pote, Joseph, *History and Antiquities of Windsor Castle and the Royal College and Chapel of St George*, Eton, 1749.

Ridley, Jasper, *Henry VIII*, London, 1984.

— *The Tudor Age*, London, 1998.

Roberts, R. S., 'Personnel and Practice of Medicine in Tudor and Stuart England', *Medical History*, 8 (1964).

Robinson, John Martin, *The Dukes of Norfolk*, Chichester, 1995.

Sandford, Francis, *A Genealogical History of the Kings and Queens of England ... 1066–1707*, 2nd edn, London, 1707.

Scarisbrook, J. J., *Henry VIII*, New Haven and London, 1997.

Sil, Narasingha Prosad, 'Sir Anthony Denny: A Tudor Servant in Office', *Renaissance and Reformation*, n.s., 8, 3 (1984), pp.190–201.

Slavin, Arthur J., 'The Fall of Lord Chancellor Wriothesley: A Study in the Politics of Conspiracy', *Albion*, 7, 4 (1975), pp.265–86.

Smith, Lacey B., 'A Tudor Tragedy' – *A Tudor Tragedy: The Life and Times of Catherine Howard*, London, 1961.

— 'Last Will' – 'The Last Will and Testament of Henry VIII: A Question of Perspective', *Journal of British Studies*, 2 (1962).

Southworth, John, *Fools and Jesters at the English Court*, Stroud, 1998.

Starkey, David, *The Reign of Henry VIII: Personalities and Politics*, London, 2002.

— (ed.), *Henry VIII: A European Court in England*, London, 1991.

Strickland, Agnes, *Lives of the Queens of England from the Norman Conquest*, 8 vols., reprinted, London, 1972.

Strype, John, 'Cheke' – *Life of the Learned John Cheke, Knight*, Oxford, 1820.

Tatton-Brown, Tim and Richard Mortimer (eds.), *Westminster Abbey: The Lady Chapel of Henry VII*, Woodbridge, 2003.

Thurley, Simon, 'The Lost Palace of Whitehall', *History Today* (January 1998).

— 'Hampton Court' – *Hampton Court: A Social and Architectural History*, New Haven and London, 2003.

Tighe, Robert Richard and James Edward Davis, *Annals of Windsor*, 2 vols., London, 1858.

Wagner, Sir Anthony, *Heralds of England*, London, 1967.

Weir, Alison, *Henry VIII: King and Court*, London, 2002.

Whinney, Margaret, *Sculpture in Britain, 1530–1830*, Harmondsworth, 1964.

Williams, Neville, *Henry VIII and His Court*, London, 1973.

Wilson, Derek, *In the Lion's Court: Power, Ambition and Sudden Death in the Reign of Henry VIII*, London, 2001.

Chronology

1491: 28 June	Henry born at Greenwich Palace, third child of Henry VII and his wife, Elizabeth of York.
1502: 2 April	Henry's elder brother, Prince Arthur, dies at Ludlow, of tuberculosis, aged fifteen.
1509: 23 April	Henry proclaimed king, aged seventeen.
1509: June	Marriage (11 June) and coronation (24 June) of Henry and Catherine of Aragon, widow of Henry's brother, Arthur.
1511: 1 January	Birth of Prince Henry, son of Henry and Catherine of Aragon. The infant dies on 22 February.
1516: 18 February	Birth of Mary, daughter of Henry and Catherine of Aragon, at Greenwich.
1521: 11 October	Pope Leo X declares Henry 'Defender of the Faith'.
1527: May	Henry starts divorce proceedings against Catherine of Aragon.
1530: November	Arrest on charges of treason (4 November) and death (29 November) of Cardinal Wolsey, Lord Chancellor and Henry's Chief Minister.
1533: ?25 January	Henry secretly marries Anne Boleyn. She is crowned on 1 June.
1533: 7 September	Birth of Princess Elizabeth at Greenwich, daughter of Henry and Anne Boleyn.

1534: 23 March	First Act of Succession, annulling Henry's marriage with Catherine of Aragon and entailing the crown on any children by Anne Boleyn.
1534: ?November	Treasons Act, making it high treason to 'maliciously wish, will, or desire by words' death or bodily harm to the king, queen or their heirs apparent, deprive them of their dignity or call the king 'an heretic, schismatic, tyrant, infidel or usurper'.
1534: November	Act of Supremacy over the Church of England – '*Anglicana Ecclesia*'.
1535–40	Dissolution of monastic houses.
1536: 7 January	Death of Catherine of Aragon, aged fifty, from cancer of the heart, at Kimbolton Castle, near Huntingdon.
1536: 19 May	Execution of Anne Boleyn on Tower Green by an executioner brought from St Omer and paid £24 for his expert services with a two-handed sword.
1536: 30 May	Henry marries his third wife, Jane Seymour, in the Queen's Closet in the Palace of Westminster.
1536: June	Second Act of Succession, nullifying Henry's two earlier marriages and entailing the crown on male children of Jane Seymour, then on boys by any future wife and finally on female children by Jane Seymour.
1536: June	Act for Extinguishing the Authority of the Bishop of Rome, making it treason to refuse an oath renouncing the jurisdiction of the See of Rome and acknowledging Henry's supremacy over the Church in England.
1536: October	Pilgrimage of Grace – a popular rising against the Dissolution of the Monasteries in the northern counties.
1537: 12 October	Birth of Prince Edward, legitimate heir of Henry and Queen Jane Seymour.
1537: 24 October	Death of Queen Jane Seymour.

1539: 28 June	Royal Assent granted to An Act Abolishing Diversity in Opinions ('Statute of Six Articles') against Protestant practices and beliefs.
1540: 6 January	Henry marries Anne of Cleves at Greenwich Palace.
1540: 9 July	Marriage to Anne of Cleves annulled by Clerical Convocation.
1540: 13 July	Parliament confirms annulment. Anne pensioned off.
1540: 28 July	Marriage of Henry and Katherine Howard. Execution of Thomas Cromwell, by beheading, on Tower Hill.
1540: 30 July	Execution of three evangelical priests – William Jerome, Robert Barnes and Thomas Garret – at Smithfield.
1541: 10 December	Execution of Thomas Culpeper and Francis Dereham, lovers of Katherine Howard, at Tyburn, for treason.
1542: 13 February	Execution of Queen Katherine Howard, by beheading, on Tower Green.
1542: 24 November	English victory over the Scots at Solway Moss.
1543: 12 July	Henry marries Katherine Parr at Hampton Court.
1544: February	Third Act of Succession, restoring Princesses Mary and Elizabeth into the line of succession to the crown after Prince Edward and his male and female heirs, subject to conditions of Henry's will.
1544: 7 May	English forces sack Edinburgh.
1544: 7 July	Commission of Regency signed appointing Queen Katherine Parr regent in England during Henry's absence in France. The king signs a new will.
1544: 14 July	Henry goes to war in France.
1544: 18 September	Surrender of the castle and town of Boulogne.
1545: 3 January	Francis I of France threatens invasion of England.
1545: early February	Henry launches pre-emptive strike against the Scots.

1545: 27 February	English forces ambushed and defeated at Ancrum Moor, near Jedburgh.
1545: 20 July	Loss of *Mary Rose* in naval action off Southsea, Hampshire.
1545: 21 July	French troops land on Isle of Wight but are driven off in a matter of days.
1545: 22 August	Death of Henry's long-time friend Charles Brandon, Duke of Suffolk, at Guildford, Surrey.
1545: September	Introduction of 'dry stamp' facsimile signature to approve state documents.
?1545: November	Plot hatched and foiled against Archbishop Cranmer.
1545: November	Economic crisis because of war costs.
1545: 24 December	Henry's last speech to Parliament.
1546: February	Whispering campaign of rumours begun against Queen Katherine Parr.
1546: 7 June	Anglo-French peace treaty signed at Campe.
1546: ?4 July	Charges against the queen drawn up.
1546: ?14 July	Lord Chancellor Wriothesley tries unsuccessfully to arrest the queen.
1546: 16 July	Anne Askew burnt at Smithfield for heresy.
1546: October	Sir Thomas Heneage dismissed as Chief Gentleman of the Privy Chamber and Groom of the Stool.
1546: November	Bishop Gardiner excluded from court.
1546: 12 December	Earl of Surrey and Duke of Norfolk taken to the Tower of London.
1546: 26 December	Henry gives instructions for a revised will.
1546: 30 December	'Dry stamp' said to have been applied to royal will.
1547: 13 January	Earl of Surrey found guilty of treason.
1547: 17 January	Henry briefly meets the Spanish and French ambassadors – last time he is seen by outsiders.

1547: 19 January	Earl of Surrey executed.
1547: 27 January	Bills of Attainder against Surrey and Norfolk given Royal Assent.
	Henry receives last communion from his confessor.
1547: 28 January	The king dies at about two o'clock in the morning.
1547: 16 February	Henry buried alongside Jane Seymour in St George's Chapel, Windsor.
1547: 20 February	Coronation of King Edward VI.

Dramatis Personae

Henry Tudor (1491–1547). King of England, France and Lord of Ireland, Defender of the Faith and Supreme Head of the Church of England.

Jane Seymour (?1509–37). Henry's third queen, whom he married on 30 May 1536 at the Palace of Westminster. Died from puerperal fever and septicaemia following childbirth at Hampton Court, 24 October 1537.

Anne of Cleves (1515–57). Henry's fourth queen. Married at Greenwich Palace, 6 January 1540. Marriage annulled by Clerical Convocation on 9 July 1540 and by Parliament on 13 July 1540. Pensioned off. Died 16 July 1557 at Chelsea. Buried in Westminster Abbey.

Katherine Howard (1522–42). Henry's fifth queen. Married 28 July 1540 at Otelands, Surrey. Beheaded at Tower Green, 13 February 1542, for treason.

Katherine Parr (?1512–48). Henry's sixth and final queen. Married 12 July 1543 at Hampton Court. Following Henry's death in January 1547, married Thomas Seymour, Lord High Admiral, probably in early June 1547. Died from puerperal fever following the birth of a daughter at Sudeley Castle, Gloucestershire, 5 September 1548.

Prince Edward, later King Edward VI, (1537–53). Legitimate son and heir of Henry and Queen Jane Seymour. Proclaimed king 31 January 1547 at the Tower of London. Died of tuberculosis, Greenwich Palace, 6 July 1553.

Princess Mary, later Queen Mary I, (1516–58). Fourth and only surviving child (from at least six pregnancies) of Henry and his first wife, Catherine of Aragon. Proclaimed queen 19 July 1553. Reintroduced Catholicism to England. Married Philip, son of Charles V of Spain, at Winchester, 25 July 1554. Died, childless, from ovarian or stomach cancer, St James's Palace, London, 17 November 1558.

Princess Elizabeth, later Queen Elizabeth I, (1533–1603). Daughter of Henry and his second wife, Anne Boleyn. Succeeded Mary as queen November 1558. Secured Protestantism as state religion. Died, unmarried, from pneumonia and dental sepsis, Richmond, 24 March 1603.

Candidates for Henry's Brides

Christina (1522–90). Daughter of Christian II of Denmark, widow of the Duke of Milan. Married François, Duc de Bar, 1541. Regent of Lorraine, 1545.

Marie of Guise (1515–60). Second wife of James V of Scotland (1512–42) and mother of Mary, Queen of Scots. Regent of Scotland during her daughter's absence in France, 1554.

Marie of Vendôme (1515–38).

Foreign Rulers and their Ambassadors

Francis I of France (1494–1547). Crowned at Reims, 1515. Died at Château-Rambouillet, thirty miles south-west of Paris, and succeeded by son Henry II.

Francis I's Ambassadors to Henry's Court:

> **Louis de Perreau, Sieur de Castillon**. Ambassador, November 1537–December 1538.

> **Charles de Marillac** (*c.*1510–60). Ambassador, 1538–43. Later Bishop of Vannes (1550); Archbishop of Vienne (1557).

> **Odet de Selve** (*c.*1504–63). Ambassador, 6 July 1546–1550.

Charles V, King of Spain and Holy Roman Emperor (1500–58). Nephew of Catherine of Aragon, first wife of Henry VIII. Acceded to Spanish throne 1516. Abdicated in favour of son, Philip (husband of Mary I of England), 1556. Retreated to monastery of Yuste, dying two years later.

Charles V's Ambassadors to Henry's Court:

> **Eustace Chapuys** (d.1556). First embassy, 1529–38. Second embassy, 1540–5.

> **Francis van der Delft**. Imperial ambassador from 1545.

Henry's Privy Chamber

William Clerk, a clerk to the Privy Seal, 1542–8. Authorised to ink in the 'dry stamp' used to sign Henry's documents from September 1545.

Sir Anthony Denny (1501–49). Powerful confidant of the king. Assisted in suppression of Kett's Rebellion in Norfolk in 1549. Accumulated substantial incomes and lands through royal favour. Died ?10 September 1549 at his home in Cheshunt, Hertfordshire.

John Gates (?1504–53). Brother-in-law to Denny. Servant to Queen Katherine Parr, 1543–5. Appointed Vice-Chamberlain of the Household 8 April 1551. Appointed Chancellor of the Duchy of Lancaster 7 July 1552. Executed as supporter of Northumberland, 22 August 1553.

Sir Thomas Heneage (1480–1553). Chief Gentleman and Groom of the Stool. Knighted 1537. Abruptly dismissed and succeeded by Denny in 1546 after thirty years' service to the Crown.

Sir William Herbert (?1501–70). Appointed one of the Gentlemen of the Privy Chamber in 1546. Married Katherine Parr's sister Anne. Appointed President of Wales 1550. Created Earl of Pembroke 1551; joined Northumberland in proclaiming Lady Jane Grey queen in 1553 but quickly switched sides to support Mary. Appointed Governor of Calais 1556. Made Lord Steward under Elizabeth in 1568. Buried in St Paul's Cathedral.

The Royal Household and Henry's Government

Sir John Baker (d.1558). Lawyer; Attorney-General, 1535–40. Chancellor of the Exchequer, 1545–58.

Charles Brandon, First Duke of Suffolk (?1484–1545). Appointed Warden of the Scottish Marches in 1542. Commanded English army invading France in 1544. Lord Steward of the King's Household, 1541–4. Died at Guildford, Surrey, 22 August 1545. Buried in St George's Chapel, Windsor.

Sir Anthony Browne (d.1548). Master of the King's Horse, 1539–48.

Sir Thomas Cheyney (?1485–1558). Appointed Warden of the Cinque Ports 1538 and Treasurer of the Royal Household from 1539. Retained office under Edward, Mary and Elizabeth.

Thomas Cranmer (1489–1556). Archbishop of Canterbury. Supervised preparation and publication of first Prayer Book, 1549. Burnt at the stake in Oxford,

21 March 1556, for repudiating his admissions of the supremacy of the Pope and the truth of Catholic doctrine.

John Dudley (?1502–53). Created Viscount Lisle 1542. Served as Lord High Admiral, 1542–7 and 1548–9. Governor of Boulogne, 1544–6. Created Earl of Warwick on Edward's succession and appointed Lord High Chamberlain of England 1551–3. Duke of Northumberland, 1551. Married his son to Lady Jane Grey. Executed for treason – supporting Lady Jane as queen – 22 August 1553 at Tower Hill.

Sir William Fitzwilliam, Earl of Southampton (d.1542). Lord High Admiral, 1536–40. Later Lord Privy Seal. Died on active service whilst commanding the vanguard of Norfolk's expedition against Scotland, 1542.

Stephen Gardiner, Bishop of Winchester (c.1483–1555). Imprisoned from 1547 during most of Edward's reign for sedition and failure in religious conformity. Appointed Lord Chancellor by Mary I on her accession in 1553. Died at Palace of Westminster, 13 November 1555.

Sir William Paget, later Lord Paget of Beaudesert (1505–63). Protégé of Bishop Stephen Gardiner. Appointed Chief Secretary of State 1543 and later was one of Henry's chief advisers. Became an ally of radical reformers just before Henry's death. Imprisoned in 1551 and fined £6,000 for misconduct as Chancellor of the Duchy of Lancaster. Reinstated as a member of the Privy Council in 1553. Signed document transferring crown to Lady Jane Grey after Edward VI's death but was retained by Queen Mary as a Privy Councillor because of his administrative abilities and appointed Lord Privy Seal in 1556. He gave up all public office on Elizabeth's accession in 1558.

Sir William, Lord Parr (1513–71). Brother of Queen Katherine Parr. Made Earl of Essex, 1543. Appointed Marquis of Northampton, 1547. Condemned to death after Mary's accession but pardoned with forfeiture of titles and part of his estates. Reinstated marquis, 1559.

Sir William Paulet, Lord St John (?1485–1572). Treasurer of the Household, 1537–9. Lord Steward of the Household, 1545–50. Keeper of the Great Seal under Somerset, 1547. Created Earl of Wiltshire, 1550, and Marquis of Winchester, 1551. Proclaimed Mary queen on 19 July 1553 at Baynard's Castle, London. Appointed Lord Treasurer in 1549–50 and remained so until his death.

Sir William Petre (?1505–72). Created one of Henry's secretaries, 1544. Retained office under Edward, Mary and Elizabeth until 1566, when he retired from public life.

Sir Richard Rich (?1496–1567). Speaker, House of Commons, 1536. Appointed Chancellor of the Court of Augmentations, 1536–44, overseeing revenues from dissolved monastic houses. Created Baron Rich on Edward's accession. Lord Chancellor, 1548–51. After signing proclamation declaring Lady Jane Grey queen, he later switched sides to declare for Mary and was confirmed as a Privy Councillor. He was active in Essex in the prosecution of Protestants during the Counter-Reformation and was not confirmed as a Privy Councillor by Elizabeth on her accession.

John, Lord Russell (?1486–1555). Comptroller of the Household, 1537–9. Lord High Admiral, 1540–2. Lord Privy Seal, 1542, 1547 and 1553. Created Earl of Bedford, 1550.

Sir Edward Seymour (?1506–52). Earl of Hertford, 1537; made Duke of Somerset on Edward's accession. Lieutenant General in the North, 1545. Lieutenant and Captain General of Boulogne, 1546. Lieutenant General of the English army in France, 1546. Lord Treasurer, 1546–7. Lord Great Chamberlain of England, 1546–7. Declared Protector by Privy Council, 31 January 1547. Arrested on charges of conspiracy to murder Warwick, October 1551, and beheaded on Tower Hill on 22 January 1552.

Sir Thomas Seymour (?1508–49). Appointed Master of Ordnance for life, 1544. Admiral of fleet serving against the French, 1544–5. Lord High Admiral and created Baron Seymour of Sudeley, 1547. Secretly married Queen Katherine Parr, ?June 1547. Attainted for treason and beheaded on 20 March 1549 on Tower Hill.

Will Somers, fool or jester (d.1560). Retired after Henry's death but made guest appearances in masques and entertainments at Edward VI's court. Supported by Mary and Elizabeth during their reigns. Buried in St Leonard's Church, Shoreditch.

Sir Thomas Wriothesley (1505–50). Joint principal secretary to Henry VIII, 1540. Created Baron Wriothesley, 1544. Lord Chancellor, 1544–7. Created Earl of Southampton, 1547. Deprived of office in 1547, fined £4,000 for acting illegally in his use of the Great Seal and put under house arrest at his London home. Reinstated to Privy Council in 1548. Struck off list of Councillors, 1550.

Prince Edward's Household

Roger Ascham (1515–68). Tutor to Princess Elizabeth and teacher to Prince Edward. Wrote and published *Toxophilus or the School or Partitions of Archery*, 1545. Appointed Latin Secretary to Queen Mary in 1553. Tutor and secretary to

Queen Elizabeth. Given a Prebend of York, 1559. Wrote a practical treatise on education, *The Schoolmaster*, which, although unfinished, was published after his death, in 1570. Buried in St Sepulchre without Newgate, London.

John Cheke (1514–57). Regius professor of Greek at Cambridge University. Knighted by Edward in 1552 and appointed his secretary of state after he became king. Imprisoned in the Tower after Mary's accession and exiled to Switzerland and Italy.

Sir John Cornwallis (*c*.1496–1544). Steward. Died at Ashridge, Hertfordshire.

Richard Cox (1500–81). Former headmaster of Eton and first dean of Christ Church, Oxford. Imprisoned in the Marshalsea early in Mary's reign; escaped to Frankfurt in 1554. Became Bishop of Norwich in 1559 after Elizabeth's accession and shortly afterwards of Ely until 1580.

Mistress Jak. Prince Edward's wet nurse until October 1538.

Margaret, Lady Bryan. 'Lady Mistress' of the prince's household.

Sybil Penn (d.1562). Sister-in-law of Sir William Sidney. Governess to the prince. Buried at Hampton, Middlesex.

Sir William Sidney (?1482–1554). Soldier. Chamberlain from 1538; later steward and tutor. Granted Penshurst estate, 1552.

The Victims

Anne Askew (1521–46). Burnt at Smithfield for heresy after torture in the Tower of London, 16 July 1546.

Robert Barnes (1495–1540). Prior of Austin Friars, Cambridge. Involved in diplomatic negotiations for Henry's marriage with Anne of Cleves. Burnt at Smithfield for heresy, 30 July 1540.

Thomas Cromwell, Earl of Essex (?1485–1540). Lord Privy Seal and Vice-Regent for religious affairs. Beheaded for treason, 28 July 1540, on Tower Hill.

Thomas Culpeper. One of Henry's Privy Chamber favourites. Beheaded as a traitor at Tyburn, 10 December 1541.

Francis Dereham. Former lover and private secretary to Queen Katherine Howard. Hanged, drawn and quartered as a traitor at Tyburn, 10 December 1541.

Thomas Fiennes, Lord Dacre of the South (b.1517). Hanged for murder at Tyburn, 29 June 1541.

Thomas Garret. Burnt at Smithfield for heresy, 30 July 1540.

Henry Howard, Earl of Surrey (?1517–47). Son of Thomas Howard, Third Duke of Norfolk. Poet, courtier and soldier. Beheaded for treason, 19 January 1547, on Tower Hill.

Thomas Howard, Third Duke of Norfolk (1473–1554). Soldier, Earl Marshal and Lord High Treasurer of England. Commanded English forces against the Scots, 1542. Lieutenant General of English army in France, 1544. Condemned to death for treason but saved from execution by Henry VIII's death. Imprisoned in the Tower of London until Mary's accession in 1553. Presided at trial of Northumberland, 1553.

William Jerome, Vicar of Stepney, East London. Burnt at Smithfield for heresy, 30 July 1540.

John Lambert *alias* John Nicholson. After a show trial, burnt at Smithfield, 22 November 1538, for denying the 'Real Presence' – the corporeal presence of Christ in the Holy Sacrament of Communion.

Richard Mekins (1526–41). Fifteen-year-old boy burnt at Smithfield on 30 July 1541 for denying the 'Real Presence'.

Lady Jane Rochford (?1510–42). Lady-in-waiting to Queen Anne of Cleves and Queen Katherine Howard, widow of George Boleyn (executed 17 May 1536 for conducting an incestuous relationship with his sister Anne Boleyn). Beheaded for treason, 13 February 1542, on Tower Green.

Index

KH refers to Katherine Howard
KP refers to Katherine Parr

Abbey of Bexley, Kent (given to Vicary) 127
Abel, Thomas (papist, executed) 94
Act of Supremacy 83, 329
Acts of Attainder 215
   Cromwell 33
   KH 50
   Surrey and Norfolk 219, 234, 332
   Wolsey 128
Acts of Succession 212, 329, 330
Acton, Master (justice of the peace) 223
actors 70, 144, 178, 223
Adams, John (tailor, executed) 174
Aguilar, Marquis de 23
Albert, Francis (armourer) 106
alms 212
   death of Henry 224, 225
   Edward's christening 67
Alsop, Thomas (apothecary) 17, 206–7, 209
Henry's funeral 228
   Henry's will 214
Ampthill, Bedfordshire 38, 76
Anabaptists 86, 89, 162, 177
Ancrum Moor (English defeat) 113, 123, 331
Anne, Queen (child's burial) 271, 273
Anne of Cleves (fourth wife of Henry)
   24–31, 33–6, 60–1, 333
   annulment 31, 33–5, 37, 330, 333
   Barnes 338

Cromwell 25, 27, 28, 30, 93
   death 257, 333
   Denny 29, 153
   hopes of reconciliation 47–8, 52–3
   Lady Denny as lady-in-waiting 154
   Lady Jane Rochford 30, 339
   idea of marriage to Thomas Seymour
     244
   pension 33, 47, 330, 333
   pre-contract of marriage with Francis
     27–8, 31
   trumpeters impress Henry 276
   wedding 28, 330, 333
annulments of Henry's marriages
   Anne of Cleves 31, 33–5, 37, 330, 333
   Catherine of Aragon 19, 35
Antwerp
   Barnes 94
   John Lambert 82
   mercenaries 120–1
   moneylenders 119
   planned flight by Mary 256
   Vaughan 121, 124, 167
apothecaries 17, 131, 206–7, 209, 228
   Henry's will 214
archery (Edward) 63
Ardres (peace treaty) 125, 291
Armin, Robert (actor) 144
armour 105–6, 132, 137, 142
   Butts 135
   Henry's funeral 230
   jousting 137

arms (heraldic) 224–6, 228, 230, 269
    Edward 200
    Norfolk 198
    St Edward the Confessor 196, 198–9
    Surrey 196–7, 198–203
    Wolsey 262
Arran, Earl of (regent governor of Scotland) 72
Arthur, Prince (Henry's late brother) 131, 328
    death 328
    marriage to Catherine of Aragon 19, 59
    tuberculosis 19, 292, 328
Arundel, Earl of 200
Arundell, Millicent (witness against Surrey) 183–4, 194
Ascham, Roger 153, 337–8
    tutor to Edward 73, 153, 337–8
    tutor to Elizabeth 15, 73, 153, 337
Ashley, Catherine 'Cat' (governess to Elizabeth) 247
Ashridge, Hertfordshire 70, 76
Aske, Robert (attorney, executed) 192, 302
Askew (or Ascough), Anne 168–71
    executed 174, 331, 338
Audley, Lady (her fool entertained KP) 76
Audley, Sir Thomas (sees infant Edward) 69–70
Augustine de Augustinis (doctor) 128, 134–5, 293
Aurelius, Marcus (Roman Emperor) 132
Austin Friars, Cambridge 32, 338
Ayliffe, Sir John (surgeon) 136, 228, 294

Baker, Sir John (Attorney-General, Chancellor of Exchequer) 97, 98, 169, 335
Bale, John (Bishop of Ossory) 75–6, 296
Bandinelli, Baccio (sculptor) 261
Bar, Francois Duc de (married Christina of Denmark) 334
barbers 136–7
barge race on the Thames 84
Barker, Christopher (Garter King at Arms) 65, 228, 231–2
Barnes, Robert (evangelical priest) 94–6

executed 169, 330, 338
Basset, Anne 54, 280
Basset, Elizabeth (lady-in-waiting to Anne of Cleves) 52
Bateson, Giles (crossbow-maker) 77
Battle of the Spurs 55
Baynton, Sir Edward (KH's vice-chamberlain) 46–7, 279
Beachy Head, Sussex (English navy) 119
Beaton, Cardinal David (Archbishop of St Andrews) 123
Beauchamp, Viscount see Seymour, Sir Edward
Beaufort, Margaret (Henry's grandmother) 17
Beck, Thomas (pet food supplier) 76
Bedford, Earl of see Russell, John Lord
Belenian, Nicholas (priest, executed) 174
Bell, Richard (KP's household) 76
Bellin, Nicholas, of Modena (carver of Henry's effigy) 224
Belmaine, John (taught Edward French) 284
Bembridge, Isle of Wight (French troops landed) 118
Bennet, Mr (tried for heresy) 97–8
Blagge, Sir George (pardoned) 168, 195
Blount, Elizabeth (mother of Henry's illegitimate son) 127
Boleyn, Anne (second wife of Henry) 19–20, 34, 328–9
    Baynton 46–7, 279
    birth of Elizabeth 133, 328, 334
    brother executed for incest 48, 339
    burial in the Tower of London 51
    cousin of KH 35
    doctors 133, 135
    executed 19–20, 23, 34, 51, 172, 329
    failure to bear a son 66
    miscarriages 128, 137
    niece of Norfolk 43, 46, 49, 192
    syphilis 128
    wedding 58, 328
    Wolsey 262
Boleyn, George (brother of Anne, executed) 48, 339
Boleyn, Mary (Henry's mistress) 127

Boleyn, Thomas (Earl of Wiltshire, Norfolk's brother-in-law) 192

Bonner, Edmund (Bishop of London) 96, 131, 229, 230

book burning 83

Boole, John (Henry's confessor) 219

Boorde, Andrew (doctor) 136

Boulogne 330
Denny knighted 152
Hertford 119, 186–7, 337
Lisle 336
handed back to the French 125
mercenaries 120
papal Bull 89
Privy Council 185, 217
Surrey 185–7
war 106, 108, 110–20, 122, 124, 144

Bourchier, Henry (second Earl of Essex) 65, 71, 72

Bowes, Sir Martin (Sheriff of London) 95, 169

Brabant (mercenaries) 120

Bradshaw, Henry (Chief Baron of Exchequer) 159

Brandon, Charles (first Duke of Suffolk) 97, 99, 335
Anne of Cleves 34
attack on Edinburgh 104
burial 119, 290–1, 335
death 119, 331, 335
godfather to Edward 66
Henry marries KP 19
jousting 97, 119, 137
KH's arrest 50, 279
war in France 105, 110, 115–17
wife had dog called 'Gardiner' 166

Brandon, Henry (second Duke of Suffolk) 73

Bray, Lord (Henry's funeral) 226

Bridgewater, Lady Katherine (aunt of KH) 49

Brighton, Sussex (attacked by French warships) 117

Brione, Martin (gift to Edward) 75

Bristow, Nicholas (Privy Purse) 155, 157

Bromley, Sir Thomas (executor of Henry's will) 213

Browne, Sir Anthony (Master of the King's Horse) 335
Anne of Cleves 26
Edward's christening 65
Edward's succession 15
executor of Henry's will 213
Henry's funeral 228
Henry's will 211, 213, 214
Norfolk 199
religious conservatism 97
Surrey 200
wedding of Henry and KP 59

Bruges, John (tailor) 306

Bruges, Thomas (banner bearer) 227

Brussels 22, 58

Bryan, Sir Francis (Chief Gentleman of Privy Chamber) 65, 152–3

Bryan, Margaret, Lady 70–2, 338

Buckingham, Duke of (Humfrey Stafford) 256

Buckingham, Edward, third Duke of 192

Bullein, William (nurse-surgeon) 136

Bulmer, Sir John (executed as traitor) 192, 302

Bungay, Suffolk (given to Denny) 236–7

Burgavenny, Lord (Henry's funeral) 226

Burgundy (claimed by Spain) 105, 112

Burnet, Bishop 91–2

Busebridge, John (murdered) 39

Butts, Sir William (doctor) 29, 135, 284, 293–4
Cranmer 100, 135
death 205
Edward 72
Jane Seymour 133, 135

Calais 21, 25, 92, 168
Arthur Plantagenet as Captain 70
Herbert as Governor 335
Lisle 88
plague 278
war 105–6, 110, 116, 144

Callyniuod, Robert (laundry and clothing bill) 148

Campe (peace treaty) 125, 331

Canterbury, Archbishop of *see* Cranmer

Canterbury Cathedral 89, 98

Capon, John (Bishop of Salisbury) 98

card games 25, 140, 156, 205, 298

Carew, Sir Gawen (Vice-Admiral of English fleet) 118, 194

Carew, Lady Martha (sister of Denny) 118, 153

Carew, Sir Nicholas (Edward's christening) 65

Carew, Sir Wymond (Receiver-General to Anne of Cleves) 153, 189

Carwarden, Sir Thomas (pardoned) 99

Castillon, Louis de Perreau, Sieur de (French ambassador) 20–2, 334

Cathedral of Notre Dame (Mass for Henry) 234

Cathedral of St Bavo, Ghent 269

Catherine of Aragon (first wife of Henry) 19, 35, 83, 262, 328–9
   annulment 19, 35
   aunt of Charles V 133, 334
   birth of Mary 328, 333
   death 23, 329
   divorce 83, 262, 328–9
   doctors 131, 133, 134
   great aunt to Christina of Denmark 22–3, 334
   lady-in-waiting was KP's mother 55
   marriage to Henry 328
   marriage to Prince Arthur 19, 59
   planned monument 260, 261
   syphilis 127–8

Catholicism 20, 37, 83–4, 92–5, 99, 260, 329
   annulment of marriage to Catherine of Aragon 19
   Cranmer 257, 336
   Cromwell 278
   excommunication of Henry 89
   Gardiner 257
   Henry's monument 265–6
   Lisle 88
   Mary 80, 176, 178, 254–5, 257, 333
   planned invasion of England 24
   split with Rome 20, 83–4, 329
   Surrey 184

Caverley, Sir Hugh (accused Blagge of heresy) 168

Cawarden, Sir Thomas (Master of the Revels) 157

Cecil, Sir William (friend of Denny) 152, 266

Chamberlain, Thomas (mercenaries' liaison) 120

Chambre (or Chamber), John (doctor) 29, 131, 133
   Edward 72
   Henry's funeral 228

Champernown, Sir Philip (father-in-law of Denny) 154

Chantries Act 160, 161

Chapman, John (freemason) 77

Chapuys, Eustace (Spanish ambassador) 334
   Anne of Cleves 52–3, 60–1
   Augustine 134
   Dacre's execution 39
   Henry's character 142–3
   Henry's search for a consort 54–5
   Henry's wedding to KP 60
   KH 36, 42, 46, 50
   Lady Rochford 48
   morals of Henry's household 51
   retirement 115–17
   war in France 143
   war in Scotland 54

charities 160

Charles I (burial) 270, 271, 272, 273

Charles II (Henry's monument) 269

Charles V of Spain 117, 165–6, 197, 205, 334
   abdicated in favour of Philip 234, 334
   alliance with England 105, 112, 143, 165
   alliance with France 21–2
   Augustine 134
   death 234
   diplomacy of KP 116
   Henry's death 13, 16
   Henry's funeral 227
   Henry's search for wife 21–3
   mercenaries 120
   nephew of Catherine of Aragon 133, 334
   peace treaty 160
   plot against KP 166

son marries Queen Mary 333
Surrey 185
Thomas Thirlby 193
war in France 105, 143
Charles, Nicholas (Lancaster Herald) 261
Chatteras, Cambridge (Dr Wendy) 135
Cheke, Sir John (tutor to Edward) 73–4, 76, 80, 338
Denny 153
imprisoned 284, 338
inscription on Butt's tomb 294
Chelmsford Church (Gates) 256
Chelsea 106, 240–3, 245, 247–8
death of Anne of Cleves 333
Elizabeth 247
Henry's funeral 228
Paulet 266
Cheshunt, Hertfordshire
Denny 154, 256, 335
Elizabeth 246, 248
chess 140, 298
Cheyney, Sir Thomas (Treasurer of Royal Household) 155, 335
confiscation of Cromwell's assets 32, 39
Henry's burial 231
pardon for son 39
Chobham, Guildford (Henry hunting) 206
Christ Church, Oxford (Richard Cox) 73, 338
Christian II of Denmark 22, 334
Christina of Denmark (great-niece of Catherine of Aragon) 22–3, 334
Church of All Hallows, Barking (burial of Surrey) 203
Church of England 13, 83, 86, 88, 90, 97, 287
Supreme Head 163–4, 176, 329
Church of St Peter ad Vincula (Tower of London) 51
City of London
Anne of Cleves 27
Cromwell 32
Denny 153
doctors 131, 133
plague 282
sending troops 118, 121
Surrey 183, 187

Clarke, Robert (Henry's monument) 269
Clement VII, Pope 83–5, 89
Clere, Thomas (witness against Surrey) 184
Clerical Convocation (annulment of marriage) 34, 330, 333
Clerk, William (clerk to Privy Chamber) 335
dry stamp 154, 158, 214–15, 335
Henry's will 214–15
Cleves, Anne of see Anne of Cleves
Cleves, Duke William of (brother of Anne) 24, 27, 33–5, 53, 61
clothes 74, 150, 298, 306–7
Anne of Cleves 26–8, 34–5
Culpeper 41
Edward 71
effigy of Henry 224, 226
KH 47, 77
KP 56–7, 77, 81, 174, 230
Ralfe Lyons 79
Somers 147–8, 258
Cobham, Lord (case against Dacre) 39
Coke, William (Groom of the Leash) 76
Colchester, Essex (execution of Sacramentarians) 89
Coldstream, Scotland (papal Bull) 89
Collins, John (executed for heresy) 96–7
commodes 150
Commonwealth 268
Company of Pure Surgeons 131
confiscation see forfeiture of lands and assets
Constable, Sir Robert (executed) 192, 302
constipation 132, 139–40
Conyers, Lord (Henry's funeral) 226
Cooke, Anthony (education of Edward) 76
Cope, Sir Anthony (Vice-Chamberlain to KP) 76
Cornwallis, Sir John (steward to Edward) 69, 338
coronation
Edward 225, 232, 332
Elizabeth 258
Henry 55, 328
Mary 234
Corpus Christi College, Oxford (wax image of Edward) 68
costs and expenses 122–5, 155–7

alms 212
Anne Boleyn's executioner 329
annulment of marriage to Anne of Cleves 33
burial of Suffolk 119
cereals during famine 114
commodes 150
defence of Boulogne 185
Dissolution of the Monasteries 31
doctors 127, 131, 134–6, 284
Edward's handkerchiefs 69
Edward's household 70
footstools 150
Henry's funeral 221–2
Henry's monument 260–1, 263–7
Henry's trams 149
keeping Norfolk in the Tower 203
KP's household 76–7
medicines 206–7
mercenaries 119–21
monument for Henry's parents 260, 262
pottery urinals 207
Privy Chamber 154–5
Ralfe Lyons 79
St George's Chapel 212
sale of Henry's effigy 268–9
Scottish prisoners 107–8
Somers 147–8
spectacles 157
war 108, 119, 122–5, 156, 264, 331
Wolsey's monument 262
Cotton, Richard (Comptroller) 70
Council of the North 217
Court of Augmentations 156, 218, 337
Courtenay, Gertrude (Marchioness of Exeter) 23, 64, 282
Coverdale, Miles (KP's household) 81
Cox, Richard (Bishop of Norwich) 73, 80, 284, 338
Cranmer, Thomas (Archbishop of Canterbury) 97–102, 165, 168, 331, 335–6
advice during KP's regency 106
Anabaptists 86
Book of Common Prayer 257
Butts 100, 135
Cromwell 32
death warrant 208

Denny 99, 154
Edward 65, 73, 75
executed 257, 335–6
executor of Henry's will 213
Gardiner 102, 176
godfather to Edward 65, 204
Great Bible 85
Henry's death 14, 220, 221
Henry's funeral 227
Henry's will 213, 214
KH 40–1, 45–6, 168
Lambert's appeal 86–7
licence for wedding of Henry and KP 58
marriage of Henry and Anne of Cleves 28
peace treaty with France 160
prayers for war with France 121
secretary (Ralph Morice) 36, 91–2
Six Articles 90, 91–2
wife 90, 287
Crepy (peace treaty) 112
Crome, Dr Edward (preacher) 168
Cromer, Walter (doctor) 135, 209
Henry's funeral 228
Henry's will 214
Cromwell, Thomas (Earl of Essex, Lord Privy Seal) 30–3, 338
Anabaptists 86
Anne of Cleves 25, 27, 28, 30, 93
arrested for treason 30–3, 338
Augustine 128, 134
confiscation of land and assets 32–3, 39, 277
death of Jane Seymour 67
Denny 153
Edward 63, 69, 71
executed 31–3, 37, 93–4, 141, 277–8, 330, 338
Gardiner 176
Great Bible 85
Henry's constipation 140
Henry's funeral 226
Henry's jousting accident 138
Henry's monument 263
heresy 33, 92–4, 98, 278
KP's household 81
Lambert's appeal 86–8

Norfolk 30–1, 189, 192
papal Bull 89
Pilgrimage of Grace 55
religious reform 37, 84, 97
Rich informs against 97
Six Articles 92
speech from the scaffold 278
spoils of St Pancras priory 68
stripped of Garter insignia 31, 189
Surrey 37, 182, 188, 200
Tower of London (letter to Henry) 31–2,
    63
crossbows 77, 143, 183, 184
Culpeper, Thomas (Gentleman of the Privy
    Chamber) 338
    affair with KH 41–4, 47–9
    executed 49, 279, 330, 338
    pardon for rape and murder 41
    pardon for servant 40
Cumberland, Duke of (opening Henry's
    vault) 271
Cure, Cornelius (sculptor) 266–7
Cushing's syndrome 207–9

da Rovezzano, Benedetto (sculptor)
    Henry's monument 262–3
    Wolsey's monument 262
Dacre see Fiennes, Thomas
Dacres, Robert (Master of Requests) 153
dancing 38
    KP 56, 81
d'Annebaut, Admiral Claud (French navy)
    117, 118
    peace treaty 159–60
Darcy, Thomas (Baron Darcy) 192
Darknall, John (verger of St George's
    Chapel) 268
Dauphin (heir to French throne) 112
Davy, Margaret (poisoner, boiled alive) 103
Day, George (Bishop of Chichester) 76, 87
de Guaras, Antonio (Spanish merchant) 193,
    199, 202
de Leu, Sir John (royal gardener) 217
de Maiano, Giovanni (sculptor) 262
de Marillac, Charles (French ambassador)
    334

Anne Basset 54
Anne of Cleves 35, 53
Augustine 134
Edward 63
Henry's health 134, 140–2
Henry's overeating 52
KH 38, 42–3, 45, 46
de Morette, Monsieur (peace treaty) 159
de Selve, Odet (French envoy) 206, 211,
    216–17, 308, 334
de Vega, Juan (Spanish ambassador) 13
de Vere, Frances (daughter of Earl of Oxford)
    186
    married to Surrey 182
de Vere, John (playwright) 223
de Victoria (or Vittoria), Fernando (doctor)
    131, 133
debasement of currency 124, 156
deep-vein thrombosis 129
Denmark 114–15
Denny, Sir Anthony (Chief Gentleman of
    Privy Chamber) 151–8, 335
    Anne of Cleves 29, 153
    commodes 150
    death 256, 335
    dry stamp 158, 218
    executor of Henry's will 213
    Gardiner 181
    Henry's death 14–15, 235, 236–7
    Henry's funeral 226
    Henry's ill health 160
    Henry's trams 149
    Henry's will 210, 213, 214
    KP's marriage to Seymour 249
    Kett's rebellion 256
    religious factions 152, 154, 165
    succeeds Heneage 178
    summons Cranmer 99
    warning Henry of imminent death
        219–20
    wife is lady-in-waiting to KP 154, 170
Denny, Sir Edmund (father to Sir Anthony)
    152
Denny, Lady Joan (wife of Sir Anthony) 154,
    170, 249
Denny, John (nephew of Sir Anthony) 155
Denny, Mary (mother to Sir Anthony) 152

Denny, Thomas (brother of Sir Anthony) 153

dental sepsis (Elizabeth) 334

Dereham, Francis (lover of KH) 41, 45–6, 48–9, 338
executed 49, 279, 330, 338

deserters 109

d'Estampes, Madame (mistress to Francis I) 194

Dethicke, Gilbert (Norroy King of Arms) 222–3

Dissolution of the Monasteries 31, 156, 226, 263, 329

doctors (including surgeons) 38, 105, 129–43, 205–8, 214, 217, 219, 228
Augustine 128, 134–5
Ayliffe 136, 228, 294
Butts 29, 72, 100, 133, 135, 205, 284
Chambre 29, 72, 131, 133, 228
Cromer 135, 209, 214, 228
costs 127, 131, 134–6, 284
de Victoria 131, 133
diagnosis 132, 133, 208
Edward 63–4, 72, 127, 135–7
Ferris 136
Guersie 134
Henry Halford (to George III) 272
Henry's death 17
Henry's funeral 228
Henry's ulcerated legs 127, 129, 132–3
Lady Rochford 48
Linacre 131, 133
Monforde 136
Owen 133, 135, 206, 209, 214, 228
Robert Huicke 135–6, 168, 214, 250
Vicary 127
Wendy 135, 172, 206, 209, 214, 228
Wotton 133–4

Dodge, John (patronage) 155

Doloenus, Glaterus (gift to Edward) 75

Dormer, Sir Michael (Lord Mayor) 48

Dorset, Marchioness of (Edward's christening) 281

Dorset, Marquis of see Grey, Henry

Douglas, Lady Margaret (niece of Henry) 38, 59, 111

Dover, Kent 25, 121, 140

dry stamp 154, 157–9, 181, 217–18, 331, 335
Henry's will 214–16, 331
Mary 299

Dudley, John (Viscount Lisle, Earl of Warwick, Duke of Northumberland, Lord High Admiral) 197–8, 209, 290, 336
Edward Seymour's conspiracy to murder 337
executed 255, 336
executor of Henry's will 213
Gardiner 176, 181
Gates 335
Henry's death 236–7
Henry's will 210, 213, 214, 215
Lambert's appeal 88
Norfolk 199, 339
Paget 256
peace talks with France 124
playing cards with Henry 205
Somerset toppled 254
son married to Lady Jane Grey 255, 336
stepfather of Anne Basset 280
succession 255
Surrey 200–1
Thomas Seymour 58

Edinburgh (attacked) 104–5

Edward IV 65, 70, 212, 264
Wolsey's tomb 262

Edward, Prince (later Edward VI) 63–78, 80, 333, 337–8
arrangements for after Henry's death 210
Ascham as tutor 37, 73, 153
Barnes 95
birth 20, 64, 67, 329, 333
ceremony ratifying peace treaty 159
Cheyney 335
christening 64–7, 281
coronation 225, 232, 332
custody 209–10
death 255, 257, 265, 292, 333
doctors 63–4, 72, 127, 135–6
education 73–6, 80, 284
Elizabeth 15, 65–6, 70–1, 73, 80, 253
Gardiner 71–2, 256–7, 336

Hampton Court 20, 64, 67, 68, 80, 106, 108, 333
Henry's death 15–16, 234–7
Henry's deteriorating health 203–4, 205
Henry's need for a consort 52
   Henry's will 211–13
   heraldic arms 200
   Hertford (later Somerset) 15, 66, 187, 225, 254
   KP 59, 74–8, 203–4, 234–5
   KP's grave 251
   KP's marriage to Seymour 241, 244–5
   marriage plans 72–3, 104, 284
   mercenaries 121
   monument 267
   music 73–4, 284–5
   Norfolk and Surrey 193, 195, 197, 201
   Paget 235, 256, 336
   parents' monument 264–5
   Petre 336
   planned investiture as Prince of Wales 218
   portraits 146, 147
   Protestants 71–2, 73, 75–6, 160, 256, 265
   regency 213
   Rich 337
   Somers 258, 337
   Somerset 254
   succession 15–16, 212, 221, 231–5, 245–5, 254–5, 308, 330, 333
   syphilis 128
   Thomas Seymour 193, 241, 244–5, 252–3
   tuberculosis 254, 333
   Warwick 254, 336
Eleanor, Lady (daughter of Henry's sister) 213
Elizabeth, Princess (later Elizabeth I) 76, 79–80, 334
   Anne of Cleves 34
   Ascham 15, 73, 153, 337–8
   attempt to marry her off 79
   becomes queen 334
   birth 133, 328, 334
   Cheyney 335
   coronation 258
   Cox 338
   death 334

   doctors 127, 133, 136
   Edward 15, 65–6, 70–1, 73, 80, 253
   Edward's christening 65–6
   Henry's death 15
   Henry's monument 266–7
   Henry's will 214
   Herbert 335
   KP 58–9, 77, 79–81, 246–8, 249
   need for Henry to find consort 52
   Paget 256, 336
   Petre 336
   portrait 147
   public speaking 161
   Rich 337
   Shakespeare 144
   Somers 258, 337
   succession 79–80, 212, 254, 330
   syphilis 128
   Thomas Seymour 247–8, 252–3
   Thomas Wilson 146
   warships 213
Elizabeth of France (daughter of Henry II) 284
Elizabeth of York (Henry's mother) 18, 260, 328
Elyot, Sir Thomas (diplomat and scholar) 132
enemas 132, 140
Englefield, Sir Francis (Privy Councillor) 265
Enterprise of Paris 105
Essex, Earl of *see* Bourchier, Henry; Cromwell, Thomas; Parr, Sir William
evangelism 82–3, 97, 160, 162, 165–8, 223
   Butt 100
   Denny 154
   Gardiner 176
   KP 166
   priests executed 94–6, 169, 330, 338–9
Evers, Sir William (Lord Warden of Eastern Marches) 109, 113, 122
excommunication 89, 260
executions 14, 23, 39–40, 83, 88–97, 107
   Anabaptists 89
   Anne Askew 174, 331, 338
   Anne Boleyn 19–20, 23, 34, 51, 172, 329
   Anne of Cleves' fear 34

Barnes 169, 330, 338

Bulmer 192, 302

Constable 192, 302

Cranmer 257, 335–6

Cromwell 31–3, 37, 93–4, 141, 277–8, 330, 338

Culpeper 49, 279, 330, 338

Dacre 39, 278, 338

Dereham 49, 279, 330, 338

Edward Seymour 254, 337

evangelical priests 94–6, 169, 330, 338–9

for imaging Henry's death 126, 138, 219

Gates 256, 335

George Boleyn 48, 339

Germain 99

Henry Pole 23, 138, 292

heresy 88–90, 92–7, 102, 94–5, 174, 274, 286, 331, 338–9

Hungerford 37, 278

insanity 48, 51, 97

KH 49, 50–1, 55, 172, 330, 333

Lady Jane Grey 255

Lady Rochford 48, 51, 339

Lambert 88, 339

Lassels 40, 168, 174

Norfolk's planned 202, 203, 221, 233, 339

Northumberland 255, 336

papists 94–5, 99

poisoners 103

Sacramentarians 89

Six Articles 89–90

Smithfield 89, 94, 96, 103, 174, 330–1, 338–9

Surrey 202, 203, 332, 339

Thomas Seymour 253, 337

threatened for KP 172

treason 51, 94–5, 97, 192, 274, 302

Wolsey 134, 328

famine 114

Fane, Sir Ralph (liaison officer with mercenaries) 120

Fausterne, (KP's property let by Somerset) 245

Featherstone, Richard (papist, executed) 94

Fermer, Richard (Northamptonshire merchant) 145, 295–6

Ferris, Richard (surgeon) 136

Field of the Cloth of Gold (1520) 13

Fiennes, Thomas (Lord Dacre of the South) executed 39, 278, 338

Filmer, Henry (tailor, tried for heresy) 97

Fisher, John (Bishop of Rochester) 103

Fitzroy, Henry (Duke of Richmond; illegitimate son of Henry) 127

   Anne of Cleves seeking reconciliation 47–8

   Butts 135

   death 201

   death of Elizabeth 334

   marries Mary Howard 182

   tuberculosis 301

Fitzwater, Lord (Henry's funeral) 226

Fitzwilliam, Lady Jane (wife of Sir William) 170

Fitzwilliam, Sir William (Earl of Southampton) (Lord Privy Seal) 97, 336

   Anne of Cleves 25, 34

   Cromwell 31

   Edward 71

   Henry's health 134, 293

   KH 41, 50

   wife as lady-in-waiting to KP 170

Flaxman, John (sculptor) 261

fleet see navy

Fleet Prison 136, 182, 184, 256

food 14, 36, 38, 52, 54, 64, 66, 136, 139–40

   Edward 68, 72

   mercenaries 120

forfeiture or confiscation of lands and assets 23, 90

   Cromwell 32–3, 39, 277

   Culpeper 41–2

   Norfolk 49, 189, 191, 202, 234

   Surrey 202, 236

Forster, Bridget (rocker of Edward's cradle) 70

Forth Estuary (attacked) 105

Fowler, John (Groom of the Privy Chamber) 244, 253

Fox, Edward (KP's household) 77

Framlingham Church (burial of Norfolk
    and Surrey) 234, 304
France 105–24
    alliance with Denmark 114–15
    alliance with Scotland 109, 114–15, 124
    alliance with Spain 20, 21–2, 24, 104, 112
    apple trees 217
    cost of war 108, 119, 122–5, 156, 264, 331
    death of Henry 13
    did Henry contract syphilis 127
    Fitzroy and Henry Howard 182
    fleet threatening Pevensey castle 248–9
    Henry's new will 210
    Hertford 337
    Mary, Queen of Scots 73
    Norfolk 191, 193
    Paget 164
    papal Bull 89
    peace treaty 124–5, 159–60, 291, 331
    search for wife for Henry 20–2, 53–4
    succession 212
    Surrey 185–6, 193
    Thomas Seymour 337
    threatened invasion 24, 109, 114–15, 118,
        143, 330
    war 55, 80, 105–25, 127, 143–4, 156,
        185–6, 210, 226, 330–1, 335, 337
Frances, Lady (daughter of Henry's sister
    Mary) (Duchess of Suffolk) (succession)
    213, 254
Francis I (King of France) 334
    Anne of Cleves 27–8, 31, 53
    battlefleet 122
    birth of Edward 67
    death 234
    death of Henry 234
    Edward succeeds to the throne 308
    Henry's ill health 140, 217
    Henry's jousting accident 138
    KH 42, 46
    mistress 194
    Norfolk and Surrey 193
    peace treaty 160, 291
    search for wife for Henry 21–2, 54
    threatened invasion of England 109,
        114–15, 330
    war 105, 114, 119

Franklin, William (Dean of Windsor) 98
Fuggers banking 119, 124, 156
Fuller, Thomas (divine) 176

Gage, Sir John (Constable of the Tower)
    199, 231
Gainsborough, Edward, Lord Borough of
    (first husband of KP) 55
Galen (Greek doctor) 132
gambling 140, 156, 298
Gardiner, Stephen (Bishop of Winchester)
    94–9, 171, 175–81, 336
    Anne of Cleves 53
    Barnes 94–6
    conservatism 97, 165–8, 171, 187, 198
    Cranmer 102, 176
    death 257, 336
    Detection of the Devil's Sophistry 177
    Edward 71–2, 256–7, 336
    excluded from court 331
    Henry's death 222–3, 225
    Henry's funeral 230–1
    Henry's jousting accident 138
    Henry's will 211
    heresy 82, 86–7, 94–9, 176–7
    imprisoned 256–7
    KH 35–7, 44
    KP 59, 166–8, 171
    Lambert's appeal 86–7
    Mary 176, 178, 257, 336
    pardon for Marbeck 98
    Six Articles 89, 91
    war in France 113
    William Huicke 135
Garret, Thomas (evangelical priest,
    executed) 94, 330, 339
Garter, Order of the 226, 261, 273
    Edward 232
    Gardiner 223
    Paget 256
    stripped from Cromwell 31, 189
    stripped from Norfolk 189
    Surrey 200
    William Parr 57
Gates, John (brother-in-law of Denny)
    154–5, 255–6, 335

dry stamp 158, 218
executed 256, 335
Gardiner 181
Henry's death 236–7
Henry's will 214
made Chancellor of the Duchy of
Lancaster 256, 335
Norfolk 189–91
Surrey 189–90
Gentlemen of the Privy Chamber *see* Privy
Chamber
George III 272
George IV (when Prince Regent) 271–2
Gerard, John (brasier) 269
Germain (Gardiner's cousin, executed) 99
Germany 83–4, 90, 260
Anne of Cleves 24, 33
cereals 114
cleric visits Henry's tomb 267
Cranmer's wife 90, 287
Lutherans 83–4, 90, 260
mercenaries 119–21
search for wife for Henry 22, 24
spectacles 157
Gloucester, Bishop of 229
Goldsmith, Mr (sought position with KP) 81
Goodrich, Thomas (Bishop of Ely) 230
Grafton, Richard *Great Bible* 85
Great Bible 85
Great Harry (ship) 117
Great Zachary (ship) 159
Green, William (bill for commode) 150
Greenwich
Anne of Cleves 25, 26, 27, 28, 330, 333
armoury 106
Edward's death 333
Elizabeth's birth 328
Henry's birth 328
jousting 137
KP 110, 196, 210, 220
Mary's birth 328
Robert Huicke 135
Scottish peace treaty 73
sermon 229
Somers 144, 258
Gresham, Sir Richard 96, 183
Greville, William (Henry's coffin) 229

Grey, Catherine (succession) 254
Grey, Henry, Third Marquis of Dorset
(father to Lady Jane) 249
death of KP 250
Henry's funeral 225, 228
war in France 112
Grey, Lady Jane (daughter of Marquis of
Dorset)
Cranmer 257
executed 255
KP 249, 252
Northumberland 255, 336
Paget 256, 336
plot against KP 172, 173
proclaimed queen 255, 335
Rich 337
succession 254–5
Grey, Margaret (Marchioness of Dorset)
Edward's christening 281
Grey, Mary (succession) 254
greyhounds 76
Grindal, William (Edward's education) 76
Guercey, Richard (wax image of Edward) 68
Guersie, Balthasar (surgeon) 134
Guildford, Surrey (death of Suffolk) 119,
331, 335
Guildhall 48, 96, 168
Surrey's trial 199, 202
gummata 127–8

haemorrhoids 132
Halford, Sir Henry (doctor to George III)
272
Hall, Edward (chronicler) 96, 111–12
Hampton Court 140, 142
Chapel Royal 40, 64–5
cost of pottery urinals 207
Denny 158
dry stamp 158
Edward 20, 64, 67, 68, 80, 106, 108, 333
Edward's birth 20, 333
Edward's christening 64–5, 67
Elizabeth 90
fountain 267
French peace treaty 159
Henry's wedding to KP 59–60, 330, 333

Jane Seymour's death 20, 67, 333
  KH 38, 40, 42, 45, 46
  KP 62, 80, 108
  Lady Rochford 48
  Mary 80
  Somers 146, 258
Hanworth (manor settled on KP) 106,
  247–8
Harman, Edmund (tried for heresy and
  pardoned) 99
Harvel, Edmond (ambassador to Venice) 59,
  155
Havering-atte-Bower, Essex 68–70
hawks 77, 207
Hedgehog (ship) 114
Heneage, Sir Thomas (Chief Gentleman of
  Privy Chamber) 140, 152, 335
  Anne of Cleves 29
  Culpeper 41
  dismissed from Privy Chamber 41, 331,
    335
  KH 45
  succeeded by Denny 178
Henry II of France 334
  plans for daughter to marry Edward 284
Henry VI (tomb) 212, 264
Henry VII (Henry's father) 328
  monument 260, 262
  portrait 18
  tuberculosis 292
Henry VIII (1491–1547) 328–32, 333, 338–9
  alleged unfulfilled intentions 235–8
  alms 212
  Anne Boleyn 19–20, 34, 328–9
  Anne of Cleves 24–31, 33–7, 47–8, 52–3,
    93, 276, 330, 333, 338
  armour 105–6, 132, 137, 142, 230
  Assertion of the Seven Sacraments 83
  attack on Edinburgh 104–5
  barbers 136–7
  birth 328
  break with Rome 83–4
  burial 212, 213, 231, 259, 261, 270–1, 332
  card games 25, 140, 156, 205, 298
  Catherine of Aragon 19, 35, 83, 262,
    328–9
  chess 140, 298

Church of England 13, 83, 86, 88, 90, 97,
  163–4, 176, 287, 329
clothes 74, 127, 150, 298, 306–7
coffin 17, 221–31, 270–2
colic 205
constipation 132, 139–40
coronation 55, 328
Cranmer 98, 99–102, 331
Cromwell 31–3, 37, 63
Cushing's syndrome 207–9
dancing 38
death 13–18, 127, 220, 221–32, 233–9,
  252, 332
Denny 152–8, 219–20
depression 207–8
doctors 38, 129–43, 205–8, 214, 217, 219,
  228
drinking 14, 54, 141, 157
dry stamp 154, 157–9, 181, 214–16,
  217–18, 331, 335
Edward 63–78, 80, 333
effigy 224, 226–7, 229–31, 261, 263,
  266, 268–9, 306
Elizabeth 76, 79–80, 334
embalming 17
evangelicals 94–7, 330
excommunication 89, 260
executors 213
exercise 14, 126, 208
fever 38, 129, 140–1, 143, 205–6, 210
fistulas 136, 138, 140, 274
food and overeating 14, 36, 38, 52, 54, 64,
  66, 136, 139–41
funeral 16–17, 221–32
gambling 140, 156, 298
Gardiner 175–6, 178–81, 331
Great Bible 85
healing powers 149, 296
heresy 82–3, 86–102
hump on his back 207–8
hunting 24, 38, 44, 119, 126, 129, 140,
  143, 159, 206
hypochondria 129
ill temper 13–14, 22–3, 25, 38, 133, 136,
  142, 144, 153, 206
immobility 148–50, 206, 210
injuries 106, 126–7, 129, 137–8

Jane Seymour 20, 67, 329, 333
jousting 66, 97, 106, 119, 126–7, 129,
    137–8
KH 35–8, 40–52, 55, 63, 330, 333
KP 19, 55–62, 76–81, 106–11, 166–74,
    175, 330, 333
KP marries Thomas Seymour 244–7
KP's grave 251
KP's regency 106–11
Lambert's appeal 86–8
last speech to Parliament 161–5, 331
malaria 38, 126
marriage plans for Edward 72–3
Mary 76, 80, 333
Mass 20, 38, 40, 140, 160
Masses said after death 221–5, 229–30
medicines 129–34, 142, 205–7, 293
melancholia 152, 158, 208
memorial plaque 273
mercenaries 105, 119–21
mercy and pardons 39–40, 41, 45, 47, 49,
    88, 98–9, 123, 158, 168, 217, 254, 336
migraines 137
mistresses 127
monument 259–70
moodiness 13–14, 141–2, 151, 153, 208
music 24, 129, 142
Norfolk 189–203, 331, 339
obesity 13–14, 17, 34–8, 51–2, 57, 61, 106,
    136, 141–3, 149, 159, 207–8, 210, 220
pain 14, 26, 126–9, 138, 141, 143–4, 150,
    206, 208, 218
paranoia 208–9
peace treaty with France 124–5, 159–60,
    291, 331
portraits 17–18, 78, 128, 142–3, 146–7,
    204, 295, 296
Privy Chamber 151–8, 331, 335
Privy Council 335–7
proclaimed king 328
prudery 21, 38
psychosis 144, 208–9
Ralfe Lyons 78–9
religion 75, 81, 82–103, 162–71, 260
ruthlessness 13–14, 23, 34, 44
search for a wife 19–25, 52–5, 334
sexual prowess 28–31, 33–4, 37–8

singing 24, 38, 132
Six Articles 89–92
Somers 144–8, 152, 257–8, 337
spectacles 157, 196
succession 79–80, 254
Surrey 182–90, 193–7, 199–203, 331, 339
sword 104, 112, 228, 230, 289
syphilis 127–9, 292
tennis 127
trams 149
treason to imagine his death 126, 138,
    149, 219, 292, 329
ulcerated legs 17, 26, 38, 41, 52, 57,
    127–9, 132–3, 138–43, 148, 150, 160,
    206–8, 210, 217, 274
vault opened 270–2
war with France 80, 105–25, 127, 143–4,
    185–6
war with Scotland 54, 104–5, 330
weddings 19, 28, 37, 58–60, 328–30, 333
will 15–16, 106, 135–6, 210–16, 237–9,
    259, 264, 330, 331
Wolsey 262, 328
wrestling 126
Henry, Prince (son of Henry and Catherine
    of Aragon) 66, 328
Hentzner, Canon Paul (German) 267
Herbert of Cherbury, Lord (Wolsey's
    monument) 262
Herbert, Anne (sister of KP) 55–6, 58, 76,
    172–3, 335
    Thomas Seymour 240–1
Herbert, Sir William (Earl of
    Pembroke)(Chief Gentleman of the Privy
    Chamber) 55–6, 76, 152, 178, 335
    brawl and murder 280
    death of Henry 15, 235, 236–7
    dry stamp 218
    executor of Henry's will 213
    Henry's funeral 226
    Henry's monument 267
    Henry's will 213, 214
    Thomas Seymour 240–1
Herd, John (porter) 227
heresy 14, 82–3, 86–102, 162, 166, 168–9,
    197
    Anne Askew 331, 338

Barnes 338
conspiracy against KP 166, 167, 171
Cranmer 257
Cromwell 33, 92–4, 98, 278
executions 88–90, 92–7, 102, 94–5, 174,
     274, 286, 331, 338–9
French and Spanish alliance 24
Gardiner 82, 86–7, 94–9, 176–7
Garret 339
Jerome 339
Norfolk 192
Six Articles 89–92
Surrey 188
Hertford, Earl of see Seymour, Edward
Hesse, Philip, Landgrave of 113, 120, 121
Hilles, Richard (writer) 102
Hobberthorne, Henry (Lord Mayor of
     London) 168, 200
Hoby, Sir Philip (diplomat) 99
Holbeach, Henry (Bishop of Rochester) 231
Holbein the Younger, Hans (painter) 275,
     295
     Anne of Cleves 24
     Christina of Denmark 22
     Denny 154
Holinshed, Raphael (chronicler) 111
Holland, Elizabeth 'Bess' (mistress of
     Norfolk) 149
     arrest of Norfolk 190, 194, 203
hounds 207
Howard, Anne (sister-in-law to KH) 49
Howard, Lord Charles (brother of KH) 38,
     43
Howard, Lord Edmund (father of KH) 36
Howard, Henry (Earl of Surrey; son of
     Norfolk) 181–90, 193–203, 339
     Act of Attainder 219
     arms 196–7, 198–203
     attempted escape from Tower 193, 200–1
     Commander-in-Chief of forces 185–6
     cost of wars 123
     Cromwell 37, 182, 188, 200
     executed 202, 203, 332, 339
     Hertford 182, 186–8, 200–2
     hooliganism 183–4, 199
     KH 38, 280
     lands distributed 236

married to Frances de Vere 182
     Tower of London 189–90, 193, 195,
          199–202, 331
     treason 199, 200, 202, 203, 331, 339
     trial 149, 199
Howard, Katherine (fifth wife of Henry;
     niece of Norfolk) 35–8, 40–52, 55, 63,
     192, 330, 333
     affairs 40–50, 64, 142, 168
     arrest 50–1, 279–80
     clothes altered for KP 77
     Dereham 41, 45–6, 48–9, 338
     executed 49, 50–1, 55, 172, 330, 333
     Lady Rochford 339
     Tower of London 50–1
     wedding 37, 58, 330, 333
Howard, Mary (Duchess of Richmond,
     daughter of Norfolk)
     arrest of father and brother 190, 194–7,
          201, 203
     married Henry Fitzroy (Duke of
          Richmond) 182
     asked to seduce Henry 166
Howard, Thomas, third Duke of Norfolk
     (KH's uncle) 48, 189–203, 277, 331, 339
     Act of Attainder 219, 234, 332
     arrest 189–97
     Augustine 134
     Boorde 136
     confession 198–9, 203
     confiscated lands and assets 49, 189, 191,
          202, 234
     Cranmer 101–2
     Cromwell 30–1, 189, 192
     death 234
     death of Henry 233, 236–7
     death of Jane Seymour 67
     death warrant 189
     execution planned 202, 203, 221, 233,
          339
     Gardiner 181
     godfather to Edward 65
     Henry's ill health 129
     Henry's jousting accident 137
     KH 35–7, 43–4, 46, 48–9, 280
     KP 166
     Latimers 55

letter from Henry 205
Mary 234, 336, 339
mistress 149, 190, 194, 203
released 234
religious factions 36–7, 97, 166, 191, 210
Scotland 336
Six Articles 89
spoils from St Pancras priory 68
Surrey 185–9, 200
Tower of London 189–92, 198, 203, 221,
    233, 331, 339
uncle of Anne Boleyn 43, 46, 49, 192
war in France 105, 110–12, 115, 119
Howard, Thomas (son of Norfolk) 167–8
Howard, Thomas (son of Surrey) 182
Howard, Lord William (step-brother of
    Norfolk) 49
Howard, Lady Margaret (wife of Lord
    William) 49
Huicke, Elizabeth (wife of Robert) 135–6
Huicke, Robert (doctor) 135–6, 168
birth of KP's daughter 250
Henry's will 135, 214
Huicke, William 135, 168
Hume, Patrick (Scottish prisoner in the
    Tower) 123
Hungary, Queen of 39, 60
Hungerford, Walter, Lord (executed) 37, 278
Hunsdon, Hertfordshire 54, 70, 74, 78
hunting 24, 38, 44, 119, 126, 129, 140, 143,
    159, 206
Edward 63
KP 77
not Anne of Cleves 24
Hussey MP, Thomas 123
Hustwayt, William (bill for cistern) 150

insanity and execution 48, 51, 97
Ireland 13, 212
Isaac (sexton's man) 270
Isle of Wight 117–18, 331
Italy 119, 260–5

Jak, Mistress (Edward's wet nurse) 70, 71,
    296, 338

James II (Henry's monument) 269
James V of Scotland (father of Mary, Queen
    of Scots) 73, 334
death 54
married to Marie of Guise 20, 275, 334
Jane (Mary's fool) 147, 296
Jerome, William (evangelical priest) 94, 339
executed 330, 339
jewellery 222, 226
Anne of Cleves 34
Cromwell's assets 32
Edward's coronation 225
Henry's will 213, 214
Jane Seymour 134
KH 45, 47
KP 56, 61–2, 81, 174, 220, 245–6, 252
Mary 54
Norfolk and Surrey 190
Johnson, Otwell (London merchant) 168
jousting 66, 97, 106, 126–7, 129, 137–8
Edward 63
Henry's injuries 106, 137–8
Suffolk 97, 119, 137

Kenninghall (home of Norfolk) 49, 189–91,
    200, 234
Kentish rebellion 234
Kett's rebellion (1549) 256, 335
King's Pensioners 59, 280–1
Knyvett, Anthony (Lieutenant of the Tower)
    170–1
Knyvett, Sir Edmund (Serjeant Porter) 195,
    231
Kyme, Thomas (husband of Anne Askew)
    169

Lambert, John (alias John Nicholson,
    executed) 339
appeal 82, 86–8, 92
imprisoned with John Collins 97
Lambeth Palace (Cranmer) 98
Lassels, John (executed) 40, 168, 174
Latimer, Lord (Henry's funeral) 226
Latimer, Lord see Neville, John
Laxton, Sir William (Sheriff of London) 95

Layton, Sir Bryan (murdered by Hume) 123
leeches 134
Leigh, Sir John (challenged to a duel by
    Surrey) 182
Leo X, Pope 83, 328
    monument 261
Liege, Bishop of 120
Lily, William (humanist) 152
Linacre, Thomas (doctor) 131, 133
Lisle, Lady Honor (wife of Arthur Planta-
    genet) 70
Lisle, Viscount see Dudley, John
Littleton (accused Blagge of heresy) 168
London, Bishop of 96, 131, 229, 230
Lorraine, Duke of (father of Francis) 27
Lorraine, Francis of (pre-contract of
    marriage with Anne of Cleves) 27–8, 31
Louise of Guise (sister to Marie) 20
Ludlow, Maurice (Groom of the Chamber)
    77
Luther, Martin and Lutherans 83–4, 90,
    260
Lyons, Ralfe (child given to Henry) 78–9

malaria 38, 126
    Butts 135
Mallard, John King's Psalter 146–7
Malt, John (tailor) 147
Marbeck, John (organist, tried for heresy)
    97–8
Marie of Guise 53, 54, 334
    married to James V 20, 275, 334
Marie of Vendome 20–1, 334
Marillac, Charles de see de Marillac, Charles
Marshalsea Prison 98, 338
Mary, Princess (later Mary I) 73–6, 333
    Anne of Cleves 34
    Ascham 337
    birth 328, 333
    called to court 54, 76
    Catholicism 80, 176, 178, 254–5, 257, 333
    Cheke 338
    Cheyney 335
    coronation 234
    Counter-reformation 75
    Cox 338

Cranmer 257
    doctors 127, 133, 135
    dry stamp 299
    Edward 63, 65, 71, 73–5, 80, 204
    fool 147
    Gardiner 176, 178, 257, 336
    Gates 256
    godmother to Edward 65
    Henry's ill health 217
    Henry's monument 265
    Henry's will 214
    Herbert 335
    imprisoning Edward's tutors 73
    KH 36
    KP 58–60, 62, 76–7, 80–1, 244, 249–50
    married to Philip of Spain 234, 333, 334
    music 74, 284
    need for Henry to find a consort 52
    Norfolk 234, 336, 339
    Paget 256, 336
    Paulet 336
    Petre 336
    planned flight to Antwerp 256
    portrait 147
    proclaimed queen 333
    Rich 337
    Somers 258, 337
    Spanish ambassador meets KP 115–16
    succeeded by Elizabeth 334
    succession 79–80, 212, 254–5, 330
    syphilis 128
    Thomas Seymour dreams of marrying
        252
Mary, Princess (sister to Henry) 213, 254
Mary, Queen of Scots 72–3, 104, 334
Mary Rose (ship) 117–18, 290, 331
measles 126, 292
medicines 129–34, 142, 205–7, 293
Mekins, Richard (boy executed for heresy)
    96, 339
Melanchthon, Philip (Lutheran) 90–1
Melrose (attacked) 113
mercenaries 105, 119–21
Mercers' Chapel 168
mercy 39, 88
    Culpeper 41, 49
    Hume 123

KH 45, 47
see also pardons
Mervyn, Thomas (porter) 227
Mewtes, Joan (nurse to Edward) 69, 283
Milan, Duke of 22, 334
Milan (surrendered to the Spanish) 112
Modena, Nicholas Bellin of (painter and carver) 265
Monforde (or Mumford), John (surgeon) 136
monkey (pet of Somers) 144, 146, 147
Monox, Henry (lute player, lover of KH) 40, 48
Montague, Sir Edward (Chief Judge of Common Pleas) 254–5
executor of Henry's will 213
Montague, Lord see Pole, Henry
Montreuil 110, 112, 185
Morant, Philip (Essex historian) 255–6
More, Sir Thomas (perjury by Rich at his trial) 97
Morice, Ralph (Cranmer's secretary) 36, 91–2
Morley, Lord (Edward's christening) 66
Mowntayne, Thomas (Protestant rector) 176–7
murder 39, 41, 123, 280
music 24, 129, 142
    Anne of Cleves 24
    Edward 73–4, 284–5
    KH 40, 42
    KP 56, 76, 77
    Mary 74, 284
    organist pardoned 97–8
Mystery of Barbers 131

navy 114–15, 117–19, 122, 213, 290
    French 117–19, 122, 248–9
    Mary Rose 117–18, 290, 331
    Thomas Seymour 58, 337
needlework (Anne of Cleves) 24
Nelson, Admiral Lord
    monument made from components of Henry's 260, 270
Neville, John (Lord Latimer, KP's second husband) 55–6, 58, 246

Neville, Margaret (stepdaughter of KP) 76
Norfolk, Agnes Dowager Duchess of (stepmother of Norfolk) 192
    stepgrandmother of KH 40–1, 46, 49
Norfolk, Duchess of 149
Norfolk, second Duke of (KH's grandfather) 36, 277
Norfolk, third Duke of see Howard, Thomas
Norfolk and Suffolk, Sheriff of 153
Norlegh, Richard (patronage) 155
North, Sir Edward (Chancellor of Augmentations)
    Gardiner 180
    Henry's will 213, 214
Northampton, Marquis of see Parr, Sir William
Northumberland, Duke of see Dudley, John

oath of allegiance 83, 89
Odell, Mary (KP's pregnancy) 248
Order of St George (stripped from Cromwell) 31
Orleans, Duke of (to marry Charles V's daughter) 112
Osiander, Margaret (wife of Cranmer) 287
Osmond (wax image of Edward) 68
osteitis 129
Otelands Palace, Weybridge 206
    Gardiner 180
    Henry's wedding to KH 37, 333
    KP 60
Owen, George (doctor) 135, 206, 209
    Henry's funeral 228
    Henry's will 135, 214
    Jane Seymour 133
Oxford, Earl of 223
    daughter marries Surrey 182

Paget, Sir John (ambassador to France) 42
Paget, Sir William (Secretary of State, later Lord Paget of Beaudesert) 164–6, 256, 336
    Anne of Cleves 52
    case of poachers and murder 39
    cost of wars 123

death 256
death of Henry 14–16, 223, 233, 235–8
diplomatic duties in France 164
dry stamp 218
Edward 235, 256, 336
executor of Henry's will 213
Gardiner 175, 180
gives dog to Chapuys 117
Henry's burial 231
Henry's ill health 217
Henry's speech to Parliament 164–5
Henry's will 210–16
KP's regency 107
made Lord Privy Seal 256, 336
mercenaries 120–1
Norfolk 193–4, 199, 202
peace talks with France 124–5
plot against KP 166–7
Privy Chamber 152
Privy Council 256, 336
Somerset 233, 238–9, 256
Surrey 186, 187, 193, 200–2
Thomas Seymour 253
war in France 113
Palace of Nonsuch, Ewell 210
Palace of Westminster 25, 79, 171, 173
bed enlarged 52
Chapuys 53
Cranmer 99
Culpeper 41, 47
death of Henry 13, 16–17, 221, 225
Denny 153–4, 157
dinner for ladies 54
Gardiner 181, 222, 257
Henry hurts a foot playing tennis 127
Henry marries Jane Seymour 329, 333
Henry's ill health 219
Henry's will 214
household accounts 148–50
KP's diplomacy with Spanish ambassador
    115–16
king's trams 148–50
Lambert's appeal 86
music 74
poaching and murder case 39
portraits 147
site of executions 40

Somers 147
Surrey 188, 194
pardons 39–40, 98–9, 336
Blagge 168
Culpeper 41, 49
Culpeper's servant 40
Denny 158
Howard family 49
Marbeck 98
Northampton 336
Sacramentarians 217
Somerset 254
see also mercy
Paris 105, 112, 122
Parkhurst, John (KP's chaplain) 76, 250
Parr, Katherine (sixth wife of Henry) 55–62,
    76–81, 106–11, 166–74, 175, 330, 333
accompanying Henry to Windsor 206
arrest warrant 171–3
birth of daughter 250, 333
books 80–1, 167
brother-in-law appointed to Privy
    Chamber 178
burial 251
death 250–2
death of Henry 220, 234–5, 239–40
death warrant 208
Denny 249, 335
diplomacy with Spanish ambassador
    115–16
doctors 135, 136
Edward 59, 74–8, 203–4, 234–5
Elizabeth 58–9, 77, 79–81, 246–8, 249
failed arrest 331
Greenwich 110, 196, 210, 220
Henry's funeral 228, 230
Henry's ill health 150, 217
Henry's will 214
heresy trials 97
Hoby 99
household expenses 76–7
Jane (Mary's fool) 296
ladies-in-waiting 154, 169–70
Mary 58–60, 62, 76–7, 80–1, 244,
    249–50
pets 61, 76–7
plot against 161, 166–74, 175, 331

pregnancy 248–50
Ralfe Lyons 79
regency 80, 106–11, 115–16, 210, 240
religion 56, 80–1, 166–73
sister of Essex 336
Somerset 106, 241–3, 245–6, 248–50
Thomas Seymour 57–9, 240–52, 333, 337
wedding to Henry 19, 58–60, 330, 333
will 136, 250
Parr of Horton, Lord (uncle to KP) 76
Parr, Sir Thomas (father of KP) 55
Parr, Sir William (Marquis of Northampton,
 Earl of Essex, Baron Parr of Kendal,
 brother of KP) 55, 57–8, 60, 336
 death of Henry 236
 Kett's rebellion 256
 King's Pensioners 281
 knighted at Edward's christening 67
 pardoned 336
 Thomas Seymour 242, 252
 Warden of Scottish Marches 57
parrot 77
Parsons, Robert (Jesuit) 169, 171
Paul III, Pope 24, 89, 90–1
Paulet, Chidock (man of arms) 230
Paulet, Sir William (Lord St John, Marquis
 of Winchester, Lord Steward) 97, 336
 Act of Attainder 219
 Augustine 293
 death of Henry 14, 17, 236
 executor of Henry's will 213
 Henry's funeral 229
 Henry's monument 266–7
 Henry's will 213, 214
 Norfolk 198–9
Paul's Cross, London 94, 168
Pearson, Anthony (priest tried for heresy)
 97
Peckham, Sir Edmund (Treasurer and
 Master of the Mint) 157
Pembroke, first Earl of (grandfather of
 William Herbert) 56
Penn, Sybil (nurse to Edward) 71, 338
Peto, Friar (later Cardinal) 307
Petre, Sir William (Secretary of State) 336
 Gardiner 178, 180
 Henry's monument 265

Henry's speech to Parliament 164
KP's regency 106
peace talks with France 125
Philip, King of Spain (son of Charles V)
 234, 334
 Gardiner 176–7
 marries Queen Mary I 234, 333, 334
Philip, John Birnie (sculptor) 309
Philip, Landgrave of Hesse 113, 120, 121
Phillips, Robert (tutor of Ralfe Lyons) 79
Pickering, William (servant to Surrey) 182,
 183
Pigott (Thomas Seymour's servant) 251
Pilgrimage of Grace (Northern rebellion)
 182, 292, 302, 329
 distraction from planning Henry's
 monument 263
 Latimers 55
Pontefract Castle 302
 Surrey 182
plague 77, 130–1, 248
 Calais 278
 London 20, 21, 60, 69, 109, 282, 130
 Marshalsea Prison 98
 Portsmouth 119
 Windsor 38
Plantagenet, Arthur (illegitimate son of
 Edward IV) 70
pneumonia (Elizabeth's death) 334
poaching 39
poisoners 103
Pole, Sir Geoffrey (Henry's health) 138
Pole, Henry (Lord Montague) 126, 138
 executed 23, 292
Pole, Cardinal Reginald (Archbishop of
 Canterbury) 265–6
Ponet, John (Bishop of Winchester) 176
Poor Knights of Windsor 212
Portinari, Giovanni (engineer) 263, 264–5
portraits 17–18, 78, 128, 142–3, 146–7, 204,
 295, 296
 Anne of Cleves 24, 25
 Denny 154
 Edward 146, 147
 Gardiner 176
 KP 56, 78, 204, 243
 search for wife for Henry 22, 24, 35

Surrey 201
Whitehall Mural 17–18
Portsmouth 117, 118, 119
Powell, Edward (papist, executed) 94
Privy Chamber 17, 151–2, 162, 165, 168,
232, 264, 335
Anne of Cleves 25–6, 29
barbers 137
Clerk 154, 158, 214–15, 335
Culpeper 41, 338
Fowler 244, 253
Gardiner 178, 180
Henry's death 17
Henry's ill health 129, 140, 216
Henry's monument 264
KH 38, 41, 43
KP's parrot 77
Lambert's appeal 86
Lord Charles Howard 43
Norfolk 189
slippers 150
Surrey 189
Thomas Seymour 67
van Wilder 74
see also Denny, Sir Anthony; Heneage,
Sir Thomas; Herbert, Sir William
Privy Council 335–7
Anne of Cleves 27, 52–3
Anne Askew 170
attack on Edinburgh 104
Boulogne 185, 217
coronation of Edward 232
Cranmer 99–102
Cromwell 30–1
Culpeper 41–3
curfew 114
Dacres 153
death of Henry 14, 221, 223, 232, 237
Dereham 41
disposable pottery urinals 207
Edward 69, 235, 237
Englefield 265
French peace treaty 159
Gardiner 177, 181
Gates 256
Henry's ill health 141, 210, 217, 219
Henry's monument 265

Henry's will 211, 213, 215–16
KH 37, 41–5, 51
KP 241, 244
KP's regency 107–8
Mary 255
Norfolk 192, 194, 196–7
Paget 256, 336
Petre 164
plot against KP 171–2
poaching and murder case 39
regency 213
religious factions 81, 83, 97, 99, 151,
164–5, 167, 181, 197–8
repaying loans 124
Richard Read 122–3
Robert Huicke 135–6
Somerset 209, 238–9, 254
succession 212, 254–5
Suffolk 119
Surrey 182–5, 187–8, 193–7
Thomas Seymour 215, 241, 244,
252–3
war with France 108, 111, 121, 156
William Parr 57
Wriothesley 238
Privy Gardens 171, 173
apple trees 217
Protestants 83, 102, 113, 166, 181, 254
Anne of Cleves 33
Bale 75
Cranmer 204, 257
Edward 71–2, 73, 160, 256, 265
Elizabeth 334
executions of evangelical priests 96
French peace treaty 160
Gardiner 176
Germany 83–4, 90, 260
Glaterus Doloenus 75
Henry's monument 269
Lassels 40
Mowntayne 176–7
plot against KP 167
Rich 337
search for wife for Henry 24
Six Articles 89, 330
Puddifant (sexton of St George's) 270
puerperal fever

Jane Seymour 20, 250, 333
KP 250, 333

quartan fever (Edward) 63

Ratcliffe, Anne (Countess of Sussex) 170,
    300
Ratcliffe, Henry (Earl of Sussex) 170
    death of Henry 274
Rattsey, Jane (lady-in-waiting to Anne of
    Cleves) 52
Read, Richard (alderman refuses to pay tax)
    122–3
Real Presence 82, 86–7, 89–90, 92, 96,
    168–9
    execution for denying 339
    William Huicke 135
regency 210
    Henry's will 213
    KP 80, 106–11, 115–16, 210, 240
    Lorraine 334
    Scotland 334
    Somerset as Lord Protector 233, 235–9
    sought by Howard family 188, 193, 195,
        197, 201
religion 162–73
    book translation 80–1
    conservatives 36–7, 59, 82, 97–9, 102,
        160, 162, 165–70, 175, 178, 187, 191, 198
    creeping to the cross 89, 138–9, 165, 295
    Cromwell 37, 84, 97
    Denny 152, 154
    differing factions 14, 162–73, 181, 197–8
    doctors 132, 135
    Edward 71–2, 73, 75–6, 160, 256, 265
    evangelism 97, 154, 160, 162, 165–8
    French peace treaty 160
    Gardiner 37
    heresy 82–3, 86–102
    KP 56, 80–1, 166–73
    Lambert's appeal 86–8
    Lassels 40
    Masses for Henry after death 221–5,
        229–30
    Norfolk 36–7, 97, 166, 191, 210

Privy Council 81, 83, 97, 99, 151, 164–5,
    167, 181, 197–8
    reformists 37, 40, 59, 75–6, 81, 83–5, 93,
        97–103, 135, 152, 154, 178–80, 195,
        209–10, 255–6
    Six Articles 89–92
    William Huicke 135
    see also Catholicism; evangelism; heresy;
        Protestants; Real Presence
Religious Injunctions 84–5
Renee of Guise (sister to Marie) 20
Reynolds, Patrick (apothecary) 206
    Henry's funeral 228
    Henry's will 214
Rhases (Arabian physician) 130
Rich, Sir Richard (Baron Rich) 236, 337
    Anne Askew 169–70
    death of Henry 236–7
    Henry's will 214
    informant against Cromwell 97
    KP 166
    perjury at More's trial 97
    religious conservatism 97, 166, 169–70
Richmond, Duchess of see Howard, Mary
Richmond, Duke of see Fitzroy, Henry
Richmond, Margaret Countess of
    (grandmother of Henry) 256
Richmond Palace, Surrey 31, 34
Roberts, John (yeoman) 219
Rochford, Lady Jane (widow of George
    Boleyn) 48, 51, 339
    Anne of Cleves 30, 339
    execution 48, 51, 339
Rogers, Edward (witness against Surrey)
    195
Roos, Richard (poisoner boiled alive) 103
Rowlands, Richard (Henry's monument)
    266–7
Royal College of Physicians 131, 133
Rumpy le Conte (French warship) 122
Russell, Jane (rocker of Edward's cradle) 70
Russell, John Lord (Earl of Bedford, Lord
    Privy Seal) 337
    Act of Attainder 219
    Anne of Cleves 26–7
    Cranmer 101
    death of Henry 236

death of Jane Seymour 67
Edward's christening 65
executor of Henry's will 213
Henry's wedding to KP 59
Henry's will 213, 214
war with France 115
Rutland, Lady Eleanor 30
Rye, Sussex (fishermen capture Scottish
    ship) 108–9

St Edward the Confessor 65
    arms 196, 198–9
St George's Chapel, Windsor
    Chambre as canon 133
    Charles I 270–2
    Commonwealth 268
    Henry's burial 212, 213, 231, 259, 261,
        270–1, 332
    Henry's funeral 221, 225, 230
    Henry's monument 261, 263–4, 266–70
    Jane Seymour's burial 20, 212, 231, 259,
        264–5, 275, 332
    memorial plaque 273
    Queen Anne's child 271, 273
    Ralfe Lyons 79
    Suffolk's burial 119, 290–1, 335
    tomb of Edward IV 264
    tomb of Henry VI 264
    vault of Henry and Jane Seymour opened
        270–2
    Wolsey 262
St James's Palace
    death of Mary 333
    Elizabeth 80
    KP 246
    Ralfe Lyons 79
    Surrey 184
    Thomas Seymour 242, 253
St John, Lord see Paulet, Sir William
St Leonard's, Shoreditch (burial of Somers)
    258, 337
St Omer (executioner of Anne Boleyn) 20,
    329
St Pancras Priory, Lewes 68
St Paul's Cathedral
    Latimer's burial 56

Linacre's burial 133
Nelson's monument 260, 270
St Thomas Becket 89
Sackville, Sir Richard (Chancellor of
    Augmentations) 265
Sacramentarians 89, 97, 99, 197
    Gardiner 177
    Norfolk 191
    pardoned 217
Sansovino, Jacopo (sculptor) 261
Savoy (surrendered to Spain) 112
Sceppurus, Cornelius (Charles V's
    councillor) 122, 167
Schore, Dr Louis (President of Council of
    Flanders) 122, 167
Schoulenburg (cook to Anne of Cleves) 34
scorbutic disease 139
Scotland
    alliance with France 109, 114–15, 124
    ambassador in Spain 117
    ambassadors meet Henry 206
    attack on Edinburgh 104–5
    English victory at Solway Moss 54, 72,
        113, 330
    English war with France 106, 113
    fishermen capture ship 108–9
    KP's regency 107, 109
    Marie of Guise marries James V 334
    marriage plans for Edward 72–3
    Norfolk 191, 336
    papal Bull 89
    prisoners held by English 107–8
    Southampton 336
    Suffolk 335
    Surrey 183
    war 54, 57, 72, 104–5, 113–14, 119, 122–3,
        156, 226, 264, 330
Scott, Sir George Gilbert (KP's grave) 251
scrofula 148
Seaford 118, 290
sedition
    Barnes 95
    Cranmer 257
    Gardiner 257, 336
septicaemia
    Edward 292
    Jane Seymour 20, 333

Sexton (fool) 145

Seymour, Sir Edward (brother of Jane,
 Viscount Beauchamp, Earl of Hertford,
 Duke of Somerset, Lord Protector)
 197–8, 233, 235–9, 337
 Act of Attainder 219
 attack on Edinburgh 104–5
 Boulogne 119, 186–7, 337
 death of Henry 15–16, 233, 235–9
 Edward's christening 66
 Edward's coronation 225
 Edward's succession 15
 evangelism 97
 executed 254, 337
 executor of Henry's will 213
 Gardiner 175, 181
 Henry's funeral 232
 Henry's will 15–16, 210, 212–16
 KP marries Thomas Seymour 241–3,
  245–6, 248–50
 KP's regency 106
 Norfolk 199, 233
 Paget 233, 238–9, 256
 peace talks with France 124
 Privy Council 209, 238–9, 254
 Thomas Seymour (brother) 241–3,
  245–6, 248–50, 252–4
 Surrey 182, 186–8, 200–2
 war in France 106, 115, 119
 wife as lady-in-waiting to KP 170

Seymour, Jane (third wife of Henry, sister of
 Hertford and Sir Thomas Seymour) 187,
 333
 Augustine 134
 brother courting KP 57
 burial 20, 212, 231, 259, 264, 265, 275,
  332
 Butts 133, 135
 death 20, 23, 36, 67, 141, 329, 333
 funeral 224
 Henry's funeral 228
 memorial plaque 273
 mother of Edward 15, 18, 20, 64–7, 133,
  329, 333
 portrait 18, 147
 puerperal fever 20, 250, 333
 vault opened 270–1

 wedding to Henry 58, 329, 333

Seymour, Mary (daughter of KP and
 Thomas Seymour) 250–1

Seymour, Sir Thomas (Lord High Admiral,
 Baron Seymour of Sudeley, brother of
 Jane) 240–52, 337
 daughter born 250
 death of Henry 236–7
 death of KP 250–2
 Elizabeth 247–8, 252–3
 executed 253, 337
 Gardiner 176
 Henry's will 214, 215
 KP 57–9, 240–52, 333, 337
 knighted at Edward's christening 67
 made Baron on Henry's death 236
 marriage to KP 240–52, 333, 337
 Norfolk 193, 199, 202
 planned marriage to Surrey's sister 194
 Privy Council 215, 241, 244, 252–3
 sent to Brussels 58
 Somerset (brother) 241–3, 245–6,
  248–50, 252–4
 Surrey 187–8, 194, 199, 202
 treason 252–3, 337

Sforza, Franceso (Duke of Milan) 22, 334

Shakespeare, William (playwright) 106,
 144, 297

Shelley, Sir William (judge) 200

Shelton, Margaret (Henry's mistress) 127

Sidney, Sir William (Chamberlain to
 Edward) 68–9, 338
 brother-in-law to Edward's nurse 71, 338

Siege of Landrecies 105

singing 24, 38, 132
 Anne of Cleves 24
 Edward 74
 Ralfe Lyons 79

Six Articles 89–92, 330

Skutt, John (tailor) 57

Slanning, Elizabeth (fringes for commodes)
 150

smallpox 126

Smithfield (executions) 89, 94, 96, 103,
 174, 330–1, 338–9

Snape Castle, Yorkshire 55

Solway Moss 54, 72, 113, 330

Somers, Will (Henry's fool) 144–8, 152,
  257–8, 337
  death 258
  Henry's funeral 228
Somerset, Duchess of *see* Stanhope, Anne
Somerset, Duke of *see* Seymour, Sir Edward
Somerset, William (Lord Herbert, son of
  Earl of Worcester) 105–6
Southampton, Earl of *see* Fitzwilliam, Sir
  William
Southsea Castle 117
Southwell, Sir Richard (MP for Norfolk)
  188–9, 193
Spain
  alliance with England 105, 112, 143, 165
  alliance with France 20, 21–2, 24, 104,
    112
  diplomacy of KP 115–16
  mercenaries 119–20
  retirement of ambassador 115–17
  search for wife for Henry 21–2
spectacles 157, 196
Speed, John *History of Britain* 261
Stafford, Sir Henry (marries Henry's grand-
  mother) 256
Stafford, Humfrey (Duke of Buckingham)
  256
Stanhope, Anne (wife of Hertford, Duchess
  of Somerset) 238
  KP 170, 242–3, 246
  Surrey 187
Star Chamber 39, 243
Sternhold, Thomas (psalmist, Groom of the
  Robes) 81
  tried for heresy and pardoned 99
Stockett, Lewis (Surveyor of the Queen's
  works) 266
Stonor, Walter (Lieutenant of the Tower)
  199, 203
Strickland, Agnes (writer) 229
Sturley, Sir Nicholas (banner carrier) 227
Sudeley Castle 248, 333
  KP's grave 251
Suffolk, Duke of *see* Brandon, Charles
Suffolk, Katherine Duchess of (lady-in-
  waiting to KP) 166, 170
  Anne Askew 170–1

dog named 'Gardiner' 166
  KP's daughter 251
  portrait of KP 243
Surrey, Earl of *see* Howard, Henry
Sussex, Countess of *see* Ratcliffe, Anne
Sussex, Earl of *see* Ratcliffe, Henry
Syon 38, 47, 50, 250
  Henry's coffin 272
  Henry's funeral 221, 226, 228–9
syphilis 127–9, 292

Talbot, Lord (banner carrier) 228
Talbot, Francis (Earl of Shrewsbury)
  Scottish prisoners 107–8
tennis 127
  Edward 63
  Fitzroy and Henry Howard 182
Testwood, Robert (singing man) 97–8
Thirlby, Thomas (Bishop of Westminster)
  106, 193
  Henry's will 211
Torrigiano, Pietro (sculptor) 260, 261, 263
torture 41
  Anne Askew 170, 174, 338
Toto, Antonio (painter) 224
Tower Green
  execution of Anne Boleyn 19–20, 329
  execution of KH 51, 330, 333
  execution of Lady Rochford 339
Tower Hill
  execution of Cromwell 37, 330, 338
  execution of Northumberland 255, 336
  execution of Somerset 254
  execution of Surrey 203, 339
  execution of Thomas Seymour 337
Tower of London 92, 94, 234
  Anne Askew 169, 170–1, 338
  Anne of Cleves' fear 34
  Augustine 134
  burial of Anne Boleyn 51
  burial of KH 50–1
  Cheke 338
  Cranmer 99–100, 257
  Cromwell 31–2, 63
  Dereham 41
  Edward's birth 64
  Edward's succession 16, 233, 333

Henry's will 213
Hume (Scottish prisoner) 123
interrogations about KH 41–2, 45
jewels 62, 220
KH 50–1
Lady Rochford 48
Norfolk 189–92, 198, 203, 221, 233, 331, 339
Thomas Seymour 252
uprising against Mary 178
Surrey 189–90, 193, 195, 199–202, 331
Surrey's attempted escape 193, 200–1
treason 14, 83, 90, 94, 255, 274, 330
Cranmer 257
Cromwell 30–3, 338
Culpeper 48–9, 330, 338
Dereham 48–9, 330, 338
evangelical priests 94
execution of insane persons 51
forging king's signature 158
Gardiner 175, 178
Gates 256
imagining Henry's death 126, 138, 149, 219, 292, 329
KH 50, 333
Lady Rochford 339
marriage to king without disclosing past 51
Norfolk 49, 192, 198, 202, 339
Northumberland 255
Somerset 254
Surrey 199, 200, 202, 203, 331, 339
Thomas Seymour 252–3, 337
Wolsey 262, 328
Triest, Anthony (Bishop of Ghent) 269
tuberculosis 148
Arthur 19, 292, 328
Edward 254, 333
Fitzroy 301
Henry VII 292
Richmond 301
Tuke, Sir Bryan (Treasurer and Henry's Secretary) 130
Tunstall, Cuthbert (Bishop of Durham) 213
Turkey 57, 105
Tyburn 330, 338
execution of Culpeper 49

execution of Dacre 39
execution of Dereham 49
execution of Surrey 202
Tye, Dr Christopher (composer, Edward's tutor) 74
Tyrwhit, Lady Elizabeth (lady-in-waiting to KP) 173, 250

Udall, Nicholas (headmaster of Eton) 81
urine 132, 137, 207

van der Delft, Francis (Spanish ambassador) 166, 209, 334
death of Henry 16, 274
Henry's funeral 227
Henry's ill health 205, 206, 210, 211
KP marries Thomas Seymour 245
king's trams 149
Norfolk 193, 196–7
plot against KP 166
Surrey 189, 193, 196–7
Thomas Seymour arrested for treason 252–3
war between England and France 117
van Wilder, Philip (Edward's tutor) 74
Vaughan, Stephen (financial agent in Antwerp) 121, 124, 167
Vicary, Thomas (serjeant surgeon) 127
von Reiffenberg, Captain Frederick (mercenary) 120–1, 291

Wallop, Sir John (military operations) 58, 105
war
Ancrum Moor 113, 123, 331
bankruptcy 221
cost 108, 119, 122–5, 156, 264, 331
France 55, 80, 105–25, 127, 143–4, 156, 185–6, 210, 226, 330–1, 335, 337
Henry's new will 210
munitions 226
peace with France 159, 331
Scotland 54, 57, 72, 104–5, 113–14, 119, 122–3, 156, 226, 264, 330

Surrey 185, 186
Turkey 57
warships 109, 117–19, 122, 213
French 117, 122
Warwick, Earl of see Dudley, John
Watkins, Richard (Henry's notary) 59
Weldon, Thomas (tried for heresy and pardoned) 99
Wendy, Thomas (doctor) 135, 206, 209
death 135
Henry's funeral 228
Henry's will 135, 214
plot against KP 172
witness to Henry's will 135
witness to Mary's will 135
Westminster Abbey
burial of Anne of Cleves 257, 333
coronation of Edward 232
monument to Henry's parents 260, 262
Tomb House 265
Westminster, Bishop of see Thirlby, Thomas
Wharton, Lord (Warden of Scottish Western Marches) 109
Whetnall, Joan (maid) 194
Whichcot, Christopher (governor of Windsor Castle) 268
burial of Charles I 270
William IV (monument) 273
wills
Edward VI 255, 265
Henry 15–16, 106, 135–6, 210–16, 237–9, 259, 264, 330–1
Henry's executors 213
Henry's new one before war in France 106
Henry's witnessed by doctors 135
KP 136, 250
Latimer 56
legacies to doctors 135–6
Mary 135
Wilson, Thomas (Elizabeth's Secretary of State) 146
Winchester, Bishop of see Gardiner, Stephen; Ponet, John
Winchester, Marquis of see Paulet, Sir William
Winchester House, Southwark 35, 44

Windsor, Lord (Keeper of Great Wardrobe) 147, 227
Windsor Castle 38
Commonwealth removes monuments 268
Edward 254
Henry's funeral 224–5
Henry's ill health 206, 210
heresy trials 97–8
Surrey imprisoned 182
see also St George's Chapel, Windsor
Wingfield, Sir Anthony (Captain of the Royal Guard) 188
Henry's funeral 228
Wolf, Morgan (royal goldsmith) 157
Wolsey, Cardinal Thomas (Lord Chancellor and Chief Minister) 328
Augustine 128, 134
death 134, 328
Gardiner 175
Henry's monument 224, 260, 262–3, 270
monument 224, 261–3, 270
monument appropriated by Henry 224
Norfolk 192
Privy Chamber 152
Somers 145–6
syphilis 128
The More (house) 77
treason 262, 328
Worcester, Earl of (father of William Somerset) 106
Worcester, Lord (king's almoner) 225
Worley, Richard (page of pallet chamber) 168
Wotton, Sir Edward (Treasurer of Calais, brother of Dr Nicholas)
executor of Henry's will 213
Wotton, Edward (doctor) 133–4
death 134
Wotton, Dr Nicholas (Dean of Canterbury and York, ambassador to France) 193
Henry's will 213, 214
peace treaty with France 124, 159
search for wife for Henry 24
wrestling 126

Wriothesley, Sir Thomas (Lord Chancellor, later Earl of Southampton) 97, 166–70, 173, 238, 337
  Act of Attainder 219
  Anne Askew 169–70
  Anne of Cleves 30, 34
  cost of wars 123–4
  Culpeper 41
  death 238
  death of Henry 14, 16, 236–7
  dry stamp 159
  executor of Henry's will 213
  French peace treaty 159
  Gardiner 170, 180, 181
  Henry's ill health 206
  Henry's will 210, 213, 214
  KH 41, 46
  KP 19, 60, 106, 166, 167, 173, 331
  made Earl of Southampton 236
  Norfolk 193–4, 198, 203
  search for wife for Henry 22–3
  Somers 147
  speech to Parliament 161
  Surrey 189, 193–5, 200, 202
  war in France 116
Wyatt, Edward (son or brother of Sir Thomas) 178
Wyatt, James (architect, Henry's monument) 269–70
Wyatt, Sir Thomas (knighted at Edward's christening) 67, 301
Wyatt the Younger, Thomas 183, 301
  rebellion against Mary 178, 234